Unexpected Death in Childhood

Unexpected Death in Childhood

A Handbook for Practitioners

PETER SIDEBOTHAM
Consultant Senior Lecturer in Child Health, University of Warwick

PETER FLEMING
Professor of Infant Health and Developmental Physiology at the University of Bristol

John Wiley & Sons, Ltd

Other Wiley Editorial Offices

John Wiley & Sons Inc., 111 River Street, Hoboken, NJ 07030, USA

Jossey-Bass, 989 Market Street, San Francisco, CA 94103-1741, USA

Wiley-VCH Verlag GmbH, Boschstr. 12, D-69469 Weinheim, Germany

John Wiley & Sons Australia Ltd, 42 McDougall Street, Milton, Queensland 4064, Australia

John Wiley & Sons (Asia) Pte Ltd, 2 Clementi Loop #02-01, Jin Xing Distripark, Singapore
129809

John Wiley & Sons Canada Ltd, 6045 Freemont Blvd, Mississauga, ONT, L5R 4J3, Canada

Wiley also publishes its books in a variety of electronic formats. Some content that appears in
print may not be available in electronic books.

Anniversary Logo Design: Richard J. Pacifico

Library of Congress Cataloging-in-Publication Data

Sidebotham, Peter.
    Unexpected death in childhood : a handbook for practitioners / Peter Sidebotham,
Peter Fleming.
      p.   cm.
    Includes bibliographical references and index.
    ISBN 978-0-470-06095-7 (cloth) – ISBN 978-0-470-06096-4 (pbk.)
    1. Grief.   2. Bereavement–Psychological aspects.   3. Children–Death–Psychological aspects.
4. Children–Death.   I. Fleming, Peter.   II. Title.
    BF575.G7S49 2007
    155.9′37–dc22

                                                                                    2007026602

A catalogue record for this book is available from the British Library

ISBN: 9780470060957 (cloth)
ISBN: 9780470060964 (paper)

Typeset by SNP Best-set Typesetter Ltd., Hong Kong

Printed and bound in Great Britain by TJ International Ltd, Padstow.

This book is printed on acid-free paper responsibly manufactured from sustainable forestry
in which at least two trees are planted for each one used for paper production.

Contents

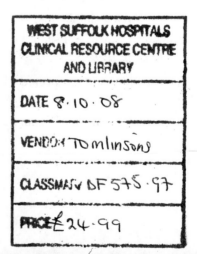

Foreword

Few of us can imagine a greater nightmare than facing the death of a child. The professionals who work with families through such a tragedy – doctors, nurses, policemen and social workers – deal with the rawest of emotions; the feelings of profound loss and despair, the rage and self-blaming, the sadness and need for comfort.

In the vast majority of cases, the causes are clear and nothing unlawful has taken place. The parents need sensitive support to help deal with their loss. However, it also is every family's right to have their child's death properly investigated. Families desperately want to know what happened, how the event could have occurred, what the cause of death was and whether it could have been prevented. This is important in terms of grieving but in some cases it also may be relevant to a family's high anxiety about future pregnancies and may identify some hidden underlying cause, such as a genetic problem. And if there happens to be another sudden child death in the family, carefully conducted investigations of an earlier death also help prevent miscarriages of justice.

In 2004, I had the privilege of chairing a joint working group established by the Royal College of Paediatrics and Child Health and the Royal College of Pathologists in the aftermath of the cases of Sally Clark and Angela Canning. Both women had been wrongly convicted of murdering their babies. The evidence had been unsatisfactory and the public outcry and media frenzy following the quashing of their convictions sent tremors through the medical profession. Many specialists involved with the unexpected deaths of children were anxious to maintain public trust, showing their desire to care for all those involved in such tragic events without undermining their commitment to child protection. They were also anxious not to lose recruits into these specialisms because of lowered morale and fear of scapegoating. It was for these reasons that they urged their colleges to take the initiative and respond positively to the events.

The task of the working group was to identify where the system had failed and to establish a protocol for the investigation of sudden infant death. When chairing any commission or inquiry there is always a steep learning curve and I acquired a wealth of information not just from the rest of the working group but from the many doctors, judges, coroners, social workers, police officers and families who had direct experience of these tragedies. Fault lay with many parts of the system, including the courts.

It was in working on this important project that I came to know a number of the authors of this vital handbook and it was from them that I came to really understand the pressures on the people who deal with these terrible deaths. My admiration for them is immeasurable.

There is still great variance around the country as to how a childhood death is handled by doctors and the police. There are 43 police forces in England and Wales, each with their own procedures and there are 28 strategic health authorities. There are also many social service departments. The geographical remits of these different agencies do not coincide with each other and they have different operational methods. The coroners who sit within these areas can also have quite distinct ways of working. This diversity creates a very complicated patchwork in which good practice can often be found but stories of insensitivity and failure are still sadly and angrily being told: parents being treated with inappropriate suspicion, numbers of policemen in uniform arriving shortly after an emergency call, children being taken straight to mortuaries and parents being given too little information or information that is communicated with little sensitivity.

However, huge progress is now being made in establishing clear procedures and protocols for the investigation of a sudden unexpected death in childhood and there is greater clarity about the role of experts. This handbook will be a vital part of that advance. Doctors have also needed clear guidance on the collection of non-biological data and instructions for history taking, with a minimum dataset. This is so that parents can access this information at any future date should genetic information be forthcoming or scientific advances take place which will provide explanations for the loss of their baby. It also means that an expert engaged at a later stage for whatever reason has a solid basis upon which he or she can base an opinion.

For innocent parents to have a child taken from them or to be prosecuted and convicted of killing a child who actually died of natural causes is unbearable. However, we must also acknowledge that in a small percentage of the cases where a baby or child dies, something unlawful will have taken place. Despite our unwillingness to accept the possibility, we have learned conclusively in the past thirty years that some mothers, fathers and other carers do induce illnesses in their children and sometimes fatally harm them. Child protection is a responsibility all of us must bear because of the special vulnerability of the youngest among us, who have no voice.

I congratulate all the authors on this wonderful handbook and have no doubt it will become an invaluable tool in their crucial work.

BARONESS HELENA KENNEDY QC

Preface

Unexpected death during childhood is a rare occurrence in the Western world. These deaths may occur as a result of sudden illness, accidents or through maltreatment. Whatever the cause, each death is a tragedy for the family and for all those involved with them. Professionals from all the caring agencies have a responsibility to help those families, offering support, investigating the cause of death, providing information and above all, seeking to prevent deaths in the first place.

Sadly, the trauma experienced by families is all too often exacerbated by inappropriate or incompetent professional responses. The devastating consequences of getting it wrong have been highlighted clearly in recent Court of Appeal cases where previous convictions have been overturned. Both families and professionals suffer as a result. It is our view that many of these situations could have been avoided if the professionals involved had been adequately trained and supported and the deaths had been responded to appropriately in the first place. In the words of Baroness Helena Kennedy, 'it is every family's right to have their baby's death properly investigated' (Royal College of Pathologists & Royal College of Paediatrics and Child Health 2004). However, this is an area where professionals often feel ill-equipped and unprepared.

It is from that perspective that we wanted to put this book together as a resource for all professionals working in this area. We have been privileged over the years to spend time with bereaved parents and families, sharing in some small way in their grief, and hopefully offering some support and understanding. These parents have been our mentors as we have learnt more about childhood death and how to respond to it. Our involvement with these families constantly highlights that we don't always get it right and we continue to learn with each death we respond to. There is no perfect or 'right' way to work with a family following the death of a child, but what we hope to provide in this book is a framework to support good practice, based on a thorough understanding of childhood death.

It is all too easy to forget, when we focus on statistics or techniques, that each child is an individual, precious son or daughter, brother, sister or grandchild. With this in mind, we start the book from the perspective of the parents and families. We are extremely grateful to Ann Chalmers from the Child Bereavement Trust, who has pulled together some of the experiences of families whom she has known. The insights and experiences she shares, as well as those of Alison Stewart and Ann Dent in Chapter 10, remind us that there is no 'right' way to grieve and that individuals will be affected in different ways. They also remind us that there are steps we can take to support families, and that even the smallest touch of compassion may make a big difference to a parent's distress.

Part I of the book provides a background to our work with families following the death of a child. The question all bereaved parents ask is 'why?' On one level, we may never be able to answer that question fully. However, if we are properly informed, we can at least provide some answers. In these chapters, we and our colleagues, Peter Blair and Jo Sibert, have attempted to explore what we know about the nature and causes of childhood death. One of the dangers of trying to put across such information in a book is the recognition that our knowledge is incomplete and may very quickly go out of date. In an era of rapid advances in molecular and genetic studies, this may be even more of an issue. What we present here is, therefore, based on best evidence at this time, but we recognise that this evidence may well change or go out of date. We owe it to families to be informed and to strive to understand more, but also to be humble enough to admit when we don't know and when we have got things wrong.

In Part II of the book we provide a framework for responding to the unexpected death of a child. The hub of this is Chapter 7, which outlines the approach we have developed through our work in the South West and West Midlands. This approach, which also draws on the experience of many others in the United Kingdom and beyond, is underpinned by two important principles: a thorough, systematic investigation of the circumstances of death based on the best available evidence, and a sensitive, caring approach to supporting the family. We believe strongly that the two are not mutually exclusive and indeed, by taking a sensitive and supportive approach, our investigation into the circumstances of death is likely to be more fruitful, which in turn will provide the basis for ongoing support for the family. Our aim here is not only to establish a 'cause of death' but to help the parents understand as fully as possible why their child died, whether that death is due to natural medical causes, circumstances in the environment or parenting, or (as is most often the case) a combination of factors. Again, we would emphasise that in many (perhaps most) cases, we cannot understand fully why that particular child died at that particular time; nevertheless, by exploring thoroughly all the circumstances of the death, we can provide some pointers to help the parents.

As Ann Chalmers points out in Chapter 1, the 'system' that swings into action when a sudden death occurs can leave parents feeling powerless, with everything out of their control. It is crucial that we do not add to their grief by prejudging or by being unprepared or ill-informed. All bereaved parents, whatever the cause of their child's death, deserve respect, understanding and care. This applies as much to the young father who in a moment of lost control

has shaken his baby, or the mother who, falling asleep on a sofa, has accidentally smothered her child, as it does to the parents whose teenage son has been
killed by a speeding car, or those parents whose severely disabled child has
succumbed to a fatal epileptic seizure. We have therefore tried to emphasise
the importance of family support throughout the book, but focus specifically
on this in Chapter 10. Alison Stewart and Ann Dent bring some invaluable
perspectives from their work with parents and other family members. As with
other chapters, much of what they put across is supported by practical resources
in the appendices.

   We have been very privileged to have worked with a large number of skilled
and motivated colleagues from a range of different disciplines, including police
officers, social workers, coroners and other health professionals. Whilst different professionals may approach the death of a child with differing priorities
and perspectives, it is very clear to us that these perspectives, far from being
conflicting, are in fact complementary. No one professional has a monopoly of
knowledge or skills and we do rely on each other in our responses. We hope
that this perspective comes across throughout this section of the book. We
have tried to ensure the book is accessible to all professionals involved in
responding to childhood deaths. Thus, although we include chapters that
convey quite detailed medical or forensic information, it is not our intention
to teach doctors to be police investigators, or social workers to interpret
autopsy findings, but rather to give all professionals an insight into where their
colleagues are coming from and what they can contribute to the process.

   The final section of the book moves on to learning lessons from child deaths.
There is an African proverb that says it takes a village to raise a child. We
would extend this to emphasise that it takes a community to bury a child. The
impact of a child's death extends beyond the immediate family and should
affect the whole community. To some extent, we all carry some responsibility
for each child's death and we owe it to children to learn from their deaths
and to strive to prevent future deaths. In the UK, we have a long history of
reviewing deaths from abuse or neglect, as outlined in Chapter 12. The new
frameworks for safeguarding children outlined in *Working Together* (HM
Government 2006b) provide a unique opportunity to build on this history and
learn lessons from reviewing all childhood deaths. We have a lot to learn in
this area from other countries where child death review processes have been
in place for a number of years. Martin Ward Platt draws on some of this experience as well as more local experiences in describing different approaches to
child death review in Chapter 11.

   Whilst we and our fellow authors are able to draw on our experience in
working with families, we do not put ourselves forward as 'experts'. There can
be no experts when it comes to responding to a child's death, any more than
there can be a perfect response. We hope, however, that the insights we share
will be of benefit to you as professionals, will help support bereaved families
and ultimately, may help to prevent future childhood deaths.

A Note on Terminology

We are well aware that when we use a word, it may mean something different to others from what we intended. This is never more so than in the field of unexpected childhood deaths, where practitioners come from a range of backgrounds, each with their own jargon, where there remain many uncertainties in the issues we are dealing with and where there exist differences both between and within countries in the way individuals apply terms. Throughout this book we have tried to be consistent in our use of terminology and to define clearly what we mean by specific terms. As far as possible we have tried to avoid the use of medical terminology or to explain it in lay terms where not avoidable. Nevertheless, because of the subject matter, this has not always proved possible, for which we apologise. We suggest that non-medics (and medics like us, who find themselves getting a bit rusty) find a friendly paediatrician or pathologist to explain those more complex medical terms, or consult one of the many on-line medical dictionaries.

A few terms deserve specific clarification:

Unexpected Deaths – an unexpected death may be defined as the death of a child which was not anticipated as a significant possibility 24 hours before the death, or where there was a similarly unexpected collapse leading to or precipitating the events which led to the death (Fleming et al. 2000). This includes Sudden Unexpected Deaths in Infancy and unexpected deaths in older children.

Sudden Unexpected Death in Infancy (SUDI) – we use this to refer to all unexpected deaths of infants up to one year of age at the point of presentation. As such, it is a descriptive term rather than a diagnosis. During the course of an investigation into the cause of death, these deaths may be unexplained, pending further investigation. At the conclusion of an investigation, they will divide into those for which we have a clear diagnosis (explained SUDI) and those for which we do not have a diagnosis (SIDS).

Sudden Infant Death Syndrome (SIDS) – we use the 1991 definition: the sudden death of an infant under one year of age which remains unexplained after a thorough case investigation, including performance of a complete autopsy, examination of the death scene and review of the clinical history (Willinger et al. 1991). We use this term consistently when those criteria are met, regardless of the presence or absence of any recognised factors, rather than using terms such as undetermined, unascertained, unexplained or border-line SIDS, which are more ambiguous. In doing so, we recognise that SIDS is not a diagnosis as such but rather an acknowledgement that we do not know why the infant has died. The label SIDS will inevitably encompass a range of causes that we have been unable to identify conclusively, including some potential deaths from asphyxia (accidental or intentional). As noted in the description of the Avon clinico-pathological classification of SUDI, within the information collected on infants whose deaths have been attributed to the overall term 'SIDS' it may be possible to identify notable, potentially contribu-tory, or probably contributory factors, which may be important, but which do not in themselves provide a complete explanation for the death (which thus remains classified overall as SIDS). Knowledge of these contributory factors may have significance in the development of preventive strategies and may be very important for the family.

List of Contributors

PETER BLAIR

Peter Blair is a Senior Research Fellow at the University of Bristol. He has worked for many years in researching the epidemiology of SIDS, in particular the investigation of background characteristics and risk factors linked with SIDS families and infants. Peter has published extensively, focusing on factors within the infant sleep environment, such as how the infant is positioned, thermal stress, infant bedding, the use of dummies and issues surrounding co-sleeping, as well as associations with infant vulnerability at birth, parental smoking and immunisation. He is an executive board member of the International Society for the Study and Prevention of Infant Death (ISPID).

ANN CHALMERS

Ann Chalmers is Chief Executive of the Child Bereavement Trust, a national United Kingdom charity founded in 1994. The charity provides specialised training and support for professionals to improve their response to the needs of bereaved families. The Child Bereavement Trust produces resources and information for children and families and all the professionals who come into contact with them in the course of their work. Ann works as a trainer and facilitator for the charity and continues to learn through her work as a trained bereavement counsellor within the NHS, providing support to families and staff, and through her work with schools, palliative care staff, police and emergency services, and those in the voluntary sector.

PHIL COX

Phil Cox is one of a team of three Perinatal Pathologists based at Birmingham Women's Hospital, who deliver the perinatal post-mortem service to 17 Trusts in the West Midlands and beyond. He and his team perform coronial post-mortems for the 11 coroners' jurisdictions in the West Midlands and also occasional cases from further afield. Dr Cox trained in perinatal pathology at St George's Hospital, London, and worked with Professor Jonathan Wigglesworth at the Hammersmith Hospital prior to his retirement. He moved to Birmingham in 2000. His interests are the pathology of genetic malformation syndromes and congenital neuromuscular diseases.

ANN DENT

Ann Dent has worked in the field of palliative care and bereavement with adults and children for nearly 30 years, in service provision, education and research. She was chairperson of the consultant panel of the Child Bereavement Network for four years. Currently she is chairperson of the Bereavement Research Forum and Bristol Bereavement Forum. She is a patron of The Compassionate Friends and Cruse Bereavement Care (Bristol). She is a co-author of several books on sudden child death.

PETER FLEMING

Peter Fleming is Professor of Infant Health and Developmental Physiology at the University of Bristol. His clinical practice is in the fields of newborn intensive care, developmental assessment and investigation and care of children with sleep-related disorders, particularly involving breathing. His research is in the areas of developmental physiology, mother/baby interactions (particularly during sleep) and large-scale studies of factors contributing to sudden death in infants. He also has a particular clinical and research interest in the provision of bereavement care to parents after the death of a baby or child. He is a world leader in research into sudden unexpected death in infancy and has published extensively on this and other topics. He has won numerous awards for his work, including a CBE awarded for services to the understanding and prevention of cot deaths. Professor Fleming is a member of the Royal College of Paediatrics and Child Health, the Neonatal Society, the British Association of Perinatal Medicine, the British Sleep Society and the Paediatric Intensive Care Society.

JOHN FOX

John Fox is a recently retired police superintendent with many years' operational experience in dealing with child homicide. At a national level, he has represented the Association of Chief Police Officers (ACPO) on various government working parties and committees concerning child abuse and related issues, and amongst other things, assisted with the production of the key national guidance documents *Working Together to Safeguard Children* and *Achieving Best Evidence* and the national police *Child Abuse Investigation Guidance* (2005). John was, until recently, the lead officer for ACPO in respect of infant deaths and in that role he chaired the working group, which produced the national ACPO guidelines concerning the investigation of infant deaths. He was appointed as the Police Service representative to the Attorney General's working party to examine the safety of infant death convictions, and he was a member of Baroness Kennedy's Intercollegiate Working Group. He was one of Lord Laming's four assessors during the Victoria Climbié Inquiry.

JO SIBERT

Professor Jonathan Richard (Jo) Sibert recently retired as Professor of Child Health at Cardiff University and as a Consultant Paediatrician working for the Cardiff and Vale NHS Trust. He now has the title of Emeritus Professor. He has been involved with the medical care of children for over 35 years. He was awarded an OBE in the 2007 New Year Honours list for services to Paediatrics and Child Health. He was awarded the Sir James Spence Medal in April 2006 by the Royal College of Paediatrics and Child Health for his contribution to extending paediatric knowledge. He has a wide research portfolio, including contributions on accident prevention in childhood – in particular the prevention of poisoning, drowning and playground injuries. He has also studied the epidemiology of child abuse and improving the evidence base in child protection, jointly founding the Welsh Child Protection Systematic Research Group.

PETER SIDEBOTHAM

Peter Sidebotham is a Consultant Senior Lecturer in Child Health at the University of Warwick. His main clinical interests are in child protection, sudden unexpected death in infancy and child development and disability. During seven years in Bristol, Dr Sidebotham helped to build up an internationally-acclaimed clinical and academic service for sudden unexpected deaths in infancy. Since moving to Warwickshire, he has built on this experience to work with colleagues in developing a local service for responding to unexpected childhood deaths. He is a council member with the Foundation for the Study of Infant Deaths and sits on the child protection standing committee of the Royal College of Paediatrics and Child Health. Dr Sidebotham is the director of the Warwick Advanced Course in the Management of Unexpected Childhood Death. He is heading up a research team with ongoing research into child death review processes.

ALISON STEWART

Alison Stewart has been involved in education, research and clinical practice over many years with families and health professionals following the death of a baby or child. This has included working with individual members of families, providing resources and support for mutual help groups, teaching in undergraduate and postgraduate nursing courses, offering professional development workshops for health professionals and undertaking research, which has included exploring the stories of bereaved grandparents.

PAUL TUDOR

After a career of 20 years with the NSPCC, Paul Tudor has been an independent Child Protection Advisor for a further 14 years. In addition to locum contracts chairing Child Protection Conferences and Looked After reviews, he has chaired 35 Serious Case Reviews and written management reviews for a further five. Some of them have been high profile (Gloucester 1994; Lincoln 2004). He has analysed 20 of these cases (referred to as 'the cohort' in the text of Chapter 12) and this analysis formed the basis of a paper accepted by and presented to the International ISPCAN Conference in York in 2006.

MARTIN WARD PLATT

Martin Ward Platt qualified from Bristol University and has worked in the North East for over 20 years. Since 1990 he has been a consultant paediatrician (neonatal medicine) at the Royal Victoria Infirmary, Newcastle upon Tyne. He has undertaken research in infant developmental physiology and sudden infant deaths, and he has been active in developing case review for sudden unexpected death in infancy across the region. He is a Reader in Neonatal and Paediatric Medicine at Newcastle University, Clinical Director of the Regional Maternity Survey Office and currently an Associate Editor of *Archives of Disease in Childhood*.

Acknowledgements

This book has been some time in its gestation and represents a collaborative effort built on a lot of support from our colleagues and friends. We are grateful for the excellent contributions from our co-authors, but also from many other colleagues who have contributed perspectives from their own agency. We are also grateful to those who have responded with us to individual children's deaths and to our faculty on the Warwick Advanced Course in the Management of Unexpected Childhood Death, which has helped us develop and refine our ideas. It would be impossible to acknowledge all of those who have contributed, but we are particularly grateful to Carol Evanson Coombe and Maggie Edmond, who have put so much into our study in the South West. We are grateful to the Foundation for the Study of Infant Deaths, the University of Warwick, and to the Department for Education and Skills for financial support for our research and training programmes. We are both extremely grateful to our wives, Helen and Jo, who have borne with us in all our work, and to Lorraine, Michelle and Ellen for their secretarial support. Above all, however, we are grateful to all the families who have taught us so much and have allowed us the privilege of getting to know them in what is undoubtedly the most difficult time any family could face.

I Understanding Childhood Death

1 A Family's Journey

ANN CHALMERS

'Ondine lived for nearly seven months and then died suddenly one night . . . The horror and shock and desperation of that discovery are difficult to describe. But in barely an hour we were transformed from a normal blessed family to three crushed individuals at the beginning of a journey of grief of which we knew nothing.'

Madeleine

The sudden and unexpected death of a child is something for which no parent can ever be prepared. Parents expect to be able to watch their children grow and develop into adulthood, and when a child's life is abruptly ended, whatever the cause, the anguish is immense. As professionals coming into contact with families at this time and in whatever capacity, we are faced with the most tragic of situations that cannot be made better. This does not mean, however, that we cannot make a difference to those families in a time of tragedy.

A parent's natural instinct is to protect their child, and the sudden and unexpected death of that child can give rise to powerful feelings of responsibility and failure as a parent, however irrational these may seem. Whilst most deaths are likely to be from natural causes, the fact that an investigation may be necessary inevitably adds to that burden of responsibility. It is paramount that parents are handled with respect, sensitivity and understanding throughout the investigative process.

The death of a child at any age is always a death out of time. As parents, our perfectly reasonable expectation is that our children will survive us. It is interesting that this expectation is so firmly entrenched in us all that no single word exists to denote a parent who has lost a child, whereas there are words for other situations of bereavement, such as for those who have lost a spouse and for a child who is left without parents.

Parents often feel a sense of stigma in relation to their child's death. The death of a child threatens the security of everyone who comes into contact with the family – concrete evidence of every parent's worst nightmare. At one extreme, the extent of their grief can be so great that others may avoid them, finding it unbearable even to come close to a situation where this has happened. At the other end of the spectrum, assumptions may be made that a little amount of life, measured by time, equates to a little amount of loss.

Unexpected Death in Childhood: A Handbook for Practitioners. Edited by P. Sidebotham and P. Fleming.
Copyright © 2007 by John Wiley & Sons, Ltd.

Professionals have an important role in acknowledging the significance of the parents' experience. Referring to their child by name acknowledges their child and the reality of what has happened.

When a child dies, the parents' lives are forever changed. Their child is still, and always will be, part of their family. There will be a gap that can never be filled. The death of a child represents not only the loss of a past with that child, but the loss of a future that will never be fulfilled, and the loss of all hopes, dreams and expectations associated with that child. The grief is not only for the loss of what was, but for what can now never be.

> 'As we held her that night, we were acutely aware that nothing could ever be the same again. Up until then had been normal life, and from that moment on represented our changed lives, which would never feel normal again. I think that this is probably a pivotal moment common to all bereaved parents. Life will go on and must go on, but it will always be different. You can resume routine over the weeks and months but your loss will permeate everything.'
>
> Madeleine

The parents' ability to survive emotionally will be impacted by what has gone before in their lives, by their own childhood experience of parenting and by what they have invested in their relationship with this child. This may have been the longed-for boy in the family, the child who caused the least trouble, the child with whom a mother was going to develop the kind of relationship never experienced with her own parents. Parents are faced with the monumental task of learning to live life without their child, and to survive this experience as best they can.

There is no 'right' way to grieve. Understanding what is happening to them in relation to what happens to anyone facing significant loss can help parents to feel 'normal' in their grief, when so many fear they are 'going mad'. Parents find it helpful to know that grief can be felt physically as well as emotionally, and is exhausting. Grief also has much anxiety and fear attached to it; one family were greatly helped by their Health Visitor who explained that people often feel frightened in grief. Part of grieving is struggling to accept the reality of what has happened. Believing it to be real and reaching any acceptance that you will live every day of your life without your child feels almost impossible to achieve, but families have been helped by professionals who avoid jargon and are honest. This helps parents accept the reality.

Each parent will grieve in their own way in their own time. Grieving the death of a child is a solitary experience. Although this is the one loss in life that, as parents of the dead child, they may share equally, each parent will have had their own unique relationship with that child and their grief may be very different in its expression and duration. Couples often experience an inability to communicate with each another and to express their overwhelming feelings. As a result, each can feel alone and isolated in their grief, particularly if partners are unable to share with each other what this loss means for them. This can drive a wedge in a relationship from which some may not recover, particularly if there were difficulties before the death happened. Others who find a way of sharing their feelings may find themselves drawn together in this shared tragedy.

Men and women often behave differently in grief. Women naturally tend to focus on the loss and are more concerned with their emotions; men in contrast are more likely to be restorative, wanting things to return to 'normal' as soon as possible. Unhelpful assumptions can be made, with women sometimes misinterpreting their partner's response as not caring about their child. Because a restorative response does not involve the 'expected' way of grieving, professionals may also place unhelpful interpretations on a person's behaviour. Yet getting in touch with the emotions associated with a loss and doing things that take you away from the enormity of that experience for a time are both very necessary components of a healthy grieving process. Men need to find ways to express their feelings about their child's death, and women need to develop ways of being restorative if they are to move forward.

Through memories the dead child remains a member of the family. Everything surrounding their child's death, including their interactions with professionals they encounter at that time, will be part of that precious memory bank for parents. Even the most difficult aspects of investigating a child's sudden death can be managed positively.

'The hospital staff, from the Paediatrician who told us Ondine was dead, to the nurses who regularly checked on us, were gentle and sensitive to our needs. Even the police, who had to come and ask questions, were dignified and kind enough to agree with me that yes, she was a beautiful baby. We could not fault anyone that night.'

Madeleine

Parents tell us that the professionals who make a real difference to them are those who do not hide behind some professional façade, but who are able to be congruent and let their own humanity shine through in their interactions with the family.

'We were fortunate to be supported by many wonderful people in those early weeks and months. Family and old friends of course, but others too, more surprising and unexpected: the funeral director whose dignity and sorrow were palpable, whose respectful hands would wash and dress our baby with a mother's tender touch; the surgery staff nurse who visited us and spoke of her vivid memories of Ondine and who even came to her funeral; the coroner's assistant who gently guided us through the inquest; the Paediatrician who spoke with such understanding and honesty.'

Madeleine

Acknowledgement of the significance of their loss is vitally important to parents, as is the feeling that others really understand the depth of the tragedy they are facing. Often, because it can seem so impossible to find 'the right words' to say, we may say nothing. A simple expression of sorrow at what has happened can go a long way.

> 'An understandably difficult encounter was with the Paediatric Pathologist. We were shocked by how unfeeling she seemed. We could acknowledge that her job was one of scientific investigation, but felt bemused as to why the few words of condolence which would have put us at our ease were never spoken.'
>
> Madeleine

In contrast, Rachel and Simon were helped by a member of the mortuary staff who explained she would take great care of the body of their little son, Ben, and that they were to think of her as their babysitter.

Memories of time spent with their child after death can be very precious. Sensitively preparing parents for what their child might look like is important, as is affording them the opportunity to do things that matter to them. Sarah greatly appreciated the mortuary technician who gently and willingly made her little child's body available for her to see each day before the funeral so she could read her stories, and the interest the technician took in the books she brought.

Parents have seldom had anything but positive feelings towards professionals who have been visibly moved by what has happened. They are often helped by seeing the professionals' reactions to the death of their child; this makes the death real and can also give parents the permission they may need to show their emotions.

> 'It was important that people saw our beautiful son and thought that this was the worst thing in the world that could have happened.'
>
> Andrea[1]

The 'system' that swings into action when a sudden death occurs can leave parents feeling powerless, with everything out of their control. Where a coroner's post-mortem examination is to take place, having no say as parents in whether or not their child undergoes the examination can be experienced as a huge violation. Unfortunately, when a death is to be referred to a coroner, the temptation for professionals in contact with the family at that time can be to present this as a fait accompli, believing that the less the parents have to think about this, the better it will be for them. Arguably, however, in cases of sudden death there is even more reason to ensure that clear explanations and information are given to parents at each stage of the process.

However well intentioned, keeping people in the dark usually only serves to increase their anxiety. Explaining gently to parents that the examination is being done to help understand why their child died, giving them the name of the pathologist who will be carrying out the examination and details of where and when it will be carried out, reassuring them that nothing will be retained

[1] From: *Paediatric Post Mortem: Communicating with Grieving Families* (Video/CD-Rom 2004) The Child Bereavement Trust

without them knowing why and for how long, and informing them what the arrangements will be if they wish to see their child afterwards can help alleviate concerns.

Another important area is making sure that parents are fully informed of the process where there is to be an inquest. If members of the press are present, families need help in understanding that aspects of the inquest may be made public. Media interest can be difficult for families to manage. While Lucy found it deeply shocking to see her daughter's picture on the front page of newspapers which were blowing around a wet and windy petrol station forecourt, Louise and Paul were helped by a sensitive coroner who allowed them to leave the inquest by the back door to avoid the waiting press.

Parents have greatly appreciated those professionals who have afforded them the opportunity to ask questions, and who have sensitively answered those questions honestly and openly. Telling parents that certain things are 'not possible' or 'not advisable' without any explanation as to why leaves them wondering and fuels their imagination, often leading them to conclusions that may be a far cry from the reality of the situation.

> 'When I asked if I could pick her up, the funeral director said he wouldn't advise it.'
>
> Natasha[2]

This left Natasha with concerns as to what had happened during the post-mortem examination, whereas a sensitive explanation of what could be expected would have been much more helpful.

Professionals need to take their lead from the family. Information should be available for those who want it. It is important not to assume that information will be too difficult for parents to manage, but equally important not to force unwanted information on them. Sensitivity is the key. Often, parents will appreciate knowing what the next stage in the process is. They have also been grateful to be given the contact number of someone they can get in touch with should they later have any questions.

Parenting instincts are not extinguished by death; they may never have spent any time apart from their child during the child's lifetime and knowing where their child is, who is with their child, being helped to understand what is and is not possible under the circumstances, and what the course of events is likely to be can be extremely helpful in lessening their understandable anxiety in being separated from their child. They need time to absorb what has happened; in their distress, information may need to be repeated several times. It can be helpful to provide some clear information in writing to back up what has been given verbally, and for professionals to take responsibility for checking whether parents have understood what they have been told.

---

[2] From: *Paediatric Post Mortem: Communicating with Grieving Families* (Video/CD-Rom 2004) The Child Bereavement Trust

Parents have appreciated being offered the choice of being involved in all aspects of their child's care, even when very difficult. Lucy and Mark watched the attempts to resuscitate their daughter Hazel, and appreciated that everything possible had been done. Supporting parents by communicating what is happening, and why, is important.

> 'I got there in time to see them working on Hazel, which is something I'll never forget – they were trying everything. Lucy had been there for 25 minutes. I arrived with new hope and thought everyone around me wasn't so hopeful, because I didn't realise.'
>
> Mark[3]

Even the most difficult of subjects, if broached sensitively, can be raised with families. When Peter and Andrea's son, Thomas, died suddenly and unexpectedly, the sensitivity of the nursing staff in raising the subject of organ donation helped them consider this choice without any pressure or agenda on the part of the staff. In fact, three adults and two other children benefited from Thomas's organs, and Andrea and Peter had some precious extra days with Thomas while recipients were found.

A major source of concern for parents whose child has died suddenly and unexpectedly is explaining to their other children what has happened. Most parents will never have had any cause to think about how they might do this, and will appreciate guidance from informed professionals.

> 'What about our surviving children? How do we explain to them something we do not understand ourselves?'
>
> Louise

Every parent's natural instinct is likely to be to protect siblings, but the issue is not whether or not to talk to them, but how this can be managed. Even very young children are aware when something significant is happening within the family, and will notice what is going on around them. Professionals can play an important role in supporting parents with this difficult task by making time to discuss with them their worries and anxieties and helping them think about how they might include siblings around their brother's or sister's death.

Acknowledging that it is natural for parents to want to protect their children, but that children tell us they want to know and be included, can be supportive of parents in parenting their other children when a tragedy has happened in the family. Very young children may have difficulty in understanding the permanence of death, but simple explanations such as 'when you're dead, your body doesn't work any more' can help children understand that death is different to being asleep (when your body works very well) and why, if they touch someone who has died, their body will feel very cold.

[3]From: *A Child Dies: Parents' Grief* (DVD 2006) The Child Bereavement Trust

If children are to be involved, preparing them for what they will see – avoiding euphemisms and using words appropriate to their level of understanding – is crucial.

No answer will ever be adequate to justify to parents why their child was taken from them; the 'why' will never be satisfactorily answered, regardless of whether or not a definitive cause of death is ultimately established. Parents are rendered powerless in the face of death, regardless of when or how that death occurs. Those feelings of powerlessness are not infrequently mirrored in the professionals who come into contact with the family.

Working to understand the needs of grieving families who experience their child's sudden death can aid us in offering appropriate support. We learn constantly from families; each one is unique and that family's 'culture' will determine their responses and actions. Similarly, as professionals, our own family culture will determine our responses to issues of death and dying, and will inevitably impact on our interactions with bereaved families. It is essential, therefore, if we are to be effective in caring for bereaved families, that we are self aware and recognise that we will bring our own feelings about our own life experiences to any encounter with grieving families. These can give us the sensitivity to engage with families. Conversely, if we do not recognise where our own feelings come from, the potential for them to get in the way is significant.

Self awareness requires us not only to be willing and able to look at what has happened in our own lives, but to recognise how those experiences have affected us, and what aspects of those experiences we might carry into our work. It also involves us looking at the impact of this work on ourselves. Emotional pain can be catching, and accessing support for our needs is vital. If we are willing to look at these things for ourselves, we will undoubtedly be better equipped to come alongside bereaved families and afford them the care they deserve.

2 Childhood Deaths in Context

PETER SIDEBOTHAM
PETER FLEMING

INTRODUCTION

In 2004, 5,000 children under the age of 16 died in the United Kingdom (UK) (Office for National Statistics 2006b). This bald figure cannot possibly capture for each one of those families the awful reality of losing their child. Nevertheless, if we are ever to make a difference in preventing childhood deaths, it is important that we understand contemporary patterns of such deaths, their nature, causes and any underlying contributory factors. In this chapter we will explore the historical and geographical context of childhood deaths in the UK and outline current patterns of child mortality. We will outline briefly the major causes and categories of childhood death, and will draw on published literature to examine underlying contributory factors. Subsequent chapters in this section will develop in more detail natural causes of childhood death (Chapter 3), sudden infant death syndrome (Chapter 4), childhood accidents (Chapter 5) and fatal child maltreatment (Chapter 6).

DEFINITIONS

It is important first to clarify the process of death certification and some definitions which will be used in this chapter and elsewhere in the book. Some important definitions, as used by the Office for National Statistics (ONS) are provided in Box 2.1. Mortality is defined as the rate of deaths per unit population within a given time period. This is usually expressed as deaths per 100,000 population per year. For child deaths, mortality is usually given as age-specific mortality within particular age bands. In infancy, mortality is more commonly expressed per 1,000 live births, and is divided into infant mortality (all deaths under 1 year), neonatal mortality (up to 4 weeks) and post-neonatal mortality (deaths between 28 days and 1 year). A further important rate is the perinatal mortality which, in contrast to the above figures, includes stillbirths and deaths under 1 week, and is calculated in relation to all births (live births and stillbirths).

Box 2.1 Definitions

Incidence

The frequency of new occurrences of a disease or condition within a defined time interval (usually 1 year).

Prevalence

The total number of cases of a disease or condition in a given population at a specific time.

Mortality

The number of deaths per unit of population within a given period of time. Usually expressed as deaths per 100,000 population per year.

Standardised mortality ratio (SMR)

A ratio of the observed number of deaths in a given population compared to the expected number of deaths based on the age profile of the population. An SMR of 100 implies the population has the same mortality as the general population, >100 implies an increased risk of death and <100 a lower risk.

Age-specific mortality rate

The number of deaths in a particular age group per 100,000 population in that group.

Stillbirth rate

The number of stillbirths per 1,000 live births and stillbirths.

Perinatal mortality rate

The number of stillbirths plus number of deaths at ages under one week, per 1,000 live births and stillbirths.

Infant mortality rate

The number of deaths at ages under one year, per 1,000 live births.

Neonatal mortality rate

The number of deaths at ages under 4 weeks, per 1,000 live births.

Early neonatal mortality rate

The number of deaths at ages under 1 week, per 1,000 live births.

Postneonatal mortality rate

The number of deaths at ages 28 days and over but under one year, per 1,000 live births.

DEATH CERTIFICATION

In England and Wales, all births and deaths need to be registered with a registrar of births, deaths and marriages. Registration of a birth is required legally within 42 days of its occurrence. This is usually undertaken by the parents of the child, although certain other people may be qualified to notify a birth. Under the National Health Service Act 1977, births must also be notified within 36 hours to the Director of Public Health in the primary care organisation where the birth occurred. This is carried out by the hospital where the birth took place, or by the midwife or doctor in attendance at the birth. Most deaths are certified by a medical practitioner, using the Medical Certificate of Cause of Death (MCCD). The forms are slightly different for neonatal and non-neonatal deaths. The doctor certifying the death must have been in attendance during the last illness of the deceased. This certificate is then usually taken to a registrar of births and deaths by a person known as the informant – usually a near relative of the deceased – within five days of the death.

In certain cases deaths are referred to, and sometimes then investigated by, a coroner (Box 2.2) (Office for National Statistics 2005c). In these cases the coroner sends information to the registrar and it is used instead of that on the MCCD to register the death. Coroners have a number of possible courses of action once a death has been referred. If they are satisfied that the death is due to natural causes and the cause is correctly certified, the local registrar is notified and they can then register the death using the cause given on the MCCD. Alternatively, the coroner may order a post-mortem examination, particularly where the death was sudden and the cause unknown, or for deaths where there were no doctors in attendance (this would include for example, all sudden unexpected deaths in infancy). If the autopsy shows unequivocally

---

Box 2.2 Conditions notified to a coroner

Deaths that should be referred to a coroner include those where:

- the cause is unknown
- the deceased was not seen by the certifying doctor either after death or within the 14 days before death
- the cause was violent, or unnatural, or suspicious
- the death may have been due to an accident (whenever it occurred)
- the death may have been due to self-neglect or neglect by others
- the death occurred during an operation or before recovery from the effects of an anaesthetic
- the death may have been a suicide
- the death occurred during or shortly after detention in police or prison custody.

that the death was due to natural causes, the coroner notifies the registrar of the cause of death, based on the information from the autopsy. If, following the autopsy, the coroner is unable to give a natural cause of death, they will hold an inquest and the death can usually be registered only after the inquest has taken place. Rarely, the coroner may hold an inquest without an autopsy, although this would be unusual in an unexpected death of a child. In most cases the inquest concludes the investigation and the death is then certified by the coroner. If it appears that someone is to be charged with an offence in relation to the death, the coroner must adjourn the inquest until legal proceedings are completed. If the inquest is adjourned, the death may be registered using a temporary code for the underlying cause of death until final information becomes available.

The cause of death, as determined by the registrar, is based on the WHO International Classification of Diseases (ICD-10) (World Health Organisation 1993). The cause of death is defined as: a) the disease or injury that initiated the train of events directly leading to death; or b) the circumstances of the accident or violence that produced the fatal injury. For neonatal deaths, a different classification system is used, based on the timing of the event or factors leading to death: whether it was before the onset of labour, in or shortly after labour, or postnatal.

THE NATURE OF CHILDHOOD

Childhood, in UK law, is defined as the period from birth up to the person's 18th birthday (HM Government 2006b). Within this, we need to recognise that there is a continuum from conception, through growth *in utero*, delivery, and subsequent growth and development through to adulthood. Childhood is an important period for a number of reasons: it is a period of change, of vulnerability and dependence, of gradually developing autonomy; it is a period in which particular rights and needs are recognised. Children are not simply small adults, or just in a process of becoming. Childhood is important in its own right, and children and young people have their own aspirations. In a recent consultation exercise in the UK (HM Government 2003), children and young people outlined five outcomes that were important to them: being healthy, staying safe, enjoying and achieving, making a positive contribution and enjoying economic well-being. We too need to recognise and value the importance of those outcomes and to recognise that death in childhood, and the circumstances that lead to that death, deny the child those opportunities.

From a physical or medical point of view, children also should not be seen simply as small adults. The child's body works differently to that of an adult; it will respond differently to the environment, to disease processes and to medical and non-medical treatments. An example of this would be in the use of drugs to treat an underlying disease: simply adjusting the dose to account for a child's weight compared to that of an adult does not reflect the different ways in which the child may absorb the drug or the immaturity of the liver in metabolising that drug, of the body tissues in responding to the drug, or the kidneys in excreting the drug. Not taking account of such differences could lead to serious under- or over-dosing of the drug in question.

THE NATURE OF DEATH IN CHILDHOOD

Death has been defined as 'the irreversible loss of the capacity for consciousness, combined with the irreversible loss of the capacity to breathe', reflecting the concept that death entails the irreversible loss of those essential characteristics which are necessary to the existence of a living human person (Royal College of Anaesthetists 2006). In most situations, the irreversible loss of consciousness goes hand in hand with the irreversible loss of the capacity to breathe and with cessation of the heart beat. However, it is possible to lose one capacity without the other: for example, a child may irreversibly lose the capacity to breathe, yet be kept alive with some conscious faculties, through the use of mechanical ventilation. Furthermore, the sequence of events may vary. In adults, sudden death often occurs as a result of a heart attack. The heart stops beating and the consequent lack of oxygen supply to the brain leads to loss of consciousness and cessation of breathing. In infants, death often occurs due to respiratory compromise which in turn leads to a lack of oxygen supply to the brain and heart. In other situations, for example traumatic brain injury, it may be the brain itself that is affected primarily, leading to loss of function, including the function of the brain stem, which regulates breathing.

Following a cardiorespiratory arrest, a doctor needs to be certain that there has been irreversible damage to the vital centres of the brain stem before he can certify death. To date there have been no standardised criteria on which to base that certainty; however, a joint working party has recently suggested some standardised criteria which should lead to improved certification of death (Box 2.3) (Royal College of Anaesthetists 2006).

Many deaths in childhood are the expected consequence of natural disease processes. This would particularly be the case, for example, in a child dying of cancer where treatment has been unavailable or unsuccessful, or in a child with a progressive neurodegenerative disorder. In such situations, palliative and supportive care can be provided to the child and family and often preparations can be made to meet the wishes of the child and family, for example in terms of where the child dies and who is with them. Other deaths, however, occur in an unexpected manner. An unexpected death may be defined as the death of a child which was not anticipated as a significant possibility 24 hours before the death or where there was a similarly unexpected collapse leading to or precipitating the events which led to the death (Fleming

---

Box 2.3 Criteria for certifying death after cardiorespiratory arrest

- The simultaneous and irreversible onset of apnoea and unconsciousness in the absence of the circulation.
- No reversible factors are causing or contributing to the cardiorespiratory arrest. Such factors include body temperature, endocrine, metabolic and biochemical abnormalities.
- One of the following is fulfilled:
  - the individual meets the criteria for not attempting cardiopulmonary resuscitation
  - attempts at cardiopulmonary resuscitation have failed
  - treatment has been withdrawn because it has been decided to be of no further benefit to the patient and not in his/her best interest to continue and/or in respect of the patient's wishes.
- The individual should be observed for a full five minutes to confirm that irreversible cardiorespiratory arrest has occurred. The absence of mechanical cardiac function can be confirmed with increasing accuracy using any one or a combination of the following:
  - absence of a central pulse on palpation
  - absence of heart sounds on auscultation
  - asystole on a continuous ECG display
  - absence of pulsatile flow using direct intra-arterial pressure monitoring
  - absence of contractile activity using echocardiography.
- Given, as above, that no further attempts are planned to restore the circulation, any spontaneous return of cardiac or respiratory activity during this period of observation should prompt a further five minutes' observation from the next point of cardiorespiratory arrest.
- After five minutes of continued cardiorespiratory arrest, the absence of the papillary responses to light, of the corneal reflexes, and of any motor response to supra-orbital pressure should be confirmed.
- The time of death is recorded as the time at which these criteria are fulfilled.

---

et al. 2000). In such situations, the event may be observed and cardiopulmonary resuscitation instituted, or the child may be discovered some time after the event. It is not unusual, if a child is observed at the point of collapse, or discovered shortly afterwards, for resuscitation to be successful in restoring cardiac output. A child's breathing may then be maintained on a ventilator with intensive care support. In these situations, it may be necessary to make subsequent decisions on withdrawal of intensive care. Such decisions should never be made lightly and should involve the full clinical team working with the parents and other family members (Royal College of Paediatrics & Child Health 2004).

CHILDHOOD DEATH IN THE 21ST CENTURY

Today, in the UK and other developed nations, death in childhood is fortunately a rare experience. It has not always been so, and even today, for many parts of the world, the loss of a child is far too common. Globally, 10.6 million children under the age of five die every year, with more than one in five children dying before the age of five in parts of sub-Saharan Africa, or South Asia (UNICEF 2006). More than half of these child deaths are caused by four communicable disease categories: diarrhoea, pneumonia, malaria, and neonatal pneumonia and sepsis, with malnutrition also contributing to more than 50% of childhood deaths (Bryce et al. 2005). In developed countries the pattern is very different, with a lower overall mortality, and with far fewer deaths related to infectious diseases.

The number of childhood deaths in the UK has fallen dramatically over the past century, from over 200,000 in 1904, to just over 5,000 in 2004 (Figure 2.1). Some of this fall in death rates can be attributed to improvements in public health, including proper sanitation and immunisation. Further improvements relate to an overall improvement in housing and standards of living, nutrition (both child and maternal), ending child labour, and to improved Health Services, including the availability of antibiotics for the treatment of infectious diseases. However, disparities still exist, with wide variations across the UK largely reflecting a strong north–south divide. In spite of an overall drop in the infant mortality rate over the past century, strong socio-economic differences persist, with infants whose fathers are in routine or semi-routine occupations having twice the mortality of those whose fathers are in managerial or professional posts (Figure 2.2); those whose fathers are long-term unemployed have a more than 30-fold increase in risk of death (Office for National Statistics

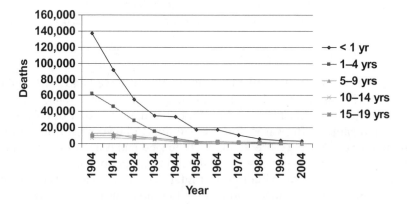

Figure 2.1 Child mortality 1904–2004
Source: National Statistics Online: www.statistics.gov.uk

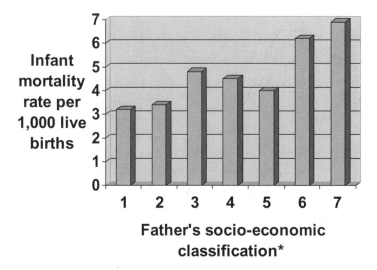

* National Statistics Socio-economic Classification (NS-SEC):
1 Higher managerial and professional occupations
2 Lower managerial and professional occupations
3 Intermediate occupations
4 Small employers and own-account workers
5 Lower supervisory and technical occupations
6 Semi-routine occupations
7 Routine occupations

Figure 2.2 Infant mortality by father's socio-economic classification (Office for National Statistics 2006b)

2006b). Similar class gradients are observed in relation to specific causes of death in older children, particularly deaths from injuries, with a seven-fold difference in deaths due to traffic collision with a pedestrian and an eight-fold difference in deaths due to fire (Spencer 1996).

The majority of childhood deaths occur in the youngest age groups. Of the 5,025 childhood deaths in 2004, 83% were of children aged under five; 72% under one year; 49% under one month and 37% less than a week (Office for National Statistics 2006b). However, whilst the highest rates are found in infancy, there is a second rise in adolescence (Figure 2.3). At all ages, there is a consistently higher mortality in boys compared to girls (Figure 2.3). Overall rates are 1.2:1 in infancy and early childhood, but rising to 2.3:1 in the 15–19 age group.

Within these different age bands, the main causes of death vary. For neonatal deaths, conditions originating in the perinatal period, including maternal factors and complications of pregnancy, labour or delivery; and prematurity or poor fetal growth, account for 79% of all deaths (Table 2.1, Figure 2.4)

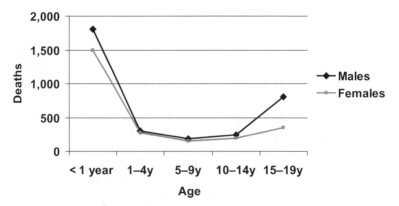

Figure 2.3 Childhood mortality, England and Wales 2003 (Office for National Statistics 2005b)

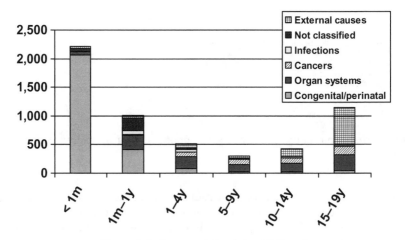

Figure 2.4 Causes of death in childhood

(Office for National Statistics 2005d, 2006b). Congenital malformations make up the next largest group (15%), with respiratory and cardiovascular disorders, including birth asphyxia, respiratory infections and respiratory distress syndrome accounting for most other deaths. Other infections and organ-specific diseases are less common causes of death. Injury, poisoning and other external causes are rare, but nevertheless important as they are potentially avoidable deaths. In this age group, sudden infant death syndrome (SIDS) is rare, with most SIDS deaths occurring after the age of six weeks.

Outside of this neonatal period, congenital malformations and perinatal conditions remain important causes, accounting for 31% of infant deaths; a

Table 2.1 Causes of death in childhood (Office for National Statistics 2005d, 2006b)

	<1 month	1 month–1 year	1–4 years	5–9 years	10–14 years	15–19 years
Congenital malformations and conditions originating in the perinatal period	2,439 (93.2%)	411 (40.7%)	81 (15.7%)	24 (7.9%)	21 (5.0%)	48 (4.2%)
Various diseases of organ systems	73 (2.8%)	250 (24.8%)	209 (40.5%)	128 (42.2%)	148 (35.3%)	269 (23.4%)
Cancers	6 (0.2%)	19 (1.9%)	73 (14.1%)	89 (29.4%)	99 (23.6%)	151 (13.1%)
Infections	1 (0.0%)	71 (7.0%)	50 (9.7%)	14 (4.6%)	15 (3.6%)	22 (1.9%)
Abnormal clinical and laboratory findings not elsewhere classified	66 (2.5%)	218 (21.6%)	22 (4.3%)	7 (2.3%)	9 (2.1%)	14 (1.2%)
External causes of morbidity and mortality	31 (1.2%)	41 (4.1%)	81 (15.7%)	41 (14.5%)	127 (30.3%)	646 (56.2%)
Total*	**2,209**	**1,010**	**516**	**303**	**419**	**1,150**

*The system of classification of cause of neonatal deaths allows more than one main cause of death to be included, therefore the figures for main cause groups add up to more than the total number of deaths.

further 44% are due to infections, cancers and other medical diagnoses. A quarter of infant deaths however are categorised as due to external causes, or 'findings not elsewhere classified', a term that encompasses the large proportion of deaths classified as SIDS. During the middle childhood years, natural causes of death predominate, with infections, cancers and other medical causes accounting for 79% of deaths. However, during the adolescent years (15–17), the pattern is strikingly different. Overall death rates rise again, and in contrast to early childhood, 52% of these deaths are due to external causes of morbidity and mortality, including accidental deaths, homicide and suicide.

AVOIDABLE DEATHS

It is arguable that all of those deaths classified as due to external causes are potentially avoidable. However, a closer look at all deaths suggests that even amongst those with a recognisable 'medical' cause of death, many could be prevented (Box 2.4). A study in Wolverhampton concluded that, of 180 deaths in children aged under five in 1996–2002, 34 (19%) were preventable (Moore 2005). Rimsza et al. (2002), reviewing 4,800 deaths in Arizona in 1995–1999, concluded that overall 29% were preventable, this figure rising to 38% if neonatal deaths were excluded. Further evidence that many childhood deaths are potentially avoidable comes from examining the disparities in mortality rates across the UK. For example, in 2004, infant mortality was 7 per 1,000 live births in Birmingham and the Black Country, compared to 3.3 in Hampshire and the Isle of Wight (Office for National Statistics 2006b). Indeed, if all regions of the country shared the mortality rates of the best, over 1,000 infant deaths and nearly 500 child deaths could be prevented each year (Office for National Statistics 2005c, 2006b).

FACTORS RELATED TO CHILDHOOD DEATH

Those who work within the child protection field in the UK will be familiar with the three domains of the *Framework of Assessment* (HM Government 2000): the child's developmental needs, parenting capacity and the wider family and environmental context (Figure 2.5). This same framework can be used to understand the interplay of factors relating to a child's death.

CHILD FACTORS

First we need to consider factors within the child, remembering that up to the point where he or she died, that child was growing and developing the same as any child. The very nature of childhood means that children, and especially

---

Box 2.4 Case study

Harvey, a three-year-old boy, was brought by ambulance to the Emergency Department one afternoon having suffered what appeared to be a severe anaphylactic reaction. Harvey had been healthy during early infancy, but at five months of age presented to hospital following ingestion of a Farley's rusk, which led to a rash but no other symptoms. Investigations confirmed an allergy to wheat, egg and nuts. He was placed on an appropriately restricted diet, with advice and support given to the parents. Harvey went on to develop recurrent wheeze and was treated with inhalers and courses of steroids. He suffered from infantile eczema but had otherwise been healthy and was growing well.

At the age of two, Harvey started attending nursery. The nursery staff was informed of his dietary needs, and was aware of his allergies and asthma. On the afternoon of the fatal episode, one of the children at the nursery had brought some fairy cakes because it was her birthday. A new staff member was looking after their group and had not been told about Harvey's allergy, so they let him have one of the cakes. Harvey started to cough, then rapidly became distressed, with difficulty breathing and clutching at his throat. By the time the ambulance arrived, Harvey was unconscious and in spite of appropriate resuscitation, he did not recover. An autopsy confirmed that the death was due to an anaphylactic (severe allergic) reaction.

In this situation, a clear medical cause of death was evident (asphyxia secondary to anaphylaxis). However, this death was potentially avoidable. The underlying allergies were known about and had been the cause of previous hospital admissions. If Harvey had not been given the fairy cake, he would not have suffered an anaphylactic reaction; equally, if prompt treatment had been instituted prior to the arrival of the ambulance, the rapid deterioration could have been halted.

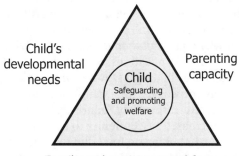

Figure 2.5 Assessment framework
Source: Crown copyright material is reproduced with the permission of the Controller of HMSO and Queen's Printer for Scotland.

younger infants, are more vulnerable than adults and potentially more susceptible to adverse environmental factors. Certain features of the child may make
them more vulnerable still. We have already mentioned the increased mortality at all ages of boys compared to girls. The reasons for this are not entirely
clear, but there may be underlying genetic susceptibilities and, at least in adolescence, the character and temperament of males may make them more susceptible through risk-taking behaviours. Premature and low-birth-weight
infants have an increased mortality at all stages and this increases in relation
to shorter gestations and lower birth weights.

There are a number of life-limiting and life-threatening conditions which
may affect children, for example cancers and neurodegenerative disorders. The
nature and progression of these conditions varies and new treatments are
being developed that may alter their course. For example, whilst cystic fibrosis
previously led to death in early childhood, the average life expectancy may
now be as high as 40 years (Staab et al. 1998). Similarly, for many children with
neuromuscular disorders, the natural progression would have led to death
from respiratory failure during adolescence. With new approaches to home
ventilation, many of these children have a longer and better quality of life. For
children with life-limiting conditions, palliative and supportive care should be
available and of a high quality to minimise any pain and distress associated
with dying.

Children may also suffer from a range of acute and chronic conditions which
are not normally fatal or life limiting. Asthma and epilepsy are long-term
conditions which can normally be managed with appropriate medication and
children with these conditions should be able to live normal lives. However,
both conditions do carry the risk of severe attacks, which may be fatal. Similarly, children with anaphylaxis may have fatal reactions following exposure
to specific allergens. Psychiatric disorders such as anorexia nervosa may be
fatal, and children with depression or other mental health problems may be
at risk of suicide or of unintentional death through risk-taking behaviours.

Disabled children are generally more vulnerable than their counterparts,
but this vulnerability depends on the nature and severity of the disability, and
it is important to remember that the presence of a disability in itself is never
sufficient to explain why a particular child has died. A disabled child may be
at risk through associated complications, for example heart failure due to an
untreatable heart defect in a child with Down's syndrome; through progression
of the underlying disease processes, for example a child with muscular dystro-
phy developing progressive respiratory failure due to the underlying muscle
weakness; or through increased susceptibility to external hazards, for example
a child with cerebral palsy choking on food due to poor swallowing and cough
reflexes. Like all children, disabled children may die of any number of natural
or unnatural causes, including infections, cancers or organ system diseases, or
accidents, homicide or suicide. However, being more dependent on their carers,
they may be more vulnerable to the effects of poor parental care, neglect or

abuse. Indeed it is well recognised that disabled children are more at risk of child maltreatment (Westcott & Jones 1999, Sullivan & Knutson 2000, National Working Group on Child Protection and Disability 2003), and such issues should be considered when a disabled child dies unexpectedly.

PARENTAL FACTORS

The issue of parental factors contributing to a child's death is a sensitive one, and we must be careful not to attribute blame inappropriately, but similarly not to ignore the influence that parents have on their children's health and well-being, and factors in the parents' nature, health or behaviour that may be amenable to change.

Some parents may lack the capacity to recognise or respond to their children's needs, for example through learning difficulties, physical disabilities or chronic ill-health. This inability to care may be exacerbated when it interacts with particular needs of the child, for example, the very young infant who is totally dependent on the parents for regular feeding, or a disabled or ill child who needs extra levels of care. Parents in these situations need adequate care and support in their parenting role from professionals and the wider community. Parents with mental health problems are a particular group where the underlying illness may impact on the ability to care for their children. This issue has been particularly realised in numerous serious case reviews of children who have died as a result of abuse or neglect (Reder & Duncan 1999). However, in considering parents with mental health problems, as with those with other health issues or disabilities, it is important not to jump to the conclusion that the death was a result of maltreatment. Deaths in these circumstances require the same thorough and systematic approach to investigation as all other unexpected child deaths.

Drug and alcohol abuse by parents may present particular risks to the child. Again this may not be through any intent to harm the child, but may be a consequence, for example, of falling asleep with a child on a sofa whilst under the influence of drugs or alcohol. Other parental behaviours, particularly cigarette smoking, may present direct risks to the child's health, with both maternal smoking during pregnancy and postnatal exposure to cigarette smoke more than doubling the risk of sudden infant death syndrome (Blair et al. 1996).

Children of young parents have an increased mortality: infant mortality amongst those born to mothers aged less than 20 is 7.7 compared to 4.9 overall (Office for National Statistics 2006b). Similarly, those infants born to single mothers have a higher mortality (6.3 for those registered singly at birth, compared to 4.5 and 5.5 respectively for those registered jointly within and outside of marriage). The reasons for these disparities are complex and probably involve a range of biological, generational, socio-economic and behavioural factors.

FAMILY AND ENVIRONMENTAL FACTORS

The socio-economic disparities in child mortality have already been mentioned. Other family factors also affect risk. Ethnicity may be particularly important. Whilst the mortality rate for infants of mothers born in the UK is 4.7, that for infants of mothers born outside of the UK is 5.8, with particularly high rates in those from Pakistan (8.9), East Africa (8.5), other African countries excluding South Africa (8.3) and the Caribbean (8.4) (Office for National Statistics 2006b).

Within the environment, various other factors may contribute to a child's death and a thorough assessment of these is essential to understanding the nature and causes of the child's death. Within the home, factors such as heating, ventilation, overcrowding or damp may all contribute to ill-health or death; hazards within or outside of the home may contribute to death from injury. Specific factors in the environment, such as where and how the child is sleeping, affect the risk of sudden infant death syndrome. These are covered in more detail in Chapter 4. Children's play environments and road safety measures all affect risk of accidental death outside of the home and will be considered in Chapter 5.

3 Natural Causes of Unexpected Childhood Deaths

PETER FLEMING
PETER SIDEBOTHAM

INTRODUCTION

Whilst most information on unexpected deaths in childhood is on deaths in the first year of life, unexpected deaths can occur at any age throughout childhood. A major problem in collecting data on the causes of such deaths beyond infancy is that the deaths will be categorised according to the attributed underlying cause, with no note of whether the deaths were sudden or unexpected. Sudden unexpected deaths that remain unexplained despite thorough investigation are uncommon beyond the age of nine months, and rare beyond the age of two years.

In a study of post-mortem findings in children and young people between the ages of 2 and 20 years over a 20-year period in Scotland, Keeling and Knowles (1989) showed that of 169 sudden unexpected deaths from natural causes, 92 (54%) occurred in children with recognised disorders to which the deaths were attributed (e.g. cardiac abnormalities, asthma or epilepsy). Amongst the 77 sudden unexpected deaths of previously apparently healthy children, infection was the most commonly identified cause, whilst only 11 unexpected deaths out of the total of 169 (i.e. 6.5%) remained unexplained.

In a more recent study in the north of England, Wren et al. (2000) investigated the registered cause of death for children and young people from 1 to 20 years of age inclusive over a 10-year period. Of a total of 2,523 deaths, 1,287 (51%) were natural, of which 270 were identified as sudden. Of these sudden deaths, 142 occurred in children with a previously recognised disorder, to which the death was attributed (e.g. epilepsy, cardiac abnormality or asthma). Of the 128 unexpected deaths in previously apparently healthy children, 49 were due to infection and 26 were due to previously unrecognised cardiovascular abnormalities. 41 (15%) of the 270 natural unexpected deaths were unexplained. This study shows that for this population the rate of sudden unexpected deaths was 3.3/100,000 population per year, with the unexpected and unexplained death rate being 0.5/100,000 population per year.

Unexpected Death in Childhood: A Handbook for Practitioners. Edited by P. Sidebotham and P. Fleming.
Copyright © 2007 by John Wiley & Sons, Ltd.

In a study from northern Spain, Morentin and colleagues (2000) investigated all unexpected non-violent deaths of children from 1 to 19 years from 1990 to 1997, and reported a very similar distribution of identified causes, giving a rate for sudden unexpected deaths in childhood of 1.7/100,000 per year, and a rate for unexpected and unexplained deaths in childhood of 0.5/100,000 per year.

Preliminary data from a study of childhood deaths in five regions of the UK currently being conducted by CEMACH (the Confidential Enquiry into Maternal and Child Health) suggests that for many unexpected deaths of older children, potentially preventable factors can be identified that may be amenable to change, with the possibility of reducing the risk of future similar deaths. Thus the conduct of a thorough multi-agency investigation may be as important in the identification of potentially significant contributory factors for unexpected but 'explained' deaths in childhood as it is for sudden infant deaths.

THE REGISTERED CAUSES OF DEATHS IN INFANCY AND CHILDHOOD

As noted in Chapter 2 (Table 2.1) the distribution of certified causes of deaths varies among age groups in childhood, but the proportion of deaths from recognised external causes rises with increasing age to reach 56% of all deaths in the 15–19 years age group.

Assessment and comparison of figures for the proportion of childhood deaths in different countries attributed to various categories is complicated by the different ways in which the data are published, as not all such data are classified according to the most recent 10th revision of the WHO International Classification of Diseases (ICD-10). Table 3.1 shows the proportion of childhood deaths attributed to trauma in published data from the US in 2004, and from Belarus over the period 1980–2000, showing remarkable similarities over a long time period.

In the study from Belarus, there was clear evidence that, as the total childhood mortality rates (per 1,000 population at risk) fell over this time period, there was a steady rise in the proportion of deaths related to trauma. Thus

Table 3.1 Proportion of childhood deaths certified as being due to trauma (accidental and non-accidental) in the US in 2004 and in Belarus in 1980–2000

Age range, years (inclusive)	US (2004) (Hamilton et al. 2007)	Belarus (1980–2000) (Gruber et al. 2005)
1–4	42%	34%
5–9	43%	52%
10–14	44%	44%

improved child health, with reduced disease-related mortality rates, was not accompanied by parallel falls in deaths from trauma – either accidental or non-accidental. In many parts of Africa and Asia these effects are even more marked, with increased mortality rates from trauma accompanying improved disease-related survival rates.

Table 3.2 shows similar data for childhood deaths in England and Wales for the period 1998–2000.

The proportion of 'unexpected' deaths amongst those attributed to infection, circulatory or respiratory causes, or to disorders of the nervous system, is not clear.

It is thus likely that, throughout childhood, unexpected deaths, including those due to a previously unrecognised identifiable cause and those that remain unexplained, together with both accidental and non-accidental trauma, in total account for between 30 and 50% of all deaths.

In a study from the Oxford record linkage system, Petrou and colleagues (2006) showed that, for the period 1979–1988, the mortality rates per 1,000 population at risk rose significantly with decreasing socio-economic status of parents, for each age group (0–6 days, 7–27 days, 28–365 days and 1–10 years) of children under the age of 10. Overall the mortality rate (13.1/1,000) for children in social class V (parents unskilled) was more than 85% higher than for children in social class II (managerial and professional).

Deaths throughout childhood from respiratory causes, notably from pneumonia and bronchiolitis, fell dramatically in the 1970s and 1980s, with the most marked fall being seen in deaths of infants less than one year of age. For example, mortality rates from bronchiolitis in infancy fell from around 150/100,000 in the early 1970s to 15/100,000 in the early 1990s (Panickar et al. 2005). Since the early 1990s, despite a continued fall in total infant mortality

Table 3.2 Main causes of child mortality: by sex and age (percentages), 1998–2000, in England and Wales

	Males		Females	
	1–4	5–15	1–4	5–15
Infections	10	4	9	6
Cancers	15	24	13	23
Nervous system and sense organs	13	15	13	16
Circulatory system	6	5	8	5
Respiratory system	11	6	9	8
Congenital anomalies	13	6	16	8
Accidents	16	27	15	17
Other*	17	13	16	16
All deaths (=100%) (numbers)	1,153	1,773	855	1,239

*Includes undetermined injury whether accidentally or purposely inflicted, homicide, mental disorders and suicide.
Source: Office for National Statistics.

rates (partly due to falls in SIDS rates), the death rates for pneumonia and bronchiolitis have fallen very little, leading to an increase in the proportion of deaths in this age group being attributable to these infections.

Overall, the infant mortality rate has fallen substantially in the UK over the past 30 years, from 13.8/1,000 live births in 1976, to 4.9 in 2005, a fall dominated by the reduction in neonatal mortality (i.e. deaths in the first month after birth) from 9.6/1,000 in 1976, to 3.4 in 2005 (Maher & Macfarlane 2004, Office for National Statistics 2006a). In 2005 a total of 3,188 deaths of infants aged under one year were registered in England and Wales, of which 2,193 (69%) occurred within the first month after birth, with 1,676 (52%) in the first week (Office for National Statistics 2006a).

CAUSES OF SUDDEN DEATH IN INFANCY

With the fall in the overall prevalence of sudden infant deaths, a greater proportion of these are now found to have an identifiable cause. The Confidential Enquiry into Stillbirths and Deaths in Infancy (CESDI) studies of sudden unexpected deaths in infancy, conducted in 1993–1996, identified 93 explained deaths out of a total of 456 SUDI (20%). The most common identified causes were trauma (39%), infection (38%) and (previously unrecognised) congenital malformations (11%). A further 5% were due to gastrointestinal conditions and 4% to metabolic disorders (Fleming et al. 2000).

In the Southwest of England, a study was conducted over the 4-year period 2003–2006 inclusive of all unexpected deaths of infants from birth to two years of age. In this Southwest Infant Sleep Scene (SWISS) study, a higher proportion of deaths was found to be explained completely than in the CESDI study a decade earlier. In a preliminary analysis of the results of the first three years (2003–2005 inclusive) of the SWISS study (Figure 3.1), the distribution of the causes of fully explained deaths (from birth to two years) is compared with that in the CESDI study (which included only deaths from one week to one year).

The proportions of explained deaths due to infection were similar in the two studies, but in the SWISS study a higher proportion was attributed to metabolic disorders and congenital anomalies, and a smaller proportion to accidental and non-accidental injury.

In Figure 3.2 the data are shown for all unexpected infant deaths in the first three years of the SWISS study, again compared to the data from the CESDI SUDI study. The proportion of unexpected infant deaths attributed to SIDS was considerably lower in the SWISS study than in the CESDI study, whilst the proportion of deaths attributed to congenital anomalies, infection and metabolic causes increased, with no identifiable change in the proportion due to non-accidental or accidental injury.

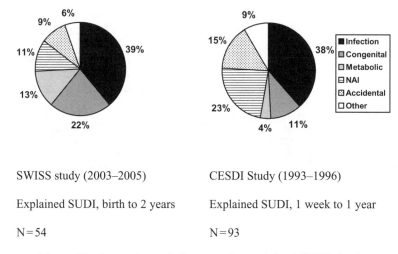

SWISS study (2003–2005)   CESDI Study (1993–1996)

Explained SUDI, birth to 2 years   Explained SUDI, 1 week to 1 year

N = 54   N = 93

Figure 3.1 Comparison of diagnoses for explained SUDI deaths

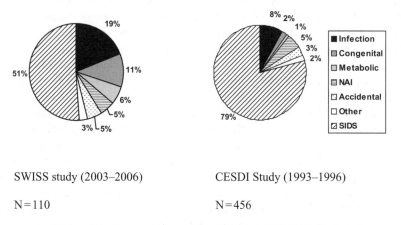

SWISS study (2003–2006)   CESDI Study (1993–1996)

N = 110   N = 456

Figure 3.2 Comparison of diagnoses for all SUDI deaths

The increase in proportion of deaths in the SWISS study attributed to congenital anomalies, and possibly to metabolic causes, may be an effect of including deaths in the first week (which included an increased proportion of both of these groups of causes). The increase in proportion of deaths attributed to infection may in part be a consequence of much improved microbiological and virological investigations being conducted as part of the routine investigation in the Emergency Department (e.g. routinely taking a blood culture and samples of spinal fluid on initial presentation, rather than these samples only being taken at post-mortem examination).

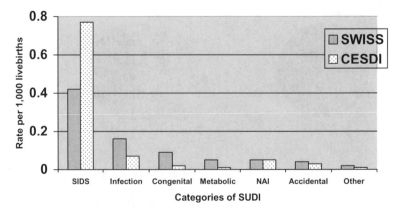

Figure 3.3 Comparison of rates for categories of SUDI

Figure 3.3 shows the data from the CESDI study and from the first three years of the SWISS study expressed as rates per 1,000 live births. It is clear that the SIDS rate for the SWISS study (2003–2005 inclusive) was lower than for the period covered by the CESDI study 10 years earlier (1993–1996). Part of this change is due to an increased proportion of deaths being attributed to specific conditions such as infections, congenital anomalies and inborn errors of metabolism in the SWISS study. As noted above, this change resulted partly from improved immediate investigation for infections and metabolic conditions, and partly from inclusion of deaths in the first week after birth, in which a higher proportion of deaths than in older infants was identified as a consequence of previously unrecognised congenital anomalies.

It is worth noting that the CESDI study took place after the 'Back to Sleep' campaign and the associated fall in the number of SIDS cases. Therefore, whilst some of the reduction in the SIDS rate between these two studies may be attributable to continuing changes in prevalent sleeping practices, this does not account for the overall decline. In contrast to many other studies (Shapiro-Mendoza et al. 2006), these studies have consistently categorised unexpected infant deaths as SIDS where the definitional criteria are met (Willinger et al. 1991) rather than using terms such as 'undetermined' or 'unascertained'. These studies included all sudden unexpected deaths, rather than only including those eventually categorised as SIDS. Thus the identified fall in SIDS rates is not related to changes in categorising these deaths.

The increased proportions of deaths attributed to infection, metabolic causes and congenital anomalies each reflect a higher estimated *rate* (per 1,000 live births) for these causes, but neither the proportion nor the absolute rate of deaths attributed to non-accidental and accidental injury shows any change.

'FULLY EXPLAINED' NATURAL CAUSES OF UNEXPECTED DEATHS IN INFANCY AND CHILDHOOD

As noted above, a wide range of conditions – both those that occur acutely, and those already present but unrecognised – may contribute to or cause unexpected deaths in infancy and childhood. The question of whether or not a particular condition or factor has a direct causal relationship to a death, is one of several potentially contributory factors, or is merely a notable factor that did not directly contribute to the process leading to death is very difficult to establish. The Avon Clinico-Pathological Classification system (see Chapter 7 and Appendix 13) for unexpected deaths is designed to establish a systematic framework within which this assessment can be made (usually at the multi-professional case review meeting) (Fleming et al. 2004).

It is also important to attempt to distinguish between a child who dies *of* a particular condition, and one who dies *with* that condition, but whose death may have another cause or causes.

A further important point in attributing death to a known pre-existing condition is that, although sudden death (e.g. from epilepsy) is well recognised in children with severe neurodevelopmental problems (e.g. cerebral palsy), these children are vulnerable to a large number of risks. For example, the pressures of caring for such children place immense stress upon their families, and such children are at increased risk of abuse. This may include so-called 'mercy killings' by parents in response to the perceived suffering of their child. Disabled children and those with chronic and life-limiting conditions may place far more demands on their parents and carers and may therefore be at risk of neglect of their basic needs, which may lead to increased vulnerability through malnutrition, impaired hygiene or inadequate responses to acute illness. Physical impairments including poor mobility and poor oro-motor control may put some children at greater risk of respiratory or other infections. Finally, whilst attitudes in society to disabled children have changed, there may still be inadequate medical or social care, thus putting these children at further risk. Disabled children and their families are entitled to the same rights as all other children, so the sudden death of a child with an underlying physical or developmental abnormality at an unexpected time warrants as full and careful an investigation as for a previously healthy child.

THE EPIDEMIOLOGY OF UNEXPECTED BUT EXPLAINED DEATHS IN INFANCY AND CHILDHOOD

In the CESDI SUDI study, the epidemiological profile of the unexpected but explained infant deaths was very similar to that of SIDS, with more deaths occurring during the winter months, several markers to suggest social deprivation including younger mothers and higher rates of exposure to tobacco smoke, and markers of infant vulnerability such as low birthweight and prematurity. The only two significant differences from 22 features measured were that more of the explained deaths occurred in the first month of life than was the case for unexplained deaths (SIDS) and that although the prevalence of parental smoking was higher in the explained SUDI than in the control infants, the prevalence in the SIDS families was significantly higher still (Leach et al. 1999, Fleming et al. 2000).

No studies have specifically addressed the epidemiology of unexpected but explained deaths in older children. It is our perception that many of the contributory factors for explained but unexpected deaths in both infants and older children are shared with those factors found in SIDS and indeed with many other causes of childhood mortality. This is an area worthy of more study.

SPECIFIC CONDITIONS THAT MAY CAUSE UNEXPECTED DEATHS IN INFANTS AND CHILDREN

INFECTIONS

Infections, particularly meningococcal or pneumococcal disease, can progress very rapidly in both infants and older children and make up the largest group of medical causes of sudden or unexpected deaths. Septicaemia, meningitis, myocarditis, encephalitis, bronchopneumonia, bronchiolitis and peritonitis have all been identified as causally related to sudden unexpected deaths of both infants and older children.

Myocarditis (inflammation of the heart muscle) may be caused by a wide variety of viruses and other infectious agents, leading to rapid and catastrophic heart failure. Whilst there may be some pointers in the history, including signs of heart failure such as poor feeding, rapid weight gain (due to fluid accumulation) and breathing difficulties, these cases may show little more than non-specific clinical signs. Diagnosis is dependent on the finding of an enlarged heart with an inflammatory cell infiltrate with myocyte necrosis at autopsy and may be supported by the finding of micro-organisms in blood or cardiac tissue (Byard 2004).

Upper respiratory tract infections including croup and epiglottitis may lead to sudden death through upper respiratory obstruction. Although typically there will be some antecedent symptoms, such as a characteristic 'barking' cough, laboured breathing and drooling, the clinical course may be extremely rapid. The incidence of epiglottitis has dropped substantially with the introduction of Haemophilus influenzae B immunisation. The incidence of pertussis (whooping cough) has also dropped because of immunisation, but it may still present in infancy with sudden death due to apnoea. Infants often do not demonstrate the classic 'whoop' following a bout of coughing and again symptoms may be non-specific or absent. Much more common are lower respiratory tract infections, including bronchopneumonia and bronchiolitis. In both of these, preceding symptoms may be mild and non-specific, including poor feeding, irritability and mild respiratory distress. Respiratory infections are however extremely common and most infants recover completely, even when radiology reveals gross changes in the lungs. Many infants with significant pulmonary infiltrates and/or consolidation present with varying degrees of respiratory distress, but survive – thus the finding of intrapulmonary pathology may reflect a contributory factor in a compromised infant rather than a complete and sufficient explanation for the death.

Meningitis may present with a rapid course and minimal or non-specific symptoms. Children, particularly those under the age of three years, may present with a minor illness during the evening, with rapid progression of the infection during sleep and unexpected death before morning. There may be both a non-specific maculo-papular (blanching) rash, and the more familiar non-blanching purpuric rash, particularly in septicaemia (blood infection) without meningitis, although these are not universally present. Haemophylus influenzae, Streptococcus pneumoniae and Neisseria meningitidis (meningococcus) are the most common infecting organisms, along with group B streptococci and enterobacteria in the neonatal period. Immunisations against H influenzae type B and N meningitidis type C have reduced the incidence of both of these organisms as causes of rapidly progressive meningitis or septicaemia, but other serotypes of meningococcus still occur. A rapidly fulminating course may result in fatal septicaemia before the onset of meningitis and the lethal effects are thought to be due to circulating endotoxins. These endotoxins may lead to pathological changes to the myocardium and adrenal glands that can be recognised at autopsy.

The diagnosis of lethal septicaemia is dependent on positive blood cultures and/or isolation of the same organism from multiple sites, preferably with microscopic evidence of disseminated sepsis, but on occasion a blood culture will demonstrate a pure culture of a known pathogen such as S pneumoniae or H influenzae, suggesting that death was a consequence of infection in the absence of any identifiable gross pathological or histological evidence of inflammation or sepsis (Byard 2004).

Blackwell and Morris have each shown the potential importance of toxigenic staphylococci as contributory agents to circulatory collapse and sudden death in infancy (Blackwell & Weir 1999, Morris 2004). Toxin production in such staphylococci increases with increasing environmental temperature and is minimal below 37°C (Blackwell & Weir 1999). SUDI victims have increased nasopharyngeal colonisation with staphylococci compared to healthy age- and community-matched controls (Morris 1999). In the prone position, or with head covering (particularly in the presence of potential rebreathing), nasopharyngeal temperature rises above the normal value of 32°C, with a resultant increase in toxin production by any toxigenic staphylococci present on the mucosal surface (Moscovis et al. 2004). Transmucosal absorption of toxins might thus lead to circulatory collapse and death without the need for invasive infection to occur. The question of whether an unexpected infant death is a consequence of such staphylococcal toxins is thus difficult to answer, but making this diagnosis with any degree of certainty will require the identification of the presence of toxigenic staphylococci together with evidence of the presence of toxins. Such investigations are, however, very seldom conducted as part of the investigation of unexpected deaths.

Certain viruses, notably the entroviruses, have been commonly identified in stool or other samples from infants dying unexpectedly and on occasion have been identified from brain or spinal fluid samples using polymerase chain reaction (PCR) techniques. The known predilection of entroviruses for the central nervous system raises the possibility that these isolates may be causally related to the process leading to death (e.g. by direct effects upon brain-stem nuclei involved in autonomic control, or as a consequence of unrecognised seizures) even in the absence of any histological evidence of CNS inflammatory changes (Grangeot-Keros et al. 1996).

CARDIOVASCULAR CAUSES

Sudden death has been reported in a wide range of congenital heart defects arising *de novo*, or following cardiac surgery. Causes of death in these situations include fatal arrhythmias, cardiac failure, infarction and endocarditis (Byard 2004). One case series found associated cardiac disease in 9.7% of sudden unexpected infant deaths (Dancea et al. 2002). In 60% of these deaths, the diagnosis had not been recognised before autopsy.

Cardiomyopathies are a group of disorders in which the ability of the heart to pump blood effectively is impaired. These may be primary or secondary to metabolic disorders and may result in sudden death. Another heart condition associated with sudden unexpected death is endocardial fibroelastosis. This may result from viral infections or arise spontaneously. At autopsy, there are characteristic changes with thickening of the heart tissue.

Sudden unexpected death has been attributed to a wide range of cardiac dysrhythmias (abnormal heart rhythms), which may occur either as a result of an acute infection (e.g. myocarditis) or as a consequence of an aberrant conduction pathway within the heart. Some of the most common dysrhythmias are listed below.

In the Wolff–Parkinson–White (W–P–W) syndrome an accessory conduction pathway in the heart bypasses the atrioventricular sulcus, and leads to faster conduction and episodes of supraventricular tachycardia (an extremely rapid heart beat), which may on occasion lead to fatal heart failure. W–P–W syndrome is inherited as an autosomal dominant condition, and the gene has been identified on chromosome 7q34-36 (Gollob et al. 2001). Several other patterns of abnormal conduction pathways in the heart have been identified by careful investigation after sudden unexpected deaths, but the proportion of sudden deaths resulting from such abnormalities is not known. There may in these cases be a history of apparent life-threatening events (ALTE) or other episodic events, such as transient colour loss or rapid breathing (Gilbert-Barness & Barness 2006).

The long QT syndrome (LQTS) is a heterogeneous group of disorders characterised by prolongation of the corrected QT interval (QTc) on the ECG, and which may lead to seizures, syncope or sudden death. The defects, a variety of channelopathies affecting myocardial repolarisation, create a vulnerable refractory period in which episodes of ventricular tachycardia (rapid and uncontrolled heart rate) may occur, with potentially lethal loss of cardiac output. At least seven different genetic variants of LQTS have been identified, all of which are inherited in an autosomal dominant manner. A small population-based study of LQTS genes in unexpected infant deaths in the US identified mutations in 3/58 white infants (5.1%) and 1/34 black infants (2.9%) (Tester & Ackerman 2005). These infants died in conditions known to be associated with increased risk of SIDS (prone sleeping and unsafe bed sharing), raising the possibility that prone sleeping may itself increase the risk of arrhythmia in susceptible individuals. Reports from Italy suggest the possibility of immaturity of the cardiac repolarisation process in some infants, perhaps as a marker of general autonomic instability, leading to a temporary condition of LQTS and increased vulnerability to unexpected infant death (Schwartz et al. 1998).

Brugada syndrome is an autosomal dominant condition characterised by right bundle branch block and ST segment elevation in leads V1–V3 of the ECG. It may lead to sudden death from polymorphic ventricular tachycardia, most commonly in young adults, but occasionally in infants or children. The gene defect, SCN5A, is allelic with LQTS type 3 (Gilbert-Barness & Barness 2006).

Arrhythmogenic right ventricular dysplasia (ARVD) is an uncommon condition in which left bundle branch block and right ventricular dilatation are present, and may lead to ventricular tachycardia, commonly precipitated by an infection. Histology of the right ventricle shows fatty infiltration, sometimes accompanied by interstitial fibrosis of the myocardium. Several genetically distinct variants of this condition have been described, mostly inherited as autosomal dominant with variable penetrance, and more common in males than females. In a study from northern Italy, 20% of young adults who died suddenly had histological evidence of right ventricular dysplasia at autopsy (Kullo et al. 1995, Gilbert-Barness & Barness 2006).

Since many cardiac conduction defects cannot be identified at autopsy, the diagnosis must rest on the clinical and family history and appropriate molecular studies, together with ECG investigation of surviving siblings and of parents. It is quite likely that a proportion of those deaths labelled as SIDS are related to underlying but unrecognised heart dysrrhythmias.

Williams syndrome, in which there is a genetically determined abnormality of elastin, is characterised by a typical facial appearance, mild growth impairment and developmental delay, and is associated with a variety of cardiac abnormalities, including suravalvar aortic or pulmonary stenosis and coronary artery stenosis. Children with this condition are at significant risk of sudden unexpected death, as a consequence of their cardiac abnormalities, and in particular some have died suddenly during the course of cardiac catheterisation (Bird et al. 1996). Other syndromes, including Down's syndrome, are known to be associated with congenital heart defects, and although these will often be picked up by antenatal or postnatal screening, this is not always the case, and we have known infants with a range of congenital heart defects that have not been identified prior to the child's death.

The witnessed death of an infant should always raise the possibility of an underlying heart defect. Although most unexpected infant deaths seem to occur during sleep and are only discovered when the parent wakes and checks the child, this is not invariably so, and it is our experience that witnessed deaths are surprisingly common. Such deaths may also result from asphyxia (accidental or inflicted), seizures, or any of the other recognised causes of sudden death. These infants may initially respond to resuscitation but may then subsequently deteriorate, or show no signs of cerebral function, leading to appropriate withdrawal of intensive care. They should be investigated thoroughly, including a very careful history of the events surrounding and preceding the fatal event. If the child does initially respond to resuscitation, it may be possible to carry out a range of investigations prior to death. However, as with unwitnessed deaths, it is not always possible to identify a cause.

GASTROINTESTINAL CAUSES

Fulminant gastroenteritis with severe dehydration and electrolyte imbalance may lead to death from cardiac arrhythmias, cerebral haemorrhage or venous thrombosis. Clinical signs may be apparent at autopsy, and analysis of vitreous humour from the eye may reveal electrolyte imbalances. Other gastrointestinal conditions, including intestinal obstruction, may occasionally present as sudden death, but will usually be obvious at autopsy (Byard 2004). Gastro-oesophageal reflux has been suggested as a possible cause of SIDS (see Chapter 4), through vagally mediated reflex effects upon respiratory control, but good evidence in support of this theory is lacking.

METABOLIC DISORDERS

Inborn errors of metabolism represent a disparate group of disorders, all of which are individually rare, but which in total may account for a substantial proportion of SUDI (Byard 2004). Features in the history that may point to an underlying metabolic disorder include failure to thrive, developmental delay, seizures, and vomiting and diarrhoea. An enlarged liver or spleen may be noted on examination, whilst at autopsy cardiomegaly (an enlarged heart), cerebral oedema (swelling of the brain) and fatty changes in the liver, kidneys and muscle may be found. However, these changes are not specific to metabolic disorders and may be found for example in acute dehydration and severe infection.

Chace and colleagues in Philadelphia conducted a retrospective study of electrospray tandem mass spectrometry for analysis of acylcarnitines on post-mortem samples of blood taken from over 7,000 infants who had died suddenly and unexpectedly, and in whom a diagnosis of metabolic disorders had not been made by other means (Chace et al. 2001). They identified 66 (1%) infants in whom a diagnosis of a recognisable metabolic abnormality could be made. The most common disorders were medium-chain and very-long-chain acyl CoA dehydrogenase deficiency (23 and 9 cases respectively), glutaric acidaemia type I (3 cases) and type II (8 cases), carnitine palmitoyl transferase type II (6 cases), severe carnitine deficiency (4 cases), isovaleric acidaemia/2-methylbutyryl-CoA dehydrogenase deficiency (4 cases) and long-chain hydroxyl-CoA dehydrogenase deficiency/trifunctional protein deficiency (4 cases). They suggested that in the US, routine national screening of neonatal blood spots by tandem mass spectrometry might lead to the diagnosis of 465 infants per year with such potentially fatal inborn errors of metabolism, many of which are treatable. If the prevalence were similar, in the UK this would equate to the identification of approximately 80 such infants per year.

In a study in Virginia in 1996–2001, in which post-mortem blood samples taken from 793 unexpected deaths of children aged less than three years were investigated using tandem mass spectrometry, a similar result was obtained, suggesting that around 1% had died of a recognised metabolic abnormality (Chace et al. 2003).

Fat oxidation disorders, of which the most common is medium-chain acyl CoA dehydrogenase deficiency (MCAD), typically present either in the first month or in later infancy, often with a minor infection. In these disorders, episodic hypoglycaemia, encephalopathy and respiratory depression with apnoea may be precipitated by viral illness or by fasting.

Sudden deaths have also been reported in glycogen storage diseases, mitochondrial respiratory chain defects, amino acid disorders and other rare metabolic disorders (Byard 2004).

The use of tandem mass spectrometry as part of the autopsy protocol for infants who died unexpectedly in the SWISS study (see above) led to an increase in the proportion of deaths identified as being due to previously unrecognised inborn errors of metabolism. Our most recent estimate is that as a whole, metabolic disorders may account for about 6% of sudden unexpected deaths in infants (see Figures 3.1–3.3 above). However, the recognition of such disorders is dependent on adequate laboratory investigation. It is certainly possible that a proportion of those deaths currently labelled as SIDS may be due to as yet unrecognised metabolic disorders. We therefore recommend that full metabolic screening should be adopted as a routine part of the autopsy protocol for all unexpected deaths in childhood.

SUDDEN UNEXPECTED DEATH DURING EPILEPSY (SUDEP)

The occurrence of unexpected death during the course of an epileptic seizure is a rare but recognised complication of epilepsy, though the incidence is unclear. In a prospective study of unexpected deaths in Victoria, Australia, Opeskin and Berkovic (2003) identified 50 individuals with known epilepsy who died during apparent seizures, of whom four were aged under 18 years, and compared the features with those of 50 people with known epilepsy who died unexpectedly of other causes. Apparent seizure-related deaths commonly occurred in bed at night, and on scene investigation there was commonly evidence of terminal seizure activity. Being on treatment with anti-epileptic drugs was not associated with an increased risk of SUDEP and may have decreased the risk. Many of these cases will show non-specific changes at autopsy, including bronchial secretions, minor aspiration or oedema (fluid swelling) of the lungs and other organs (Nashef et al. 1998, 2007), although these are not sufficient to determine the cause or manner of death. As with cases of sudden unexpected death in infancy, a full review of the history, with a scene examination and a full autopsy may help in clarifying why these children die (Nashef et al. 1998). It is important to recognise that children with epilepsy are at increased risk from accidental death through drowning, asphyxia or other accidents. Prolonged, uncontrolled seizures (status epilepticus) may themselves be fatal in spite of appropriate treatment. Children with epilepsy may also die from unrelated causes. A study in Australia of 93 deaths in children with epilepsy found that 63% of these deaths were not directly attributable to epilepsy, 20% were attributable to the epilepsy, including 11 sudden unexplained deaths, and 15% were undetermined (Harvey et al. 1993). Death was more common in those children with secondary epilepsy (i.e. epilepsy related to a primary underlying neurological disorder). Whilst there have been some anecdotal reports of deaths following febrile seizures, most population-based studies do not show any increase in mortality and this must be considered rare (Waruiru & Appleton 2004).

The occurrence of unrecognised seizures as a cause of death in individuals not previously known to suffer from epilepsy remains a possible cause of some unexpected deaths, but in the absence of direct evidence to suggest terminal seizure activity this must remain speculative.

SUDDEN DEATH IN ASTHMA

Death from asthma in childhood is rare (less than one in 10,000 affected children). Whilst most such deaths occur in hospitalised children with severe asthma, sudden and unexpected death has been described in children with previously mild asthma. In a study from Adelaide, Champ and Byard (1994) investigated 11 sudden and unexpected deaths of children with asthma over a 30-year period, and showed that 10 (90%) had severe asthma, with 8 (73%) showing growth impairment (weight or height below the 3rd centile). Most had a history of recurrent exacerbations and hospitalisation, and acute viral respiratory infections were commonly present at the time of death (Champ & Byard 1994).

Sudden unexpected death should therefore not be attributed to an acute asthma attack in a child with previously mild or moderate asthma in the absence of direct evidence (e.g. extensive airway plugging at post mortem, together with a good history of a final severe asthma attack).

TRAUMA

Deaths due to major trauma will usually be apparent from the history, examination or autopsy, and include deaths from intracranial haemorrhage, abdominal trauma with ruptured organs and multiple trauma. Asphyxia, both accidental and inflicted, may be less easy to detect. Features that may help to distinguish accidental from intentional deaths are outlined in Chapter 6.

SUDDEN INFANT DEATH SYNDROME

Sudden infant death syndrome (SIDS) remains the largest group of unexpected deaths in infancy, and is described in detail in Chapter 4.

SUDDEN UNEXPLAINED DEATHS IN OLDER CHILDREN (SUDC)

As noted above, a small proportion of unexpected deaths in older children remain unexplained but with thorough investigation of the circumstances of death and thorough post-mortem examination (including the use of modern microbiological techniques such as PCR, and full metabolic investigations), this proportion is likely to fall further in the future.

Krous has suggested the term 'sudden unexplained death in childhood' (SUDC) for this group of deaths, which has an incidence of 0.5–1.5/100,000 population per year (Wren et al. 2000, Byard 2004, Krous et al. 2005).

The rarity of such deaths means that few studies have investigated the epidemiology in detail. In a review of 36 cases of sudden unexpected deaths in childhood which remained unexplained after thorough investigation, Krous and colleagues noted that most were in the age range 1–3 years, many had a personal or family history of fever-associated seizures, the majority were male, and many were found prone, often with their face straight down into the sleep surface (Krous et al. 2005). They further emphasised the importance of thorough multiprofessional investigation after such deaths.

In a recent study, Kinney et al. have shown the presence of microdysgenesis in the hippocampus in five toddlers who died suddenly and unexpectedly, and whose deaths were otherwise unexplained. Kinney suggests that unobserved seizures during sleep may be a potential mechanism of death in these cases (Kinney et al. 2007).

As with sudden unexpected death in infancy, it is unlikely that a single causal pathway will explain all these sudden unexplained deaths. Improvements in our response to these deaths, including a full history, evaluation of the scene and circumstances of death and a thorough autopsy, should help to elucidate the causes and contributory factors. It is worth remembering that the majority of unexpected deaths in childhood are due to natural causes, but that there will often be a whole range of contributory factors that help to explain why this child has died of this condition at this time. A full understanding of a child's death needs to take account of all those factors, and not just rest with a simplistic cause of death as entered on a death certificate.

SUMMARY

In summary, unexpected deaths, though most common in infancy, may occur throughout childhood. The proportion of such deaths that remain unexplained is highest for deaths in the age range 1–6 months, and falls thereafter. Unexpected but explained deaths in childhood may be caused by a wide range of conditions, and thorough investigation is necessary to make a diagnosis, which may have significant genetic implications for the family. Sudden unexplained deaths in childhood (SUDC) are rare, and can only be diagnosed after a full multiagency investigation and multiprofessional case review process (see Chapter 7).

4 Sudden Infant Death Syndrome

PETER BLAIR

THE DIAGNOSIS OF SIDS

Sudden infant death syndrome (SIDS) is defined as the sudden death of an infant under one year of age which remains unexplained after a thorough case investigation, including performance of a complete autopsy, examination of the death scene and review of the clinical history (Willinger et al. 1991). Death often occurs unobserved, during infant sleep, with no discernable signs of a major illness.

TYPICAL DESCRIPTIONS OF A SIDS DEATH

Box 4.1 Case studies

Case 1 Male infant, four months old, born at 36 weeks. Spent two days in SCBU but had thrived since. Had a cold two days before death but otherwise described as normal and healthy by single, unemployed parent. Infant was placed in the cot by the parental bed for the night sleep, positioned on his side with lower arm extended to prevent rolling onto tummy. Parent woke in the morning to find infant dead in the prone position, face down in the mattress with covers over the head. Post mortem revealed no signs of infection or intra-pulmonary haemorrhage.

Case 2 Female infant, two months old, born term, slightly small for gestational dates but otherwise healthy. Large family, parents always co-slept with their infants for the first 12 months, mother was a smoker who breastfed. Infant was put down supine on the mother's side of the bed as usual, took a feed and then fell asleep. Mother woke in the early hours of the morning to find infant dead still in the same supine position. Interview with parents, close examination of the death scene and post mortem revealed no evidence of over-laying.

Unexpected Death in Childhood: A Handbook for Practitioners. Edited by P. Sidebotham and P. Fleming.
Copyright © 2007 by John Wiley & Sons, Ltd.

The diagnosis of SIDS is unique in that it is not a cause of death but rather an admission that we do not know why the baby died. It is a diagnosis of exclusion. A detailed parental interview and death-scene investigation are mandatory (Fleming et al. 2004) to establish the exact circumstances and potential for accidental or non-accidental death whilst pathological clues of possible infection or inborn disorders are investigated using a standardised post-mortem protocol (Krous 1995). Only when the recognised causes of infant death are excluded is the death labelled SIDS. It is not so much a diagnosis but an admission of ignorance and there are valid concerns that such labelling could create a 'diagnostic dustbin' (Huber 1993) or at the very least attribute too much homogeneity to what might be disparate causes of death (WHO 1968). The reluctance of accepting such an imprecise definition was probably reflected in the belated classification of SIDS in 1968 (Limerick 1992), which owed more to the increasing awareness of the endemic nature of the problem. In 1953 a steering committee was formed to investigate sudden death in infancy in the Cambridge and London areas (Beal & Blundell 1978), expecting to find around 200 deaths per annum in England and Wales. An interim report four years later suggested the problem was much larger, estimating 1,400 deaths per year. For the next 30 years the annual number of SIDS deaths remained around this level, accounting for over a third of the total post-neonatal mortality rate in the UK until finally a breakthrough was made that dramatically reduced the number of deaths. Despite the misgivings to accept SIDS as an international classification this decision has led to one of the most striking achievements of applied epidemiology in the twentieth century.

This chapter will review the importance of the changing epidemiology associated with SIDS, set out the debate on the contentious issues surrounding current advice and explore the potential of suggested causal mechanisms.

FALL IN THE SIDS RATE

In the late 1980s epidemiological evidence from several different countries (Davies 1985, Saturnus 1985, De Jonge et al. 1989, Fleming et al. 1990, Mitchell et al. 1991) suggested SIDS deaths could be related to infants sleeping in the prone position. In 1991 the 'Back to Sleep' campaign was initiated in the UK to encourage parents to avoid placing their infants on their front and the SIDS rate fell from a peak of 2.3 deaths in 1988 to 0.7 deaths per 1,000 live births in 1994 (Figure 4.1).

The possibility that other modifiable risk factors might be amenable to further interventions in this mysterious group of conditions has led to multiple epidemiological studies of the residual deaths. Further identification of other unsafe infant care practices, particularly within the infant sleep environment, have led to additional amendments and revision of the initial campaign message and probably helped to reduce the rate further over the past 10 years in the UK to 0.4 deaths per 1,000 live births (Dattani & Cooper 2000). This equates to the

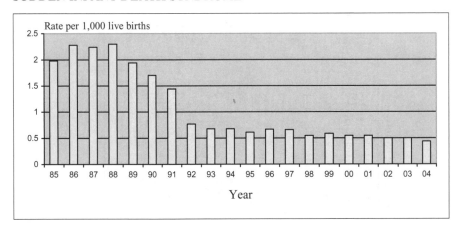

Figure 4.1 SIDS rate in England and Wales 1985–2004
Source: Office for National Statistics and the Foundation for the Study of Infant Deaths (includes deaths described as unascertained).

prevention of over 10,000 infant deaths in England and Wales alone since the campaign was first launched. Similar dramatic reductions have been observed in many other countries following such intervention campaigns (Table 4.1).

The SIDS rate varies among countries and indeed among different ethnic groups within countries. Certain indigenous cultures such as the Maoris in New Zealand, Aboriginals in Australia and Native Americans have noticeably higher SIDS rates, whilst Hispanics in the US and Asian communities in the UK have lower rates. These ethnic differences are still apparent but the number of deaths fell in all of these groups after the intervention of the 'Back to Sleep' campaign, transcending cultural boundaries. A concomitant fall in both the overall infant mortality rate and prevalence of using the prone position in the 1990s suggests the average fall in rates of 68% was due to the intervention rather than any diagnostic shift or random cyclic fluctuations amongst SIDS deaths. Recent historical evidence that active monitoring of infant mortality rates in the former Soviet Union identified the prone sleeping position as a dangerous infant care practice as early as 1972 is supported by a pre-unification SIDS rate in East Germany of 0.02 per 1,000 live births in the 1980s (Vennemann et al. 2006). East Germany is one of the few countries where the SIDS rate has increased (0.4 in 2000), most probably due to the influence of Western infant care practices.

The more recently reported decline in SIDS deaths since the beginning of the new millennium, however, is subject to a plausible diagnostic shift (Fleming & Blair 2005, Sheehan et al. 2005, Shapiro-Mendoza et al. 2006). The dramatic fall in deaths during the 1990s has prompted several major changes in the epidemiological characteristics of SIDS (Blair et al. 2006c), not least the proportional increase of deprived families and co-sleeping deaths. Some pathologists are becoming reluctant to use the diagnosis of SIDS in certain cases when

Table 4.1 Fall in SIDS rates after the 'Back to Sleep' intervention campaign in different countries

| Country | Year of campaign | SIDS rate per 1,000 live births | | | | | % fall |
| | | Before the campaign | | After the campaign | | |
		Period	Rate	Period	Rate	
Australia[1]	1991	1987–90	1.83	1997–2000	0.51	72%
Austria (Kiechl-Kohlendorfer 2003)	–[2]	1988	1.69	2000	0.51	70%
Canada (Rusen et al. 2004)	1995	1985–89	0.97	1994–98	0.54	44%
Denmark (Ponsonby et al. 2002)	1989	1987	2.00	1995	0.17	92%
Finland (Ponsonby et al. 2002)	1989	1987	0.60	1995	0.35	42%
France (Ponsonby et al. 2002)	1994	1987	1.85	1997	0.49	74%
Germany (Vennemann et al. 2006)	–[2]	1990	1.60	2000	0.60	63%
Ireland (McGarvey et al. 2003, 2006)	1992	1980–1993	2.00	2005	0.70	65%
Netherlands (L'Hoir et al. 1998b)	1987	1984	1.20	1997	0.17	86%
New Zealand (Ponsonby et al. 2002)	1990	1987	4.30	1997	1.50	65%
Norway (Oyen et al. 1997)	1989	1988	2.69	1995	0.48	82%
Sweden (Ponsonby et al. 2002)	1989	1987	0.90	1995	0.41	54%
Switzerland (Ponsonby et al. 2002)	1993	1989	1.23	1997	0.44	64%
United Kingdom[3]	1991	1988	2.30	2005	0.41	82%
United States (Ponsonby et al. 2002, Mathews & MacDorman 2006)	1994	1987	1.37	2003	0.53	61%

[1] Source: Australia Bureau of Statistics.
[2] No national campaign; regional campaigns at different times.
[3] Source: Foundation for the Study of Infant Deaths (FSID).

alcohol or illegal drugs have been consumed or overlaying is suspected although not proven, preferring to use the term 'unascertained' (Limerick & Bacon 2004). Current recommendations from the Office of National Statistics in the UK suggest unascertained deaths should be added to SIDS deaths when trying to quantify accurate SIDS rates (Corbin 2005).

EPIDEMIOLOGICAL CHARACTERISTICS PRIOR TO THE FALL IN SIDS

Many studies were conducted prior to 1991 and there was broad agreement on some of the epidemiological findings. The majority of deaths occurred within the first nine months of life, with a peak around the third and fourth months. Many of the deaths also occurred during the night sleep although there was no discernable increase in prevalence on a particular day of the week across studies (Froggatt et al. 1971, Fedrick 1973, Rintahaka & Hirvonen 1986, McGlashan 1989). More deaths occurred in males and in winter months. SIDS occurred across the social strata but was more common in the socio-economically deprived groups and particularly amongst parents who smoked. Hospital records showed that many of the SIDS infants had lower birth weight, shorter gestation and more neonatal problems at delivery. Maternal factors were important. There was a strong correlation with young maternal age and higher parity and the risk increased with multiple births, single motherhood or a poor obstetric history.

It had been assumed generally that these factors were specific to SIDS to the extent that the syndrome has been described as an 'epidemiological entity' (Daltveit et al. 1997). However, many of the factors associated with SIDS were also closely associated with other infant deaths. A direct comparison of the above background factors revealed that only the distinctive age distribution and high prevalence of tobacco exposure distinguished SIDS infants from infants who died suddenly but of explained causes (Leach et al. 1999). Deaths from congenital malformations decrease steadily from early age whilst deaths from respiratory or infectious diseases remain relatively constant over the first year of life (Bouvier-Colle et al. 1989). In general the highest prevalence of infant deaths is in the first weeks after birth when infants are at their most vulnerable (Wagner et al. 1984, Kraus et al. 1989). However, the evidence from SIDS studies suggested that few deaths occurred in the first month, with a large peak at three to four months and a steady decline thereafter. Even amongst the sudden unexpected deaths in infancy (SUDI) there is a marked difference in age distribution between the unexplained SIDS deaths and deaths due to unrecognised rapid infection that eventually are explained at post mortem (Figure 4.2).

Given the socio-economic indicators describing SIDS families it was not surprising for studies to report an increased prevalence of smoking during

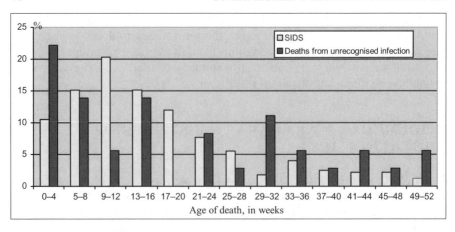

N.B. The deaths due to unrecognised infection were sudden and unexpected but explained at post mortem.

Figure 4.2 Age distribution of SIDS infants and infant deaths from unrecognised infection
Source: CESDI SUDI study 1993–96. N=325 SIDS deaths and 36 deaths due to unrecognised infection.

pregnancy amongst SIDS mothers, although it was unusually high even for such a group.

It is perhaps in the infant sleeping environment that the epidemiological study of SIDS has had the most success. Prone sleeping was actively encouraged in most countries from the 1950s (Beal 1995) to improve infant posture and skeletal growth (Anon 1961), prevent flattening of the skull (Greene 1930, Abramson 1944) and avoid the perceived risk of aspiration in the supine position (Spoelstra & Srikasibhandha 1973). This was also a time when special care neonatal units were quickly expanding and apparent benefits of using the prone position were found amongst pre-term infants, including a discernable increase in quiet sleep (Martin et al. 1979), better gastric emptying (Victor 1975), better oxygenation (Schwartz et al. 1975, Victor 1975) and a more effective ribcage and abdominal coupling with a decreased work of breathing (Fleming et al. 1979). What was best for the relatively small number of pre-term infants was not necessarily beneficial for the rest of the infant population. The historical references to infant sleeping position in images of art and early medical texts suggest the use of the prone position was an aberration of the twentieth century (Hiley 1992) and it took a number of years and many deaths before we realised the potential danger of such an infant-care practice. Population-based studies identified both the prone sleeping position and thermal stress as major factors associated with SIDS. SIDS infants tended to be wrapped warmer than surviving control infants (Gilbert et al. 1992, Ponsonby et al. 1992) and discovered in warmer rooms (Klonoff-Cohen &

Edelstein 1995); in combination with other risk factors these findings yielded significant interactions. Gilbert found that the combination of viral infection and heavy wrapping was associated with a high relative risk (Gilbert et al. 1992) whilst in a study from Tasmania, Ponsonby et al. (1992) found the risk associated with the prone position was potentiated by overnight heating, swaddling, recent infection and mattress type. Williams confirmed these findings in a study from New Zealand and found a small additive effect if the mother smoked (Williams et al. 1996). Although positioning and wrapping were not sufficient to fully explain the cause of death they could be linked to some causal chain of events and an intervention campaign to advise parents against these practices was instigated.

EPIDEMIOLOGICAL CHARACTERISTICS SINCE THE FALL IN SIDS

DISTAL FACTORS

The intervention campaigns in different countries were conducted at different times during the 1990s but common to all was the dramatic fall in SIDS rate and concomitant fall in the use of the prone position. Less publicised was the change in infant wrapping; studies of control infants in Avon prior to and after the 'Back to Sleep' campaign (Gilbert et al. 1992, Fleming et al. 1996) suggest the thermal resistance (tog value) with which we dress and cover infants for sleep has halved in the wider population, reflecting perhaps the withdrawal by manufacturers of heavy infant duvets. Certainly the winter peaks of SIDS deaths have all but disappeared and the reduced cohort has brought further major epidemiological changes amongst the deaths. SIDS no longer straddles the socio-economic divide but is now largely confined to deprived families.

Data from a longitudinal study conducted in Avon (Blair et al. 2006c) shows that the high proportion of social classes IV, V and long-term unemployed amongst SIDS families has risen from 47% to nearly 75% in the past 20 years (Figure 4.3). The change in socio-economic status has led to some expected changes in the background characteristics of SIDS families: an increase in single mothers, younger mothers, mothers who smoke and lower-birth-weight infants. However, the prevalence of maternal smoking during pregnancy amongst SIDS mothers (80–90%) is twice the level expected amongst control mothers with similarly deprived socio-economic backgrounds (Fleming et al. 2003), lending support to the hypothesis that infant exposure to tobacco smoke is some part of a causal mechanism. Studies have demonstrated a clear increase in risk with the number of cigarettes smoked (Haglund & Cnattingius 1990, Mitchell et al. 1993a, Klonoff-Cohen et al. 1995) both to the prenatal and postnatal infant (Blair et al. 1996), whilst a recent review by Mitchell and Milerad suggests this risk has grown despite advice against smoking in the

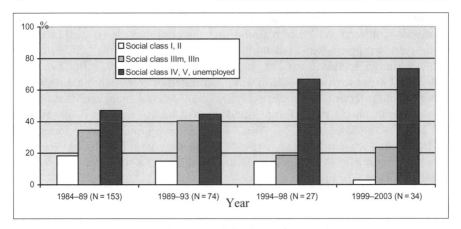

Figure 4.3 Socio-economic trends of SIDS families in Avon 1984–2003
Source: Avon Longitudinal Study

earlier intervention campaigns (Mitchell & Milerad 2006). The proportional increase in maternal smoking may be related to the increasing prevalence of pre-term infants, which has now tripled; over a third of SIDS infants are now pre-term, compared to a UK population prevalence of 5% (Blair et al. 2006b). Evidence suggests that the combined effect of known modifiable risk factors in the infant sleeping environment and the vulnerability of pre-term infants in the first few weeks of life may account for some of this increase. Other changes in the established characteristics of SIDS families includes parity; the occurrence of SIDS amongst larger families has been well-documented although longitudinal data from Avon now suggests that SIDS is most common amongst first-time mothers (Blair et al. 2006c). These distal factors may have limited use in terms of immediate prevention but studying the changes in patterns may have implications in terms of potential causal pathways.

PROXIMAL FACTORS

Further evidence of risks within the infant sleeping environment has brought about modifications and additions to the advice we now give to parents.

The risk of positioning infants on their side to sleep

Before the 'Back to Sleep' campaign, few studies had looked at the use of the lateral sleeping position and the findings were inconclusive (Kahn et al. 1984, Tonkin 1986, Mitchell et al. 1992, Klonoff-Cohen & Edelstein 1995); the side position with the lower arm extended to avoid infants rolling on their front was suggested as a safe alternative to sleeping prone. More recent studies

(Fleming et al. 1996, Scragg & Mitchell 1998, Skadberg et al. 1998, L'Hoir et al. 1998a, Li et al. 2003, Carpenter et al. 2004) suggest the side position carries a similar degree of attributable risk to being placed prone, mainly because of the inability of young infants who roll from side to prone to extricate themselves from this position. Certain infants, notably those with abnormalities of the upper airway (e.g. Pierre Robin syndrome) are at risk of lethal upper-airway obstruction if placed supine, and should therefore be placed in the prone or possibly the side position for sleep. With the exception of such rare conditions, most countries now recommend supine sleeping only but it is questionable whether the impact of the new guidelines has been as pervasive as the initial campaigns. Reports suggest that the use of the side position has increased (Cullen et al. 2000, Kiechl-Kohlendorfer et al. 2001) and although few maternity units use or recommend the prone position many still advocate the side position as a safe alternative, citing either outdated SIDS guidelines or fear of aspiration, cyanosis or apnoea when the infant is placed supine (Rose et al. 1998, Nelson et al. 2000, Hein & Pettit 2001, Pastore et al. 2003). Yet the forensic and epidemiological evidence does not substantiate these fears. A review of 196 infant deaths in South Australia found an extensive amount of gastric content in the airways and alveoli of three infants but all were found face down in the prone position (Byard & Beal 2000). Similar findings linking aspiration with the prone rather than the supine position have been found in the UK (Fleming & Stewart 1992), whilst a large cohort study of over 8,000 surviving UK infants showed no association between the prevalence of vomiting and infant sleeping position (Hunt et al. 1997). A recent study from New Zealand (Hutchison et al. 2003) has linked the increase in sleeping supine with nonsynostotic plagiocephaly, recommending that parents should vary the infant head position when putting them down to sleep and give their infants five minutes of supervised 'tummy time' each day. Placing infants to sleep on their backs has not been linked to apnoea or cyanosis (Ponsonby et al. 1997) and no demonstrable increase in symptoms or illness amongst supine sleeping infants has been shown in a recent large US study (Hunt et al. 2003). More worrying is the cited misconception of many health professionals who still believe placing infants in the side position protects against SIDS. Placing babies prone or on the side in hospital should be viewed as a potentially hazardous intervention, carrying a higher risk than most medications used in infancy, and one that should be used only for clear medical indications. A media-led campaign is needed to educate both health professionals and parents that the 'Back to Sleep' campaign needs to be taken literally (Blair 2002).

The risk of soft sleeping surfaces

Soft mattresses and other malleable surfaces have been associated with an increased risk of SIDS (Mitchell et al. 1996, Fleming et al. 2000, Geib & Nunes

2006) and there is some evidence that this risk is even higher in combination with established risk factors such as the prone sleeping position (Flick et al. 2001, Hauck et al. 2003) and infant thermal stress (Sawczenko & Fleming 1996). Pillows, cushions and bean bags have been used not just as a sleep surface but also as a prop to maintain the body position of a sleeping infant or provide easier access to bottle feeding. This practice presents the additional risk, even to supine sleeping infants, of such objects potentially covering the external airways (Scheers et al. 1998). This includes the adult-size V-shaped pillows used to accommodate breastfeeding (Byard & Beal 1997). The current advice is to sleep infants on a firm mattress and away from soft objects.

The risk of bedding covering the infant

It is not uncommon for SIDS infants to be discovered dead with bedclothes covering the head and face; indeed 'accidental mechanical suffocation' was a term used to describe these deaths prior to the SIDS classification (Abramson 1944). However, studies in the late 1940s rejected the idea that a child could be suffocated by 'ordinary bedclothes', largely based on the lack of post-mortem findings to support asphyxia as a cause of death (Davison 1945, Wooley 1945, Werne & Garrow 1947, Bowden 1950). Uncontrolled observations from early studies (Bass et al. 1986, Nelson et al. 1989a, 1989b, Wilson et al. 1994, Beal 2000) suggesting that around a fifth of SIDS infants were found with bedding covering the face or head were thus ignored or interpreted to be part of the agonal struggle just prior to death. Subsequent findings of reduced arousability during the sleep of SIDS infants (Horne et al. 2002) and lack of such a struggle during live recordings of several SIDS infants who died whilst on a monitor (Poets 2004) do not support the idea that head covering is just a consequence of the terminal event. The difficulties with determining infant asphyxia at post mortem (Dix 1998) have cast doubts on the earlier claim that head covering is not an important characteristic of an SIDS death (Bowden 1950, Thach 1986). Recent studies suggest the prevalence of head covering amongst SIDS victims still remains at over 20% (Schellscheidt et al. 1997, L'Hoir et al. 1998a, Fleming et al. 2000, Hauck et al. 2003, Carpenter et al. 2004, Nelson et al. 2005), ten-fold higher than the prevalence amongst age-matched controls and highly significant despite adjusting for other risk factors. Studies have linked head covering to loose bedding (Fleming et al. 2000), infant movement down under the covers (L'Hoir et al. 1998b, Fleming et al. 2000) and the use of duvets (Markestad et al. 1995, L'Hoir et al. 1998b, Fleming et al. 2000) or quilts (Ponsonby et al., 1998). In 1997 a 'Feet to Foot' campaign was launched in England and Wales by the Foundation for the Study of Infant Death to encourage parents to tuck the bedding in firmly, avoid using duvets or pillows and place the feet of the infant at the foot of the cot (FSID 2006). This advice has subsequently been endorsed by a policy statement from the American Academy of Pediatrics (2005).

The risk associated with unobserved sleep

SIDS occurs most often unobserved during infant sleep and the peak incidence was at a time when parents were actively encouraged to sleep their infant in a separate room despite scant epidemiological evidence that this provided any benefit to the infant (Spock & Rothenberg 1985, 219; Leach 1980, 93–94). Anthropologists have documented how infants in the past were raised in a consistently rich sensory environment and that the solitary experience in Western societies was a recent development (McKenna 1986). Reports from New Zealand in 1996 were the first to suggest that room sharing was protective against SIDS (Scragg et al. 1996), backed up by subsequent evidence from the UK (Fleming et al. 2000, Tappin et al. 2005) that the safest place for the infant to sleep was the cot by the parental bed. Further analysis of the UK data also suggests that parental supervision for daytime sleeps is equally important (Blair et al. 2006a). Parental presence during infant sleep does not guarantee the infant will be observed constantly, nor indeed that parental intervention will prevent death from occurring. However, having the sleeping infant nearby during the day may alert parents to circumstances such as young infants rolling from the side to the prone position or bedclothes covering the infant's head or face. Such advice for daytime infant sleep has not yet been implemented and scrutiny would have to be given to safe infant-sleeping environments in the daytime setting as well as the wording of such advice so as not to make parents feel they have to constantly watch over the sleeping infant.

The risk associated with bed sharing

Although more commonly known as 'cot death', SIDS can occur in any infant sleeping environment and is discovered more often in the parental bed than expected. Recent case-control studies suggest as much as half of the deaths take place when infants co-sleep with an adult (Tappin et al. 2002, Hauck et al. 2003, McGarvey et al. 2003, Carpenter et al. 2004). This rather alarming proportional rise in co-sleeping SIDS deaths has led some countries and organisations to recommend against bed sharing, including the American Academy of Pediatrics (2005). However, longitudinal data from Avon over the last 20 years shows that this apparent rise in prevalence is more due to the effectiveness of intervention campaigns in reducing SIDS deaths in the solitary sleeping environment (where deaths have fallen to one sixth of their previous levels) than an increase in deaths when bed sharing (Blair et al. 2006c). As Figure 4.4 shows, the *proportion* of bed-sharing deaths has risen from an average of 16% of all SIDS deaths prior to the 'Back to Sleep' campaign to 34% after, yet the *number* of SIDS deaths in the parental bed in Avon has almost halved over the same time period. Bed-sharing SIDS deaths have fallen, but not at the same rate as those occurring in the cot, and this may be explained

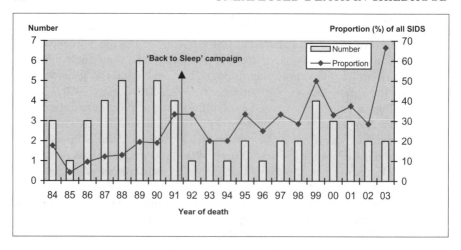

Figure 4.4 SIDS deaths in the parental bed in Avon 1984–2003
Source: Avon Longitudinal Study (N=300 SIDS deaths).

partly by the ineffectiveness of a campaign aimed at bed-sharing mothers who were already positioning their infants supine to breastfeed. More worrying is the rise in both prevalence and number of SIDS infants with a parent on a sofa (not included in Figure 4.4), with two such deaths in Avon prior to the intervention campaign but nine deaths subsequently. This is particularly important because any mother who wants to avoid the potential risk of bringing the baby into bed to breastfeed and inadvertently falling asleep may put the infant at greater risk by getting out of bed and sitting in a chair or on a sofa.

Bed sharing is perceived to be and treated as a risk factor in the field of SIDS epidemiology and, dealt with in this rudimentary way, there is ample evidence to advise against such a practice. On closer inspection however there are several things to be considered. Adjusting for potential confounders specifically associated with the adult co-sleeping environment in our UK study, such as recent alcohol consumption, sleep deprivation, overcrowded conditions and the large duvets used, rendered bed sharing as a non-significant risk factor, suggesting it is not bed sharing itself but the particular circumstances in which we bed share that puts an infant at risk (Blair et al. 1999). An intriguing aspect of this debate is that in certain cultures where mother–infant co-sleeping is common, such as Japan (Takeda 1987) and Hong Kong (Davies 1985), the cot-death rates are very low, corresponding to findings in the Bangladeshi (Gantley et al. 1993) and Asian (Farooqi et al. 1994) communities in the UK and the Pacific Island communities in New Zealand (Tuohy et al. 1993). In other mother–infant co-sleeping cultures, such as the Maoris in New Zealand and Aboriginal populations in Australia, the SIDS rates are noticeably higher. It is not bed sharing that distinguishes these cultures; there are other mediating factors such as parental alcohol consumption and smoking (Connor et al. 2005, Chikritzhs & Brady 2006) that may combine with co-sleeping and play a role in SIDS deaths. Another aspect is that of generalisation – the majority of bed-sharing SIDS mothers smoke whilst the majority of bed-sharing mothers in the population do not. The magnitude of any increase in risk for non-smoking breastfeeding mothers who are bed sharing on a firm flat surface, and who have not taken alcohol or other drugs, is unclear, but certainly small (Blair et al. 1999, Carpenter et al. 2004, Wailoo et al. 2004, Fleming et al. 2006, McGarvey et al. 2006). There is also the wider debate beyond the field of SIDS in terms of the potential advantages associated with bed sharing. Before the last century – and in most non-Westernised cultures today – the normative practice was for the primary caregiver – usually the mother – to share the bed with the infant (Mosko et al. 1993). Postulated physiological benefits of close contact between infants and care-givers include improved cardio-respiratory stability and oxygenation, fewer crying episodes, better thermo-regulation, an increased prevalence and duration of breastfeeding, and enhanced milk production (Anderson 1991, Ludington-Hoe et al. 1991).

There has been little in the way of direct observational data until recently, but it is becoming clear that bed sharing both for infants and mothers results in complex interactions which are completely different to isolated sleeping and which need to be understood in detail before applying simplistic labels such as 'safe' or 'unsafe' (McKenna 1996, Ball et al. 1999). The unusual level of criticism and hostility (Bartick 2006, Eidelman & Gartner 2006, Gessner & Porter 2006, Pelayo et al. 2006) generated by the recent policy statement by the American Academy of Pediatrics against bed sharing (American Academy of Pediatrics 2005) is a testament to the current polarised debate. Current advice in the UK does not warn against bed sharing but describes particular circumstances when bed sharing should be avoided. Co-sleeping with an infant on a sofa should always be avoided.

The apparent protective effect of infant dummy use (pacifiers)

The current debate on bed sharing holds many parallels with the debate on dummy use (pacifiers). Several studies have examined the prevalence of infant dummy use and shown a reduced risk for SIDS (Mitchell et al. 1993b, Fleming et al. 1999, L'Hoir et al. 1999, Brooke et al. 2000, Hauck et al. 2003, McGarvey et al. 2003, Carpenter et al. 2004, Vennemann et al. 2005, Li et al. 2006), with one recent study from California (Li et al. 2006) going so far as to suggest that the risk of SIDS would be reduced by 90% if all infants used a dummy. Some countries, such as Holland and the US, actively encourage such a practice, although, like the advice on bed sharing, this has again been met with hostile criticism (Bartick 2006, Buzzetti & D'Amico 2006, Eidelman & Gartner 2006) mainly concerning the potential adverse effects regarding breastfeeding. The evidence of a significant association is not in dispute but whether this association is causal in itself is still being debated (Blair & Fleming 2006). The mechanism by which pacifiers might reduce the risk of SIDS, or by their absence increase the risk, is unknown, but several ideas have been postulated. These include avoidance of the prone sleeping position (Righard 1998), protection of the orophayngeal airway (Cozzi et al. 1979, 2002), reduction of gastroesophageal reflux through non-nutrient sucking (Mitchell et al. 1993b) or lowering of the arousal threshold (Franco et al. 2000). These mechanisms, however, assume the presence of a dummy in the infant's mouth, when the evidence suggests dummies generally fall out within 30 minutes of the infant falling asleep (Franco et al. 2000, Weiss & Kerbl 2001) whilst many of the night-time deaths are thought to occur much later during the sleep (Golding et al. 1985, Blair et al. 2006a). Alternatively, dummy use may be a marker for some protective factors that have eluded measurement. The physiology of not only infant dummy use, but also non-use amongst routine users and infant thumb sucking deserves further investigation.

Before recommending the use of dummies, the potential disadvantages must also be considered. There appears to be a clear relationship between frequent or continuous dummy use and a reduction in breastfeeding from observational studies (Barros et al. 1995, Righard & Alade 1997, Howard et al. 1999, Vogel et al. 2001). Dummy use has been associated with a significantly higher risk of infective symptoms, especially otitis media (Uhari et al. 1996, Warren et al. 2001) and oral yeast infection (Mattos-Graner et al. 2001). Other potential disadvantages include accidents (airway obstruction (Simkiss et al. 1998), strangulation by cords tied to the dummy (Feldman & Simms 1980), eye injuries (Stubbs & Aburn 1996)) and dental malocclusion (Adair et al. 1995). The current advice in the UK no longer discourages the use of dummies but falls short of recommending them as an SIDS deterrent.

RECURRENT SIDS

Subsequent siblings of SIDS victims are at an increased risk of SIDS although the recurrence rates appear to be similar to infant deaths from other causes. Population studies conducted prior to the fall in SIDS rates in both the US (Guntheroth et al. 1990) and Norway (Oyen et al. 1996) report a five- to six-fold relative risk of recurrence. The degree to which the recurrence rate is attributable to the same environmental risk factors, covert homicide or some genetic component is less well understood.

Although some factors associated with SIDS infants and families are modifiable the majority are not, especially those factors linked with social deprivation and infant vulnerability. Families identified as being high risk for SIDS usually remain at high risk after a death has occurred. Younger mothers, unmarried mothers and those with lower incomes are usually living in similar circumstances if they decide to have another child. The risks of prematurity, low birthweight or neonatal problems are mediated by the same genetic and familial predispositions. Even modifiable risk factors often remain unchanged; positioning infants in the prone position to sleep might now be uncommon but is still a feature of current SIDS deaths, whilst the prevalence and risk of maternal smoking during pregnancy has increased, despite continued advice against this practice (Blair et al. 2006c). Given that SIDS now occurs increasingly amongst socio-economically deprived families it is perhaps to be expected that subsequent siblings will be at an increased risk.

SIDS is a diagnosis of exclusion; of trying to rule out the probable causes of death to eventually conclude that we don't know why the baby died. The evidence is limited to parental testimony often of a death that was unobserved, a scene investigation several hours after the event and a finite number of pathological tests. There is thus always the possibility that something has been missed and SIDS has been diagnosed when there is an explanation due to natural or unnatural causes. Levene and Bacon (2004) estimate that around 10% of SIDS deaths are potentially misdiagnosed and could be due to covert homicide or maltreatment. Although multiple infanticide is rare it is widely reported especially when the deaths have been misdiagnosed as SIDS (Begley 1997, Bergman 1997, Bohnert et al. 2004). When a second SIDS death occurs in the same family there must always be a very thorough investigation of the circumstances but the assumption that death was most likely due to unnatural causes is not necessarily a correct one. A recent thorough review of 46 such deaths in the UK (Carpenter et al. 2005) concluded that 80–90% of the cases were natural deaths, despite recurring in the same family, while the others were probable homicides.

The risk of recurrent SIDS is sufficiently low to exclude the possibility of simple genetic inheritance. However, there is growing evidence that a number of genetically controlled pathways may be involved in at least some cases of SIDS (Weese-Mayer et al. 2007). Preliminary findings from our most recent investigation of SUDI suggest the rate of explained deaths due to metabolic disorders has more than trebled in the past 10 years. Increasingly, inherited metabolic disorders are being recognised as the cause of death in infants who have originally been classified as having died of SIDS. However, the complexity of the diagnosis of these disorders, combined with a general lack of expertise and resources to proceed with comprehensive metabolic investigation in cases of SUDI, results in some cases being under-investigated (Loughrey et al. 2005). Cote et al. (1999) report that a non-SIDS diagnosis was reached three times more frequently in centres with expertise in paediatric pathology, thus inherited metabolic disorders or other genetic disorders may be under-diagnosed as a cause of SUDI in less specialist centres.

On a population basis, the risk of SIDS is greater amongst subsequent siblings. The possibility of covert homicide needs to be considered, but equal if not more weight should be given to a careful search for an inherited disorder.

POTENTIAL CAUSAL MECHANISMS

The 'triple risk' hypothesis – which envisages SIDS occurring as a result of a final insult (one which is not usually fatal on its own) that affects a baby with an intrinsic vulnerability (arising from genetic or early developmental factors), at a potentially vulnerable stage of physiological development (e.g. immunological, respiratory, cardiovascular or thermal), has been proposed in various forms by a number of authors over the past 15 years (Tonkin 1986, Filiano & Kinney 1994, Guntheroth & Spiers 2002). This seems to fit with the proposed pathogenesis of established risk factors and known physiology.

Infant sleeping positions have an effect on physiology, and a number of patho-physiological mechanisms for the increased risk of SIDS have been proposed, though evidence in favour of each is indirect. Clearly it is possible that more than one mechanism may be involved. In the prone position babies are potentially more vulnerable to the effects of re-breathing expired gases, particularly if sleeping on soft bedding (Bolton et al. 1993, Kemp et al. 1994b, Kemp & Thach 1995). A further effect of the prone sleeping position is that the arousal threshold is higher (Franco et al. 1998); response to adverse events such as hypoxia may have more profound and lethal effects in the prone position. Blackwell and Weir have suggested a possible mechanism by which the prone sleeping position, heavy wrapping and the presence of a viral infection might predispose to the development of a secondary infection leading to the lethal development of shock (Blackwell & Weir 1999). Whilst the final sequence of events leading to death is not known, physiological recordings of some infants prior to death (Meny et al. 1994, Poets 2004) suggest a cardiovascular rather than a respiratory event as the primary trigger for the final collapse. One possible physiological explanation for such a pattern might be a catastrophic fall in blood pressure as a consequence of sudden peripheral vasodilatation – e.g. in response to toxins or as a consequence of heat stress (Morris 1999). Head covering may cause death by the effects of thermal imbalance. Thermal modelling of clothed infants over a wide range of environmental temperatures suggests that the most important determinant of heat loss is not the quantity of insulation (unless extreme) but the area of exposed skin, particularly that of the head (Nelson et al. 1989b, Jardine 1992). Rectal and peripheral temperature rises in infants when the head is covered, even if there is a drop in metabolic rate (Marks et al. 1985), whilst maturation of the infant thermal system does not occur until the third month of age, around the peak incidence of SIDS. Blackwell and Morris have each shown the potential importance of toxigenic staphylococci as contributory agents to circulatory collapse and SIDS (Blackwell & Weir 1999, Morris 2004). Toxin production in such staphylococci increases with increasing environmental temperature and SIDS victims have increased nasopharyngeal colonisation with staphylococci compared to healthy-age and community-matched controls (Wigfield et al. 1993). In the prone position, or with head covering (particularly in the presence of potential re-breathing), nasopharyngeal temperature is likely to rise above the normal value of 32°C, with resultant increase in toxin production by any toxigenic staphylococci present on the mucosal surface (Dashash et al. 2006). Transmucosal absorption of toxins might thus lead to circulatory collapse and death without the need for invasive infection to occur.

The mechanism by which exposure to tobacco smoke increases the risk of SIDS is not clear, though there are several possibilities. Tobacco smoke affects infant apnoea rates and may contribute to deficient hypoxia responses (Lewis & Bosque 1995), may impair the development of the autonomic function (White et al. 1995) and increases the prevalence of respiratory infections throughout childhood (DiFranza & Lew 1996). The increased pervasiveness of smoking amongst SIDS parents is becoming such that it would be difficult to generalise any new advice about infant care practices to non-smoking parents.

The circumstances in which co-sleeping SIDS victims are discovered would suggest that entrapment or accidental overlaying may be the primary mechanism, especially if alcohol or other sleep-inducing drugs are involved, although it would be wrong to assume this for the majority of cases. Cot death is not the preserve of the cot but happens in different sleeping environments. In England on any one particular night nearly a quarter of parents bring the infant into the parental bed (Blair & Ball 2004), thus one would expect a certain proportion of SIDS to be discovered co-sleeping. Apart from possible signs of intra-pulmonary haemorrhage, suffocation cannot be detected at post-mortem investigation. The diagnosis of overlaying would require supportive evidence from the death-scene investigation and parental interview.

Elevated levels of interleukin 6 in the cerebrospinal fluid of SIDS victims compared to age-matched controls dying of known causes raised the possibility of a vigorous pro-inflammatory response being part of the pathophysiology of SIDS (Vege et al. 1995). Drucker has recently shown that common polymorphisms, leading to high levels of pro-inflammatory cytokines (e.g. interleukin 6 and VEGF) or low levels of anti-inflammatory cytokines (e.g. interleukin 10) are associated with increased risk for unexpected deaths in infants (Dashash et al. 2006). A high pro-inflammatory response to infection, with vigorous sympathetic activity including peripheral vasoconstriction and pyrexia, might indirectly lead to further toxin production in the nasopharynx. Vascular endothelial growth factor (VEGF), in addition to being a potent pro-inflammatory cytokine, is also an important factor in normal lung growth and development, particularly mesenchymal proliferation (Dashash et al. 2006).

The relationship between the pro-inflammatory cytokine IL1-β and the risk of SIDS is complex, and Moscovis et al. (2004) have shown potentially important ethnic differences in the patterns of gene polymorphisms. In both Aboriginal Australian and Bangladeshi infants a particular polymorphism (TT) is found that is uncommon in infants of European origin. This polymorphism is associated with a marked increase in IL1-β production, and increased pro-inflammatory responses on exposure to tobacco smoke. This may partially explain the major difference between Aboriginal Australian infants with high maternal smoking rates and high SIDS rate, and Bangladeshi infants, who are genetically similar with regard to IL1-β, but have very low rates of maternal smoking and very low SIDS rates. The potential interaction between genetic and environmental factors is further exemplified by the anti-inflammatory cytokine IL10, production of which is markedly decreased by exposure to tobacco smoke (Moscovis et al. 2004).

The recent developments in our knowledge of environmental, immunological, genetic and physiological factors in infants, and recognition of the changes in all these systems that occur during the first few months after birth support a 'triple risk' model of causation for most unexpected infant deaths, including some for which a partial or even a complete 'explanation' can be identified on thorough investigation. This approach to understanding the pathophysiological processes that may contribute to unexpected infant deaths holds great promise for targeted interventions to further reduce the number of such deaths.

CAUSAL THEORIES LACKING EVIDENCE

Many plausible theories are put forward to explain SIDS but the media attention given to these claims is sometimes disproportionate to the evidence available in the scientific literature.

Assertions that vaccination causes unexpected infant death (other than anaphylaxis) are inconsistent with epidemiological research. The peak age of SIDS, between two and five months, occurs around the same time as many infant immunisation programmes. However, several studies have shown that vaccinations are not associated with an increased risk of SIDS; indeed, some studies have shown a reduced risk (Hoffman et al. 1987, Mitchell et al. 1995, Fleming et al. 2001, Jonville-Bera et al. 2001, Brotherton et al. 2005, Vennemann et al. 2007).

The 'toxic gas' theory has previously received considerable media attention in the UK and New Zealand, but has not been substantiated (Kelley et al. 1992, Warnock et al. 1995, Pery 1998). According to this theory, toxic gases are produced by the fungus *Scopulariopsis brevicaulis* as it metabolises chemicals containing arsenic, antimony and phosphorus in cot mattresses. Proponents of the theory recommend wrapping cot mattresses in polythene, but this is potentially dangerous if done wrongly in view of the evidence that plastic sheeting in a baby's sleeping environment can cause death through suffocation (Kraus 1985).

There is now little support for the (central) apnoea hypothesis, which was the major mechanism postulated in the 1970s and 1980s. The use of home apnoea monitors has not been shown to be of value in preventing SIDS (Freed et al. 2002, Committee on Fetus and Newborn 2003, Fleming & Blair 2003) and there is no evidence to support the practice of routinely offering home monitors to the families of pre-term infants. Whilst such monitors may help some parents to relax and cope with the demands of their infant, the false alarms may be very stressful for other families and there is no evidence of any direct benefit to the infant. However, the importance of maintaining adequate oxygenation in infants may be critical for such conditions as bronchopulmonary dysplasia.

CURRENT RECOMMENDATIONS

The scientific rigour with which data are gathered is not easily applied to the dissemination of the results, and formulating advice can be a subjective exercise of weighing up the available evidence and constrained by attempts to simplify the message. The debate on the safety, advantages and disadvantages of infant-care practices must be informed not just by epidemiological evidence from one narrow field but from many disciplines from different fields if it is to become more than the exchange of mere opinion. The advantages when we get this advice right are evident in the dramatic fall in SIDS deaths but it should be remembered that it was probably getting the advice wrong in the first place that started the process. The current advice in the UK (Figure 4.5) tries to strike a balance between a cautious approach to what we have learnt in SIDS research and what we have learnt from other related fields and disciplines.

Reduce the risk of cot death

1. Place your baby on the back to sleep.
2. Do not let your baby get too hot.
3. Cut smoking in pregnancy – fathers too! Do not let anyone smoke in the same room as your baby.
4. Never let a baby sleep on a pillow, cushion, bean bag or waterbed.
5. Keep your baby's head uncovered – place your baby in the 'feet to foot' position.
6. Keep the baby's cot in the parents' room for the first six months.
7. Never sleep together with a baby on a sofa.
8. If parents bring the baby into their own bed for a cuddle or a feed, they should put the baby back into the cot before going to sleep.
9. Parents should also avoid sleeping with their baby if they are smokers, take any form of drugs or medication which makes them sleep more heavily, have recently taken alcohol, or if they are extremely tired.
10. If your baby is unwell, seek medical advice promptly.

Figure 4.5 Current UK advice on the prevention of SIDS
Source: Reproduced by permission of FSID.

Despite the decline in SIDS it is still one of the major causes of post-neo-natal infant death. It is a complex disorder and continued research is needed to fully understand the subtle interactions between different factors. The SIDS rate will decline further if the current recommendations are followed. How to disseminate these guidelines, especially amongst high-risk families, encourage putting them into practice and increase our understanding of the potential causal mechanisms are the future challenges.

5 Deaths from Unintentional Injuries

JO SIBERT
PETER SIDEBOTHAM

Accidents are the most frequent cause of death in children over one year of age in the UK and Europe and thus are a challenge to any efforts to reduce mortality in childhood (Morrison & Stone 1999). In 2004, 249 children aged under 15 died as a result of accidents in England and Wales (Office for National Statistics 2005a). These unintentional deaths have reduced over the years in keeping with the general reduction in mortality in childhood. For instance, 703 children died from drowning in England and Wales in 1901 (incidence 6.6/100,000 children) compared with 45 in 1999 (incidence 0.45/100,000 children). This is probably the result of better health care of children and a much safer environment. Children are also not exposed to injury as much as they were. Far fewer children walk unsupervised to school now, for instance.

What causes these accidental deaths? Road traffic injuries remain the most frequent cause of death by injury in children Britain and Europe (Adamson et al. 2000). Particularly important here are deaths among child pedestrians but children also die on bicycles and in cars. Many children drown, as well as die in house fires. Usually the differential diagnosis between accident and abuse is a definite one. Sometimes, however, particularly with such entities as suffocation and head injuries in very young children, this can be difficult. There is a wider differential diagnosis in some cases: accident, neglect or physical abuse. Is the 10 month old who drowns in the bath after being left unsupervised a victim of an accident, parental neglect on leaving him or her alone or a deliberate act of submersion?

WHAT FACTORS PREDISPOSE TO ACCIDENTAL DEATHS IN CHILDHOOD?

Poverty is a factor in many childhood accidental deaths. Road traffic injuries to children are five times more common and deaths in house fires 16 times more common in the poorest families compared to the most well off. Similar findings are seen in other injuries to children, with disadvantaged children having more injuries. There are very few exceptions – horse-riding accidents are one. Why is this so? Poorer families usually live in more dangerous environments; for example, it is much easier for a child to have a road accident if his house opens straight on to a main road in the inner city than if he lives in a detached house with a garden. Psychosocial stress factors are also involved in the aetiology of many childhood injuries, particularly road traffic injuries and accidental childhood poisoning (Sibert 1975).

The question of personality in childhood accidents and whether children can be injury prone is difficult. There is evidence that attention deficit disorder predisposes to accidents (Hoare & Beattie 2003, Swensen et al. 2004). However, it is more likely that injury proneness is related to the environment, both physical and social, rather than to personality factors. It is probably more correct to speak of an injury-prone community than an injury-prone child. When assessing risks or evaluating factors contributing to childhood accidents, the 'triangle of assessment' (HM Government 2000) can provide a useful framework, looking at factors intrinsic to the child, the parental background and behaviour, and wider environmental factors. Of these, it is the wider environmental factors that are the most important.

DEATHS FROM TRAUMA

Traumatic childhood deaths may occur through a number of different pathways. Severe direct damage to vital organs, including the brain, chest and abdominal organs may result from road traffic accidents, falls from a significant height, crush injuries or severe child abuse. These children will usually die immediately as a consequence of the overwhelming damage. Other children die from respiratory failure secondary to respiratory obstruction, for example a blocked airway in an unconscious child or airway burns, or from respiratory failure secondary to respiratory depression caused by head injury with raised intracranial pressure. The other major pathway leading to death is circulatory failure caused by fluid loss. Any trauma may lead to significant blood loss, even if there is no apparent bleeding – fractures and abdominal trauma may cause internal bleeding, leading to shock. Burns result in substantial fluid loss that can lead rapidly to circulatory failure. Trauma may also cause circulatory failure through maldistribution of body fluids. This may happen when there is secondary infection, or through failure of various body organs.

ROAD TRAFFIC INJURIES

Children may die on the roads as pedestrians, passengers in cars, cyclists, or as under-age drivers. Over half of all accidental childhood deaths involve transport accidents and these account for 9% of all childhood deaths from 1 to 14 years. Traffic fatalities are strongly linked to vehicle speed, with 85% mortality in pedestrians hit by a car travelling at 40 mph, 45% at 30 mph and 5% at 20 mph (Child Accident Prevention Trust 2004). Children may be at particular risk because of their size, making them less visible and also affecting the part of the body hit by a car; and because of their behaviour, having less awareness of traffic dangers and being less able to judge distance and speed. Children who are unrestrained or inadequately restrained in vehicles are also at particular risk.

Unexpected deaths of children from pedestrian road traffic accidents are always distressing. There is always the feeling that they could have been prevented. Pedestrian road traffic injuries are not random events and they are much more common in poorer families and in the inner city. The reasons for this are complex and are related to exposure of children to traffic. The interaction of a poor environment with stress is probably involved in many injuries.

Children under 10 years are particularly at risk from pedestrian road traffic injuries. Boys between five and eight years are at maximum risk as they are unable to estimate the speed or dangers of traffic. Parents may overestimate the ability of their children to handle traffic and let them go out on the road unsupervised. Sharples et al. (1990), looking at deaths from head injuries in the northern region, found that 72% of these deaths occurred between 3 pm and 9 pm and mostly to boys playing after school.

Although very occasionally abuse can be covered by a fabricated road traffic accident, usually the history is only too clear and can be confirmed by many people, including the police.

THERMAL INJURIES TO CHILDREN

House fires

Thermal injuries are a significant cause of accidental death in childhood. The majority of children die in conflagrations in private dwellings. Younger children are at greater risk of thermal injuries. Many children die from smoke inhalation rather than by direct heat. There have been striking reductions in the number of children who have died from fire in recent years. Despite this, the death rate from fires is unacceptably high. A major component of the reduction has been the fall in the number of deaths from the ignition of clothing following flame-proofing regulations and the reduction of open fires. Many conflagrations are caused initially by smoking. Many children have died in house fires because of the flammability of upholstered furniture and from the toxic fumes produced when it burns. House fires are a particular problem in poor families and they are occasionally caused by arson. Sometimes there is a question of whether there is an element of neglect in their aetiology (Squires & Busuttil 1995).

The extent of thermal injuries is related to both the temperature and the contact time. Burns may be caused by flames, contact with a hot object (solid, liquid or gas), or by caustic liquids and gases. Any external burn will destroy the skin's protective layer, leading to fluid loss from the underlying tissues and creating a potential portal for entry of infection. Most children dying of thermal injuries do so because of the accompanying fluid loss causing circulatory or other organ failure, or through secondary infection.

Scalds in children

Although scalds are a major cause of morbidity in childhood, accounting for 70% of all thermal injuries (Child Accident Prevention Trust 2002), deaths are rare and are mainly caused by scalding in the bath. They are usually caused by unsupervised children falling in the bath (Yeoh et al. 1994) but the differentiation between accident and abuse can be difficult to determine (Chapter 6).

DROWNING IN CHILDHOOD

Drowning is an important cause of death from injury in children in the UK, with only road traffic accidents causing consistently more deaths. In 1988/89 Kemp and Sibert (1992) reviewed drowning deaths in the UK and in 1998/99 they reviewed what progress had been made in 10 years (Sibert et al. 2002). Overall drowning deaths had fallen significantly from 149 in 1988 and 1989 to 104 in 1998 and 1999. Boys drown more frequently than girls (75% in both series). This probably reflects their different behaviour patterns. Most of the children were less than five years of age. Approximately the same numbers of children are admitted after near drowning as drowning. Drowning incidence is much higher in warmer parts of the world such as California or Australia than in the UK.

Modes of drowning by development and by site

Children can drown indoors and outdoors, and in deep or shallow water. In many cases the site of drowning is associated with a definite age range and stage in child development.

Babies and developmentally-delayed older children may drown when they are unable to sit up when down in the water. A typical example is bath drowning occurring at a stage in development where a child is able to sit but unable to right themselves when they fall (8 to 18 months). A similar mechanism applies to older children who have an epileptic fit. Babies can drown in quite shallow water and should not be left unattended. The possibility of non-accidental drowning should be remembered in young children (Kemp et al.

1994a). Accidental bath drownings tend to occur in children between 6 and 18 months.

Toddlers and children, particularly those with learning or behaviour difficulties, may wander off to unprotected water. In the UK, that happens in garden ponds, in Australia and California, in domestic swimming pools and in the Netherlands, in small canals. Indeed, toddlers can wander off and drown in any type of water and in quite small, shallow ponds. The most common story is of an unsupervised toddler in a neighbour's garden or when visiting friends or relatives. Toddlers can also drown in pails, farm slurry pits, cattle troughs and puddles. The number of children drowning in garden ponds has increased in the UK, probably because of the increased number of water features in gardens.

Older children playing near open water may fall in and may be unable to rescue themselves in that situation. They may also be swimming where there is no lifeguard or an inadequate lifeguard: examples are open water, public and private pools. Deaths from public-pool drownings are a minor problem in the UK following health and safety regulations introduced in 1985, which insist that there is a high level of supervision of children in such pools. Drownings in public pools are at a level of one per year in the UK, a tribute to the level of supervision (Kemp & Sibert 1992, Sibert et al. 2002). This level of supervision may be unavailable elsewhere, however, and many children die in pools abroad not supervised by lifeguards (Cornall et al. 2005). Drowning in rivers, canals and lakes is predominantly a problem of older boys who play unsupervised and get into trouble in deep water (Kemp & Sibert 1992). Many are unable to swim. The number has fallen over the 10 years from 1988/89 to 1998/99. These boys correspond to the boys in Australia who drown in creeks. A few children drown at sea in England and Wales, some from falling into docks, some being lost at sea in boating accidents and some from swimming in the sea.

DEATHS FROM FALLS

Falls cause some deaths in childhood and are also the most common cause of presentation to the Accident and Emergency Department. The most common cause of fall deaths in childhood is from falls from buildings, usually through the window. Vish et al. (2005), in a study from Chicago, have demonstrated that this is not only a problem of high-rise buildings. Thankfully, deaths from falls in playgrounds are very rare. Very occasionally children die from falling down stairs. The danger of falls from baby walkers has been highlighted and they can no longer be advised for children's use (Gleadhill et al. 1987).

As with road traffic accidents, deaths from falls may occur as a result of major head injury, chest or abdominal trauma, or through multiple trauma at different sites. The differential diagnosis for accidental death between falls and abuse in children can sometimes be difficult (Chapter 6). There are studies, however, that can be helpful – for instance, in abdominal injury, small bowel injury in under fives has not been demonstrated to be due to a fall (Barnes et al. 2005).

ACCIDENTAL SUFFOCATION, CHOKING AND STRANGULATION IN CHILDHOOD

Accidental mechanical asphyxia is a significant cause of death in children. Nixon and his colleagues (1995) reviewed deaths registered as choking, suffocation or strangulation in a total population study for the two years 1990–1991 in England and Wales. Rather similar findings were ascertained by Altmann and Nolan (1995) in Australia. Some of these incidents are not true accidents and there may be problems of classification, with inhalation of vomit, non-accidental injury and the co-existing diagnosis of SIDS. Nixon et al. found an overall annual incidence of 0.7 per 100,000 children at risk, with two modal peaks at less than one year of age and in the early teenage years, because of boys being found hanged. Children die from choking on food and on non-food items. Few children now suffocate on a toy and that emphasises the importance of Standards for Toy Safety. They also die from inhalation of vomit, often associated with medical conditions. Children die from strangulation. They may be younger children who are strangled by cords, clothing and accessories and by poorly maintained cots. Parents of young children should be discouraged from using poorly maintained cots, telephone wires or window cords near cots and necklaces or dummy cords when in cots. Some boys die from hanging; this may be deliberate but is probably not true suicide on the whole.

CHILDHOOD POISONING

Poisoning in children may be accidental, non-accidental, iatrogenic or, in older children, a result of deliberate self-harm. This chapter will deal with deaths from accidental poisoning, which is predominantly seen in children under the age of five years, although older children may be involved if they are developmentally delayed. The peak age is between one and four years. More boys than girls take poisons accidentally. Some children die from poisoning each year (Craft 1983), but the number of deaths has fallen over recent years, probably because of better treatment and because of the child-resistant container (CRC) regulations. Furthermore, fewer tricyclic antidepressants are prescribed. Petridou and her colleagues (1996) found that socio-economic factors were not important in the aetiology of childhood poisoning but not having both parents in the home was. Perhaps surprisingly, the availability of poisons does not appear to be a major factor in accidental child poisoning. There is evidence that family psychosocial stress and behavioural problems, such as hyperactivity, predispose towards child poisoning (Sibert 1975) and these family and personality findings have importance for the prevention of child poisoning.

Children may take a variety of substances accidentally. These are conveniently divided into medicines (prescribed and non-prescribed), household products and plants. The majority of children who take poisons do not have serious symptoms. Medicines that may cause death include iron and tricyclic antidepressants. Again, most of the household products children take are relatively non-toxic but a few, such as caustic soda, soldering flux and paint stripper, may cause serious harm. The most common household product that children take is white spirit and turpentine substitute. About 10% of these children have patchy chest X-ray changes. In developing countries, paraffin (kerosene) poisoning is a particular problem as it is used as a cooking fuel and is often kept in open containers. These incidents are common in poor social circumstances and in summer, and are probably largely related to thirst. Kerosene may cause serious aspiration pneumonitis and death. Again, most of the plants children take accidentally are relatively non-toxic; however, some, such as arum lily, deadly nightshade and yew, can cause serious symptoms and even, very rarely, death.

DEATHS FROM AGRICULTURAL INJURIES

Children on farms are in a unique situation: they live in a place of work. They are thus particularly liable to injury and even death from accidents. Cameron and his colleagues reviewed fatal farm accidents in the UK over the four years from April 1986 to March 1990 (Cameron et al. 1992). Thirty three deaths were notified, eight related to tractors and allied machinery and ten related to falling objects. They concluded that the farm remains a dangerous environment for children. Enforcement of existing safety legislation with significant penalties and targeting of safety education will help reduce accident rates. A study by Stueland and his colleagues (1996) from Wisconsin found that the significant variables that predisposed towards injury were the hours the child worked, the presence of a disabled safety device and feeding cows by grazing. Children who are not working on farms are also exposed to risk (Pickett et al. 2005).

DOG BITES

Dog bites to children are extremely common and as many as one in 100 children a year presents to an Accident and Emergency Department with this problem. Sacks et al. (1996) estimated an incidence of 18/1,000 in the US. Many of the accidents occur in the home or with dogs well known to the children. The majority of dog bites are minor, but severe lacerations, particularly facial lacerations, may occur and there are occasional deaths, mainly of children exposed to guard dogs. There has also been concern about potentially dangerous breeds of dog kept in the home. A randomised control trial (RCT) has shown an educational intervention was effective in modifying children's behaviour with dogs (Chapman et al. 2000).

INVESTIGATING FATAL CHILDHOOD ACCIDENTS

As with other unexpected childhood deaths, all accidental deaths come under the jurisdiction of the coroner and need to be investigated thoroughly. Police have a duty to investigate any road traffic collision involving injury or fatality and will assign a senior investigating officer (SIO) along with a collision investigator. A national form (MG NCRF or MG NSRF) is used to ensure consistency of investigation (HM Government 2006a). Information collected during the reporting of a road traffic collision allows the collision to be investigated properly, provides a record of the occurrence and provides statistical data which can be used by police to inform intelligence-led enforcement, by highway authorities for casualty reduction purposes and by government departments to underpin research and legislative changes.

Following any collision, the scene must be made secure to ensure a safe environment for emergency services and the public and to enable a thorough investigation to take place. The first priority is obviously to save lives and respond to any casualties. Once initial rescue and treatment work has ceased, a systematic approach to investigation must be undertaken in order to establish fully the circumstances of the death. Where a child has died, a family liaison officer will be appointed to support the family during the investigation. The investigation will involve a thorough analysis of the scene, including road and driving conditions, weather and any hazards; assessment of all vehicles and drivers involved; verbatim accounts, where available, from those involved and from witnesses; consideration of breath tests and seizing of mobile phones. The information is then analysed to determine any contributory factors including factors relating to the environment, the vehicles, actions on the part of any driver or rider, and actions on the part of any pedestrian. A thorough investigation of this nature is very much in keeping with the principles of child death review (Chapter 11) and is essential for effective preventive work. However, as they stand, the investigations do tend to focus on the immediate (proximal) contributory factors. There is further scope for extending the investigation to draw in multi-agency teams and to look at wider, more distal factors. For example, examining the past educational or medical history, or the social circumstances of a fatally-injured child pedestrian, may reveal information on behaviour or supervision which may have led to the child being in a dangerous situation in the first place.

Although police procedures are very well developed in relation to collision investigations, a similar thorough approach could be applied to the investigation of any injury-related death. The same multi-agency approach outlined in Chapter 7 should be carried out, involving a thorough history and evaluation of the scene, and including, where appropriate, a reconstruction of the scene and a post-mortem examination.

HOW DO WE PREVENT ACCIDENTAL CHILDHOOD INJURIES?

We clearly would like to prevent accidental deaths in children, although they are unlikely to be prevented by campaigns covering all types of accidents, as is sometimes advocated. However, well researched multidisciplinary action on individual types of accidents can be successful (Jarvis & Sibert 1998). In preventing a particular injury, a methodological approach is needed – looking first at the size and nature of the problem, then deciding what preventive solutions are possible, implementing and evaluating them on a small scale and then introducing them more widely when they have proved to be effective. Randomised control trials are increasingly being used in injury prevention. Of course, there are difficulties regarding which unit to randomise, and schools and areas are increasingly being randomised, rather than individual children.

The use of systematic reviews on the prevention of childhood injury is important and is increasing, the work by Towner and Dowswell (2002) being particularly helpful. There are three main strategies for injury control: changing the environment, enforcing changes in the environment by law and educating children and parents. Research suggests that whilst in some fields education is important, such as in teaching children to swim, most successes in prevention have followed environmental change. Moreover, research suggests that educational campaigns by themselves are only of limited value.

ENVIRONMENTAL CHANGE

There is considerable evidence that environmental change can prevent injuries. This has been shown, for example, in the use of child-resistant containers to prevent childhood poisoning, smoke detectors, child safety seats to prevent injury in passenger car accidents, fences around private swimming pools to prevent drowning and the flame-proofing of nightdresses to prevent burns. There are many other examples.

Child-resistant containers (CRCs) were first suggested in 1959 by Dr Jay Arena in Durham, North Carolina (Arena 1959). These containers were evaluated in a community in the US by Scherz (1970) and were found to be successful. They were then introduced into the US for aspirin preparations, with successful results. Following this work in the US, child-resistant closures were introduced by regulation in 1976 in the UK for junior aspirin and paracetamol preparations. This resulted in a fall in admissions of children under five years after salicylate poisoning (Sibert et al. 1977). In 1978, CRCs were introduced by regulation for adult aspirin and paracetamol tablets. Child-resistant containers or packaging are now a professional requirement of the Royal Pharmaceutical Society and are regulated for a number of household products (e.g. white spirit and turpentine substitute).

Smoke detectors are widely used in many countries for the prevention of death and injury due to house fires and have been found to be effective, particularly for children (Runyan et al. 1992, DiGuiseppi et al. 1998). They have an important role in the prevention of injury from house fires and their use should be enforced both in public and private housing. The effectiveness of education programmes to use smoke alarms has been less clearly established. In a recent systematic review of controlled trial interventions to promote smoke alarms, DiGuiseppi and Higgins (2000) suggest only modest potential benefits from education to promote smoke alarms. Giving away smoke alarms will not necessarily increase the prevalence of functioning alarms (DiGuiseppi et al. 1999).

Poor window catches and designs have allowed a number of accidents through falls. The introduction of safety catches or window guards could reduce these. In New York City, a programme providing free window guards (The Children Can't Fly Program) has been successful in preventing window falls in a poor area of New York (Spiegel & Lindaman 1977).

Reducing the temperature of hot water in domestic systems could prevent bath scalds, as was illustrated in the classic paper by Feldman et al. (1978). This can be done in two ways: by reducing the thermostat temperature in domestic hot water tanks and, more expensively, by thermostatically controlled mixer taps. However, there is little evidence that the distribution of devices to control hot water temperatures is effective (Katcher et al. 1989).

There is evidence that fencing with self-shutting gates to prevent children from having access to domestic pools can prevent drowning. In Canberra, private swimming pools have to be fenced by law but there was no such legal sanction in Brisbane at the time of one study: only one child died in the Australian capital from a swimming pool accident over a five-year period, compared with 55 in Brisbane. Fencing has now been introduced by regulation into Australia, South Africa, New Zealand and parts of the US. Parents should also be told about the dangers of drowning in garden ponds and families with young children are well advised to fence or cover these (or better still, not have them at all). Much could be done to insist on protecting children from access to these ponds, particularly in garden centres.

LEGISLATIVE CHANGES

Whilst environmental measures, such as seat-belts for cars or fencing garden pools may be effective, often they are not fully used by the population and have to be enforced by law. There is now legislation in the UK to ban the use of inflammable materials for children's clothing, and to ban the foam which causes dangerous fumes in furniture and replace it with safety foam. The full effects of this latter legislation will take many years to come through because of the long life of furniture in homes. The compulsory use of seat-belts in cars in the UK has undoubtedly led to reductions in fatal injuries, and the more recent introduction of legislation on the use of child booster seats could lead to further reductions.

EDUCATION

Most drowning accidents occur with children too young to be able to swim. The prevention of bath accidents involving babies should be part of the Health Visitor's programme of education for mothers. It should be emphasised that it is unsafe to leave young children unsupervised in the bath even for short periods. Children with epilepsy should always shower and not bath.

Being unable to swim probably increases the risk of drowning. Asher and his colleagues (1995) found that the swimming ability and safety skills of young pre-school children can be improved by training. Teaching children to swim may reduce the number of deaths among 5 to 14 year olds. Certainly, there has been an overall fall in the number of deaths of children from drowning, which has coincided with better swimming training. Life jackets and buoyancy aids are important in helping to prevent children from drowning if they fall overboard when using use boats and canoes. Getting children to wear them is difficult but boat and canoe clubs can insist that their members wear them. Bennet et al. (1999) in Seattle demonstrated a significant, although modest increase in life vest use and ownership amongst children after an education programme.

The evidence that educational programmes by themselves can prevent accidents is, however, sparse (Towner & Dowswell 2002). For instance, an education campaign in Cardiff using posters and literature only sensitized the population to trivial accidents (Minchom et al. 1984). There is evidence, however, that Health Visitors visiting the home giving specific attention to accident prevention can make a difference to the way that families behave, in particular with regard to the installation of safety equipment. A study in Canada (King et al. 2005) showed the modest effectiveness of an intervention (home safety visit) aimed at improving home safety. Health education therefore must be directed either on a one-to-one basis by people such as the Health Visitor or general practitioner, or to educate public opinion to institute environmental change.

SECONDARY AND TERTIARY PREVENTION

Primary preventive methods such as those described above aim to reduce the risk of accidents occurring in the first place. Secondary prevention aims to minimise the effects of an accident. The use of seat belts in cars and helmets for cycle users would be examples of secondary prevention. Tertiary prevention aims to restrict the damage caused by injuries sustained in an accident. Such prevention requires appropriate emergency responses including resuscitation, rapid transfer to hospital and intensive care management.

Deaths from trauma fall into three categories: those who die immediately with massive injuries; those dying within a few hours from progressive respiratory or circulatory failure, or from the effects of raised intracranial pressure; and those who die later as a consequence of secondary infection or organ failure. Deaths in the second and third categories may be prevented by appropriate emergency management, including stabilisation of the airway, fluid resuscitation and thorough assessment and treatment of all injuries (Mackway-Jones et al. 2005).

PREVENTING DEATHS FROM TRAFFIC ACCIDENTS

The most effective means of preventing pedestrian road traffic accidents is by modification of the environment. Residential areas can be redesigned to give priority to pedestrians and to separate them from traffic. The speed of traffic can be reduced by speed bumps and safe crossings can be provided. There is now good evidence that area-wide engineering schemes and traffic-calming schemes reduce injuries (Towner et al. 2001). A recent study in Wales (Jones et al. 2005) concluded that traffic calming is associated with absolute reductions in child pedestrian injury rates and reductions in relative inequalities. The provision of play areas will reduce the number of children on dangerous streets.

Some children can be taught pedestrian skills. One approach is designating safer routes to school. Two randomised trials (Ampofo-Boateng & Thomson 1991, Anon 2000a) have shown improvements in children finding safe places to cross the road. There is little evidence that these programmes have actually gone on to prevent injuries. Roberts et al. (1994) concluded that safety and traffic education are unlikely by themselves to prevent road traffic injuries. School-based traffic clubs have not been shown to be effective.

The death of children whilst passengers in cars remains a serious problem throughout the world. A major part of prevention is the development of child-restraint systems and seat belts. Much of the research on seat belts has been on adult passengers and there is good evidence that seat belts are effective in preventing death and serious injury. Child-restraint systems have the unexpected bonus of improving children's behaviour and this probably improves driving standards. The problem is getting adults and children to use them.

In young children and babies the barrier to the use of child restraints has in many cases been cost, and child-restraint loan schemes have been developed to help poorer families. They appear to be an effective strategy to increase the number of children transported safely in cars (Towner et al. 2001). However, an RCT of demonstrating restraint use did not appear to increase correct use (Christophersen et al. 1985).

Educational campaigns used to persuade children to wear seat belts have had mixed results. Miller and Pless (1977) found no significant differences in seat-belt usage, however Macknin et al. (1987) found a campaign effective in the short term. Most countries have believed that legislation is needed to ensure seat-belt usage. Serious injuries fell by 20% following the 1983 legislation in the UK compelling the wearing of seat belts in front seats. A systematic review (Towner et al. 2001) of nine studies in the US evaluating seat-belt legislation concluded that it was associated with reductions of injuries and death and increases in the numbers of children using restraints. Many children remain unrestrained, however.

Bicycle injuries are a significant cause of death in children. There are factors in bicycle design which are vital to safety; for example, the high-rise bicycle that was introduced into Britain in the late 1960s and early 1970s had features that made it more dangerous than standard models. The prevention and reduction in severity of bicycle injuries may involve education and environmental change. There is now some evidence that bicycle skills training can improve riding behaviour. Van Schagen and Brookhuis (1994) in an RCT in the Netherlands showed improved behaviour in the intervention children.

However, the use of helmets is now accepted as a key part of preventing bicycle injuries and deaths. There are at least five case-control studies that show the effectiveness of cycle helmets in preventing head injury. A key case-control study was by Thompson et al. (1989) in Seattle, where cyclists were shown to have an 85% reduction in their risk of head injury by wearing helmets. What is more difficult is getting children to wear them. One RCT (Cushman et al. 1991) showed no difference in helmet wearing after an intervention. However, a case-control study in Reading showed the benefit of a health promotion campaign (Lee et al. 2000). In some places, such as parts of Australia and the US, helmets have been introduced by legislation, with a resultant reduction in injuries.

Rivara and his colleagues (1997) in Seattle emphasised that the prevention of serious injuries cannot be accomplished by helmet use alone and 'may require separation of cyclists from motor vehicles and delaying cycling until children are developmentally ready'.

ACTION ON CHILDHOOD INJURIES

The basis of any programme of injury control is surveillance. This needs close liaison between the Emergency Department and local clinicians. Once an injury has happened it may happen again. For instance, a dangerous balcony that allowed a fall should be repaired straight away, together with others like it.

A number of organisations are involved in the prevention of accidental deaths to children. In England, in 1977, Donald Court and Hugh Jackson were instrumental in the formation of the Child Accident Prevention Trust (CAPT).

The Royal Society for the Prevention of Accidents also works with children, particularly on water and leisure accidents. There are similar organisations in Europe and throughout the world. These organisations bring many disciplines together to foster action and research on injuries to children.

As well as national action on injury prevention and control, local action is needed. In Sweden, public health physicians led by Svanstrom (1997) from the Karolinska Institute in Stockholm developed local action through the concept of Safe Communities. There have been doubts about how effective the programmes actually are (Sibert & Kemp 2002) and one study in Australia showed no benefit (Ozanne-Smith et al. 2002). However, Lyons et al. (2006) demonstrated that local politicians are effective advocates for enhancing safety in their areas.

6 Fatal Child Maltreatment

PETER SIDEBOTHAM

INTRODUCTION

When she died at the age of eight, Victoria Climbié was found to have 128 individual injuries over her body. Victoria spent much of her last days, in the winter of 1999–2000, living and sleeping in a bath in an unheated bathroom, bound hand and foot inside a bin bag, lying in her own urine and faeces. In the report on his inquiry into Victoria's death, Lord Laming summarised that in the space of just a few months, Victoria had been transformed from a healthy, lively and happy little girl, into a wretched and broken wreck of a human being (Cm 5730 2003).

INCIDENCE OF FATAL CHILD MALTREATMENT

Although some high profile cases capture a lot of media and public attention, the true incidence of fatal child maltreatment is unknown. It is widely stated that one to two children die each week in the UK at the hands of their carers, although the basis for this figure is unclear and the true incidence is likely to be much higher (Green 1998). The annual figure for the number of Serious Case Reviews in England and Wales is around 80–120, although some of these relate to serious but not fatal abuse, and not all maltreatment-related deaths will be subject to a Serious Case Review (Reder & Duncan 1999, Brandon 2007, Rose & Barnes 2007). Home Office statistics suggest homicide rates varying from 2.3 per 100,000 (1989) to 7.6 per 100,000 (1974) in children under 1; 0.7 per 100,000 (1980) to 1.4 per 100,000 (1979, 1991) in children aged 1–4; and 0.2 per 100,000 (1983, 1993) to 0.6 per 100,000 (1985) in children aged 5–15 (Creighton 1995). Rates in the US may be even higher, with a total of 3,312 infant homicides reported between 1989 and 1998 (8.3 per 100,000) (Paulozzi & Sells 2002). Studies consistently show that the highest risks are in infancy and particularly within the first days of life. It has been estimated that the risk of homicide on the first day of life may be as much as 10 times greater than at any other stage (Paulozzi & Sells, 2002). Worldwide, an estimated 57,000 children die each year as a result of maltreatment, with the highest rates being

Unexpected Death in Childhood: A Handbook for Practitioners. Edited by P. Sidebotham and P. Fleming.
Copyright © 2007 by John Wiley & Sons, Ltd.

in low- to middle-income countries (Krug et al. 2002). Whilst most other causes of childhood death have fallen and continue to fall in developed countries, rates of fatal child maltreatment and homicide have remained static or in some cases risen (Christoffel 1984, Creighton 1995). However, many commentators have argued that official statistics are limited in their ability to provide accurate information on the number of child fatalities caused by abuse (Kotch et al. 1993, Wilczynski 1994, Creighton 1995, 2001, Gellert et al. 1995, Crume et al. 2002, Webster et al. 2003). This may be due to under-ascertainment related to covert homicide, inadequate investigations failing to recognise maltreatment, underreporting of abuse, and differences in definitions and criteria for registration (Jenny & Isaac 2006).

PATTERNS OF FATAL CHILD MALTREATMENT

Maltreatment-related deaths do not form one homogeneous group, but rather fall into a number of distinct but overlapping subgroups (Christoffel 1984, Reder et al. 1993). My own experience suggests that maltreatment-related fatalities can be classified in five broad groups, which differ in relation to the characteristics of the victims and perpetrators, the mode of death and the intentions behind the death (Box 6.1). These groups may not, however, be mutually exclusive and there are almost certainly overlaps between them. Further study is required to determine whether this classification could be useful in understanding and responding to fatal maltreatment or in preventive efforts. It is, however, important to remember that every child fatality is a unique event that will carry its own characteristics.

Box 6.1 Categories of fatal child maltreatment

A Infanticide and 'covert' homicide.
B Severe physical assaults.
C Extreme neglect/deprivational abuse.
D Deliberate/overt homicides.
E Deaths related to but not directly caused by maltreatment.

The highest risk for fatal child abuse is in early infancy (Overpeck et al. 1998, Rohde et al. 1998, Brookman & Maguire 2003). This pattern of increased risk in younger infants may reflect the overall vulnerability of the infant (Reder & Duncan 1999), although other factors, including parental stress and specific triggers, may also be important. The overall age distribution is heavily influenced by the strong bias towards younger victims in categories A (infanticide and covert homicide) and B (severe physical assaults) and may be less marked in the other forms of fatal maltreatment.

INFANTICIDE AND COVERT HOMICIDE

Although the term 'infanticide' has a precise legal definition in the UK, I use it along with the term 'covert homicide' to describe a group of fatalilties, usually of very young infants, many shortly after birth and typically perpetrated by the mother using non-violent means. These differ significantly from the group of severe physical assaults that make up the majority of Serious Case Reviews in the UK. Studies of infant fatalities have found that female perpetrators are more likely to use asphyxiation, drowning, strangulation or poisoning (Schloesser et al. 1992, Reder & Duncan 1999). Indeed in Reder and Duncan's study of 'Part 8' inquiries in the early 1990s (Reder & Duncan 1999), they distinguished 23 deaths from physical assaults, in 80% of which the perpetrator was male, compared to eight children who were strangled, smothered or drowned, all with female perpetrators. In many cases the perpetrator holds a soft object over the infant or child's nose and mouth, preventing breathing and holding it there until all struggling ceases. Other cases may involve the perpetrator holding a hand over the mouth and nose, pinching the nose, using a plastic bag, or compressing the chest to prevent breathing.

One of the greatest challenges to professionals in these deaths, particularly those occurring in infancy, is their covert nature. Smothering, particularly when using a soft object, may leave no external signs of injury, and autopsy findings are typically non-specific so that it may be difficult to distinguish homicide deaths from other sudden unexpected deaths in infancy (SUDI). Estimates of the proportion of SUDI caused by homicide vary considerably although many authors suggest up to 10% may be frank homicide, with maltreatment (abuse or neglect) being a contributory (though not necessarily causal) factor in a similar proportion (Fleming et al. 2000, Levene & Bacon 2004, Bajanowski et al. 2005, Sidebotham et al. 2005). In the CESDI SUDI study of 456 SUDI in 1993–96, maltreatment was thought to be the main cause of death for a total of 25 infants (6%), and a secondary or alternative cause of death for a further 32 infants (7.7%) (Fleming et al. 2000).

Neonatal deaths may form a specific subgroup within the overall category of infanticide, reflecting unwanted or concealed pregnancies (Rohde et al. 1998). Many of these mothers are young and unmarried (Herman-Giddens et al. 2003) and may have a history of mental health problems including childhood abuse and psychotic or dissociative symptoms. Whilst the most common mode of death in these neonatal killings seems to be smothering with a pillow or other soft objects, others involve drowning or abandonment and withdrawal of care, or more violent means. In the UK, this distinct profile is recognised in the official classification of infanticide. The Infanticide Act 1938 (DRSD 1938) defines this as the death of a child under the age of 12 months whose mother causes their death by a wilful act or omission, but whose mother's balance of mind is disturbed by either not having recovered from childbirth, or experiencing the effects of lactation. It is important to recognise, however, that not all mothers who kill their children are suffering from mental illness and that the vast majority of mothers who are suffering from mental illness do not even entertain thoughts of killing their infants. Fathers or other family members can also be responsible for neonatal killings. Whilst the highest risks are undoubtedly in infancy, older children may also be killed in a similar manner.

There appears in these deaths to be an intent to end the child's life, which may be associated with distorted perceptions of the child or with the mother either not wanting the child or believing that by ending the child's life she is somehow acting in the child's best interests. Within this group there may be an overlap with so-called 'mercy killings' of disabled or chronically ill children, the parent in these cases wanting to relieve the child's suffering or spare them from further suffering.

It is questionable whether a criminal prosecution for murder is an appropriate response in most of these cases, particularly where there may be doubt surrounding the nature or mode of death, the degree of intent, or the capacity or perceptions of the perpetrator. It is nevertheless essential to investigate these deaths thoroughly and, where the investigation suggests homicide, to acknowledge it as such in order to appropriately support both the perpetrator and other family members, and to protect other children from possible harm.

SEVERE PHYSICAL ASSAULTS

This is probably the largest group of maltreatment-related deaths, and certainly the most well-recognised. In studies of Serious Case Reviews in the UK, the majority of cases involve severe physical violence with or without associated neglect (Reder et al. 1993, Reder & Duncan 1999, Brandon 2007, Rose & Barnes 2007). These deaths extend throughout childhood, but again the highest risks are in infancy. In most cases the perpetrator is a family member (Kotch et al. 1993), more commonly the father or father figure (Lucas et al. 2002, Bourget & Gagne 2005), although other carers may be implicated and in some cases both parents are involved. The mode of death in these cases is typically a violent assault, most commonly an inflicted head injury, including shaking and shaking-impact injuries, but also multiple injuries and abdominal injuries. Other deaths involve the use of firearms, beatings, stabbings and strangulation (Bourget & Gagne 2005). Many of these killings appear to be impulsive outbursts in response to specific triggers, including a crying baby, disobedience in older children, or wider family or environmental triggers, including marital disagreements (Levine et al. 1994, Brewster et al. 1998, Lucas et al. 2002, Lyman et al. 2003). There may be indications of unrealistic parental expectations, leading to excessive and uncontrolled physical punishment. However, it is probably unusual for such outbursts to be totally unprecedented and often there is a pre-existing history of physical abuse or other domestic violence. The carers in these cases are typically, though not exclusively, young parents of low socio-economic status; there may be a history of mental health problems (Rohde et al. 1998, Bourget & Gagne 2002, 2005, Lucas et al. 2002) and the families are often known to social support or child protective services (Reder et al. 1993, Sanders et al. 1999). The families are typified by a high degree of disorganisation, often with multiple partners and with evidence of intrafamilial violence. Alcohol or drugs may be implicated in some deaths, but surprisingly this does not appear to be a feature in most (Lucas et al. 2002, Bourget & Gagne 2005).

Whilst in most cases there is probably no intent to kill the child, a substantial proportion will show evidence of persistent or escalating violence towards the child, with previous child abuse investigations, or with old fractures or other injuries discovered at autopsy. Many also show signs of neglect with evidence of malnutrition, cold injury or poor hygiene. This presumably reflects an ongoing pattern of abusive and neglectful care, which may be focused on one 'scape-goat' or may be part of a broader pattern of family interaction.

EXTREME NEGLECT/DEPRIVATIONAL ABUSE

Although neglect appears to be one of the most prevalent forms of maltreatment, the mortality associated with it appears to be low. In Reder and Duncan's study, neglect was the primary cause of death in just six cases (12%), three of which involved abandonment at birth, though a much higher proportion had evidence of neglect in association with physical abuse (Reder & Duncan 1999). However, this may in part be related to issues around defining maltreatment-related deaths and attributing cause of death to omissions in parental care. Indeed, it has been argued in the US that more children die of neglect than any other form of maltreatment, with 40% or more of maltreatment-related deaths being due to neglect or a combination of abuse and neglect (Levine et al. 1994, Douglas & Finkelhor 2007). In some of these deaths, the neglect may be a reflection of parental incompetence, related to learning difficulties, physical or mental ill-health, or other environmental circumstances. However, such cases are probably rare and I believe should more appropriately be considered as deaths related to but not directly caused by maltreatment (category E). The more extreme forms of neglect appear to have an element of intent to deprive the child of his or her needs, and may be better referred to as 'deprivational abuse' (Golden et al. 2003). These children are typically seen as unwanted or in some other way perceived as different and may be treated by their carers as though they do not exist (Reder et al. 1993). Victims are often shut away and denied food, warmth, clothing, hygiene and medical care. Death may result from extreme malnutrition or electrolyte imbalance, or from hypothermia, often leading to multiple organ failure. In other cases, neglect of the child's hygiene needs may lead to systemic infections.

Disabled children or those with chronic illness may be particularly at risk, where their carers perceive the children as placing additional or unreasonable

demands on them as carers. These children may not receive the medical thera-
peutic or educational input they require and this in turn may lead to further
disability or ill-health and can prove fatal if medication is withheld or given
inappropriately.

DELIBERATE/OVERT HOMICIDES

This fourth group of fatalities overlaps with the first category of infanticide/
covert homicide, in that there would appear to be an intent to kill the child;
but differs from it and other groups in the age profile, in the victim and perpetrator characteristics and in the typical mode of death. Whilst most infanticides involve the mother killing her infant, in this category the perpetrator is
typically male. In contrast to deaths in younger children, an increasing number
of homicides involving older children and adolescents occur outside the home
by perpetrators outside the immediate family (Christoffel 1984, Creighton
1995). However, even in adolescents, the majority of killings are by people
known to the victim, whilst in younger children stranger killings are extremely
rare (Moskowitz et al. 2005). Killings of older children and adolescents more
typically involve stabbings and firearms (Christoffel 1984, Lucas et al. 2002).
Some of these deaths are associated with sexual assaults (Kotch et al. 1993)
and there have been a number of high-profile cases of young girls being
abducted, sexually assaulted and finally murdered by unrelated adults.

The motives leading to these homicides may not always be clear. In some
cases, the killing can be a form of revenge against an estranged spouse and
may include multiple killings, or arson leading to house-fire fatalities (Squires
& Busuttil 1995). In a study in Quebec, a high proportion of homicides (23%)
involved multiple victims and in 18% the offender also killed his spouse
(Bourget & Gagne 2005). About 60% of total homicides were followed by an
attempted suicide, this rising to 86% in those involving multiple killings. Similarly, in six cases of multiple killings perpetrated by mothers, all were followed
by maternal suicide (Bourget & Gagne 2002). These 'extended suicides' may
be a distinct subgroup, the perpetrators being older than those of other categories, with a much higher incidence of mental health problems, and possibly a
bias towards higher social classes (Rohde et al. 1998).

DEATHS RELATED TO BUT NOT DIRECTLY
CAUSED BY MALTREATMENT

A number of reviews of sudden unexpected death in infancy have revealed
a significant proportion of deaths where issues around parental care are
identified but not felt to be causal (Fleming et al. 2000, Bajanowski et al. 2005).
These include families where there have been previous child protection concerns in the index child or siblings; infants with evidence of previous physical
abuse or neglect, but with no indication of abuse as a cause of death (either

presenting with an identifiable medical cause of death, or meeting the criteria for SIDS); or where there are concerns around parental care, but not sufficient to label as neglect. We know that many SIDS deaths occur in chaotic family or home environments (Chapter 4), and where an infant dies, for example, whilst co-sleeping on a sofa with a parent who has taken alcohol or drugs, there may be issues around parental care that need to be addressed, but it may not be appropriate to pursue a criminal line of culpable neglect. In other circumstances, however, such a line may be appropriate – for example, where the carers have clearly been made aware of the risks they are posing to their children, but actively chose to ignore or go against the advice of professionals.

It is well recognised that many of the risk factors for child abuse and neglect also increase the risks of other adverse outcomes (Newberger et al. 1977). It is therefore hardly surprising that issues around abuse and neglect are likely to be found in a proportion of children dying of a range of natural disorders. In all cases it is essential to evaluate carefully all of the circumstances surrounding the death, to acknowledge where there are issues around parental care, or where abuse or neglect are contributory factors, but not to label the death as caused by abuse or neglect when this cannot be substantiated.

One particular group where this is important is those children involved in fatal accidents where there may be issues of parental supervision and care. A lack of developmentally appropriate supervision may place children at risk from traffic or domestic accidents, including accidental ingestion of drugs or other household substances, drownings, falls, electrocution, gunshot wounds and fires (Bonner et al. 1999). Deaths from burns and house fires, discussed in Chapter 5, comprise a group within which there are often indicators of neglect. In a study of 168 child deaths in 118 house fires in Scotland (Squires & Busuttil 1995), 30% of incidents were started by children playing or experimenting with matches, fires or flammable liquids, almost invariably in situations where there was inadequate parental supervision, or where the child was in an unsafe environment with access to fire hazards. Other deaths involved smoking, chip pans or electrical equipment. A large proportion (28%) involved the parents or carers consuming large quantities of alcohol. Similarly, young children left unsupervised in baths or near water may be at risk of drowning. The issue here is the level of supervision required in relation to the child's developmental abilities and the parents' appreciation of those needs.

A further group includes those children dying of natural causes whose parents may not have sought medical intervention early enough. This may have been through a failure to recognise the severity of the child's condition, or through prioritising the parents' needs above those of the child. In all cases, there should be a careful and sensitive evaluation of the history and presentation.

Maltreatment may also play an indirect role in a wide range of deaths throughout childhood. It is well recognised that children who have been abused have a higher subsequent risk of death than their non-abused counterparts. Sabotta and Davis in Washington State showed that children on the child abuse registry were nearly three times more likely to die before their 18th birthday than their peers (Sabotta & Davis 1992). Some of these deaths may be direct deaths from maltreatment, perhaps particularly where physical abuse is involved. Other deaths, however, may be a reflection of the underlying vulnerability of these children and families to a host of adverse circumstances, or deaths as a secondary consequence of the abuse, for example death from an overwhelming chest infection in a child severely disabled by a non-accidental head injury. All forms of maltreatment, but particularly sexual and emotional abuse, may have long-term consequences in the mental health and behaviour of young people. Victims of abuse are recognised to have higher rates of depression and suicide (Dube et al. 2001, Ystgaard et al. 2004), and may also be more prone to risk-taking behaviours including substance abuse, which puts them at risk of accidental and medical causes of death (Bensley et al. 1999). A study of over 16,000 young people in the US found that 31% of previously abused adolescents had ever attempted suicide, compared with just 10% of their non-abused counterparts (Perkins & Jones 2004). Furthermore, members of the abused group were more likely than their peers to have used alcohol, tobacco and drugs, to have engaged in sexual activity, and to display antisocial behaviours.

PREDISPOSING FACTORS

It would be both inaccurate and inappropriate to characterise a 'typical' profile of a fatal child abuse case, particularly given the different patterns of death outlined above. Nevertheless, several factors have been shown repeatedly to increase the risks, and many of these overlap with recognised risk factors for non-fatal child maltreatment (Creighton 1992, Belsky 1993, Kotch et al. 1999, Sidebotham & Heron 2006) and indeed with other causes of childhood death, including sudden infant death syndrome (Chapter 4) and accidental deaths (Chapter 5). In evaluating possible maltreatment-related deaths, as with any child deaths, it is important to take a broad ecological view, incorporating factors intrinsic to the child; factors around the parents and parental care; and factors in the wider family and environmental context, including any services provided to or needed by the family (Figure 6.1) (HM Government 2000, 2005a, Sidebotham 2001).

In a national study in the US, the strongest risk factors for fatal maltreatment in the first year of life were a maternal age of less than 17 years, a second or subsequent birth for a mother 19 years old or younger, and no prenatal care (Overpeck et al. 1998). Low maternal education and single status were also important risk factors. These factors have been found repeatedly in relation to most forms of fatal maltreatment (Jason & Andereck 1983, Schloesser

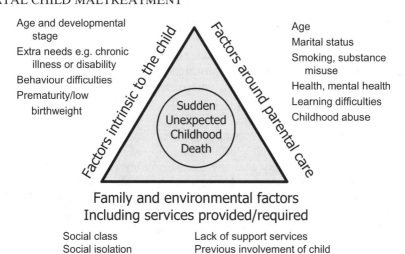

Age and developmental stage
Extra needs e.g. chronic illness or disability
Behaviour difficulties
Prematurity/low birthweight

Age
Marital status
Smoking, substance misuse
Health, mental health
Learning difficulties
Childhood abuse

Family and environmental factors
Including services provided/required

Social class
Social isolation
Unsafe environments
Family violence

Lack of support services
Previous involvement of child protective services
Inadequate antenatal care

Figure 6.1 Factors affecting risk of fatal maltreatment (based on HM Government 2000)
Source: Crown copyright material is reproduced with the permission of the Controller of HMSO and Queen's Printer for Scotland.

et al. 1992, Overpeck et al. 1998, Herman-Giddens et al. 2003). Parental mental illness is a feature in many studies (Reder et al. 1993, Rohde et al. 1998, Reder & Duncan 1999, Bourget & Gagne 2002, 2005, Lucas et al. 2002, Herman-Giddens et al. 2003). Family interactions play an important role, perhaps most notably in those deaths from severe assaults where a history of family violence and marital disagreement is common (Brewster et al. 1998, Lucas et al. 2002). Chaotic or disorganised family arrangements are frequently noted (Reder et al. 1993, Reder & Duncan 1999).

Factors intrinsic to the child are less easily defined. The age and developmental stage of the child is clearly important and affects risk differently in relation to the different forms of maltreatment-related deaths. Infants and young children who are in any way different or perceived to be different by their parents may be at higher risk, particularly in relation to infanticide and covert homicide. This includes those infants born prematurely or of low birthweight, those with chronic illness or disability and those who are unwanted. Those with behavioural difficulties may be at particular risk of severe physical assaults, where the child's behaviour may act as a trigger for an impulsive outburst by the parent. In American studies, blacks and American Indians appear to be more at risk (Levine et al. 1994, Overpeck et al. 1998, Lucas et al. 2002, Herman-Giddens et al. 2003, Lyman et al. 2003), although associations with ethnicity in this country are less clear and indeed in many cases ethnicity is not recorded, making it difficult to ascertain any differences in

prevalence or patterns of maltreatment-related deaths between different
ethnic groups (Rose & Barnes 2007). It is possible that different patterns of
maltreatment-related deaths predominate in different subgroups of the population, but I have found few data exploring this. There does not appear to be
any clear pattern for victim gender, with different sex ratios reported in different studies, although overall, most studies suggest a slightly higher rate
amongst males (Jason & Andereck 1983, Schloesser et al. 1992, Brewster et al.
1998, Lucas et al. 2002). One particular issue which may be of relevance in
some cultures is selective female infanticide and sex-selective abortion, which
have been reported in many countries, most notably China and India, where
male offspring are highly valued (Hesketh & Xing 2006, Jha et al. 2006). There
are no published data on such practices in this country, although it is widely
thought that this may be practiced amongst some immigrant groups, with some
travelling overseas to obtain selective abortions.

Several studies have demonstrated evidence of previous maltreatment
in many cases (Reder et al. 1993, Sanders et al. 1999), although this is not
universal and a large proportion will present having had no pre-existing concerns (Lucas et al. 2002). A study from Los Angeles found that 43% of child
homicides and 38% of unintentional injury deaths came from families with
previous contact with social or child protection services, however, those dying
of homicides were over three times as likely to have had a documented history
of child maltreatment and social service need prior to the death (Sorenson &
Peterson 1994).

NATURE OF FATAL CHILD ABUSE AND NEGLECT

Having explored some of the patterns of maltreatment-related deaths, and
factors contributing to those deaths, we will now examine some of the more
common immediate causes of death, and address some specific areas of difficulty for the practitioner.

NON-ACCIDENTAL HEAD INJURY

Non-accidental head injury is the most common cause of fatal child maltreatment (Schloesser et al. 1992, Kotch et al. 1993, Hicks & Gaughan 1995, Kasim
et al. 1995, Pollanen et al. 2002, Graupman & Winston 2006, King et al. 2006).
A population-based study from North Carolina found an incidence of inflicted
traumatic brain injury in children under two of 17 per 100,000 per year, with
a case fatality rate of 22.5% (Keenan et al. 2003). Distinguishing accidental
from non-accidental head injury may not always be easy, but certain pointers
may suggest child abuse. Children suffering inflicted head injuries tend to be
younger and have more severe injuries than those with accidental injuries
(Keenan et al. 2003). In contrast to accidental head injuries, for which there

appears to be no gender difference, inflicted injuries are more common in male than female infants (Keenan et al. 2003).

Skull fractures occur as a result of direct trauma to the head, either through being struck by an object, or as a result of a fall, or impact with a surface. Both abusive and accidental skull fractures are more common in younger children (Welsh Child Protection Systematic Review Group 2005). Most skull fractures, both accidental and abusive, are simple, linear fractures confined to one of the bones of the skull. Multiple or bilateral fractures, or those that cross suture lines (the joints between different skull bones) are more likely to be inflicted (Hobbs 1984, Meservy et al. 1987). Skull fractures may have associated bruising or overlying boggy or swollen areas on the scalp. These boggy areas of swelling may take some hours or days to develop, and can persist for many weeks. In some cases, they will harden around the edges, giving a hard rim overlying the skull. However, fractures may be present with no external signs of injury, and proper X-rays with both antero-posterior and lateral views are essential to diagnosis. It is important to realise that a skull fracture of itself is not a cause of death, but may be a pointer to underlying brain injury, or to other injuries. Unlike other bones in the body, the skull bones do not follow the same pattern of healing, and it is not possible to date skull fractures in the same way as other fractures.

Subdural haemorrhage (SDH) may be one of the strongest pointers to non-accidental head injury. This is a collection of blood found in the subdural space within the skull vault. The dura is a thick membrane covering the surface of the brain. The space between the dura and the brain surface is crossed by tiny bridging veins which may rupture when stretched, leading to bleeding into the subdural space. Such injuries are thought to happen most commonly when there are rotational or shearing forces on the brain, as may happen when a baby is shaken (Case et al. 2001). In such situations the baby's brain may rotate at a different rate to the head, exacerbated by the relatively large head size and the relative weakness of neck muscles. Subdural haemorrhage is thought to be more likely where there is shaking followed by an impact, but it can occur in the absence of impact. Subdural haemorrhages may also occur as a result of a wide variety of medical conditions including clotting disorders, infections and metabolic disorders, and following birth trauma (Box 6.2; Kemp 2002) although for most medical causes there will be other pointers in the history or examination findings. An Australian study of subdural haemorrhages in children under two years found that non-accidental injury was the most common cause, accounting for 55% of cases, compared to 39% for accidents and 6% (two cases) from other causes (Tzioumi & Oates 1998). The most extensive study in this country found that 82% of cases were highly suggestive of abuse (Jayawant et al. 1998). The overall incidence of subdural haemorrhage was 12.8 per 100,000 children per year rising to 21 per 100,000 children per year for children under a year. Most cases are in children aged less than two, although occasional cases are seen in older children.

Box 6.2 Causes of subdural haemorrhage

Intentional injury	Shaken baby syndrome
Non-intentional injury	Major trauma, e.g. road traffic accident, serious falls
Neurosurgical complications	Following any neurosurgical intervention
Perinatal/Foetal	Antenatal or following labour*
Cranial malformations	Spontaneous bleeding from vascular malformations
Cerebral infections	Meningitis
Coagulation and haematological disorders	Leukaemia, sickle cell anaemia, disseminated intravascular coagulation, haemophilia, Von Willebrand's disease, haemorrhagic disease of the newborn, idiopathic thrombocytopenia purpura
Metabolic disorders	Glutaric aciduria, galactosaemia
Biochemical disorders	Salt poisoning, hypernatraemic dehydration

*Several recent studies have shown a significant incidence of SDH in infants after both traumatic delivery (e.g. forceps) and normal delivery – the great majority are non-symptomatic and resolve by one month of age, but there are no good data on the age distribution at the time of complete resolution of such SDH.

In addition to subdural haemorrhages, the full constellation of shaking or shaking-impact injuries includes retinal haemorrhages and traumatic brain injury with or without other associated injuries, including skull fractures, metaphyseal fractures (occurring at the ends of the long bones of the arms or legs), rib fractures and bruises to the arms or trunk. Typically they will present acutely unwell following a sudden deterioration, with loss of consciousness and impaired breathing. There may be a history of the child collapsing or choking, but there is rarely an initial history of shaking or other injury. Often it is only when confronted with the news that a head injury has been found that the parents will reveal a history of minor injury or of shaking the baby in an attempt to resuscitate.

Subdural haemorrhages are typically small and do not directly cause death. The cause of death in these cases is thought to be a combination of three processes: direct trauma to the brain tissue (diffuse axonal injury) as a result of the acceleration/deceleration forces; trauma to the breathing centres of the brain stem, leading to impaired breathing and hypoxia (lack of oxygen); and secondary brain swelling, reducing the blood (and therefore oxygen) supply to the brain.

There is considerable uncertainty as to the degree of force required to cause a significant head injury. Whilst there is some controversy over whether infants and children may suffer a fatal head injury from low-level falls (Byard & Cohle 2004), most clinicians would agree that this is unusual. Fatal head injuries are more likely to occur following falls of greater than 1–2 metres or road traffic accidents, or through abuse. Moreover, infants rarely sustain serious or fatal injuries from accidents in the home or from normal child-care activities (Chadwick et al. 1991, Wilkins 1997, Duhaime et al. 1998, Tzioumi & Oates 1998).

OTHER FATAL INJURIES

Blunt abdominal injuries are an uncommon but important cause of child-abuse fatalities (Pollanen et al. 2002, King et al. 2006). Such trauma may lead to massive haemorrhaging, resulting in shock, or to intestinal perforation, causing peritonitis (Kasim et al. 1995). In a series from the US, excluding motor-vehicle accidents, child abuse was the most common cause of blunt abdominal trauma and carried a high mortality (Trokel et al. 2006). It was found that 11% of the sample had co-existing undernourishment. Many of these children will have other injuries, including traumatic brain injuries, although they may present with isolated abdominal trauma. Trauma as a cause of abdominal pain or other gastrointestinal symptoms is not easy to detect in the absence of a history; the finding of unexpected abdominal trauma at post mortem should be thoroughly investigated. Other children may die as a result of strangulation or stabbings (Kotch et al. 1993). Although skeletal injuries, including rib and long bone fractures, are common in children dying of abuse, they are rarely the cause of death (Ellis, 1997). Nevertheless, they may give pointers to patterns of maltreatment, particularly where injuries of different ages are identified. Similarly, patterns of bruises or other skin and soft-tissue injuries in unusual sites, of specific shapes or with no feasible explanation should suggest the possibility of non-accidental injury (Maguire et al. 2005).

FABRICATED AND INDUCED ILLNESS

Fabricated and induced illness (FII; previously known as Munchausen syndrome by proxy, MSbP) represents a poorly defined and diverse spectrum of situations where a child suffers significant harm through the fabrication or induction of illness by a parent or carer (RCPCH 2002). It is a rare condition with a reported incidence of around 0.4 per 100,000 per year in those aged less than 16, rising to 2.8 per 100,000 per year in infants (McClure et al. 1996). The spectrum encountered in FII encompasses exaggeration of symptoms, through fabrication of signs, symptoms and history, falsification of hospital charts and records or specimens, and interfering with treatments, to induction of illness by a variety of means including poisoning, administering medication and smothering. FII overall has a reported mortality of around 10% (Rosenberg 1987). It is probably only the more severe end of the spectrum which is potentially fatal. Deaths from fabricated and induced illness are almost exclusively due to suffocation or poisoning and this group of infants may be very difficult to distinguish from infants dying of sudden infant death syndrome (McClure et al. 1996). Rosenberg's review of 117 published cases found 10 deaths, all aged less than three years, with three deaths from suffocation and five from poisoning (Rosenberg 1987).

The more severe end of the spectrum of FII is concentrated in younger children. Most cases of smothering occur in the first three months, whilst cases of poisoning tend to occur slightly later, with most cases being between one and five years (RCPCH 2002). Whilst the majority of cases of FII involving the less severe end of the spectrum (exaggeration or verbal fabrication only) do not progress to more extreme manifestations and the risk of death is therefore low, there may be an escalation observed in some cases with more extreme manifestations or an increasing frequency of presentation.

There is some overlap with those situations described under the category of infanticide above, and the distinction is probably semantic (Rosenberg 1987, Meadow 2002). Rather than trying to categorise such deaths into distinct boxes, it is more important to obtain a full picture of all aspects of the death and the circumstances surrounding it. Indeed, whilst a significant proportion of deaths from smothering or poisoning occur in the context of other pointers to FII, many do not (McClure et al. 1996, Meadow 2002), and such deaths with no previous pointers to FII should probably not be labelled as such. Other deaths may occur as a result of medical intervention in response to fabricated and induced illness, for example through complications of surgery or anaesthesia; these deaths should again be considered as maltreatment-related deaths, even though there may have been no intent to kill on the part of either the parent or the health staff involved.

Fabricated or induced illness arises when several factors coincide: factors in the child, the fabricator, the family, social circumstances and the health-care arena. One of the distinctive features of FII is that in the majority of cases, the perpetrator is the mother (Rosenberg 1987, McClure et al. 1996). However, where a male perpetrator is involved, the cases are often at the more severe end (Meadow 1998, RCPCH 2002). There is no typical profile of the perpetrator. However, some characteristics have been found to be common in many case series, including pre-existing mental-health or personality difficulties, a childhood history of abuse and some previous paramedical training or knowledge (Rosenberg 1987). There is an increased risk of attempted suicide and deliberate self harm by the perpetrator, both before and after the event (Rosenberg 1987). Frank psychosis is unusual, and Munchausen syndrome per se is uncommon, although more general abnormal illness behaviour may be more common (Rosenberg 1987, McClure et al. 1996, Meadow 2002, RCPCH 2002). In contrast to many other causes of unexpected death, there does not appear to be any socio-economic gradient in FII. Failure to thrive and feeding difficulties are common in the children, along with frequent hospital admissions and unexplained illnesses, including apparent life-threatening events (ALTE) (Rosenberg 1987, Meadow 1999). Amongst the siblings of children suffering from FII there is an increased mortality, with both previous infant deaths, some of which may have been categorised as SIDS, and subsequent deaths (Rosenberg 1987, RCPCH 2002). Fabricated pregnancies and reported previous stillbirths and infant deaths which cannot be confirmed have been noted. Such factors may not always be apparent when taking a history from the parents, and it is therefore essential in any unexpected death to review both hospital and primary care records to gain a full picture of the previous medical history.

POISONING

A literature review of published cases of fabricated and induced illness identified two groups of poisoning: poisoning of low toxicity involving prescribed or over-the-counter drugs such as emetics, laxatives and diuretics; and poisoning of high toxicity (RCPCH 2002). Children in the low-toxicity group tend to present with symptoms such as diarrhoea, vomiting or dehydration. Poisoning with these substances would rarely be fatal unless treatment was not sought or given. The high-toxicity group includes poisoning with salt, insulin or other drugs causing hypoglycaemia, and a variety of substances which may lead to neurological symptoms including seizures, coma and sudden death.

There is a wide variety of agents that may cause high-level toxicity, including both prescribed drugs and various household products. It is important to realise that accidental poisoning in the under-twos is rare, but becomes increasingly common in the older pre-school group, once toddlers become mobile and able to manipulate bottle tops and so on (Chapter 5). Deliberate or accidental poisoning may occur with drugs prescribed for the child, for example through a carer giving excess insulin to a child with diabetes, inducing hypoglycaemia. Where a child or family member is known to be on prescribed medication, consideration should be given to seizing remaining stocks of all medications and checking dates and amounts prescribed by the GP or other doctors. Similarly, where over-the-counter medicines are noted, consideration should be given to seizing these for further investigation. Clues to the possibility of poisoning may come from the history, with previous apparent life-threatening events, unexplained hospital admissions, fitting or drowsiness preceding the death, or knowledge of prescribed medicines or substance abuse in the parents or other family members. There may be no specific features, however, either in the history or post-mortem findings, and unless the possibility of toxicity is considered and specifically looked for, such a cause may easily be overlooked.

There may be some indications on examination pointing towards the possibility of poisoning, including rashes, unexplained puncture marks in the skin (emphasising the importance of documenting all interventions during resuscitation) or caustic burns around the mouth. Investigations essential to identifying poisoning include blood-sugar measurement, measuring electrolyte levels in blood and in the vitreous humour of the eye, and taking samples of blood, urine, stomach contents and bile for toxicology. However, indiscriminate screening of samples with no specific pointers is complex, expensive and likely to have a very low yield. Toxicology screening may therefore best be targeted where there are particular concerns from the history or examination, or where there are unexplained disturbances in biochemical analysis. Analysis of remains of feeds in a baby's bottle may also prove helpful if poisoning is suspected.

SMOTHERING

Smothering presents particular difficulties in the differential diagnosis of SIDS as such cases may leave no visible external marks and no specific pointers at autopsy. Clues in these cases may include inconsistencies in the history, a previous history of apnoeic spells or apparent life-threatening events, and delays in presentation. The baby should be examined carefully for injuries or bruises, including petechial bruising around and inside the mouth and nose or over the face and neck, and for any other signs of abuse or neglect. At autopsy there may be internal petechiae of the thymus, heart and lungs, although such findings are non-specific and may be found even when there is no concern about smothering (Chapter 9). Findings such as internal petechiae, large pulmonary haemorrhage and haemosiderin-laden macrophages may point towards the possibility of smothering or previous hypoxic events, but cannot distinguish between hypoxia due to smothering and that from other causes, and must be interpreted in the light of the full clinical picture.

MANAGEMENT OF FATAL CHILD MALTREATMENT

When considering the possibility of maltreatment as a cause of unexpected childhood death, practitioners are faced with a particular dilemma. On the one hand, if they fail to recognise death from maltreatment, other children may be put at risk of further or future harm; on the other hand, parents may be wrongly accused of killing their children, compounding the suffering already experienced by these families, and potentially leading to miscarriages of justice. This dilemma is particularly pertinent in sudden unexpected death in infancy, where covert homicide may be a factor in a proportion of deaths. The dangers are compounded where more than one infant has died in the same family, leading to increased suspicion of unnatural deaths. Indeed, where there has been one homicide in a family, the risk of future homicides is increased, and in some cases, parents have confessed to multiple homicides. However, other risks are also increased and it is dangerous to presume that more than one SUDI in a family implies that the infants have been murdered. For children dying of natural or unexplained causes, including SIDS or other explained causes of SUDI, the underlying risks may well persist in the family, making subsequent children more at risk of natural deaths. More specifically, where there are genetic or metabolic factors (which may or may not have been recognised) leading to the death, there may be a direct increased risk to subsequent siblings. It is thus imperative that all unexpected deaths are thoroughly and systematically investigated and reviewed by a multi-agency team, to ascertain as far as possible any identifiable cause of death, and to consider any possible indicators of maltreatment or other concerns around parental care.

Recognition of maltreatment-related deaths is not the province of one professional or group of professionals working in isolation, but rather is crucially dependent on collaboration among all professionals including the coroner, the police forensic team, the pathologist, the paediatrician and other health and social care professionals. It is important to approach all unexpected deaths with an open mind, being aware of the possibility that maltreatment may play a role, but not prejudging on the basis of social class, or parental age or education. As highlighted above, a thorough history is crucial, including a detailed account of the 24 hours leading up to the child's death, or discovery of the body. Any discrepancies in the history should be noted, bearing in mind the effects of stress and grieving on a parent's ability to give a coherent account. Certain factors in the history, examination, autopsy or scene review may raise further suspicions (Box 6.3), but none of these are diagnostic and all should be interpreted as one piece of a jigsaw of information.

A full examination of the child is essential to look for injuries, although many will present with no external injuries (Pollanen et al. 2002). Anogenital injuries should specifically be looked for. Growth parameters including length, weight and head circumference should be taken and plotted on a centile chart looking specifically for wasting and stunting as evidence of both short- and long-term undernourishment. Every unexpected infant death and all child deaths, where there is the possibility of child abuse, should be investigated with a full skeletal survey to detect possible fractures which may not otherwise be picked up at post mortem (Mendelson 2004). All cases require a thorough post mortem, ideally undertaken jointly with a forensic and a paediatric pathologist. Other investigations will be dictated by specific findings or concerns identified either through the history and scene review, or through findings at autopsy.

In all cases, where suspicions are raised, there should be an immediate Section 47 strategy meeting involving Social Services, the police child abuse investigation team, the paediatrician and other professionals involved. There must be close liaison with the coroner and the pathologist. The purposes of the strategy meeting are to share information, including on the past history and care of the child, and any previous concerns relating to the child or other family members; to plan the ongoing investigation, including consideration of

---

Box 6.3 Concerning features

(Note that these features may serve to raise suspicions; they are *not* in themselves diagnostic.)

History

- previous recurrent cyanosis, apnoea, ALTE
- age – outside of the typical profile
- previous unexplained SUDI (siblings or other infants in care of parent)
- simultaneous twin deaths
- blood from nose or mouth*
- changing or inconsistent history
- previous child protection concerns.

Examination

- injuries:
  unexplained or suspicious bruises, lacerations, burns
  consider site, extent, patterns
- poor growth, poor hygiene, signs of neglect.

*It is important to distinguish fresh blood from blood-stained fluid, which may look very similar. Heavily blood-stained fluid from the mouth or nose is common and does NOT indicate an unnatural cause. Copious fresh blood is very unusual and most commonly occurs as a consequence of resuscitation – especially intubation by an unskilled operator – hence a very careful history of resuscitation attempts and information on when the blood was first noted is very important. Blood mixed with surfactant (from the lungs) will spread over a much larger area than blood usually does and it may therefore appear as if there has been a lot of blood when only a small amount was present on the surface.

---

any criminal investigation; to consider the needs of any other children in the family; and to review the support needs of the wider family. Even where a death is related to maltreatment, the carers will be grieving and this may be compounded by feelings of guilt, disbelief and mistrust. All these situations need careful handling both to enable a thorough investigation to take place and to support the family and ensure that other children are protected. There may be an increased risk of suicide amongst perpetrators, particularly in relation to induced illness, and in situations of multiple homicide (Rosenberg 1987, Bourget & Gagne 2002, 2005).

How such cases are handled raises particular difficulties. Craft and Hall (2004) propose that complex child deaths and child protection cases should normally be handled by civil proceedings rather than through criminal prosecution. This may be appropriate in many cases, given our poor understanding of the nature of such deaths and the motives underlying them. However, there is also a need to uphold justice and to protect other children. In cases of overt homicide, or of death resulting from severe assaults or severe deprivational abuse, it would normally be appropriate to pursue a criminal prosecution. Whilst a criminal investigation should take place for infanticide, covert homicide and deaths related to but not caused by maltreatment, these families and the wider public may be better served by an approach that recognises the complexity of issues and seeks to understand and support both the perpetrator and the wider family.

Where maltreatment is identified as a causal or contributory factor in relation to a child's death, that does need to be acknowledged and the potential risks to other and subsequent children very carefully assessed. There may be a need to remove other children from the family or to arrange appropriate supervision, even if a criminal line is not being pursued. It is appropriate that the threshold for protecting children should be lower (based on a balance of probabilities that maltreatment contributed to the child's death) than that for securing a criminal conviction (based on proving beyond reasonable doubt that a particular perpetrator has caused the death). Any child protection investigation should be led by Social Services. In all cases, should the mother become pregnant again, consideration should be given to holding a pre-birth case conference to assess any potential risks to the unborn child. This relies on all professionals being aware of these risks and of putting in place adequate systems of monitoring and notification.

Finally, it is essential that all maltreatment-related deaths are reviewed in order to learn lessons about interagency working and about factors and circumstances leading to such deaths. The processes of reviewing these deaths are covered in Chapters 11 and 12. It is my view that these Serious Case Reviews should cover all deaths in which maltreatment plays a role, and not just those where abuse or neglect has clearly been shown to be the cause of death, or those where the families were previously known to safeguarding agencies. Ultimately all maltreatment-related deaths are potentially avoidable deaths and it is our responsibility as professionals to investigate these deaths thoroughly, to pursue appropriate lines of criminal investigation, to support the families themselves and to take steps to prevent such deaths in the future.

II Responding When a Child Dies

7 Responding to Unexpected Child Deaths

PETER SIDEBOTHAM
PETER FLEMING

When a child dies unexpectedly, the question that is almost invariably upper-most in the minds of the parents is: 'Why did my child die?' As professionals, we may approach sudden unexpected deaths from different perspectives, or with different responsibilities (Box 7.1), but essentially the same question lies at the root of all of our endeavours: why did this child die?

Box 7.1 Differing needs and responsibilities in unexpected deaths

- Family – need for information, understanding and support
- Coroner – to establish the cause of death and particulars of the death (who, when, where and how)
- Paediatric/public health – to identify the cause of death and factors that may have contributed; particularly to identify issues that may have impli-cations for others, e.g. infectious diseases, genetic/metabolic diseases; to support the family and provide appropriate and accurate information; to understand this and other deaths with a view to preventing future deaths
- Police/forensic – information gathering to establish the cause of death, in particular the early recognition of potentially suspicious deaths; pres-ervation of evidence in appropriate cases; carrying out a thorough and timely investigation with the minimum intrusion; upholding justice and protecting others
- Pathologist – identifying disease processes and cause of death; interpret-ing findings
- Primary care – ongoing support for the family; bereavement care
- Social Services – need to safeguard the welfare of children, including other children in the family; providing support to the family; assessing needs; investigating cases of possible child abuse or neglect
- Religious leaders – to support and comfort the family.

Unexpected Death in Childhood: A Handbook for Practitioners. Edited by P. Sidebotham and P. Fleming.
Copyright © 2007 by John Wiley & Sons, Ltd.

Rather than being seen as conflicting needs or responsibilities, these factors are in fact complementary. Thus it is possible and indeed essential for different professionals to work together with the family to seek to understand why their child has died and to support them in their grief. Two important principles underlie our approach to an unexpected death in childhood: a thorough, systematic investigation of the circumstances of death, based on the best-available evidence, and a sensitive, caring approach to supporting the family. In responding to an unexpected death we recognise the rights of the individual child, even in death; we respect the needs and views of the parents and wider family; we value diversity; and we respect and value the contribution of all professional and lay persons.

In this chapter, we describe a framework for responding to an unexpected death (Fleming et al. 2004). This approach has been developed and used over a number of years in Avon and Somerset and elsewhere in the UK, and forms the basis of the Kennedy Report (Royal College of Pathologists and Royal College of Paediatrics and Child Health 2004) and of government guidance (HM Government 2006b). Joint-agency protocols using this approach have tended to focus on responding to sudden unexpected death in infancy, although the same principles can be applied to unexpected deaths at any age. In this chapter we outline the different stages of this approach, discuss the rationale behind it, describe how to develop local protocols based on this approach, and explore how the principles can be extended to unexpected deaths in older children.

THE JOINT-AGENCY APPROACH

The approach to investigating and managing an unexpected childhood death can be divided into three stages: immediate, early and late responses (Figure 7.1), leading to three basic outcomes: establishing the cause or causes of death, identifying any contributory factors, and supporting the family. There are four essential components to this process:

1. a careful history – taken by a skilled and experienced professional
2. a detailed and careful scene investigation – in the light of knowledge of social and cultural norms for that community
3. a post-mortem examination – carried out according to an evidence-based protocol
4. a multiprofessional case discussion meeting.

It is important to remember that at all stages, this involves professionals from a range of agencies and that no one individual can possibly meet all the needs and responsibilities involved in responding to an unexpected death.

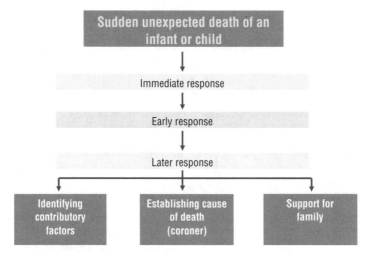

Figure 7.1 The joint agency approach to unexpected childhood deaths
Source: Reproduced by permission of University of Warwick.

IMMEDIATE RESPONSES

The responses of professionals within the first hours of an unexpected death can play a crucial role in ensuring that the death is properly investigated and the family adequately supported. Inappropriate responses can seriously jeopardise any investigation and could result in the family being further traumatised. Conversely, a thorough, sensitive approach in the first hours can set the scene for engaging with and supporting the family and ultimately for clarifying the cause of death. The aims of these immediate responses are:

- to provide care and support to the bereaved family
- to collect full and accurate information on what has happened
- to ensure that all investigations that may help to understand/explain the death are carried out to a high standard
- to ensure that all agencies work together effectively
- to meet all statutory requirements.

Typically, in a sudden unexpected death in infancy, the baby will be discovered by a parent or carer where they have been put down. In most cases, the person finding the infant will pick him up to establish any responsiveness and may attempt resuscitation prior to contacting the emergency services. Occasionally, a general practitioner will be the first on the scene, in which case the GP should notify the emergency services and follow the same processes outlined below. When the call comes through to the emergency services, the respondent needs to gain basic information rapidly and despatch an ambulance to the scene. In most cases the police will be notified as well and may

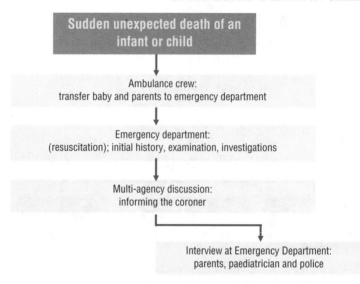

Figure 7.2 Immediate responses to an unexpected death
Source: Reproduced by permission of University of Warwick.

attend the scene alongside the ambulance crew. The police have a particular role in relation to security of the scene, specifically to ensure the safety of the public and to preserve evidence. These roles are covered in more detail in Chapter 8. Local procedures will vary in relation to how the police are notified; however, there are distinct advantages to all unexpected childhood deaths being dealt with by the police child protection team (see Chapter 8). These officers are normally trained detectives who are experienced both in working with other professionals to investigate potential crimes and in working with families in difficult circumstances. They are highly skilled in approaching difficult issues in a sensitive manner and in balancing the often competing demands of criminal investigation and family support. It is particularly important that any police response to an unexpected child death is carried out by non-uniformed officers in unmarked cars, and a detective of at least inspector rank should lead the investigation from the police perspective. Where there are clear suspicions early on or at any stage in the process, the police will need to take a more direct and active role, and many of the normal processes described in this chapter will need to be amended.

The emergency providers attending the scene should assess the child and, unless it is clearly inappropriate (e.g. where a baby is obviously dead with signs of rigor mortis or livido set in) should attempt resuscitation and transfer the child to hospital. We recommend that, unless there are pressing reasons to do otherwise, the child, even if dead, and parents/carers are transferred to the nearest Emergency Department with paediatric facilities. This helps to ensure a number of vital components of the response:

1. Resuscitation can be continued appropriately according to relevant guidelines (Royal College of Paediatrics and Child Health 2004, Mackway-Jones et al. 2005) and any decision to stop resuscitation can be made by an experienced practitioner in conjunction with the emergency care team and the parents.
2. The death of the child can be confirmed. This can only be done by a qualified medical practitioner and should follow national guidelines (Royal College of Anaesthetists 2006).
3. Appropriate help and support can be offered to the family – Emergency Departments can be equipped with a SUDC kit with appropriate information and contact details, and a designated member of staff can remain with the family to support them and help them through the processes involved.
4. The process of investigating the death can be initiated in a co-ordinated manner, including multi-agency liaison, the taking of a history, examining the child, and taking appropriate investigations.
5. The scene where the child died can be secured so that a thorough evaluation can take place at the subsequent home visit. Taking the parents to the hospital will normally ensure preservation of the scene, however if one or more family member is left at the home, it is important to stress to them that the scene must be left as it is until the team has had an opportunity to return. There may be situations where more specific steps need to be taken to secure the scene, but in our experience, this can usually be done in an unobtrusive and sensitive manner.

HOSPITAL PROCEDURES

On arrival in hospital, the most senior member of the Emergency Department team should take responsibility for leading the resuscitation and all aspects of the management. A member of the nursing staff should be allocated to support the family. This person will stay with the family throughout any resuscitation and subsequent management, to support the family, answer questions and help them through the process. Ideally, the same nurse will stay with the family for the whole of the time they are in the department, however this may not always be possible because of changing shifts or other demands. If any change is required, there should be a thorough handover from one nurse to another and the new support nurse should be introduced personally to the family. The support nurse should ensure that basic identifying information is recorded, including the child's name and date of birth, the address and details of all other family members, and who has parental responsibility for the child.

Any resuscitation should proceed according to agreed procedures, where appropriate allowing the parents to be present if they so wish. If the family are present for the resuscitation, the support nurse should remain with them to explain what is going on and to answer any questions. The decision to stop resuscitation should be made by the most experienced practitioner present, in consultation with the family and with other members of the team. It is important to emphasise that this decision is never taken lightly, but neither should resuscitation be prolonged once it is clear that the child is not responding and any reversible causes have been excluded.

Once resuscitation has stopped, a qualified medical practitioner should confirm that the child is dead. This requires the practitioner to confirm that there is no neurological response to any stimuli, no respiratory effort and no cardiac activity (assessed by auscultation or by cardiac monitoring) over a period of at least five minutes. During these five minutes, a thorough examination of the child can be carried out, as can the basic investigations listed below.

HISTORY

An initial brief history should be obtained on arrival from the mother or whoever accompanies the child. This initial history should concentrate on establishing the immediate events leading to the death or collapse; how the child was discovered; any pre-existing medical conditions and any medication the child might have been taking; and any possibility of injury, poisoning or drugs.

Further information should be sought, before they leave the department, from the ambulance crew/paramedics, and a copy of their call-out sheet should be retained in the notes. This should include:

- time of call out, arrival and departure from the scene, and time of arrival at A&E
- any history obtained, including what action was taken when the child was found
- their observations of the child, including any signs of life, the appearance of the child, any rigor mortis or dependent livido (including its distribution), any injuries observed
- if any resuscitation was started, and any other treatment given
- their description of the scene, how and where the child was found and any notable features
- the demeanour, presentation and behaviour of carers.

Following cessation of resuscitation, a full history should be obtained from the accompanying parents or carers. Ideally, this should be carried out by a senior paediatrician, together with a police officer. This full history is combined with other aspects of parental support and should not be rushed. The parents may want some time to be alone with their child before undergoing an in-depth interview, or may wish to have another family member or friend present with them for support. These wishes should normally be met unless there are pressing reasons to expedite the process. It is our practice to allow the parents to hold their child whilst we carry out the interview, although this should be offered as a choice and not imposed. It is essential that the interview is carried out in a quiet room where any interruptions can be avoided. Those carrying out the interview should switch off any pagers or mobile phones, or pass them to another member of the team to hold. A member of the nursing staff or a bereavement worker should also be present to support the parents. Consideration should be given to including a junior member of the team (specialist registrar, trainee nurse or police constable) in the interview for training purposes, but this should be done sensitively and the number of professionals present should be kept to a minimum. It is not helpful to the parents for lots of new faces to be involved at each stage of the process, so whilst changes are necessary at times, these should be kept to a minimum and any new professionals meeting the parents should be introduced by someone who has already met the family.

There are a number of key elements to a full history following an unexpected childhood death:

1. A detailed narrative account of events leading up to the death. This will include a detailed sequential account of events in the past 24–48 hours and past few weeks, including any changes from usual practice. For a sudden unexpected death in infancy, the parents should describe the events leading up to the baby being put down for the last sleep, including details of their last feeds (how much they were offered, of what and by whom, and how much they took); when they were last changed; how and when the baby was put to sleep; the position in which they were laid down (supine, prone, side; position in the bed); in what sleeping environment (cot, Moses basket, adult bed, sofa and so on); where other family members were sleeping and when they went to sleep; whether the baby was observed, fed or changed during the night; when and how they were found, including details of their position and whether that had changed from when they were put down; who found them; what they noticed about the child's appearance; and what resuscitation, if any, was attempted.

   We usually find that, given the opportunity, parents are generally very keen to describe all these events in detail and often need very little prompting. However, it is important to ensure that all aspects of this narrative account are covered and it may be necessary to go over the events more than once in order to clarify details. For those who are unfamiliar with the process, a checklist can be a useful aide-memoire (see Appendix 2), but should never form the sole basis of the history, as working through a checklist can never capture the full, rich narrative that comes from allowing the parent to describe things in their own way.

   For deaths in older children, the details required in this review of the circumstances leading to death will vary according to the nature of the death and the age of the child. However, as with infant deaths, it is important not only to explore the events immediately around the death, but to consider events in the hours, days and even weeks prior to the death as this may give further clues as to why this child died in this manner at this time.

2. The child's medical history – including details of the pregnancy and birth; the neonatal period, including any neonatal resuscitation or special care; feeding and weaning along with any feeding difficulties; the child's growth, development and behaviour (often we find that this gives a very helpful opportunity for the parents to remember all the positives about their child: they may want to show photographs, or describe with pride their baby's first smile, or how they would sing along to nursery rhymes). Details of any illnesses should be noted, complete with dates, how the child presented and any assessment or treatment they received. Any contact with the GP, health visitor or other health professionals should be detailed. The dates of any immunisations should be recorded and any adverse effects specifically asked for. Any medication the child was taking or had previously taken should be documented and at the same time a note should be made of any medication others in the house might be on.

3. A detailed family and household history. It is important to establish who the family members are, who is normally resident in the household and who was resident in the household at the time of the child's death, bearing in mind that these may not be the same. The family history should include any medical and mental-health history of the parents, any recent or concurrent illnesses in other family members and any recent travel abroad. The parents should specifically be asked about any previous childhood deaths, stillbirths or miscarriages, any congenital anomalies in siblings or other family members, and any other children who might have suffered apparent life-threatening events or other acute episodes of collapse.

4. The social history, including the parents' and other household members' use of alcohol, cigarettes and other substances, both routinely and in the time immediately prior to the child's death. We find that asking low-key questions such as: 'does anyone in the household smoke?' and similar questions in relation to alcohol and other substances allows parents to discuss this without feeling they are immediately being blamed. The parents should be asked to describe their home and environment and be given the opportunity to express any concerns they may have. Details of any employment should be obtained and the family should be offered support in informing their employers, and ensuring they are given compassionate leave. Any contact with Social Services or other agencies, including any previous child protection concerns, should specifically be asked about. This will be checked as part of the routine information-sharing procedures, but it is helpful for the parents to be able to discuss this themselves, rather than to feel things are being done behind their backs. For older children, details of any nursery, playgroup or school attendance should be sought, along with any out-of-school activities.

As any medical student will tell you, taking a thorough history is the most important part of any diagnostic process and the same holds true for the history following an unexpected death. It is important that the parents aren't subjected to repeated questioning by different professionals covering the same material; however, there is nothing wrong with taking the history in stages over time, and indeed this may well be necessary in order to get a full account. Similarly, whilst the initial account should ideally be a narrative led by the parents, it is usually necessary to probe in detail into different parts of the history in order to clarify points and seek further information. Providing this is done in a non-directive way, using open questioning whenever possible, it will not jeopardise any police investigation if concerns are later identified.

During the course of the interview, the parents' manner and presentation should be noted. It is important to note any conflicting accounts, inconsistencies or changing histories as these may give rise to concerns regarding the veracity of the account. However, it is important to remember that the unexpected death of a child is an extremely stressful event, and in their panic, parents may not remember clearly what happened or be able to explain why they took certain actions. The history they give may well change with time as they are able to reflect back on the sequence of events and make more sense of it, or may change depending on what questions they are asked and by whom – for example, asking about cigarettes or drugs in an aggressive, accusatory way at the start of an interview may lead the parents to deny or minimise their use, whilst the same questions asked sensitively and in a non-judgemental manner once the family have got used to the team, may yield a more accurate picture.

EXAMINATION

As with the history, the examination of the child should begin during the resuscitation, and will be supplemented by a more thorough examination once the child has been confirmed as dead. A note should be made of the following features:

- overall appearance: note any lividity, pallor, facial expression – mouth open/closed, eyes open/closed – position of arms, hands and legs
- any blood/frothy fluid around face, nose or mouth
- stiffness of limbs, face or hands
- any injuries apparent: recent or old
- any rashes, abrasions or skin lesions
- core body temperature (using a low reading thermometer).

Following the resuscitation attempt, a senior practitioner should examine the body thoroughly and document all findings clearly. The overall appearance of the child should be noted, including any dysmorphic or unusual features. The child should be weighed and measured, including the head circumference, and a note made of the overall state of hygiene and nutrition, including any signs of muscle wasting. A note should also be made of the child's clothing and any wrappings. These should normally be retained with the child in case they are needed for forensic investigations. The child should be fully undressed and the entire body, including head and neck, trunk, genitalia and limbs (including the soles of the feet) should be examined for any rashes, skin markings or injuries. This examination should be done sensitively with respect for the child and for any family members. It may be appropriate to undress and examine one part of the body at a time; however, it is essential to ensure that no part of the examination is overlooked. The parents may wish to be present during this examination, although usually we find it is appropriate to suggest that the parents wait in another room whilst we examine their child and carry out a few important investigations. The mouth should be examined with a torch and spatula, noting whether there are any torn fraenae or other intraoral injuries, and the state of the teeth. The abdomen should be palpated for any masses or organomegaly. Palpation may prove difficult if muscle rigidity has set in or if the abdomen is distended. Fundoscopy should be attempted, looking particularly for any retinal haemorrhage, although if the child has been dead for some time, the corneas become clouded and it may no longer be possible to view the retina. Any external findings should be recorded on a body chart and with clear descriptions.

The distribution of any dependent livido should be noted. This is usually deep purple in colour, although the depth and degree may vary and may be influenced by underlying skin colour. Livido develops due to gravity-assisted pooling of the blood so will take on a distribution corresponding to dependent parts of the child's body. Typically it begins to develop during the first two hours of the child's death, but does not become fixed for 4–6 hours. In young infants, livido develops quickly – it starts to appear within 30 minutes of death and may be quite marked on initial arrival in the Emergency Department. Although livido develops quickly, it also fades very quickly if the position is changed – so, for example, a child who died in the prone (face-down) position will have livido on the face and front of the body initially, commonly accompanied by areas of pallor over pressure points (e.g. the tip of the nose or one cheek). During resuscitation the child will always be placed on his or her back, so the appearance at the end of the resuscitation may be quite different from that at the beginning. Thus it is very important to note the appearance and site of any livido seen on arrival in the Emergency Department, as well as whether this changes during the course of resuscitation. The pathologist will commonly see livido related only to the child having been placed on his or her back in the mortuary, as the effects from the initial position may have faded. Livido that is still present on the front of the body when the pathologist sees the child (commonly two to three days after death) suggests that the child was lying on his or her front for at least four hours after death before any resuscitation attempt or the child was moved to the mortuary.

Rigor mortis, a generalised stiffness of the muscles, again develops during the first two hours.

Any medical interventions, including all attempts at venous, arterial or intraosseous cannulation, should be documented and recorded on the body chart. Any such lines can be removed, as can any orogastric or nasogastric tubes. Puncture marks from cannulation may continue to bleed or ooze serous fluid after removal and it may be appropriate to cover with a small plaster. If the child has been intubated, the position of the endotracheal tube should be confirmed and documented by a medical practitioner other than the one who intubated, using direct laryngoscopy. The tube can then be removed. It is important that this is done at an early stage, rather than leaving the tube *in situ* for the autopsy, as it can easily become dislodged during handling and transport. Although some coroners are known to require that endotracheal tubes are left *in situ*, this is distressing for families and provides no evidence of the site into which the tube was originally inserted, as tubes commonly become dislodged during movement of the child after death. Such insistence by a coroner should therefore be challenged by medical staff.

INVESTIGATIONS

During the course of resuscitation, investigations including blood sugar and blood gases may have been made. Any extra blood obtained should be used for blood cultures, full blood count and electrolytes, and any residual separated and frozen for possible future use (e.g. for metabolic investigations or for toxicology). After death has been confirmed, the body comes under the jurisdiction of the coroner and any further investigations can only be done with his or her consent. It helps to agree with the coroner in advance a standard set of investigations that can be done on all sudden unexpected deaths in infancy, so that time is not wasted trying to seek consent for individual cases. Most post-mortem investigations can be done at autopsy, however we recommend a minimum set to be taken in the Emergency Department as delays in obtaining these specimens may affect the value. A single femoral puncture should be used to obtain blood for blood cultures (both aerobic and anaerobic, with the priority on aerobic if insufficient blood is obtained), with any extra being sent for a full blood count, electrolytes, metabolic studies, cytogenetics and toxicology. Cardiac puncture should not be used as this will damage the heart tissue and may make interpretation of the autopsy findings difficult. A lumbar puncture should be undertaken and cerebrospinal fluid sent for microscopy and culture. It is often necessary to aspirate the cerebrospinal fluid as it will not always flow freely post-mortem. Since the bladder is usually empty following an unexpected infant death, we do not recommend catheterisation or suprapubic aspiration; any urine should be collected at autopsy instead. If there is urine in the nappy, a piece of filter paper can be inserted and the nappy squeezed around it to obtain a sample that can be sent for metabolic studies and toxicology. A nasopharyngeal aspirate should be obtained along with swabs from the throat and from any identifiable lesion. Finally, a skin biopsy for fibroblast culture should be taken from the skin of the upper, inner arm where it will not affect the appearance of the child. This can easily be obtained by lifting a small fold of skin with forceps and slicing cleanly using a scalpel. The biopsy should be sent to the laboratory in a suitable transport medium. The wound can be fixed with a Steristrip or covered by a small plaster. Liver biopsies are best left until the autopsy unless there is likely to be a delay of more than a couple of days, in which case support from a surgeon should be sought. A full list of recommended investigations is provided in the Table 7.1.

PARENTAL CARE AND SUPPORT

Parental and family care and support is an ongoing process from the moment services are notified of a child's death. It is not something that can be done and ticked off, but should remain a core aspect of all responses by the professionals to unexpected deaths. Parents and other family members respond individually to the death of a child and there are no set patterns that should be considered normal or abnormal. A more in-depth review of different approaches to supporting families is provided in Chapter 10, but some key principles are outlined here.

Once resuscitation has stopped and the child's death has been confirmed, the parents need time to come to terms with this. Normally, we would allow the parents and other family members to be alone with their child or on their own in a quiet, private room with comfortable furniture. It is good practice for the supporting nurse or another member of staff to be present at all times to offer support and help. Depending on the circumstances of the death, this may be required by the police or coroner, though it can usually be done discreetly and sensitively. A clear explanation of what has happened should be offered to the family, explaining what has been done with respect to attempted resuscitation and the decision to stop. It is important to address the parents by name (ask first how they would like to be addressed as some prefer first names, while others would find this intrusive), and always refer to the child by name. It is usually helpful to allow the parents to hold their child whilst you are talking with them, although again not all parents will want this. With older children, providing a room with a bed where the child can be laid can help. Whilst it is sometimes argued that parents should not be allowed to touch or hold the child in case they contaminate forensic evidence, there is no rational basis for this, as the parents will have held and moved the child prior to coming to hospital.

The family may be offered the opportunity to wash and dress their child. As with allowing the parents to hold their child, this should not interfere with any forensic investigations. However, a full examination of the child, with

Table 7.1 Laboratory investigations

Sample	Send to	Handling	Test
Blood cultures – aerobic and anaerobic 1 ml	Microbiology	If insufficient blood, aerobic only. May be obtained from femoral puncture. **Do not attempt cardiac puncture**	Culture and sensitivity
Blood	Haematology	Normal	Full blood count. Consider carboxyhaemoglobin.
Blood	Clinical chemistry	Normal	Electrolytes
Blood (serum) 1–2 ml	Clinical chemistry	Spin, store serum at −20°C	Toxicology
Blood from Guthrie card (if available)	Clinical chemistry	Normal (fill in card; do not put into plastic bag)	Inherited metabolic diseases, carnitine
Blood (lithium heparin) 1–2 ml	Cytogenetics	Normal – keep unseparated	Chromosomes (if dysmorphic)
Cerebrospinal fluid (CSF) (a few drops)	Microbiology	Normal	Microscopy, culture and sensitivity
Nasopharyngeal aspirate	Virology	Normal	Viral cultures, immunofluorescence and DNA amplification techniques*
Nasopharyngeal aspirate	Microbiology	Normal	Culture and sensitivity
Swabs from any identifiable lesions	Microbiology	Normal	Culture and sensitivity
Urine (if available)	Clinical chemistry	Obtain on filter paper by squeezing nappy. Spin, store supernatant at −20°C	Toxicology, inherited diseases
Urine (if available)	Microbiology	Normal	Microscopy, culture and sensitivity
Throat swab	Microbiology	Normal	Microscopy, culture and sensitivity
Skin biopsy	Will need co-ordination with on-call pathology team	Unless autopsy will be done within 24 hours	Fibroblast culture
Liver biopsy	Will need co-ordination with on-call pathology team to process and freeze specimen	Usually done at autopsy, unless there is likely to be a significant delay	

*Samples must be sent to an appropriate virological laboratory.
Source: Reproduced by permission of The Royal College of Pathologists and The Royal College of Paediatrics and Child Health.

careful documentation of the findings, should be carried out before the child is cleaned or dressed and if any concerns are identified, washing the child may not be appropriate. This may be particularly important if there are signs of neglect with poor hygiene or inappropriate clothing and in those circumstances photographs should be taken to back up the documentation. Families from different religious groups may have particular practices they wish to follow in cleaning their child or preparing the body. This should be facilitated where possible. The taking of mementoes (hand and foot prints, a lock of hair and photographs of the child) should be offered to all parents, though not all will want these. Practical details around offering parents time with their child and the taking of mementoes and photographs are given in Appendix 10.

It is our usual practice to dress and wrap the child in the clothing and blankets they arrived in for transfer to the mortuary, unless these items are damaged or soiled, in which case alternative suitable clothes and wrappings should be provided. In this way, the clothing is available for forensic examination if required, whilst the child is treated with respect as a child rather than simply a body. However, it is important to check with the family what they would like done with these items after the autopsy – they may wish them to be returned or for the child to be buried in them. Ensure that the parents' wishes are conveyed to the pathologist and that someone takes responsibility for ensuring that they are followed through.

One of the major needs of parents at this stage is for information. An experienced paediatrician should be prepared to spend some time with the family, discussing what has happened, informing them of the processes that need to be followed, acknowledging their grief and answering any questions they may have. At this stage, it will not be possible to give the parents a cause of death and it is important not to hazard a guess at the cause or offer assurances that may not be correct. If there are clear pointers from the history or examination towards a specific cause of death, it is appropriate to tell parents that this seems the most likely explanation, although even in these circumstances, it must be emphasized that we need to carry out various procedures in order to investigate fully the death and try to determine the cause of death. For infants, we explain that this is what we refer to as a sudden unexpected death in infancy, and that for a large proportion we are able to identify a specific cause, but others turn out to be what is commonly called a cot death, or sudden infant death syndrome. We can then discuss what this means, whilst explaining that we will do everything we can to try and identify if there is a specific underlying cause.

It is important that families understand what will happen next and the process of the multi-agency investigation. We would normally go through this briefly at the beginning of the interview when we introduce the different members of the team, and then again before leaving the parents. We explain that because the death was unexpected it needs to be referred to the coroner and that there needs to be a police investigation. We then explain that we work very closely together as paediatricians and police officers, along with other health staff and Social Services, so that we can look into every aspect of the child's death and ensure that a thorough investigation is carried out to find the cause of death, and that by working together in this way, we try to keep to a minimum the number of different people the family need to talk to. Most families seem to understand and find this approach helpful, and feedback from bereaved families suggests that they don't find the joint presence of police and paediatricians in the emergency room or at the home visit intrusive, but rather that this can be very supportive and reassures them that their child's death is being evaluated thoroughly.

During the course of the interview we explain the different components of the investigation, including the examination of their child, the investigations that have been carried out in the Emergency Department, the home visit and the autopsy, ancillary investigations, and liaison among all professionals. We emphasise that a post-mortem examination will be required, that their child will be treated with care and respect throughout and that this will be carried out by a specially trained paediatric pathologist. Many families do not realise that a pathologist is a doctor, so this may also need to be explained. It is important to inform the parents where and when this is likely to take place, particularly if it is going to necessitate their child being transferred to another hospital. The parents should be informed what will happen to their child before and after the autopsy and what arrangements there are for them to visit and spend time with their child. A specific name or number for a bereavement support worker or clinical co-ordinator whom the parents can contact for information should be given. We normally explain briefly what the autopsy will involve, in particular explaining that tissue samples will be taken (and what these are), but that no whole organs will be taken without informing the family. Since the autopsy is required by the coroner in all unexpected deaths, it is not appropriate to seek parental consent, but the family should nevertheless be fully informed. We do not routinely go into any more detail about the process of the post mortem, but offer to do so if the parents want to know more details. It is important that parents recognise that results of the autopsy will not be available immediately afterwards, and that some investigations can take several weeks; however, we would always strive to let families know information at the earliest opportunity as it becomes available.

Before leaving the parents, arrangements are made for the home visit, clarifying who will be there and at what time. We provide the family with written names and contact details for the different team members and give them appropriate information packs.

DOCUMENTATION

In all cases of unexpected childhood death it is important to keep thorough, accurate contemporaneous notes. All members of the multidisciplinary team should keep their own records, although these may be shared amongst the team. All entries should be in black ink, should record the date and time and should be signed with clear identifying details provided. Where details of the history are recorded, a note should be made of who the history was obtained from, and where possible, verbatim accounts should be included. Following the initial management in the Emergency Department, a written or typed summary of the history, examination findings and any interventions should be provided for the coroner's officer and the pathologist who will carry out the autopsy. This is essential for the pathologist to be able to interpret the autopsy findings in the knowledge of the full context of the presentation. This may be supplemented with details of the home visit and scene examination. This summary would normally be produced by the paediatrician who took the history and examined the child. An example is provided in Box 7.2.

The senior investigating officer (SIO) or deputy will need to record further specific details, to enable them to identify key informants, and the sources of all information gleaned.

Box 7.2 Sample case report

Re: Annie Bowden   Date of birth: 20.1.07
                                                    Date of death: 11.2.07

Background and contact with the family

Annie was admitted to the emergency department on 11.2.07 following a cardiac arrest at home. I met Annie's family on 11.2.07 and explained the purpose and approach to investigating the death, including the nature of the post mortem and retention of small tissue samples. A joint home visit by the paediatrician, police sergeant and health visitor was carried out on 11.2.07.

Family history

Annie was the first child of Jenny and Peter, both of whom are reportedly healthy. There is no family history on the father's side of deaths in infancy or other serious illnesses. Jenny has five siblings, one of whom has a chromosome 22 abnormality with severe learning difficulties. There is a family history on the mother's side of four stillbirths and one infant death. Both parents smoke.

Birth history

Annie was born at 38 weeks' gestation following a spontaneous labour and rapid delivery. The pregnancy was uncomplicated and all routine checks were normal. Annie weighed 5 lb 12 oz at birth. I understand the cord was wrapped around her neck and she may have required some resuscitation. Annie was reported to be a generally quiet baby who rarely cried initially. Annie was bottle fed, took her feeds well and was reported to be developing appropriately. She had experienced some problems with constipation, but no other health problems. Her weight had increased to 5 lb 15 oz on 30.1.07 and to 6 lb 6 oz on 5.2.07. Annie's normal sleeping pattern was that during the day she would tend to be in a bouncer in whichever room the parents were in. At night times she would sleep in a Moses basket crib in her parents' room.

Events leading up to death

On the Friday night (9.2.07) Annie had been repeatedly sick. This subsequently settled. During the day on Saturday, Annie remained well. She did not have a temperature or any other signs of illness. She fed normally during the day. At 10pm she was given a bottle, which she took normally. About 1am, the parents put Annie down in her crib, but she did not settle and cried after five minutes. The parents tried feeding her but as she would not settle, put her in the bed between them. Annie was wearing a vest and a babygro, with thin socks and mittens. Annie was placed on her back on the bed between her parents, partly up on the pillows and with her bottom half covered with the duvet.

Jenny woke at about 6am on Sunday. She noticed straight away that Annie was dead. Annie was still in the same position between Jenny and Peter. She was floppy at that time and lifeless with no sign of breathing. There was no response to initial resuscitation by the parents under the direction of ambulance control. The ambulance call was received at 6.10am, and the crew arrived at 6.14am. Their observations on arrival record a clear airway with no signs of breathing or of circulation. She was pale and totally unresponsive. There was some blood recorded over her face. The ambulance crew continued resuscitation with oxygen via a bag and mask. They left the scene at 6.17am and arrived at hospital at 6.29am. At no stage was there any response to resuscitation and Annie was pronounced dead at 7.10am.

Death scene investigation

Annie's parents live in a small one-bedroomed ground-floor flat. There is a small living room with a sofa and chair, which is where Annie had been during the evening. The bedroom was approximately 3×3.5 metres with a small double bed and various wardrobes and cupboards in the room, with very little room to move around in. There were a large number of cuddly toys around the room. There was a single radiator in the bedroom beneath the window and no other heating. Peter reported that the radiator was on during the evening, but off from 10pm to 6am whilst Annie was in the room. Peter described where the cot had been beside his side of the bed. He described where both he and Jenny had been lying and where they placed Annie between them, partly up on the pillows and partly covered by the duvet. The duvet appeared quite a heavy duvet and Peter thought it was 13.5 tog. There was a patch of blood on the carpet where Peter had tried to resuscitate Annie. A video recording was made of the death scene.

Impressions

The clinical history and findings are suggestive of sudden infant death syndrome. There were no suspicious findings on examination or on the investigations carried out in hospital. There were no suspicious findings on death scene investigation.

MULTI-AGENCY DISCUSSION

The investigation and management of any unexpected childhood death requires a multi-agency approach as no one professional has the requisite skills, knowledge or information to cover all aspects of management. A crucial part of this is an early multi-agency discussion involving the investigating police officers, paediatric and other hospital staff, Social Services and primary care. Ideally, this will involve an actual meeting of the relevant professionals at the earliest opportunity after presentation, although there will be occasions where it is not possible to get all professionals together, and a series of discussions may take place either in person or by telephone. This initial multi-agency discussion serves to:

- Share initial information available, including details of the initial presentation, history and examination.
- Determine what further information is required and how this will be obtained, including arrangements to obtain and review further health, Social Services and police records.
- Plan the process of ongoing investigation into the death, including who should be interviewed and by whom; who will undertake the home visit and scene investigation and when; where and when and by whom the autopsy might be conducted.
- Consider whether there are any immediate suspicions or child-protection concerns and plan any further investigation or management based on that, including considering the need for a formal Section 47 child-protection investigation; it may also be necessary to formally secure the scene or to

follow more specific criminal investigations governed by the Police and Criminal Evidence Act (1984) guidelines.

- Consider any risks to the health or well-being of siblings or other family members: where the death involves a twin, or there are other infants in the household, it may be appropriate to admit them to hospital for a period of observation; if there are immediate suspicions, a formal strategy meeting should be convened to consider the risks to other children; parents with mental health or drug abuse problems may be at particular risk of self-harm or worsening of their condition and specific support should be considered.
- Consider the support needs of the family: what information needs to be provided; any practical support issues (including, for example, notifying employers, helping a breastfeeding mother stop the production of milk); what bereavement support can be offered, and whether there are any particular religious or cultural needs.
- Make plans for further information sharing and future multi-agency meetings, bearing in mind that inter-agency liaison is not a one-off event but an ongoing process.

Each professional should record all discussions with other professionals in their own notes. For each formal multi-agency discussion, one person should take the lead in documenting the outcomes of the discussion and a written summary of the action plan should be agreed at the time by all present, and should include any actions to be taken, who is responsible, and the time frame for those actions. We find it helpful for Social Services to take the lead in chairing these meetings and producing notes of these multi-agency discussions, as they are usually less directly involved at this early stage, and so are able to take an independent, objective view. If concerns do arise, the transition to a formal Section 47 strategy meeting is easy.

EARLY RESPONSES

Following on from the immediate management in hospital, the focus of the response to an unexpected death is on gathering information to try and ascertain the cause or causes of death, whilst providing ongoing support to the family. Three processes are prominent in the first 24–48 hours following a death: the scene visit and investigation of the circumstances of death; the autopsy; and multi-agency information sharing.

INVESTIGATION OF THE CIRCUMSTANCES OF DEATH

As soon as possible after the death, a home visit is arranged. We aim to carry this out within 12 hours of presentation. The home visit is greatly enhanced

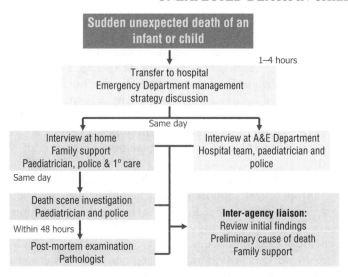

Figure 7.3 Early responses to an unexpected death
Source: Reproduced by permission of University of Warwick.

by the joint presence of a police officer and a paediatrician, as this is not so much a 'crime scene' investigation, as an holistic evaluation of the circumstances of death. There may be situations where, for pragmatic reasons, or because of the nature of the death, a joint visit is not possible or appropriate, or where the police need to visit the scene of death early to gather forensic evidence. However, even where that is the case, consideration should be given as to whether a subsequent joint visit may add further useful information or contribute to family support. It is helpful to have present a member of the primary care team who knows the family, to help with ongoing support for the family.

The home visit gives the opportunity to review the history taken in the Emergency Department. Often, in a more relaxed environment and having had some time to get over the initial shock, the parents will open up more and provide a lot more detail about the events leading up to the death. Whilst it is not necessary to go over the full history again, it is valuable to go through the circumstances leading up to the death in detail and to clarify other points from the history where there may have been gaps or uncertainties in the initial history. Again, it is important to let the parents go at their own pace in describing events and this process should not be rushed. Usually, this review of the history takes place in a living room, which may or may not be the room where the baby died. When the parents are ready, at least one of them should accompany the team into the room where the child died.

It is essential to take a structured approach to evaluating the scene. We start by observing the room itself: its size, orientation (noting, for example, where the sun might shine at different times), layout, heating and ventilation. A digital thermometer should be used to record the temperature in a drawer – this gives a reasonably robust measurement of the temperature over the preceding hours. The parents should be able to describe what heating was on and whether the windows and doors were open or closed. We assess the tidiness and cleanliness of the room, noting the proportion of available (i.e. excluding furnishings) floor space which is visible; whether there is a surface (e.g. bed or chair) on which to sit, or on which to place a baby for changing; whether there are pointers to negligent care such as overflowing bins, excrement on the floor, accumulated unwashed dishes or mouldy food left out. We also note evidence of cigarette use, alcohol or drug use in the room and elsewhere in the house.

Box 7.3 Questions to ask about the room

1. Is the room cramped?
   - Is there space for an adult to stand comfortably beside the cot/bed?
2. Is the room cluttered?
   - Is more than 50% of the floor space visible (excluding fixed furniture); is there at least one clear surface for placing things on?
3. Is there evidence of neglectful care?
   - Is there rubbish on the floor/surfaces; is there excrement on the floor; are there accumulated unwashed dishes or food?
4. Are there any hazards in the room?
   - Is there a smell of gas; is there damp or mould; are there any faulty appliances or fixings?

Attention is then turned to the sleeping environment. We start by observing the bed or cot, its location in the room and relation to other furnishings, including proximity to heaters. We check the safety and appropriateness of the sleep surface and environment – whether the cot is on a secure base; whether it has a firm, appropriately fitting mattress; any gaps around the bed or cot; the nature and cleanliness of the bedding; any other objects (including pillows and soft toys) in the bed or cot. Finally, we ask the parent(s) to describe in detail the sleeping arrangements – how, when and where they put their child down; what the child was wearing; what layers they had around and over them; the position they were in when put down; how, when and where any other family members went to sleep; any events overnight; then how, when and where they found their child – what position they were in, whether that had changed, whether anything was covering their face, their appearance when found. It can be helpful for parents to use a doll or other object to demonstrate where and how their child was lying and often parents will do so spontaneously. There are anatomically-weighted dolls that can be used for this purpose, but these can be cumbersome and unpleasant for some parents and we do not use them routinely.

Box 7.4 Questions to ask about the sleep environment

1. Is there any evidence of over-wrapping or over-heating?
   - How many layers was the baby wrapped in?
2. Is there any restriction or potential restriction to ventilation or breathing?
   - Is the sleeping space cluttered; is there space all round where the baby lies; is there adult-sized bedding, cushions or pillows?
3. Is there any risk of smothering?
4. Are there any potential hazards?
   - Is the cot, Moses basket or pram on a secure base; are there gaps between the mattress and other objects; if in a pushchair, is the baby strapped securely and safely; is there anything overhanging the sleeping space other than a fixed cot mobile; are there any other identifiable hazards in the room?
5. Is there any evidence of neglectful care?
   - Is the bedding unduly dirty or worn?

Both the paediatrician and the police officer attending the scene should make detailed notes from their review of the circumstances of the death, along with a sketch plan with measurements of the room. Photographs or video-

---

Box 7.5 Tips for successful video-recording of a sleep scene

- Start with identification and date/time.
- Keep on a wide angle and keep any movements slow and smooth.
- Take a sweep around the room at waist height and below, staying at the same level.
- Focus in on any items of note in the room, providing commentary as necessary.
- Take specific views of the sleep environment – orthogonal views from the side, end and above are helpful; plus the view underneath and above the sleep environment.
- Focus in on any items of note in the sleep environment.
- Ask a parent to describe the sleep environment and circumstances around putting the child to sleep, what happened overnight, and how they found the child.

recordings can be extremely useful in capturing information that is otherwise difficult to convey or record. Given the nature of these investigations, the best approach is for the police officer to take and retain any photographs or videos, but it is helpful for the whole team to review these subsequently.

BEREAVEMENT CARE

The joint home visit contributes to ongoing care of the parents and other family members. This includes both practical and emotional support. If a mother has been breastfeeding, she will need advice on how to stop. This can often be achieved by simple analgesics and breast support, although for some mothers, the use of bromocriptine or cabergoline may help. Parents may need help in informing employers or obtaining sick notes, in contacting funeral directors and registering their child's death. It is worth exploring how other members of the family are coping and offering help in breaking the news, particularly for children (see Chapter 10). The GP can be extremely helpful in providing support over the ensuing days and weeks, particularly helping with symptoms related to grieving such as headaches, sleep disturbance or loss of appetite.

One of the key needs of parents at this stage is for information. Often, after the initial shock, they will have many questions. Professionals attending the family need to be well-informed and also need to be prepared to be frank when they don't know the answers to some of the parents' questions. Parents will often ask about the different causes of sudden infant death, including sudden infant death syndrome. We find it helps to talk through some of these, although emphasise that at this stage we do not know why their child has died, and that we will need to bring together all the information from our investigation and the post-mortem examination before we can provide any specific answers. Parents also need information about the process, what is involved and what they need to do. This information often needs to be repeated, or supported in writing.

OBTAINING OTHER INFORMATION

The investigation of an unexpected childhood death can be likened to putting together a jigsaw, where different people hold different bits of information (Hobbs et al. 1999). In order to understand the full picture, all sources of information need to be pulled together. The parents provide the central part of this, with their knowledge of the child's history, their own background, and the circumstances around the death. The emergency medical and paramedical services will have information obtained immediately following presentation. The GP, midwife and Health Visitor will be able to provide further details of the past medical history, including routine checks and any consultations prior to the child's death. For a school-aged child, the teachers may be able to provide information on the child's progress in school, their well-being, demeanour and behaviour, along with any concerns raised. Social Services and the police should undertake background checks, including checking for any active or previous Social Services involvement, any criminal records for any family or household members on the police National Computer and any reports of domestic violence incidents. Social Services, the police and the paediatrician should work together in seeking out and compiling this information. Information sharing and inter-agency liaison is not a one-off event, but rather an ongoing process or approach that may require repeated telephone consultations or meetings to pull it all together.

AUTOPSY

The process and outcomes of the autopsy are described in detail in Chapter 9. In all unexpected childhood deaths there should be a full autopsy, directed by the coroner. This should be undertaken by a trained paediatric pathologist, supported where necessary by a forensic pathologist. As with other aspects of the investigation, the autopsy should be thorough and systematic, and not stop if a potential cause of death is found, as there may well be further information to add in terms of other contributory factors.

The pathologist should be briefed fully as to the initial history and circumstances of death, including any significant findings from the home visit. We find it helps to provide a written summary of these initial findings, and where possible, to talk directly with the pathologist prior to the autopsy. There should always be a discussion after the autopsy between the paediatrician and the pathologist, in order to interpret the findings and to agree where possible a cause of death, or to determine what further investigations need to be conducted. This information should be fed back directly to the coroner, and with the agreement of the coroner and the senior investigating police officer, to the family. We usually do this through a second home visit, as the information can be complex and difficult to convey over the phone.

SUBSEQUENT MANAGEMENT

Once the initial results of the autopsy are known, the management may proceed along one of three main routes:

1. The history, scene examination, autopsy and initial investigations point towards a specific natural cause of death, for example an overwhelming infection or a cardiac anomaly. The paediatrician becomes the lead professional, working closely with the primary healthcare team. The coroner may be able to issue a certificate of cause of death. Further involvement of the police, Social Services and the coroner may be minimal, although they may

contribute to ongoing support for the family, and will remain involved in the late stages. At this stage the body can usually be released for cremation or burial.

2. The findings suggest a possible death from maltreatment, such as a skull fracture or intracranial haemorrhage. In these circumstances, the police become the lead agency, under the direction of the coroner. Other professionals from all agencies will remain involved to assist the police in their investigations and to contribute to ongoing support for the family.

3. There is no clear cause of death. At this stage the death is classified as 'unexplained pending further investigation'. There will need to be an inquest, although usually the funeral can proceed. All agencies remain involved and in close communication.

SECTION 47/CRIMINAL INVESTIGATIONS

At any stage of the investigation, concerns may come to light as to possible child abuse or neglect. In such circumstances, the police need to take the lead in any further investigation, although they should be supported in this by the health team and by Social Services. Social Services should, at the point where concerns first come to light, convene a Section 47 strategy discussion (HM Government 2006b). As well as agreeing the ongoing approach to investigation, consideration should be given to other children in the family or household. There may need to be a separate investigation in relation to their welfare. The case should also be referred to the Local Safeguarding Children's Board for a Serious Case Review (Chapter 12).

LATE RESPONSES

The final stage of the inter-agency response centres around pulling together and collating all information from the investigation in order to facilitate the three outcomes of establishing the cause of death, identifying contributory factors and supporting the family. The focus of this is the multi-agency case discussion, which is usually held 2–3 months after the death. Although this may seem a long time, it is nevertheless important. Following the initial autopsy results, there may be further investigations that need to take place, including specific histological, metabolic, toxicology or genetic studies as indicated. In addition, there may be further police investigations in suspicious cases. These investigations may take several weeks or months to complete, and it is important that all members of the team and the family are kept informed of progress. There needs to be close liaison with the coroner and co-ordination with the inquest and with any criminal or child-protection investigation that may be ongoing. For the family this may be a very anxious and frustrating time during which it is easy to feel that they have been forgotten. It is helpful during this

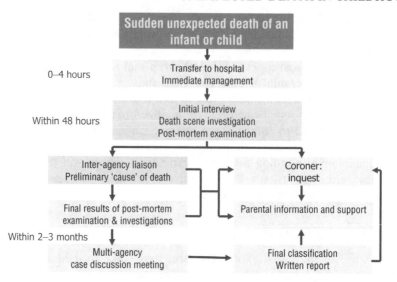

Figure 7.4 Late responses to an unexpected death
Source: Reproduced by permission of University of Warwick.

stage to have one professional who acts as the key link with the family and helps to co-ordinate information gathering and support. This may be the paediatrician, or may more appropriately be a member of the primary care team, the coroner's officer, a bereavement support worker or the police family liaison officer.

The case discussion is a multiprofessional meeting and serves a number of important functions (see Box 7.6). It is usually helpful to set the date for the case discussion soon after the death as people's diaries can get filled quickly, although there may need to be some flexibility over the date depending on the timing of the inquest or of any police or medical investigations. Our approach is to hold the discussion over a lunchtime at the GP's surgery as the involvement of the primary care team is essential. All other members of the multiprofessional team should be invited including the coroner's officer, the police team, any hospital staff involved, paramedics, the pathologist and the social worker, if involved. Consideration should be given as to how the family should be involved. We do not normally invite the family to attend the case discussion, so that the professionals can discuss the case and their involvement freely and frankly. However, there may be situations where it would be appropriate for the family to be present, or they may wish to discuss their views or any issues that have arisen with a member of the team beforehand, or may wish to meet with all or some of the team before or after the meeting. Normally we would contact the family before the meeting and arrange for one or more members of the team to visit shortly afterwards to feed back to the family the outcomes of the meeting.

Box 7.6 Functions of the multi-agency case discussion

1. It gives the opportunity to review all findings from the history, scene examination, autopsy and any investigations.
2. On the basis of a full review of all information, it establishes the cause or causes of death.
3. It identifies any contributory factors – these may be factors intrinsic to the infant or related to parental care or wider family and environmental factors (Figure 7.5).
4. It specifically addresses any evidence of child abuse, neglect or poor parental care.
5. It identifies the continuing needs of the family, including information and care of current or subsequent children.
6. It provides support for all professionals involved.

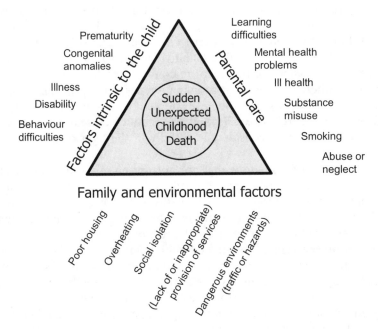

Figure 7.5 Identifying contributory factors (based on Framework of Assessment, HM Government 2000)

Source: Crown copyright material is reproduced with the permission of the Controller of HMSO and Queen's Printer for Scotland.

The case discussions should normally last no more than an hour. Each person should make their own notes of the discussion, but it is helpful if one person completes and circulates a summary. The chair (usually, but not necessarily the paediatrician) should explain the purpose of the meeting and each person should introduce themselves and describe their role in responding to the death or in support of the family. We then review the different aspects of the investigation, including the history, examination findings, scene visit and any police investigation and the post mortem with any ancillary investigations. The GP and Health Visitor can often contribute valuable information about the family and the infant prior to the death. The information is then used to consider any causal or contributory factors. We use the Avon Clinico-Pathological Classification for this (Figure 7.6, Appendix 13). This allows us to evaluate factors from each domain of the investigation: history, including the child's past medical history, any family history, the social circumstances and the circumstances leading to death; examination; scene examination; and the autopsy, including all aspects of the pathology and associated investigations.

Three levels are used for the classification of factors in each domain: level I, where there are no causal or contributory factors (this is subdivided into IA, where no factors are identified at all and IB, where factors are identified but not considered relevant to the death); level II, where possible contributory factors are identified (subdivided into IIA and IIB according to the likely significance of the factor in contributing to ill health or death); and level III, where that factor or combination of factors provides a complete and sufficient cause of death. Some examples of how different factors are classified are provided in Boxes 7.7 and 7.8, although these are not exhaustive and each factor must be considered carefully in the light of the full clinical picture.

Level IB is used for features that are not normal, or which may possibly contribute in some way to an increased vulnerability of the baby or family, but are not linked in any obvious way to the pathway by which an infant may have become ill or died – e.g. minor malformations, preterm birth, being a twin or triplet; a maternal history of postnatal depression; overcrowded accommodation; or the presence of a presumed contaminant in a blood-culture bottle. Factors in this category are either those that may be markers of some form of potential compromise of some aspect of the infant's growth or development before or after birth, or are factors that have been shown to be significantly associated with an increased risk of SUDI, though are not sufficiently strongly associated to suggest direct causality.

In general, the presence of more than one factor that is usually graded as IB will still lead to an overall classification for the case as IB. However, where several related factors are present and might have an additive effect – e.g. a preterm infant with history of previous apparent life-threatening event (ALTE)

Classification	0	Ia	Ib	IIa	IIb	III
Contributory or potentially 'causal' factors	Information not collected	No factors identified	Factors not likely to have contributed to ill health or to death	May have contributed to ill health, or possibly to death	Certainly contributed to ill health; probably contributed to the death	Provides a complete and sufficient cause of death
History						
Examination						
Scene examination						
Pathology						
Abuse/neglect						
Overall classification						

Figure 7.6 Avon Clinico-Pathological Classification
Source: Reproduced by permission of The Royal College of Pathologists and The Royal College of Paediatrics and Child Health.

bed sharing with a non-smoking adult – this may lead to a grading of IIA. Any such combination of potentially additive factors must be reviewed carefully at the local case discussion in the light of all available information, and the grading changed to IIA only if the consensus view is that the combination of factors was sufficient to contribute significantly to the likelihood of the baby being ill or dying.

Level II is used for features that possibly (IIA) or probably (IIB) contributed to significant illness or death in the infant but which are not, in their own right, identifiable as a sufficient or complete cause of the infant's death – e.g. evidence (pathological +/– clinical) of significant illness at the time of death; significant alcohol consumption by a bed-sharing adult; or an otherwise dangerous sleep environment. Factors in this category are those that have been shown consistently to be associated with an increased risk of SUDI, and for which a possible contribution to the causal pathway may be implicated, though the association is not strong enough to suggest direct causality or that the factor in itself is a complete and sufficient cause. These factors will lead to a classification of IIA or IIB depending on the perceived significance of the factor in an individual case.

Level III is used for features which, on their own, constitute a complete and sufficient 'cause' of death, or which are likely (on balance of probability) on their own to have led directly to death in a large proportion of infants with this factor – e.g. overwhelming infection; major cardiac abnormality or major head injury (with brain injury). Normally these are factors identified at post mortem or through associated investigations.

In order to understand fully why this child has died at this time, it is very important to review all aspects of the investigation. Even where a sufficient cause of death is identified at autopsy, there may still be other contributory factors that help explain why this child has died where others with a similar condition have survived. For example, a child with evidence of an overwhelming pulmonary infection has an identified cause of death, with evidence from the autopsy and from microbiological investigations. If that child was also undernourished, or had been born prematurely, that may have led to increased vulnerability to the infection; there may also have been factors in the parents or family environment, such as drug misuse or a chaotic lifestyle, which meant that the seriousness of the child's illness was not picked up on or responded to early enough.

Following the case discussion it is important to feed back to the parents the outcomes. We usually arrange a further home visit at this stage and provide the parents with a letter summarising the key findings from the investigation and our conclusions on the cause of death and any contributory factors. This needs to be done in a non-judgemental but nevertheless honest and frank manner. For example, where the parents are smokers it is important to point out that, while this was not the cause of their child's death, it does increase vulnerability and it is something that they could do something about for future pregnancies to reduce the risks for subsequent children. This home visit would normally involve the paediatrician and a member of the primary care team. As well as being able to discuss the results of the case discussion, this gives an opportunity to respond to any ongoing questions the parents may have, and to review how they are coping and any practical or emotional needs that may have arisen. We specifically discuss the possibility of future children, although we emphasise that all parents differ in whether and how soon they may want to consider this. Often the parents will ask what they can do to reduce any risks for future children and this should be discussed clearly and confidently, drawing on the advice outlined in Chapter 4. We advise increased surveillance during pregnancy, then Health Visitor and paediatric support and monitoring throughout the first year. Where a CONI (Care Of the Next Infant) scheme is operating, a CONI Health Visitor may give further support alongside the family Health Visitor.

Box 7.7 Avon Clinico-Pathological Classification: factors from the history

Factors normally classified as IB (notable factors, unlikely to have contributed to ill health or death):

- past maternal depression (brought to medical attention)
- past depression (brought to medical attention) in another primary carer
- minor malformations or deformations – e.g. talipes, dislocated hips, antenatal renal pelvicalyceal dilatation
- multiple birth (twin, triplet or higher order)
- preterm birth (<37 weeks) or low-birthweight infant (<2,500 g)
- intrapartum asphyxia needing resuscitation but with apparent full recovery
- significant perinatal illness leading to admission to NICU/SCBU
- respiratory tract infection, with symptoms in past week but appeared fully recovered before the time of the last sleep
- past urinary tract infection or other fully treated infection
- previous perinatal or child death to either of these parents (but see below)
- previous SUDI or apparent life-threatening event (ALTE) in cousin, aunt, uncle
- known genetic or familial illness in parent, sibling or other close relative (but not recognised in this baby)
- major change in family routine affecting baby in recent past (e.g. travel, family separation, illness in other member of family)
- any previously raised concerns about child protection issues with any child in the care of either of these parents, or other primary carer of this baby.

Factors normally classified as IIA (may have contributed to ill health or death), or possibly IIB if severe (certainly contributed to ill health and probably contributed to death):

- symptomatic depression in mother or other primary carer at the time of the last sleep
- respiratory infection (the presence of two or more of: cough, fever, wheeze, grunting respirations, runny nose, off feeds, sneezing, recession, tachypnoea) still present at the time of the last sleep
- other evidence of significant illness with symptoms and/or signs present at the time of the last sleep
- evidence of significant neurodevelopmental compromise or neurological abnormality recognised prior to the last sleep
- history of fits or other apparent life-threatening events in this baby
- previous SUDI in sibling
- apparent life-threatening events in siblings or parents
- known potentially significant genetic or familial illness in this baby (not necessarily symptomatic before last sleep)
- this child previously the subject of child-protection procedures or subject of significant cause for concern re child-protection issues.

Box 7.8 Avon Clinico-Pathological Classification: factors from the household or sleep environment

Factors normally classified as IB (notable factors, unlikely to have contributed to ill health or death):

- parental alcohol consumption on the last night: ≤2 units by mother, or ≤3 units by partner (if not bed sharing with baby)
- any smoking (tobacco or cannabis) by parent or primary carer, inside or outside of the home
- smoking by other persons in the baby's sleep environment
- maternal age less than 18 at time of baby's birth
- baby bed sharing (in an adult bed) with adult or sibling (not in combination with alcohol use, smoking or drugs)
- overcrowded sleeping environment (overall more than one person per room in home, excluding kitchen and bathroom)
- inappropriate sleeping environment (single factor – see below)
- damp/mould in baby's sleep environment
- put down to sleep on side or front in otherwise safe sleep environment.

Factors normally classified as IIA (may have contributed to ill health or death), or possibly IIB if severe (certainly contributed to ill health and probably contributed to death):

- very heavy smoking in the infant's sleep environment, smoking drugs of abuse (other than cannabis) in the sleep environment
- parental alcohol consumption: >2 units by mother, or >3 units by partner (if bed sharing with the baby)
- excessive parental alcohol consumption (i.e. sufficient to have probably or certainly affected parent's ability to care for the child safely) whether bed sharing or not
- bed sharing with an adult or older child on a sofa, waterbed or other inappropriate or potentially dangerous surface
- bed sharing with an adult who smokes or has been taking other drugs of abuse, or substances that are likely to affect conscious level
- baby sleeping in an inappropriate or potentially hazardous place (two or more of: very soft surface, excessively heavy wrapping/clothing, head covered, excessive heating or in direct sunshine so potentially overheated, inappropriately cold room, waterbed, adult bed alone, on soft cushion, pillow or bean bag)
- put down to sleep on front or side on soft surface e.g. pillow or cushion, waterbed, beanbag, head covered.

INQUEST

In England and Wales, the coroner is mandated by the Coroners' Act (HM Government 1988) and the Coroners' Rules (1984) to investigate all unexplained or unnatural deaths. Rule 36 requires the coroner to establish the identity of the deceased; when, where and how the deceased came by death; and certain registration particulars. Following an unexpected death, the coroner will usually order an autopsy. The pathologist, following the autopsy, will provide the coroner with a provisional report and, if possible, a provisional cause of death. If the death appears to be from natural causes, the coroner will issue a form 100B (known as a 'pink B') and release the body to the family. If, however, the pathologist cannot give a cause of death, the coroner will open and adjourn the inquest pending the gathering of further information. The evidence at this first hearing is normally confined to identification. The coroner's officer (either a civilian officer or a police officer acting on behalf of the coroner) will gather information from the family, as well as from the general practitioner and other health professionals who know the child, and any police officers or other professionals involved in responding to the death. The coroner may choose to seize records and other items as evidence for the inquest.

When all enquiries are complete, the inquest will be resumed for a full hearing, at which the parents would normally be present, and other witnesses (including professionals involved in the investigation) may be called by the coroner to give evidence. Inquests are public hearings held in a courtroom contained in either a public court building or within a civic building. The coroner's officer will have warned the family that the press are likely to be present. The evidence at the inquest is directed solely at establishing the particulars outlined above, and it is not the role of the coroner to apportion blame in the case of an unnatural death. However, where a coroner believes that particular persons may be responsible, whether that be through acts of commission or omission, he may refer the case for further criminal investigation. Having heard and considered all the evidence, the coroner must then reach a verdict on the cause of death. This may be a standard form (e.g. accident, natural causes) or may be in the form of a narrative verdict, a brief factual statement describing how the death arose. Where gross neglect has caused or contributed to the death, the verdict will reflect this. Where the coroner believes that action should be taken to prevent similar deaths, he or she may report the circumstances to a person or body in a position to effect changes (Rule 43).

Where an inquest is held after the multi-agency case discussion, the report from that discussion will be extremely helpful to the conduct of the inquest and should always be made available to the coroner. Conversely, if the inquest is held beforehand, the coroner may identify issues that are beyond his jurisdiction, but which he can refer on to the multi-agency group to consider further.

EXTENDING THE PROCESS TO DEATHS
IN OLDER CHILDREN

Although these processes have been developed in the context of sudden unexpected death in infancy (Fleming et al. 2004), it is our firm belief that the basic principles can and should apply to all unexpected childhood deaths. Whilst some local authority areas have made some steps in this direction, there is still a lot to be learned. To build in appropriate responses to unexpected deaths in older children requires co-operative working between all agencies, and indeed draws in other professionals who might not be involved in infant deaths, such as teachers, police accident investigators, and child and adolescent mental health services.

Whether a child dies unexpectedly following an accident, a suspected homicide or suicide, or through a catastrophic natural event, the child and family deserve a thorough and systematic investigation of all that led to the death, and appropriate ongoing support for the family, friends and wider community. Following accidents or unnatural deaths, the child may not be brought to an Emergency Department, but rather the police may be called directly to the scene; conversely, following a sudden, natural death, hospital staff may not think to contact the police. It is therefore even more important that procedures are put in place to ensure that appropriate staff are notified and able to respond to the death. We would recommend a home visit, even where the child did not die at home, as this gives the opportunity to discuss things with the family, obtain a full history and answer questions that may arise. It may be appropriate to arrange a joint visit to the scene of death, and this should be agreed in an early multi-agency discussion. Again, we would stress the importance of a complete autopsy, full information sharing among all professionals and a final case discussion meeting.

CONCLUSIONS

In this chapter we have outlined the processes involved in responding to an unexpected death in infancy or childhood. Whilst we have divided the process into immediate, early and late responses, there are no clear boundaries between these different phases. It is important that close inter-professional communication is maintained throughout the process, and that the family are involved and kept fully informed. As far as possible, there should be continuity in the professionals involved. Often, however, there will need to be a handover, for example from the police officer who first meets the family, to a family liaison officer who will provide ongoing support throughout the process, or from an acute paediatrician involved in the immediate response, to a designated SUDI paediatrician who may become involved at the stage of the home visit or at the final case discussion. It is less important who takes responsibility at these different stages than to ensure that someone is taking responsibility and has the appropriate competencies, that there has been a clear and thorough handover, and that any new professional is introduced to the family.

By investigating all unexpected childhood deaths in a thorough and systematic manner, we ensure that as far as possible any cause of death is identified accurately, along with any potential contributory factors; that the family is informed and supported throughout; and that the professionals themselves are supported.

8 Police Investigation in Unexpected Childhood Deaths

JOHN FOX

THE WAY WE WERE

The police response to SUDI has come a long way since the mid 1990s. Up until that time there was no special training, no multi-agency protocol, and often little guidance given to officers about the need for sensitivity when attending the scene of an incident which, by its nature, would usually be far more traumatic for a family than the sudden death of an older person.

Anecdotal evidence from the Foundation for the Study of Infant Deaths (FSID) suggests in many police force areas it would not be unusual for one or more marked patrol cars to be sent to the child's home, and even if experienced detectives attended, their basic training in crime scene investigation would sometimes cause them to over-react, thereby causing great distress to bereaved parents, most of whom were innocent of any wrongdoing. When faced with an uncertain situation for which they hadn't been trained, and for which there was no specific guidance, the natural course of action for many police first responders was to take what they would consider to be the safe course of action: secure the scene, seize bedding, baby bottles etc, and ensure the infant isn't moved until a senior colleague arrived. This would be good, standard practice for officers attending the scene of any crime, but since we can now confidently say that a large majority of SUDI cases at that time did not involve a crime, there was clearly a need for a more measured and specialised response by the police. A balance had to be struck in carrying out a thorough, yet sensitive investigation into the circumstances of the death. To do this, the police needed to integrate and work with colleagues in other agencies, notably paediatricians.

CATALYSTS FOR CHANGE

Faced then with police forces which would frequently send untrained, uniformed personnel to the scene of these incidents, and worse still, officers who

Unexpected Death in Childhood: A Handbook for Practitioners. Edited by P. Sidebotham and P. Fleming.
Copyright © 2007 by John Wiley & Sons, Ltd.

felt that attending so-called 'cot deaths' ranked with domestic violence incidents as the calls to avoid at all costs, it is quite understandable why, in 1999, the Foundation for the Study of Infant Deaths decided that they needed to publish a draft document containing advice for police and coroner's officers on the handling of SUDI cases (FSID 2003).

Spurred on in part by this minor embarrassment, the Association of Chief Police Officers' (ACPO) Homicide Working Group recognised that the police service itself should be issuing national guidance to its own officers rather than relying on a charitable organisation to do so.

Police officers have to deal with a wide range of incidents and when problems arise, the trouble can frequently be traced back to a lack of training and familiarity. This can manifest itself in a lack of confidence, poor decision-making and over-reaction. The primary aims of the ACPO guidance were firstly, to ensure that officers with the appropriate training attended the scene and secondly, to ensure that whoever attended was confident about what needed to be done and, importantly, what did *not* need to be done.

The document was produced by a small working group of police officers and academics but with very wide consultation amongst the medical profession, coroner's service, children's social care, government officials and the FSID. Several years have now passed since its publication and research conducted by the Home Office on behalf of the ACPO Homicide Working Group has indicated that it is being used widely to improve practice in England and Wales (ACPO 2002).

Recent events such as the Victoria Climbié Inquiry (Cm 5730 2003), two high-profile cases in the Court of Appeal, the Attorney General's Review (Goldsmith 2004) and Baroness Kennedy's Intercollegiate Working Group (Royal College of Pathologists & Royal College of Paediatrics and Child Health 2004) – which will all be discussed in depth later – have served to underline the importance, in policing circles, of dealing with potential crimes against children much more professionally and effectively than was the case in the past; and in that context, there is no more important task than ensuring that sudden and unexplained deaths involving children are investigated sensitively but thoroughly.

IS SUDI REALLY A POLICE PROBLEM?

Very few people in the UK ever suffer a serious criminal assault, but research has shown that if a person is unfortunate enough to become a victim of homicide, it is most likely to happen during their first year. In fact, in England and Wales, infants under one year of age face around four times the average risk of falling victim to homicide (measured as per 100,000 population) (Brookman & Maguire 2003).

Children are people and as such have the same right to life and the services of the police as adults. The Human Rights Act 1998 places an absolute duty on the police, and other public bodies, to preserve the right to life of all people as well as protect them from torture or inhumane treatment.

It is widely accepted that within the number of cases that have over the years been classified as SIDS, SUDI or cot death there is always a hidden proportion that are in fact the result of maltreatment or deliberate harm. Estimates of the proportion of SUDI caused by homicide vary considerably, although many authors suggest that up to 10% may be frank homicide, with maltreatment (abuse or neglect) being a contributory (though not necessarily causal) factor in a similar proportion (Fleming et al. 2000, Levene & Bacon 2004, Sidebotham et al. 2005). For policing purposes, it doesn't really matter what the proportion is, but rather it should be considered unacceptable for there to be *any* deliberate killing of a human being that does not attract a full and professional investigation.

It is significant that the overall number of SUDI-type classifications was much higher when that research was being conducted than it is today. The steep decline from a peak of 2.3 deaths per 1,000 live births in 1988 to 0.7 per 1,000 live births in 1994 (Chapter 4) can largely be attributed to the excellent education and awareness campaigns instigated by the FSID. Indeed, to underline the point, the director of the Foundation for the Study of Infant Death said in 2006: 'Over 14,000 lives have been saved in the UK since the advice to reduce the risk of cot death was introduced in 1991' (FSID 2006). The number of explained SUDI cases and the number of deaths due to maltreatment has remained stable and therefore the proportion of hidden homicides within the overall SUDI cohort is likely to be greater now than it was in the mid 1990s. Whatever the actual numbers, no one can seriously doubt that occasionally, some carers deliberately kill their infant children, and the expert services of the police are crucial in discovering when this has happened.

The ACPO guidance (ACPO 2002) is quite clear on the point that the majority of SUDI cases are entirely non-suspicious. The police accept this without question, but it is also accepted within police circles that an officer attending an SUDI incident today is more likely to be at a crime scene than he or she would have been 15 years ago when the overall number of SUDI cases was much higher. It can perhaps be argued that the real way to reduce the hidden number of homicides is to become far better at investigating, together with colleagues in medicine and children's social care, the cause of death, thereby exposing without doubt the natural from the unnatural and the suspicious from the non-suspicious. This should be an aspiration of the Police Service in England and Wales.

THE IMPACT OF THE VICTORIA CLIMBIÉ INQUIRY

It is generally accepted that the publication of the Victoria Climbié Inquiry Report (Cm 5730 2003) led to the biggest shake-up in child-protection policing, certainly since the 1980s, and arguably the biggest shake-up there has ever been. The evidence that emerged during the inquiry showed overwhelmingly that the police were confused about their role when dealing with potential child-abuse cases, and that although there were child-protection units in all police forces, they were often staffed with inexperienced investigators with inadequate training and a lack of resources. Clearly, in the context of dealing with a potential homicide involving an infant, this was a major shortcoming. The child-protection units were simply not able to tackle what were, in effect, the most important cases within their sphere of interest. Upon publication of the report, a great deal of pressure was brought to bear on chief constables to overhaul radically their child-protection units. In line with a recommendation by Lord Laming, the ACPO urged all its members to ensure that child-protection units were staffed by detective officers, and indeed, since 2006 a prerequisite for becoming an accredited Specialist Child Abuse Investigator is that an officer must have completed successfully the Initial Criminal Investigators Development Programme, which is the minimum entry standard for anyone wishing to join the CID.

The national child-abuse investigation guidance document (Association of Chief Police Officers & CENTREX 2005) suggests that the lead investigator for cases involving the sudden or unnatural death of a child could be a senior officer from the force child-abuse investigation unit, or at the very least, accredited child-abuse investigators should be closely involved in the investigation. This aspiration will only be implemented in all parts of England and Wales when there are sufficient skilled and trained personnel working within child-abuse investigation units (CAIU), but in some police forces, including London's Metropolitan Police and the Hampshire Constabulary, the investigation of all SUDI cases is exclusively the responsibility of the CAIU. The benefit this will bring for doctors, social workers and so on, is that the investigating officer, provided by their local police force, is likely to be very experienced at working within a multi-agency setting. Whereas they will be expert in detecting those cases which have an element of suspicion, they will also be sensitive to the needs of both the families and the other professionals with whom they will need to work. Doctors will often know the officer personally because he or she will have been involved with them in multi-agency meetings and investigations about a whole range of less serious cases involving potential child victims.

THE INTERCOLLEGIATE WORKING GROUP AND ATTORNEY GENERAL'S REVIEW

During 2002 and 2003, several high-profile cases involving infant-homicide convictions were heard at the Court of Appeal and it was considered possible that the judgements could have a significant impact on the investigation techniques used in infant-death cases. Such was the public disquiet over the fact that there may be undiscovered miscarriages of justice, the Attorney General felt it prudent to conduct a review of every infant-death case in the previous ten years where a conviction for murder, manslaughter or infanticide had been upheld. The review identified just fewer than 300 such cases, and a multi-disciplinary team set about examining the safety of those convictions. When all the dust had settled after this intense scrutiny, the scale of the problem was found not to be as great as some had originally feared. Out of the 300 cases examined by the Attorney General, about 8% were initially identified as potentially having some cause for concern, and in the end a much smaller percentage resulted in a successful appeal (Goldsmith 2004).

In the meantime, the Royal College of Pathologists and the Royal College of Paediatrics and Child Health asked Baroness Helena Kennedy QC, a leading human rights lawyer, to chair what became known as the Intercollegiate Working Group. This group was set up to review how sudden deaths in infancy should be investigated, with the 'overriding concern that steps should be taken to prevent miscarriages of justice, while protecting the interests and safety of children' (Royal College of Pathologists & Royal College of Paediatrics and Child Health 2004).

The report of the Intercollegiate Working Group had four major areas of importance for the police investigator:

- The drafting of a framework for the proposed national protocol, which has now been included largely in the latest edition of *Working Together to Safeguard Children* (HM Government 2006b).
- A section on the role of the expert witness, which crucially made the strong point, 'The courtroom (should not be) a place used by doctors to fly their personal kites, or push a theory from the far end of the medical spectrum'.
- A recommendation that all police investigators who handle SUDI cases receive special training.
- The full endorsement, and inclusion as an appendix, of the existing ACPO Infant Death Guidelines.

THE CANNINGS JUDGEMENT

On 19 January 2004 the Court of Appeal gave detailed reasons for the decision announced in December 2003 that it was allowing the appeal of Angela Cannings against her conviction for the murder of her two children.

It would be useful for all those involved in the investigation of infant deaths to understand the implications of the Appeal Court judgement in the Cannings case, because it gave certain guidelines as to when it would not be appropriate to prosecute someone in circumstances where there had been one or more SUDI cases within a household.

The judgement ruled that, 'in relation to unexplained infant deaths, where the outcome depends exclusively, or almost exclusively, on a serious disagreement between distinguished and reputable experts and natural causes cannot be excluded as a cause of death, it will often be unsafe to proceed'.

This should in no way prevent a full and thorough multi-agency investigation into every infant death. The primary purpose for all professionals should be simply to establish how the child died, and of secondary concern is a decision to be made as to whether or not a prosecution is appropriate.

In cases where, in addition to expert opinion, there is forensic, physical or medical evidence which points to maltreatment, the Cannings judgement would not normally apply. Only when the sole evidence for the court to consider is disputed expert evidence as to the cause of death, and such disagreement is both 'serious' and 'between distinguished and reputable' experts, would it normally be unsafe to proceed. In response to this judgement, the Attorney General, Lord Goldsmith, instructed that the Crown Prosecution Service (CPS) and the Association of Chief Police Officers must implement new guidance in all cases on the way the prosecution team instructs expert witnesses. The guidance sets out tougher requirements on expert witnesses in terms of: disclosure of material, certification of their credibility and competence, and in limiting opinion to their own specific area of expertise (Goldsmith 2004).

One of the key messages from the Kennedy Report (Royal College of Pathologists & Royal College of Paediatrics and Child Health 2004) is that there should be a series of professionals' meetings during the investigation process. No decision to prosecute should be made by the police or Crown Prosecution Service without taking into account the views of other colleagues during the multiprofessional review process.

THE ANATOMY OF A POLICE SUDDEN DEATH INVESTIGATION

It may be helpful at this point to examine why and how the police investigate all sudden and unexpected deaths involving people in the UK.

The history of the police role begins in 1829. Sir Richard Mayne, one of the two architects of the first professional police force, set as its primary roles the protection of life and property and the prevention and detection of crime. The prevention and detection of the crime of homicide must rank as the most important work the police are tasked with. An effective way to prevent homicide and thereby preserve life is to catch and convict those who deliberately kill people and in doing so, stop them from killing others. The consideration for the police in cases of infant death, therefore, must be as much for current or future siblings of the deceased, as for the subject child. This is so whether or not there are any suspicious circumstances, because as part of that primary duty, the police should be eager to help other professionals, such as doctors, establish the cause of an unexpected death in order to help avoid preventable deaths in the future.

The police have traditionally attended any case of sudden death resulting from an unknown cause, and their duties can include the verification of death and the submission of a report to the coroner. In England and Wales, coroners are independent judicial officers who hold office under the Crown. They are either doctors or lawyers by profession and they have a statutory duty to inquire into the cause of all sudden, unexpected, violent or unnatural deaths. The office of HM Coroner is an ancient one, dating back at least to 1194, but their duties and responsibilities are now governed in the main by the Coroners Act 1988 (HM Government 1988).

Coroners are generally supported by a number of coroner's officers, who are often ex-police officers actually employed by the local police force, although according to a 1998 Home Office study on the Coroner Service (Tarling 1998), there is a gradual shift taking place towards full civilianisation of the post of coroner's officer, and their training is being improved to include some element of death-scene investigation and assessment. In most parts of the country, coroner's officers do not normally attend the scene of a potential crime under investigation by the police. They do, however, attend the hospital or mortuary where the body is being held and liaise between the police and the coroner over the arrangements for the autopsy. Otherwise, they have no role during a criminal investigation but if, as was suggested by Dame Janet Smith in her third Shipman Inquiry Report (Smith 2003), the police withdraw from their traditional attendance at sudden death scenes where there are no apparent suspicious circumstances, the coroner's officer will play an ever more important role in triggering a fuller investigation when appropriate.

Whatever the outcome of the debate about saving police time by not attending all sudden deaths, a clear distinction must continue to be made with SUDI cases. These cases are now relatively rare and should never be considered by the police as 'natural and inevitable events' in the sense that elderly people die as a matter of course. 'Healthy children are not meant to die, and when they do these children deserve the right to have the death fully investigated in order that a cause of death can be identified, and homicide excluded' (ACPO 2002). It should be standard practice that whatever a police force's general policy about police attendance at sudden deaths may be, in every case involving the sudden or unexpected death of a child, the police should immediately deploy a detective officer of at least inspector rank to carry out an investigation.

Whilst investigating a sudden or unnatural death, any police officer is, for the time being, acting as a 'coroner's officer'.

Apart from their general responsibility to establish whether a crime may have occurred, the police also have an interest in establishing the circumstances surrounding a sudden or unexpected death, in order to assist the coroner's inquest. Early contact will be made with the coroner's office and upon completion of the investigation, a file will be passed to the coroner to share whatever evidence and information may be relevant.

SUSPECTED HOMICIDE CASES

Frequent watchers of US detective movies could be forgiven if they thought a murder was solved by a lone investigator, largely unsupervised and working all hours. Even if such a picture were accurate in the US, it is very much not the case in England and Wales.

Homicide investigation is at the pinnacle of police work and the process by which it is carried out is highly systemised and methodical, and involves the co-ordination of many people from different disciplines.

The principle investigator, known as the senior investigating officer (SIO), now undergoes a nationally-accredited development programme which involves a three-week initial course, several months' workplace assessment and a further week's immersive training. He or she will lead a dedicated team of officers, which will include several key specialists such as crime-scene investigators, police-search advisors, analysts, major-crime indexers, family liaison officers, as well as the general enquiry team made up of experienced detectives.

The SIO will be supported by a senior management team, and the whole enquiry is likely to be managed using a computer-based information and indexing system known as HOLMES.

The two key national documents which guide the police in the investigation of suspected homicide cases are the *Major Incident Room Standard Administrative Procedures* (MIRSAP) (ACPO 2005) and the *Murder Investigation Manual* (MIM) (ACPO 2006).

The MIRSAP is a huge manual that advises on a wide range of administrative matters including the roles and responsibilities of all staff in an incident room, such as the document reader, office manager, and so on. Standardised guidance on information management, the management of property and exhibits and the financing and resourcing of a major enquiry can be found within it. The MIM gives the investigator a great deal of information about what research tells us about the commission of homicide.

Updated in 2006, the MIM is a comprehensive set of guidelines to assist the SIO in the conduct of the investigation itself. It outlines the three distinct strategic phases of a homicide investigation:

1. **Instigation and initial response.** This involves the deployment of officers to the report of an incident, which may be a homicide, and the action they take to preserve life, secure the scene and secure other material.
2. **The investigation.** This involves developing investigative strategies aimed at gathering the material needed to establish whether the incident is a homicide, identifying suspects and gathering material for a prosecution.
3. **Case management.** This involves post-charge enquiries, preparing the material gathered for the prosecution and the defence, and managing witnesses and exhibits through the trial process.

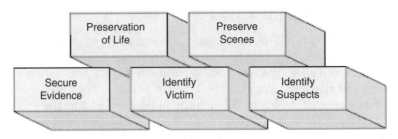

Figure 8.1 Five building-block principles

Figure 8.1, reproduced from the MIM (ACPO 2006), illustrates the five building-block principles which the investigator will consider in every suspected-homicide case.

The initial five key questions in a senior investigating officer's mind at the outset of an investigation should relate to:

- The preservation of life. Is there anything that can be done immediately to save other lives?
- The preservation of the scene. What should be done to ensure the integrity of the scene of a possible homicide in order that as accurate as possible a record can be made of exactly how things looked at the time of the events leading to the death?
- The securing of evidence. What important information or evidence will be lost forever if it is not seized, photographed or noted as soon as possible?
- The identity of the victim. Who is the person who died, and why would anyone have wanted to kill them?
- The identity of the suspects. Who could have killed the victim and who had any reason to do so?

The MIM outlines the theory and methodology which should be employed in an investigation. Figure 8.2, also reproduced from the MIM (ACPO 2006), graphically explains what else a police investigator will be considering in terms of their decision-making process.

Police investigation techniques are now highly professionalised and these two important documents (MIRSAP and MIM) are likely to be followed closely by every senior investigating officer, thus other professionals can be confident that wherever they work in England and Wales, the police will be investigating homicide to this high, national standard.

One of the most important attributes a police investigator needs to maintain is the 'healthy scepticism' to which Lord Laming referred (see above). Like many professions, the Police Service has a wide range of acronyms to help remind employees about aspects of their job. The senior investigating officer will have been taught to keep in mind both the ABC acronym (Assume

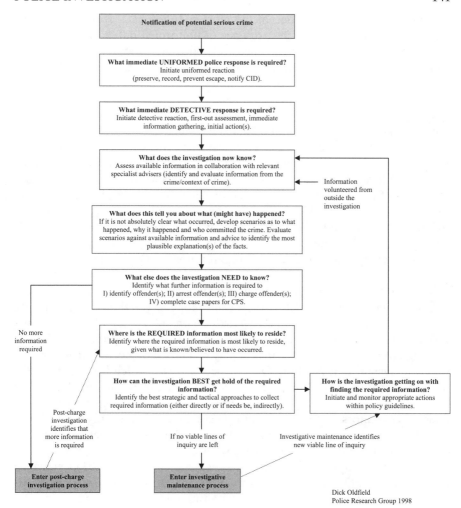

Figure 8.2 Model of 'idealised' investigative decision-making process

nothing, Believe no one, Check everything), as well as the 5WH acronym (who, what, where, when, why and how). Those working with the police ought not to be surprised if issues, which may appear to be safe assumptions, are challenged and subjected to rigorous examination.

SPECIFIC GUIDANCE IN RELATION TO SUDI

The first key point to make in this section is that although a senior detective should attend every SUDI case, it is recognised that most such events will turn out not to be suspicious deaths.

According to the FSID, one of the most common causes of upset for the families of SUDI victims is the presence of uniformed police officers at their house. Most families accept the need for police involvement and are willing to help any professional who is trying to find out the cause of their child's death. Those parents who have done no wrong will usually be co-operative if treated with dignity and respect.

The purpose of ensuring that a detective inspector takes charge from the outset is to maximise the likelihood that a thorough and professional investigation is carried out in a forensic sense, whilst at the same time ensuring the highest level of sensitivity and support for the bereaved family and providing the highest level of assistance to other professionals who are trying to establish the cause of death. It is felt that a senior detective is best placed to achieve these aims, and if that officer is also a trained specialist child-abuse investigator, as recommended by Baroness Kennedy (Royal College of Pathologists & Royal College of Paediatrics and Child Health 2004), the police are likely to have done everything possible as an organisation in order to provide the best response.

Some police forces would argue that they don't have the resources to field a child-protection-trained detective inspector for every SUDI case. In a climate where the police have been trying to demonstrate a highly professional response to so-called 'critical incidents', and generally to professionalise the investigation of all potential crimes, it may be more and more difficult for such forces to sustain that position. One particular force, which has around 3,800 police officers and would therefore be considered a medium-sized UK police force, ensures that a cadre of four detective inspectors – all experienced child-abuse investigators – work a call-out rota system to attend every single SUDI case. If Baroness Kennedy's suggested high standard is to be realised, then this sort of model could be considered elsewhere.

I will not attempt in this chapter to replicate the entire ACPO guidance document (ACPO 2002), although much of this particular section is drawn from it. The full document should be considered essential reading for any officer who is likely to be responsible for the investigation of SUDI cases. The full document should be embedded in each police force's policy and procedures manual, but in any case it is available to police officers and others in the criminal justice community at the National Centre for Policing Excellence's 'Genesis' website and on the interactive CD ROM issued with the 2006 edition of the MIM (ACPO 2006). Furthermore, it is likely that each Local Children's Safeguarding Board will have in existence a multi-agency protocol for the management of SUDI cases. These will vary from area to area but in every local protocol the section on the role of the police should reflect closely what is contained in the ACPO guidance. It is crucial that senior police investigators know of the existence of these documents and have a good understanding of their contents, and it is important that both police forces and safeguarding boards ensure good training complements the guidance and protocols.

Guiding principles which should underpin the work of the police when dealing with SUDI cases include:

- To maintain a sympathetic and sensitive approach to the family, regardless of the cause of the child's death. Police action needs to be a careful balance between consideration for the bereaved family and recognising the potential of a crime having been committed.
- To keep an open mind.

Perhaps the most important section of the ACPO guidance is the practical checklist. It is certainly my experience that when at the scene of an SUDI case, particularly in those cases where the body is still *in situ*, the police officer simply doesn't know what signs should cause him or her to be concerned that a crime may have been committed. It is quite possible to deliberately kill a very young person leaving no bruising or sign of a struggle, which might usually be found when the victim is older. Conversely, there may be some quite alarming signs present on or around the body of an infant, which in fact are quite innocuous yet may cause an investigator to over-react.

The full, confidential version of these guidelines contains important information about some factors that may be present when death occurs as a result of a deliberate act. Conversely, because none of these factors are present, it does not mean the death cannot be suspicious. The purpose of this list is to act as a guide for investigators, but it should not prevent a thorough analysis of all the circumstances surrounding the death.

There are two bullet-point lists in the ACPO guidance entitled 'Factors which may increase suspicion' and 'Factors common in most infant deaths' (as an example, the latter list is reproduced in Box 8.1) and together they are, in effect, a practical crib sheet to help the senior investigator assess the death scene. It would be good practice for these tips to be reproduced onto a laminated card and carried in one's briefcase.

In April 2006, the UK government published a revised edition of *Working Together to Safeguard Children* (HM Government 2006b). This is the key multi-agency guidance used by police, health and social care professionals in England and Wales. It is updated every 5–10 years and all Local Safeguarding Children's Board child-protection procedures should closely reflect the guidance in *Working Together*. Chapter 7 of the document provides guidance on procedures for a rapid response from professionals to all unexpected deaths of children, and this follows very closely the national protocol suggested by Baroness Kennedy and the Intercollegiate Working Group (Royal College of Pathologists & Royal College of Paediatrics and Child Health 2004).

Immediate responses

The police are most likely to hear about an SUDI incident from either the ambulance control or a member of staff at a hospital Emergency Department.

Box 8.1 Factors common in most infant deaths

- Froth emerging from the mouth and nose. This froth results from the expulsion of air and mucus from the lungs after death. Sometimes the froth may be bloodstained – this does not mean that the death was unnatural.
- Small quantities of gastric contents around the mouth. This does not mean that the death was caused by inhalation of vomit. Often there is slight regurgitation immediately after death.
- Purple discolouration of the parts of the face and body that were lying downwards. This is not bruising, but is caused by the draining of blood in the skin after death. For the same reason the parts that were lying upwards may be very pale.
- Covering of the child's head by the bedclothes. This has often been a feature of cot death in the past, and probably contributes to death through accidental asphyxia or overheating, although if drink or drugs are a known factor, the possibility of wilful neglect must be considered.
- Wet clothing or bedding (this is usually caused by excessive sweating before death).

It is very important that staff in police control rooms are aware of the immediate response requirements. Most, if not all, forces will have computerised command and control systems, and providing the category of incident is properly identified, a drop-down menu should help the control room operator deploy the appropriate resources. It is important, therefore, that information regarding SUDI response is pre-programmed into the computer system so the police do not instigate a disproportionate or improper response.

Local protocols may vary, but if *Working Together* is being adhered to, an ambulance crew attending a home following a report of SUDI should attempt resuscitation and remove the child immediately to an Emergency Department. Only if they are able to verify death, *and* there are clear signs of maltreatment, should the body be left *in situ*. Once a child has been removed to the Emergency Department, the lead clinician will involve either a designated or on-call paediatrician who will, if resuscitation has failed, contact key agencies, including the police. Hospitals need to have clear and easily-accessible guidelines for staff in Emergency Departments about how the police should be informed, but typically the initial call should be made straight to the police force central control room, which is staffed 24 hours a day. In this initial contact, there should be no ambiguity about the fact that the sudden and unexpected death involves an infant.

Early responses: history taking, investigating the circumstances of death

The ACPO guidance (ACPO 2002) provides advice on the initial action which should be taken at the death scene. Part of this includes a list of questions which should be asked when taking a history from the carers. The process of taking the history is an important opportunity for the police investigator to use their intuition and experience to assess the veracity of the story and gauge the reaction and attitude of carers. If done jointly with a paediatrician, the history taking will include a great deal more information from a medical perspective and will, in most cases, be more informative for the rest of the multi-agency team. It is not good practice, from the police perspective, for a paediatrician to be the sole history taker from those who last saw the child alive.

In accordance with guidance in the MIM (ACPO 2006), where there are any suspicious circumstances the police lead investigator may give the person who last saw the child alive the designation 'significant witness'. If this is the case, arrangements may be made to videotape the history taking so that an exact record of what was said can later be transcribed and, if necessary, turned into a witness statement. Bearing in mind the distress that an SUDI case will cause, it is important for professionals to explain clearly to the carer that the videotaping of their interview does not imply in any way that they are being considered a suspect and in any case, videotaping can only be used if the witness agrees.

In every sudden-death investigation, the police will take statements from family members on behalf of the coroner. Sometimes these statements will be used to inform a coroner's inquest and it should be explained to families that this is normal practice. If a family liaison officer has been deployed, they may well be the best person to obtain statements from family members. The police may also need written statements from professionals involved with the case. Paramedics, Emergency-Department nurses and doctors may all be asked to provide a statement detailing their involvement with the child or family. Although many doctors, particularly those involved in emergency medicine, are used to writing their own statements, in any case involving something as potentially serious as homicide, a member of the police investigation team should review the statement with them directly or write it to their dictation. Professionals often have anxiety about giving statements to the police. If possible, it is good practice to involve a designated or named child-protection professional when statements are being taken from hospital staff members who are less experienced in the criminal justice process.

If one or more carers are considered to be suspects in the potential commission of a crime, they must be treated fairly and in accordance with the Police and Criminal Evidence Act 1984. It will be necessary for any police interview to be conducted under caution and only after they have been allowed certain safeguards, such as access to a solicitor. The taking of a history, therefore, may sometimes necessarily form part of an 'official' police interview, and be recorded as such. What cannot be acceptable is for a carer privately to be considered a suspect by professionals, but then, when they are perhaps lulled into a false sense of security, be asked to give an account of the hours leading up to the body being discovered. This is not only unfair on the carer, but would certainly lead to the exclusion of potentially vital evidence.

If a carer is considered to be a suspect they will almost certainly be arrested and interviewed on tape at a police station. The investigative interviewing of suspects is now a highly specialised area of police work and in a suspicious infant-death case it is likely that two detectives, and a supervisor known for this purpose as an interview advisor, will be involved in the process. There is no reason in law why a clinician should not be involved in an interview process involving a suspect but such an arrangement would have to be agreed in a discussion with the lead paediatrician, the senior investigating officer and the interview advisor. It is fairly common practice in cases involving a suspicious death for a support team of expert advisors, which may include a behavioural psychologist, to assist the police interviewers. Sometimes, such advisors may monitor the interview from an adjacent room in order that they can provide a real-time evaluation of answers given and perhaps suggest lines for the interviewers to take. In suspicious SUDI cases, a trained and experienced clinician may be an extremely useful asset within such an interview support team.

Family care and support

A common complaint from parents and professionals has been that the police were sometimes intransigent when it came to a request for the bereaved parents to be allowed to hold their baby or receive mementoes such as a lock of hair or fingerprints. Good training will help senior investigators become confident about what they can and cannot allow, and this should lead to less over-reaction and inflexibility. During the consultation process that led to the publication of the ACPO guidance (ACPO 2002), the view of the Forensic Science Service was sought, and they were reassuring that in most cases no harm would come from allowing these basic human requests from the family. A simple precaution such as ensuring that a professional, for example a nurse, is present when the parent holds the child will negate a possible suggestion that any injuries found during the autopsy could have been caused at this time.

Whether or not the police have suspicions about the case, proper consideration and respect for the family of the deceased child is important. The MIM (ACPO 2006) underlines the principle that: 'One of the most important considerations throughout a homicide investigation is providing support to the family of the deceased. It is of paramount importance that families are treated appropriately, professionally, with respect and consideration given to their needs.' It will often be good practice to deploy a trained family liaison officer, and certainly in any case where homicide is suspected the MIM (ACPO 2006) gives clear guidance that the 'appointment of a family liaison officer is essential in all homicide investigations'. Where one is deployed, however, the family liaison officer is first and foremost part of the investigation team. Many people are under the mistaken impression that they are there simply to provide care and support to the family. They are trained to be sensitive and to ensure as much information as possible is relayed to the family about the investigation, but they cannot take the place of properly trained bereavement counsellors or therapists. The family liaison officer has the specific responsibility of acting as an interface between the family and the SIO. They will at all times be available to members of the immediate and extended family and keep them updated about the progress of the case. They will be able to explain why certain procedures and delays may be necessary, whilst at all times helping to gather evidence to establish how the child died.

The term 'family' may well include extended family or even close friends, and police investigators will endeavour to identify those people who can provide information about the circumstances leading to the death of the child and those who have a genuine need to be kept informed of progress.

Scene investigation

The scene, or scenes, in a possible homicide investigation will be designated by the investigating officer. It is very likely that there will be more than one scene – for example, the body itself is always designated as a scene, and it is possible that an ambulance used to transport the body may also be a scene. In most cases however, the location designated as Scene 1 will be the actual place where the body was discovered. In cases of SUDI where there are no suspicions, police are likely to take a very low-key approach to scene attendance and involve only the people thought to be absolutely necessary, such as the lead investigator, a crime-scene investigator and a photographer. In cases where suspicions are increased, however, the following is a list of people who may be deployed:

- cordon officers
- crime-scene loggists
- crime-scene examiners
- exhibit officers
- crime-scene managers (csm)
- pathologists
- photographers/video-camera operators.

Other specialists whose services might be required include:

- a crime-scene co-ordinator (if there are multiple scenes)
- forensic scientists

- a police search advisor (polsa)
- a scientific advisor (sa)
- a plan drawer.

An important element of the *Working Together* protocol is the proposal that in any case involving the unexpected death of an infant at home, there should be a joint home visit by a senior investigating police officer and a health-care professional (experienced in responding to unexpected child deaths, normally a paediatrician). Their purpose is to visit, talk with the parents and inspect the scene. They may make this visit together, or they may visit separately and then confer, but in any case this should be done within 24 hours (HM Government 2006b).

When investigating a possible homicide, police will sometimes refer to the period of time immediately following the discovery of a body as the 'golden hours' to describe the principle that '... effective early action can result in securing significant material that would otherwise be lost to the investigation' (ACPO 2006). In cases involving SUDI, a careful and proportionate judgement needs to be made about whether urgent steps should be taken to secure the premises or at least the room where the child died. Where necessary, this might involve ensuring a police officer guards the scene or else making sure that the premises are locked and sealed until a proper examination can be carried out with crime-scene investigators and the relevant health-care professional. Clearly, such actions could cause some distress to the family and a clear and honest explanation as to how this may help discover how the infant died is important.

Bearing in mind the five initial building blocks of any potential homicide investigation, the implication for some police senior investigating officers is that they may be concerned about losing vital evidence if a scene visit is not carried out immediately. Whereas it will usually be advantageous to make the visit together, if the health-care professional is not available, and is not likely to be available within a reasonable time scale, then the police investigator may go ahead separately and discuss the findings at the scene later on with health colleagues. The possibility that evidence may be lost, however, must be weighed against the significant advantages of having colleagues from police and health jointly assessing the death scene. A compromise in terms of when the scene is visited may be beneficial to ensure as much information as possible is obtained from the family and the environment in which the infant died, as well as a clear interpretation of the findings at the scene.

Investigators, particularly perhaps specialist crime-scene investigators who may be called in to examine the scene, sometimes consider the need to seize any bedding and the cot in which the child died. Apart from this rarely being of any help in a forensic sense, it is very important for the combined police/paediatric team to see the bedding *in situ*. Issues such as accidental overheating need to be considered and because the paediatrician is attending to help assess the scene, things should to be left as intact as possible pending the joint visit. Indeed, to underline this point, the MIM (ACPO 2006) advises that the three priorities at any potential homicide scene are:

- identify
- secure
- protect.

Removal of any articles prior to a full multi-agency assessment should therefore only be considered in the light of this guidance.

Autopsy

The post-mortem examination is a very important part of the overall investigative process and this is dealt with in some detail elsewhere in the book (Chapter 9). From the police perspective, however, it is important for senior investigators to understand the desirability of having a paediatric pathologist carrying out the autopsy. Research commissioned by the ACPO Homicide Working Group (Reeder & Nicol 2004) revealed that less than half of the police forces in England and Wales have a paediatric pathologist based in their area. It may well be necessary, therefore, to obtain permission from the coroner to move the body to a location where a paediatric pathologist can be found. Careful thought must be given to any delay this may cause, but it is incumbent upon police managers to identify a location within relatively easy reach of their district, and to predetermine that a paediatric pathologist is willing to carry out the autopsy on any SUDI cases from outside their normal catchment area. In any case where the death is suspicious, a Home Office pathologist will carry out the autopsy, preferably working with a paediatric pathologist.

In every SUDI case, part of the examination before autopsy should include a full set of bodily X-rays (skeletal survey), ideally taken in a hospital radiology department with good-quality equipment, as opposed to using a portable machine in a mortuary. The films should then be interpreted by a paediatric radiologist and the results given as part of the briefing to the paediatric pathologist. Whenever a 'full skeletal survey' is requested and carried out, it is vital that every bone in the body has a good quality image taken of it – a single 'babygram' does not give the quality of images required.

In 2004, after consultation with the Royal College of Radiology, ACPO published a good-practice guide concerning radiology in child-abuse investigations (ACPO 2004). The document stressed the importance of the recommendations of the British Society of Paediatric Radiology (BSPR) for cases of suspected non-accidental injury (NAI) (which can be found at www.bspr.org.uk). The ACPO good-practice guide should be referred to by officers dealing with any SUDI case. They should identify these guidelines as representing good medical practice and providing a standard for appropriate forensic investigation.

It is normal practice for the police senior investigator to attend the post mortem and to brief the pathologist fully about the apparent circumstances of the death, ideally using scene photographs or video footage.

Further investigations

In all cases of SUDI, the police should carry out the following checks and, where appropriate, share the results with colleagues in the multi-agency team:

- Check police records for all family members, including the Police National Computer, force intelligence systems, crime-recording system, incident logs, command and control records, domestic-violence logs.
- Check police child-protection database.
- Liaise with the relevant children's social-care department to ensure their records are checked, including the child-protection register or national children's database.

During the consultation period for the Kennedy Report (Royal College of Pathologists & Royal College of Paediatrics and Child Health 2004) some police officers expressed concern that under the new guidelines the forensic investigation might be compromised. This does not need to be the case and overall the mindset should be that complying with the ACPO guidelines is not a license to carry out a half-hearted forensic examination, but rather for a more thorough and systematic investigation to be carried out in a sensitive manner. A supportive, sensitive approach can go hand in hand with a thorough forensic examination and in order to maximise the information harvest, it is clearly advantageous that the investigating officer maintains a good relationship with the immediate and extended family.

Inter-agency working

Amongst the other things listed above, the ACPO guidelines (ACPO 2002) mention the following as additional guiding principles that must underpin the work of all relevant professionals dealing with a sudden unexplained child death:

- To ensure a co-ordinated and timely inter-agency response, particularly in respect of information sharing.
- To share information.

To have the best chance of identifying successfully how a child died unexpectedly, all the key professionals involved in the enquiry must trust each other and share information at every stage. The importance of the Local Safeguarding Children's Board organising multi-agency training in respect of SUDI cannot be overstated. It is much easier to work together with a colleague from another agency if one understands their point of view and there has been an opportunity to iron out any areas of tension. The investigation of SUDI should be kept firmly within the spirit of the local child-protection procedures, which will undoubtedly promote good communication between agencies as well as close co-operation.

The protocol outlined in *Working Together* (HM Government 2006b) suggests that when a child dies unexpectedly, a paediatrician (on-call or designated) should initiate an immediate information-sharing and planning discussion between the lead agencies (i.e. health, police, LA children's social care) to decide what should happen next and who will do what. The police senior investigator should make every effort to attend this initial meeting. A further meeting should be held as soon as possible after the post-mortem examination and although normally toxicological tests may take several days to be finalised, this should not delay an interim meeting of key professionals to discuss the findings emerging from the autopsy.

CASES OF A CLEARLY SUSPICIOUS NATURE

A multi-agency team approach to investigation is vital in all SUDI cases, and professionals from different agencies will naturally bring to the team different perspectives, experience and training. In his report (Cm 5730 2003), Lord Laming made this important and fundamental observation: 'I believe that the police should bring to the child protection arena a healthy scepticism, an open mind and, where necessary, an investigative approach.'

This is exactly what the detective inspector needs to be mindful of when attending an SUDI incident. Whilst most deaths will remain non-suspicious, some will either be caused deliberately, or be the indirect result of some form of wilful maltreatment or neglect. In the latter category a crime will have been committed, and even if a homicide charge is not appropriate, other lesser charges may be, and thus the evidence gathering needs to be rigorous and thorough. It is perhaps in these less clear-cut incidents where death may have occurred as an indirect result of maltreatment that the importance of the investigator having received specialist child-abuse training will become most apparent.

An example of this could be a case where the infant has been suffocated after sharing a bed or sofa with a carer. Although such a death may on the face of it seem like a tragic accident, if there is evidence that the carer had been seriously impaired by alcohol or drugs, and particularly if they have been warned previously about the dangers, it is quite possible that a criminal offence of wilful neglect under Section 1 of the Children and Young Persons Act 1933 may have been committed. Such a scenario underlines the point that a thorough knowledge of child-abuse investigation and the evidence-gathering techniques employed in that area of policing could be considered essential for the senior police investigator in an SUDI case.

If, after carrying out the initial investigation, the death is thought to be suspicious, then the attending detective inspector must inform a senior investigating officer immediately.

The SIO is a senior detective; usually a detective chief inspector or detective superintendent, who has, as outlined above, been trained specifically to investigate homicide cases, and accredited by their force to a standard agreed with the National Centre for Policing Excellence under the Professionalising the Investigative Process (PIP) programme. To meet the investigative and management challenges, SIOs should have completed the SIOs' Development Programme and be registered at PIP Level III or above. The *Murder Investigation Manual* (ACPO 2006) makes the following additional comments about the person who performs that role:

SIOs need to be skilled and experienced investigators who are able to develop investigative strategies based on the unique circumstances of each case and continually modify them as new material becomes available. In particular they must have:

- knowledge of:
  - the criminal law
  - the circumstances in which homicides are committed (including the ways in which offenders, witnesses and others with information about the incident are likely to behave)
  - local and national policies in relation to criminal investigation, including MIRSAP and the use of information management systems such as HOLMES and the Paper System
  - the principles of criminal investigation and supporting disciplines
- skills and experience in applying the techniques of homicide investigations
- decision-making ability.

As I have already mentioned, the ideal situation is that each police force will ensure it has sufficient senior detectives who are both accredited as SIOs and trained as specialist child-abuse investigators. Where that is the case, there would be no reason why the police investigator who initially attends the scene should not remain as the lead investigator in cases where a full homicide investigation is to be carried out.

Where this is not possible, it is likely that the case would be taken over by a senior detective from the force major investigation team.

In order to be compliant with the MIRSAP (ACPO 2005) guidance, it is the responsibility of the force chief officers to ensure there are 'sufficient appropriately trained resources available to deal with the incident'. This will typically mean that a team of between 10 and 20 detectives is assigned to the case until such time as all possible enquiries have been carried out. Best practice in infant-death cases will be that the SIO appoints a team of detectives that includes specialist major-crime investigators and specialist child-abuse investigators. Certain key roles within the team, such as the exhibits officer and disclosure officer, are generic to all homicide investigations, and specially-trained officers should fulfil them.

Once the investigation is complete, a file of evidence will be presented by the police to the Crown Prosecution Service (CPS). Assisted by the view from the multi-agency team, the CPS will, using their own guidance, known as *The Code for Crown Prosecutors* (CPS 2004), decide what, if any, charges are appropriate.

THE WAY WE ARE

Events of the past few years have brought about a huge improvement in the way police respond to child-protection issues generally, but more specifically there is a real desire to ensure that the sudden or unexpected death of every child attracts a highly professional approach. The type of scenario described at the beginning of this chapter, when untrained uniformed officers were deployed with little regard for the needs of the family and little chance of ensuring a skilled evidence-gathering process, have been left behind.

A professional, sensitive investigation to a national standard, and with a high level of multi-agency involvement and information sharing, is the way to reduce to an absolute minimum the number of cases where, after everything has been done, it is still unclear how a particular child died. The police contribution to the multi-agency investigation into SUDI is an important one and it will often provide useful data for the team trying to discover why a child died.

In the conclusion to her report, Baroness Kennedy firmly reminded us of the nightmare scenario when a carer is wrongfully accused of killing their child. She also made the point that, hard as it is to sometimes accept it, 'we have learned conclusively in the last 30 years that some mothers, fathers and other carers do fatally harm their children. Child Protection is a responsibility all of us must bear because of the special vulnerability of the youngest among us, who have no voice'. (Royal College of Pathologists & Royal College of Paediatrics and Child Health 2004).

9 The Paediatric Post-Mortem Examination

PHIL COX

INTRODUCTION

Post-mortem examination is one of the mainstays in the investigation of sudden and unexpected death in infancy (SUDI). It provides vital information for the public authorities and also for the family, who need to know why their child died and what, if any, actual or potential implications there are for other children in the family.

It is essential that the autopsy is conducted to the highest of standards, which requires a pathologist with special expertise in the area of infant death. Since the death by definition is sudden and unexpected, the autopsy will, in most countries, be performed under the jurisdiction of the legal authorities, for example the coroner or fiscal, who may not be interested in the medical needs of the family. This brings with it specific challenges if both the legal and medical aspects of the examination are to be fulfilled.

THE SIZE OF THE PROBLEM

It is not possible to collect information easily on the number of SUDIs that occur each year in the UK. This is because there is no precise definition of what constitutes an SUDI and since it is not a registerable cause of death, no population statistics are collected routinely. If one takes as an SUDI any death of a child under one year of age that is clinically unexpected (excluding post-operative deaths) then approximately 80 such deaths occur in the West Midlands Region in the UK, an area with a population of 5.27 million (Government Office for the West Midlands 2007) and around 66,000 births per year (West Midlands Perinatal Institute 2006). All of these deaths will fall under the jurisdiction of the legal authorities, namely Her Majesty's Coroner. Despite some consolidation in recent years, the West Midlands area is still divided into 12 separate coronial districts. The larger metropolitan districts may deal with 30 or more SUDIs per year, whereas small rural districts may see only one or

Unexpected Death in Childhood: A Handbook for Practitioners. Edited by P. Sidebotham and P. Fleming.
Copyright © 2007 by John Wiley & Sons, Ltd.

two. There is a danger that cases will be dealt with differently dependent upon which coroner's jurisdiction they fall under.

THE KENNEDY REPORT

Following a number of high-profile SUDI cases in the UK, in which the standard of investigation was called into question, a working group was convened jointly by the Royal College of Pathologists and the Royal College of Paediatrics and Child Health, chaired by the eminent lawyer, Baroness Helena Kennedy QC, to look at all aspects of the handling of cases of SUDI. The resulting report (Royal College of Pathologists & Royal College of Paediatrics and Child Health 2004) proposed a national protocol for the management of cases of SUDI, with a multi-agency approach, laying down the role and responsibilities of the various agencies – police, paediatrician, pathologist, coroner, Social Services and lawyer. A number of aspects of the Kennedy report have a direct bearing on the post-mortem examination. The protocol recommends that the baby should be examined by a consultant paediatrician as soon after death as possible. As detailed a history as possible should be taken at this stage as well as a number of standard samples. This should be followed by a home visit by a paediatrician and police officer within 24 hours of the death. A full report should then be prepared and this should be supplied to the pathologist prior to commencing the autopsy. This represents a huge advance over the previous situation, where often the examination was performed based on a few lines produced by the coroner's officer on the circumstances of death. The report also recommends that SUDI autopsies should be carried out only by pathologists with expertise in this field and should follow a standard protocol (Royal College of Pathologists & Royal College of Paediatrics and Child Health 2004, Bajanowski et al. 2007) (see below). Finally, there should be a multi-disciplinary team meeting to review all of the available information, once the final post-mortem report is available, and the findings regarding the cause of death and any implications thereof should be fed back to the family by the paediatrician. Where this protocol has been implemented, there is generally a feeling amongst the professionals involved, in particular the pathologists, that it represents a major step forward in the investigation of these challenging cases.

THE POST-MORTEM EXAMINATION IN SUDI

The majority of post-mortem examinations performed under the jurisdiction of HM Coroner in the UK are undertaken on adults. However, the expertise required in this area is not readily transferable to the situation of SUDI. In fact, many pathologists who deal with adult deaths are unwilling to undertake SUDI autopsies.

The SUDI autopsy differs from its adult counterpart in a number of ways. Firstly, the individual being examined is much smaller. This requires the use of smaller instruments and may also make it more difficult to recognise pathological changes with the naked eye. The range of diseases causing death is quite different from that seen in adults. Other than bacterial infections, there is little overlap with the pathology of adult deaths. Even bacterial infections in infants can show differences in their presentation and the interpretation of the pathology compared to adults. Congenital malformations and a range of genetic disorders may be present, which are rarely seen in adult practice. There is also the possibility that any SUDI might be a concealed homicide. Getting the balance right between identifying cases that are suspicious and not raising unnecessary concerns about ones that are not can prove very difficult.

The biggest difference between an SUDI autopsy and an adult one is the involvement of the parents. Whilst the death of any close relative is undoubtedly traumatic, the sudden and unexpected death of a small baby must be one of the most devastating experiences imaginable. The carers have a need to know why their precious baby died and may well be concerned that there could be implications for their other children or those that they may have in the future. The healthcare needs of the family can be overlooked if the case is dealt with in a purely legalistic manner. They may also be under suspicion for having some hand in the death, and even if this is not the case, they are very likely to be feeling under suspicion given the usual involvement of police and other authorities, however sensitively this may be handled.

As a result of these complicating factors, it is essential that autopsies in cases of SUDI are undertaken by a pathologist with special expertise in this area. In the UK, this will either be a specialist paediatric/perinatal pathologist, or a general histopathologist who has had special training in this area. Unlike an adult autopsy, the pathologist will usually perform the entire examination, ideally in a mortuary designed for paediatric/perinatal work or an area of a larger facility set aside for this purpose. The Kennedy report (Royal College of Pathologists & Royal College of Paediatrics and Child Health 2004) recommends that whenever possible, the autopsy should be performed within 48 hours of death. Our experience is that this can prove difficult and it may take up to five days to arrange the examination. Prior to the examination it is mandatory that a full skeletal X-ray survey is performed and reported by a radiologist, preferably one with experience in the field of non-accidental injury. Almost invariably a full post-mortem examination will be required, including examination of the cranial contents. Whereas a cause of death can be identified with the naked eye with reasonable confidence in the large majority of adult deaths, it is possible to give a cause of death after the initial examination in only around 5% of cases of SUDI.

Histological examination of all of the major organs and a battery of ancillary tests must be performed routinely. Table 9.1 lists the minimum histological

Table 9.1 Recommended minimum histological samples to be taken at autopsy in cases of SUDI

Organ	Samples
Lung	All lobes (5); consider Perls' stain
Heart	L & R ventricles and septum (3)
Thymus	1
Liver	L & R lobes (2)
Kidney	L & R (2)
Spleen	1
Pancreas	1
Adrenals	L & R (2)
Lymph nodes (mesenteric/thoracic)	1
Trachea/thyroid	1
Costochondral junction	1
Muscle (psoas)	1
Diaphragm	1
Brain	12

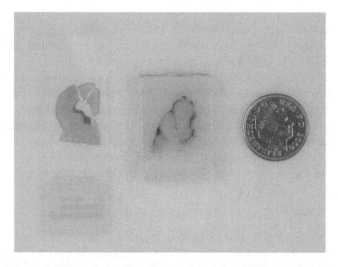

Figure 9.1 Histological section (slide) and paraffin tissue block

samples taken routinely in our department. Additional samples may be necessary depending on the autopsy findings.

The samples taken for histology are fixed in 10% formalin solution and then processed to produce paraffin wax blocks. The size of the pieces of tissue varies depending upon the organ, but they are no bigger than a British 2p coin (or a 1€) in area and up to 2 mm in thickness (Figure 9.1). Thin sections from these blocks, approximately 4 µm in thickness, are cut, mounted on glass slides and stained with dyes to visualise the cellular detail. The sections are protected

with a thin glass cover slip and are then ready for examination by the pathologist. Histological sampling of the brain should ideally be taken following a
period of fixation of the intact brain. A minimum of three days is necessary to
achieve sufficient fixation, provided a strong solution of formalin (20%) is
employed and the fixation is performed at 37 °C rather than at room temperature. Fixation will take longer if 10% formalin is used or if it cannot be performed at the higher temperature. If fixation of the entire brain is not possible,
it may be acceptable to take slightly larger samples of the areas required for
histology and to trim these to make tissue blocks after they have been fixed.
However, this approach may lead to some loss of quality of the histological
sections and should be avoided when there is a likelihood of major neuro-
pathological abnormality.

In addition to the samples taken for paraffin blocks, small samples of liver,
kidney, skeletal muscle and heart should be frozen, and sections prepared from
these samples are stained to demonstrate fat (which would be removed by
processing for the paraffin blocks). This is a useful screening test for abnormalities of fat metabolism (fatty acid beta-oxidation defects), which may cause
SUDI.

Once all of the histological samples have been taken, it is strongly advised
that all remaining tissue from the internal organs be returned to the body,
prior to it being released for burial or cremation.

Besides the samples for histology, tests should also be submitted to look for
bacterial and viral infection, metabolic disease and chromosome disorders.
Samples should also be sent routinely for toxicology tests. Table 9.2 lists the
samples sent routinely in our department. Other tests should be sent as indicated by the clinical situation and post-mortem findings. It is also advisable to
store a small sample of tissue, such as liver, frozen at −20 °C as a source of
DNA should the autopsy suggest a genetic disease.

INVOLVEMENT OF A FORENSIC PATHOLOGIST

It is probably not necessary to have a forensic pathologist in attendance at
every SUDI autopsy. However, if anything in the history, external examination,
home visit or circumstances of the death causes concern that the death may
not have been due to natural causes, then a qualified forensic pathologist,
along with scene-of-crime officers, should be present at the autopsy. Whilst in
many cases the initial suspicions may prove unfounded, it is important that
correct procedures relating to the gathering and documentation of evidence
are followed, in the event that there are subsequent criminal proceedings. It
also helps to protect the parents from unfounded speculation if nothing is
found despite the fullest of investigations.

Should an autopsy on a supposedly non-suspicious SUDI reveal a cause for
concern, it is vital that the examination be suspended and the coroner informed
immediately. Completion of the autopsy should await the attendance of offi-

Table 9.2 Routine diagnostic samples required at autopsy in cases of SUDI

Laboratory	Organ/tissue	Container
Bacteriology	Blood (heart)	Blood culture bottle
	Lung	Swab (transport medium)
	Cerebrospinal fluid	Plain universal
Virology	Nasal swab	Plain universal
	Tracheal aspirate/washings	Plain universal
	Lung tissue	Plain universal
Biochemistry	Blood (acyl carnitines ± amino acids)	Plain universal/Guthrie card
	Bile (acyl carnitines)	Plain universal/Guthrie card
	Urine (organic acids)	Plain universal
	Vitreous humour (sodium and urea) if dehydrated	Plain
Cytogenetics	Skin	Transport medium
Toxicology	Blood	Plain universal
	Gastric contents	Plain universal
	Liver	Plain universal

Notes: CSF may also be useful for measuring sodium and urea.
Bowel contents may be submitted for bacteriology and virology if gastroenteritis is suspected.
It is usually necessary to submit cardiac rather than peripheral blood for toxicology. This should be screened for major drugs of abuse, antidepressants, sedatives and common medicines. It may be helpful to agree a standard protocol with your laboratory.

cers from the relevant police force, the scene-of-crime officers and the forensic pathologist.

In cases of intracranial injury, including possible shaking or suspected suffocation, it is usually necessary to fix the brain for longer than the usual few days and to refer it to a specialist neuropathologist for examination. As a result, the brain cannot be returned to the body for burial, unless the police retain the body for several months. If shaking is suspected it is also necessary to remove the eyes for examination by a specialist in ophthalmic pathology and to send the skeletal survey for specialist review.

Following a joint autopsy, the two pathologists may submit a joint report, or alternatively they may produce separate reports detailing the findings and focusing on their particular areas of expertise.

RETENTION OF TISSUES

Under the Coroners Rules for England and Wales (HM Government 2005b) and the Human Tissue Act 2004 (HM Government 2004b), the pathologist is allowed only to retain such tissues as bear on the cause of death. Any additional tissues may only be taken with the consent of the next of kin – in the case of SUDI, the parents. In the majority of cases this is not a problem, as the initial examination usually does not provide a cause of death. Therefore, it is necessary to take a full set of histology and other samples. In the occasional case where the cause of death is clearly evident at the autopsy, it is often still desirable to retain tissues for histology and other tests, to confirm the diagnosis and to provide the parents with more information than is required by the coroner. In such circumstances, consent must be sought for such retention, by either the paediatrician, police or the coroner's officer.

Despite the recommendations of the Kennedy report, that histological samples from SUDI cases should be retained routinely as part of the medical record, subsequent changes to the Coroners Rules and legislation in the form of the Human Tissue Act 2004 (HM Government 2004b) have made it an offence to retain these samples once the coroner's jurisdiction has ceased. This is in contrast to the legislation in Scotland, which follows the recommendations of Kennedy. In England and Wales, these samples may be retained only with parental consent. How, when and by whom this consent should be obtained and what form it should take has not been laid down, leading to a very unsatisfactory situation. In general, it is in the parents' best interests that the pathologist retains these tissue samples. In many cases of SUDI, a definitive diagnosis is not reached. A diagnosis of sudden infant death syndrome (SIDS) is, after all, only a means of coding an infant death as unexplained. Even when a cause of death is reached, there is often a degree of doubt, or there may be areas where questions still remain. Review of these tissues at a later date may help to resolve outstanding issues. In the fortunately rare case of families who suffer a second SUDI, it is absolutely vital that the histology from the previous death is available for comparison with the later case. There is often suspicion that both deaths may have been caused deliberately and review of the previous case can help to support or refute that view. In occasional cases, the parents may wish to pursue a civil case regarding a missed diagnosis or inappropriate treatment and the histology can help to further the case or defend against it. The tissue samples may also, with specific parental consent, form a valuable resource for teaching, audit and research. Many parents find it helpful to think that their loss may not have been entirely in vain and that by consenting to teaching and research, their baby may have been able to help others. It is therefore important that the parents of a case of SUDI are given the opportunity and information to enable them to make an informed decision regarding consent to retention of the tissue samples, for their own benefit and for that of others. The practice of routinely advising parents that the samples should be destroyed is to be deplored and harks back to the paternalistic practices of the past.

THE AUTOPSY PROCEDURE

Prior to commencing the autopsy it is essential that a full skeletal survey has been performed. This skeletal survey should be done according to standard protocols for skeletal surveys in suspected physical abuse (British Society of

Paediatric Radiology) and should be reported on by a paediatric radiologist; a single 'babygram' carried out using portable equipment in a hospital mortuary is not sufficient. Initial results should be available prior to the autopsy. The identity of the body must be confirmed, either by checking name tags on the body, or by formal identification by a police officer or similar individual.

The unclothed body is then weighed and the height, crown–rump length and head circumference recorded. The body must be examined carefully for bruises or other marks of injury and also puncture marks and others relating to resuscitation and sample collection after death. The face should be examined for dysmorphic features and the body for rashes, moles and other skin lesions, and congenital abnormalities. Particular attention should be given to looking for petechial haemorrhages on the face, neck, conjunctivae and oral mucous membrane as a sign of possible asphyxia and for damage to the oral frenulae. The child's genitalia and anus should be examined, looking for possible signs of sexual abuse.

Providing nothing suspicious has been identified, routine photographs or digital images should be taken of the front and back of the body and close-ups of the face and any rashes or other abnormalities.

At this stage a skin biopsy can be taken for cytogenetics, a nasal swab for viral culture and a sample of cerebrospinal fluid for bacterial culture via the foramen magnum (and biochemistry/virology). The latter may be omitted if there is any suspicion of intracranial injury, as there may be a possibility of creating artefactual haemorrhage.

The body is opened by a Y-shaped incision starting at the tip of each shoulder, meeting over the manubrium and continuing in the midline to the pubic symphysis. The body cavities are opened and the internal organs inspected and removed. Care should be taken to inspect the ribs, since fractures are occasionally missed in the skeletal survey. The organ weights are recorded and the organs are incised.

To examine the brain, the skin of the scalp is incised posteriorly and reflected. Any bruises are recorded. The skull is examined, in particular to exclude fractures, and then opened. In infants of less than three months of age it is usually possible to open the skull along the suture lines. In older babies the skull has to be opened with a cranial saw. The brain is examined *in situ* and then removed. The pituitary is examined and the middle ears should be opened and inspected. If there is evidence of infection, a swab should be taken. In general, the brain should be fixed intact prior to sampling for histology (see above).

The above description relates to a non-suspicious SUDI. In cases where there are suspicions of smothering or shaking, or for example if unexplained bruises or injuries are found, the forensic pathologist may have to perform a more extensive examination of the subcutaneous tissues. It may also be necessary to remove the eyes for examination by a specialist ophthalmic pathologist.

Once all of the tissues have been sampled for histology, the remainder of the organs are returned to the body and the incisions are repaired, prior to release of the body for burial or cremation. Following the autopsy, once the child is dressed and lying prone, the incisions will normally not be visible.

It is usual for the pathologist to produce a preliminary report within two to three working days of the examination. This details the findings of the initial examination and should include relevant negatives as well as positive findings. It is commonplace at this stage for the cause of death to be given as 'awaiting the results of further tests' or something similar. The final report, which includes the description of the histology and results of the additional tests, will generally be completed in six to eight weeks, although it may take longer if the case proves to be complicated. This is particularly true of cases where a metabolic disorder is suspected, since the necessary investigations may take a number of months to complete. The final report should give a summary of the findings, together with a commentary and a medical 'cause of death' if possible. If the cause of death is unequivocal, for example, an overwhelming bacterial pneumonia with extensive involvement of both lungs and positive cultures of a single pathogen from lung and blood, this is straightforward. However, in a proportion of cases the cause of death is not clear-cut and it can be very helpful to discuss the findings with other members of the multi-disciplinary team involved with the case. This may be informally, or in the forum of a formal multi-disciplinary team meeting. Viewing the findings in the context of a more detailed understanding of the clinical history and circumstances of death may assist in clarifying whether individual autopsy findings or the results of the other tests are likely to be relevant or not. It may be necessary to indicate in the final report the probability of the proposed cause of death being correct.

INTERPRETATION OF FINDINGS – SOME PROBLEM AREAS

Determining the medical cause of death of a small infant is often not straightforward. In around 20% of cases the autopsy will demonstrate an obvious and unequivocal cause for the death of the baby – either at the initial examination (albeit rarely) or based on the findings of histology and the other ancillary tests. Another proportion will be classical SIDS cases. They will have been found dead in a cot, having slept on their back without evidence of overwrapping. There will be no concerns raised about the circumstances of death and the autopsy will show only the classical features of SIDS (Table 9.3). The ancillary tests will be entirely negative. Unfortunately, in a substantial group of cases there will be one or more clinical feature or autopsy finding that causes difficulty in assigning the cause of death.

Some of these areas are:

- 'minor' pathological changes
- positive microbiology and negative/minimal pathology
- deaths due to cardiac arrhythmia
- co-sleeping deaths
- fresh pulmonary haemorrhage
- pulmonary haemosiderin.

Table 9.3 Classical features at autopsy in SUDI

Petechial haemorrhages on thymus, heart and lungs
Pulmonary congestion and oedema
Liquid blood in the heart
Lightly blood-stained fluid in nose
Often minor inflammation in airways/lungs

MINOR PATHOLOGY

Many cases of SUDI show some pathological findings at autopsy, particularly on histology. This is particularly true of the lungs, where lymphocytic bronchitis and foci of lymphocytic alveolitis are very common. Typically, this is mild and not associated with an alveolar exudate; however, on occasion the lymphocytic infiltrate may be more extensive and it can be difficult to assess whether it is sufficiently extensive to account for death. Virological studies are occasionally positive, with isolation of viruses such as RSV, adenovirus or influenza. RSV infection in very young babies may lead to apnoeic spells (Kneyber et al. 1998) and by implication possibly SUDI, and there may be very little inflammation or involvement of the alveolar parenchyma, as the mechanism is thought to be central respiratory depression. Therefore, determining whether this is the cause of death is, to some extent, a matter of speculation. The relevance of isolating other respiratory viruses, in the presence of minor or no inflammation, is open to greater question still.

Small foci of acute bronchopneumonia may also be identified on histology in otherwise apparently normal infants, but this is unlikely to be significant unless there is evidence of systemic infection. Other findings of doubtful significance include microscopic hepatitis, unilateral choanal narrowing and minor foci of gliosis or periventricular leukomalacia. None of these would be sufficient to lead to death, but they may be markers of an infant more susceptible to unexpected death/SIDS.

POSITIVE MICROBIOLOGY WITH MINIMAL/ABSENT HISTOLOGICAL INFECTION

As noted above, viral cultures from the respiratory tract may be positive in infants who show little or no histological evidence of inflammation in the airways or lungs. Apart from RSV, the evidence is lacking to show that such pathologically-insignificant infection can lead to death. RSV is associated with reflex apnoea in premature and very young infants and may occasionally be isolated from the respiratory tract of infants presenting as SUDI, in the absence of significant bronchiolitis (Church et al. 1984).

Bacterial cultures from the lungs may also be positive without apparent acute inflammation. If multiple organisms are isolated, this is likely to represent post-mortem contamination (Morris et al. 2006). Isolation of a single pathogenic organism, such as *Streptococcus pneumoniae*, Group B Streptococcus or *Staphylococcus aureus*, may be more problematic. The early stages of overwhelming pneumonia may be difficult to recognise histologically. A proteinaceous alveolar exudate may be present, and distribution of bacteria in small groups, diffusely through the exudate adds weight to the diagnosis. Neutrophil polymorphs may be scanty at this stage. It is very helpful to assess the pathology alongside the full clinical picture with the multi-disciplinary team. In the absence of some clinical evidence of infection, such as a cough, fever and so on; unequivocal pathological changes; or culture of the same organism as a pure isolate from the blood or elsewhere; the diagnosis of early, overwhelming pneumonia based purely on positive microbiology should be made with considerable caution.

Pure isolates of pathogenic organisms from the blood may sometimes be relevant to the cause of death (Zorgani et al. 1999, Morris et al. 2006). Septicaemia may overwhelm small infants rapidly and thus the presence of a serious pathogen in the blood should be given serious consideration. Ideally, the microbiology should be assessed by the multi-disciplinary team to reach a judgement of its significance, in the light of the full clinical background to the case. The identification of a possible portal for the infection is, of course, helpful.

There has been interest in the role of toxins from bacteria such as *Staphylococcus aureus* and *Escherichia coli* as a cause of unexpected death in infants. It is suggested that the toxins act as superantigens and stimulate an overwhelming immune response in the baby, which leads to death. Some studies have found evidence of *Staphylococcus aureus* toxins in around one half of SIDS victims (Newbould et al. 1989, Zorgani et al. 1999). Testing for these toxins is not generally available and there appear to be no diagnostic histological changes, thus it is difficult to confirm this hypothesis in routine material. Evidence for a role for *E. coli* endotoxin as a cause of SUDI is less convincing.

Isolation of single pathogens from other sites, such as cerebrospinal fluid, is rare in the absence of pathological changes and thus such isolates should be treated with caution. In general, samples are taken only from other sites for bacterial culture if there is evidence of infection at autopsy and thus any positive cultures should be interpreted accordingly.

DEATHS DUE TO CARDIAC ARRHYTHMIA

Whilst it is relatively straightforward to recognise those deaths that are a result of congenital heart disease, cardiomyopathy and overt myocarditis, the identification of cases of death due to cardiac arrhythmia with a structurally and histologically normal heart are much more of a problem. The clinical history may be helpful, as cardiac deaths tend to present as an observed collapse. However, cardiac death during sleep may also occur and is likely to present as a cot death. If a cardiac cause of death is strongly suspected, for example in a child with previous episodes of collapse, it is probably advisable to attempt to examine the cardiac conducting system, although abnormalities are probably rare. Examination may require the help of an expert in this field, who may request that the heart is retained intact. The considerable work involved precludes routine examination of the conducting system in all cases of SUDI.

A number of groups have been interested in the role of abnormalities of cardiac potassium and sodium channels, leading to a long or short QTc interval and a propensity to cardiac arrhythmia. Some authors have claimed that neonatal screening shows prolonged QTc is present in up to 50% of infants who subsequently die of SIDS (Schwartz 2001). This view is not accepted by all (Guntheroth & Spiers 2005). Estimates of the frequency of mutations in SIDS range from 2% (Ackerman et al. 2001) to 10% (Arnestad et al. 2007), suggesting that it may be appropriate to test all cases; however, there are several genes and multiple mutations as well as a number of allelic variants of questionable significance, and testing is not generally available. If there is a family history of unexplained sudden death in children or adults, ECG screening or genetic testing should strongly be considered.

CO-SLEEPING DEATHS AND FRESH PULMONARY HAEMORRHAGE

Epidemiological studies of SUDI and SIDS clearly show that co-sleeping, i.e. bed sharing with one or more adults, is a risk factor for SIDS, at least in some circumstances (see Chapter 4). This is particularly true when co-sleeping occurs on a sofa. Concern is frequently raised that the death may have been a consequence of overlaying by one of the adults. In the majority of such cases the pathology does not provide support for a diagnosis of overlaying, but often the pathology alone cannot entirely exclude it either. Most babies who die whilst bed sharing do not show overt features of asphyxia, such as petechial haemorrhages on the face, mucous membranes of the mouth or conjunctivae, or suffusion of the face and upper body. Internally, petechial haemorrhages may be present on the thoracic organs (Figure 9.2), but typically they are not more numerous than in non-co-sleeping SUDI. It has been suggested that fresh pulmonary haemorrhage may be more widespread in babies who die as

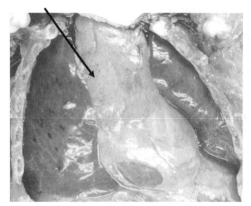
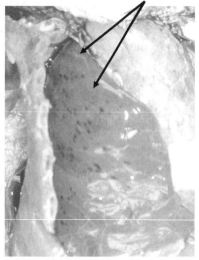

Figure 9.2 Petechial haemorrhages on the thymus and lungs of an infant presenting as SUDI

a result of accidental or deliberate asphyxia than in non-asphyxiated babies (Yukawa et al. 1999). However, the available evidence does not provide much support for this idea. In a study from New Zealand, the strongest association of pulmonary haemorrhage was young age at death (Becroft et al. 2001). Since the pathology of asphyxia is non-specific (Mitchell et al. 2002), the clinical background to the case needs to be elucidated carefully. The position of the baby when put to sleep, the coverings and relation to pillows and to the adult(s) in the bed is important. If the baby is found beneath one of the adults that is likely to be significant, but this is rarely the case. A history of consumption of alcohol or illicit drugs should ring alarm bells; however, unless there is evidence of intoxication when the sleep commenced this should not be taken as proof of overlaying. For example, if the adult has taken one unit of alcohol or a single cannabis joint six hours earlier, they are unlikely to be significantly intoxicated when they take the baby to bed with them.

As a general rule, the diagnosis of overlaying should not be made unless there is strong pathological evidence to support it, along with other corroboration in the history. The harm caused to the co-sleeping parent(s) by suggesting that the death may have been a result of overlaying, when there is little or no evidence to support it, is immeasurable. Some pathologists will not give SIDS as a cause of death if the baby has died whilst co-sleeping, since they cannot entirely exclude overlaying based on the pathology (Howatson 2006). However, if a clear history is obtained of the baby being found in the same position as placed to sleep, and not in close contact with, or particularly beneath the adult(s), who were not intoxicated at the time of the sleep, and no other evidence of asphyxiation exists, then the case meets the criteria for SIDS and should be labelled as such, recognising the conditions where co-sleeping is a risk factor.

PULMONARY HAEMOSIDERIN

Haemosiderin is a breakdown product of haemoglobin that appears in the lungs 2–3 days after an episode of haemorrhage (Sherman et al. 1984). It is visible in H&E stained sections as brown, granular material and can be stained by Perls' Prussian blue method, which recognises the Fe III within the granules, staining them dark blue. Perls' stain is more sensitive than H&E in demonstrating haemosiderin, showing up finely-divided as well as crystalline forms. Once formed, haemosiderin persists in the tissues for weeks or months, only gradually being removed by the action of phagocytes.

There has been considerable interest in the recognition of haemosiderin in the lungs of cases of SUDI as a marker of previous pulmonary haemorrhage (Becroft & Lockett 1997, Byard et al. 1997, Schluckebier et al. 2002). Whilst fresh haemorrhage may be explained as a consequence of the agonal events or attempted resuscitation, haemosiderin within macrophages in the alveoli or interstitium of the lung tissue indicates an episode of haemorrhage at least three days prior to death.

Since imposed airway obstruction may lead to pulmonary haemorrhage it has been proposed that haemosiderin in the lungs may be a marker for previous episodes of deliberate partial asphyxiation (Stewart et al. 1985). The research evidence supporting this is stronger than for fresh haemorrhage as a marker of a suspicious death, but there is still a shortage of well-conducted, definitive studies. The earliest study, by Stewart et al. (1985), suggested that haemosiderin in the interstitial and subpleural connective tissues of the lung was a marker for previous (possibly imposed) asphyxial episodes. However, a recent study found the strongest associations were with young age, increasing birth weight and increasing gestation (Becroft et al. 2005). Interstitial haemosiderin was only found in infants who had been subject to vaginal delivery. It would appear that interstitial haemosiderin is likely to be a consequence of the normal forces of labour in relatively large infants.

The literature regarding the significance of haemosiderin within alveolar macrophages has recently been reviewed (Forbes & Acland 2004). The authors conclude that there is insufficient published evidence to support the notion that the presence of haemosiderin in alveolar macrophages, if otherwise unexplained, is a marker of suspicious death. More recently, Krous et al. (2006), in a study of cases from the San Diego SIDS and SUDC Research Project, found that known accidental and deliberate suffocation cases did not show higher counts of haemosiderin-laden alveolar macrophages than SIDS cases. They showed a wider range of counts in SIDS cases. The highest count was in an SIDS case with no suspicious features. The authors concluded that the number of haemosiderin-laden alveolar macrophages couldn't be used as an independent variable to ascertain past attempts at suffocation. Thus, whilst the presence of large numbers of alveolar haemosiderin-laden macrophages may possibly be a cause for concern, it must be viewed in the light of the full background of the case, preferably by the multi-disciplinary team, and certainly cannot be used in isolation as grounds for prosecution.

MULTIPLE SUDI

Studies of SUDI/SIDS show a death rate of 0.5–2% in subsequent infants. Whilst recurrent deaths in a family may truly be unexplained and therefore classified as SIDS, recurrence increases the likelihood of finding an explanation for the deaths. Potential explanations for recurrent deaths include repeated poor parenting practices, deliberate harm, inherited disease and chance. Investigation of any case of a second or higher multiple of SUDI in a family should be even more thorough than in a single SUDI. It is strongly advised that a paediatric and a forensic pathologist should perform the autopsy jointly, with police and scene-of-crime officers in attendance. Prior to the autopsy, a detailed interview with the family should have taken place to elucidate the circumstances of death, family history and so on. In addition, the background to the previous death and post-mortem findings should have been reviewed. It is, of course, essential that the full post-mortem protocol be followed, with all ancillary tests. It may be necessary to focus on any areas of uncertainty thrown up by the previous examination. Samples must be stored for DNA extraction in case subsequent genetic tests are indicated. A multi-disciplinary review by all of the professionals involved is particularly important in cases of second deaths.

Available evidence suggests that some 10% of cases of multiple SUDI are a result of deliberate harm, whilst a further 10–20% may have some features that raise concern (Wolkind et al. 1993). Therefore, it is particularly important that cases are investigated thoroughly by the police and other professionals involved, in order that as many as possible of the unnatural deaths are identified and prosecuted, and deliberate harm is excluded with as much confidence as possible in the remaining cases.

A number of inherited disorders can account for multiple deaths in a family. As a result, inherited metabolic disease should be excluded as far as possible. It is therefore important that the post mortem in recurrent SUDI is undertaken within 48 hours of death. A review of the findings of the previous death may provide some clue to a metabolic disease, such as fatty change in the liver and other organs, failure to thrive or subtle changes in the skeletal muscle or brain. Fibroblast culture should be set up, and ideally samples of liver and muscle snap frozen for future testing, although protracted post-mortem delay may render analysis unhelpful. The threshold for performing metabolic studies on fibroblasts or the frozen tissues should be relatively low. If in doubt, a specialist in inherited metabolic disease should be consulted.

As noted above, there has been considerable interest in the role of cardiac channelopathies in SUDI. This is particularly relevant in cases of recurrent SUDI. If there is a family history of unexplained sudden death, it may be appropriate to refer the parents and other family members to a clinical geneticist or cardiologist for further investigations.

If the deaths appear to have been the result of infection, the possibility of immune deficiency should be considered. However, investigation post-mortem may be difficult.

Families who have suffered recurrent SUDI in which no suspicious features were identified and no natural disease has been identified, undoubtedly warrant a great deal of support from the health-care and Social Services in an effort to prevent further deaths.

CONCLUSIONS

Post-mortem examination is a critical part of the investigation of SUDI. The post mortem should be performed by a specialist paediatric pathologist, if necessary with the help of a forensic pathologist, and should follow a standard protocol, which includes a range of ancillary investigations. Long-term retention of tissues from SUDI autopsies is extremely important, but in England and Wales can occur only with the parents' consent. In the author's opinion, the law in this area does not serve the best interests of the family or of the state.

There are a number of difficult areas in the interpretation of the pathological findings in cases of SUDI. An understanding of the importance of such findings is probably best achieved if the various agencies consider them together in the light of their combined knowledge of the individual case. The published evidence relating to alveolar haemorrhage and haemosiderin as markers of unnatural death is at best inconclusive and certainly should not be relied upon as the sole evidence of maltreatment.

Extra effort should be invested in the investigation of recurrent SUDI, to identify evidence of deliberate harm and to diagnose inherited disease. In such cases a multi-disciplinary approach to the investigation is particularly vital.

10 Supporting Families

ALISON STEWART
ANN DENT

'It is undoubtedly the worst thing that ever happened to me and to my family. And what I still think about 10 years on, is that I knew that children died for a whole host of reasons, but I always believed that it happened to other people, not to me. Then one day I came home and there was the police officer telling me that my daughter had been killed on her way to school. That day it happened to me and I became part of that "other group" of people. I never wanted to join them but I can never go back.'

Mary, whose daughter Kirsty died five years ago

INTRODUCTION – SCENE SETTING

Chapter 1 offers a glimpse of the grief resulting from the death of a child. The relative rarity of child death in Western society (discussed in Chapter 2) emphasises for families and professionals the 'untimeliness' of such deaths. They occur outside the expected sequence of events where elderly grandparents die before their children (parents), who in turn die before their children (grandchildren).

Professionals, faced with the strong feelings of family members such as anger, distress, confusion, disbelief and guilt, can feel uncertain:

- 'I felt so helpless, I didn't want to go and visit.'
- 'I didn't know what was the right thing to say or do.'
- 'Despite all the training I have had, I felt very unconfident about how to support the family.'[1]

Despite extensive education and years in practice, many professionals feel ill-equipped to work with bereaved families. This chapter does not provide a recipe for working with bereaved families. Rather, it draws on selected literature (some of which provides an historical context), research[2] and practice, in

---

[1] Examples which illustrate the type of comments that we hear at the many workshops we have run for professionals.
[2] Dent et al. (1996) conducted a national study in the UK to ascertain bereaved parents' perceptions of support after sudden child death. As a result of the findings, a framework was devised and evaluated to guide Health

---

Unexpected Death in Childhood: A Handbook for Practitioners. Edited by P. Sidebotham and P. Fleming.

order to identify principles and strategies that professionals can use to suit different events, situations and people. The ideas presented in this chapter are discussed in more detail in our text Dent and Stewart (2004), and specifically with babies in Stewart and Dent (2005).

STRUCTURE OF THIS CHAPTER

As the earlier chapters indicate, there is a range of situations where unexpected child deaths occur. These include different locations (e.g. home, roads, leisure activity settings), different causes (e.g. infection, congenital abnormality, accident, suicide) or no identified cause (e.g. SIDS) and the involvement of different family members being absent or present at the time of death. Therefore, each particular combination of cause, location and people creates a unique context for each child's death. Within the scope of this chapter it is not possible to develop in detail issues of grief associated with particular deaths such as road traffic accidents or SIDS. There are many specialist texts, some of which we have cited. The chapter has three sections:

- experiences of grieving family members
- perspectives on grief
- working with bereaved families.

Throughout, we have included comments from families and professionals, with their permission,[3] as a means to locate this discussion in the everyday reality of working with bereaved families.

EXPERIENCES OF GRIEVING FAMILY MEMBERS

Comments from family members, such as those in Chapter 1 and from Mary at the beginning of this chapter, can help us, as professionals, to sharpen our awareness of the depth and complexity of grief following the unexpected death of a child. Whilst we cannot claim to understand another person's experience, our awareness can guide the ways in which we work with others in a respectful and caring manner. There are different members in each bereaved family, as Figure 10.1 illustrates; these include parents, siblings and grandparents.

A RIPPLE THROUGH FAMILY AND COMMUNITY AND ACROSS TIME

Many metaphors and images have been used to symbolise the experience of bereavement. In 1993, Jordan, Kraus and Ware (Jordan et al. 1993, 425) used

---

Visitors especially in supporting bereaved families (Dent 2000). Stewart (2000) explored grandparent bereavement as constructed in the stories of grandparents (n = 16), parents (n = 7) and health workers (n = 3). Twenty-three participants lived in New Zealand (NZ) and three grandparents lived in the United Kingdom (UK).
[3] Pseudonyms have been used unless otherwise requested by family members or professionals.

Figure 10.1 Image of family members
Source: Reproduced by permission of Suzanne Thornton.

Figure 10.2 Ripple of bereavement at time of death
Source: Reproduced by permission of Suzanne Thornton.

the term 'death ripple'. This image can help us appreciate that, like dropping a stone into a pond, a child's death creates a ripple of bereavement that extends out to parents, siblings, grandparents, other family members, friends, neighbours and the local community (Figure 10.2). The ripple also extends forward over time for each individual family member (Figure 10.3). For example, a grandmother whose daughter was stillborn was reminded afresh of the raw pain when, 25 years later, her grandchild died soon after birth; or parents whose child died in an accident described their fears about letting their other children take part in similar activities to those that led up to the death, whether going in a car or going out to a party.

For professionals, the 'death ripple' is a reminder that:

- A child's death affects more people than we might initially identify.
- The effect of that death can extend into people's future encounters with professionals, who may initially be unaware of the past bereavement.

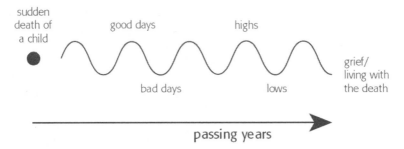

Figure 10.3 Ripple of bereavement over time
Source: Reproduced by permission of Suzanne Thornton.

Figure 10.4 Parents
Source: Reproduced by permission of Suzanne Thornton.

Next, we look at some aspects of parent, sibling and grandparent grief, making no claim that everyone experiences grief in these ways.

PARENTS

As Rando (1986, 6) wrote, 'The loss of a child through death is not quite like any other loss known. Ask adults what they dread most and the majority will state that . . . the loss they fear they could never cope with is the death of their child.' Such a death can challenge parents' sense of identity: 'Am I still a mother when my firstborn child died soon after birth?'

The intensity and range of feelings can be unimaginable for outsiders and can include a roller-coaster of shock, disbelief, anger, guilt, blame, sadness, weariness and hopelessness (e.g. Riches & Dawson 2000, Rosenblatt 2000). The unexpectedness of a child's death can mean that when told of the death, parents deny the possibility. The shock and disbelief may last days and weeks as they try to adjust the world that they knew when their child was alive, with the world that changed in a moment. A father explained, 'When you first hear, your response is to block it out, and to pretend that everyone is wrong, that there is a terrible mistake here' (Silverman 2000, 132). When a child has died in an accident, parents may want to know the details of who was involved and what, how and where it happened. In some situations, such as an accident or suicide, parents may have feelings of guilt: 'It was because I did not do [. . .] that he died.' There may be constant feelings of sadness, loss of hope and uncertainty in the future. 'It's not something that goes away. . . . You don't move on like you do with the death of a sibling or a parent or a close friend. You don't move on in the same ways that people expect. . . . It's forever and it's so deep that it doesn't feel okay really ever' (Rosenblatt 2000, 117).

Feelings come, go and return again. The enormity of grief requires bereaved people to make a huge mental effort of grappling with a changed world. Unsurprisingly, this can mean that people have difficulty listening to others, remembering what professionals said to them or concentrating on everyday activities like making toast. A mother described the first few weeks after the death of her daughter: 'It felt like being behind a thick pane of glass or in a fog. The world felt numb and black for weeks with moments of anger and crying. Then one day I saw the sun shine in a moment of colour, I felt glad. Then it was gone and life was black again. That was so frightening. I wondered if that was how it would always be. Even now, eight years after her death, the black days come but they are amidst the days of sun. I realised later it was all about hope. I had lost hope and it only came back slowly and not in the same way as before.'

Many parents experience physical and behavioural changes such as a racing heart, sickness in the pit of the stomach, insomnia and loss of appetite. In some situations, parents describe vivid visual and auditory hallucinations of seeing or hearing their child in the room or nearby. These changes can be frightening and people may not recognise that these are associated with the enormous stress of bereavement and may think that they are becoming ill or 'mad'.

So how do parents cope with the death of their child? Parents are generally members of a family group, whether with a partner who is a parent/step-parent to the child, or a solo parent with grandparents or siblings. Other family members may offer support as well as being grievers in their own right. They may share memories, learn ways of coping and share the effort of organising a funeral with each other. However, the individuality of grief may mean that each family member has different regrets, feelings or wishes. This may draw the parents together or it may create tensions (e.g. Rosenblatt 2000, Stewart

2000). One father described his experience: 'I find it hard to come to terms with my daughter's death. Sometimes I can't talk to anyone. I try not to bring it into conversation. When my partner talks about it, I find it hard to talk and try to avoid it by going out.'

At the same time that parents are living with their own grief, they are often also responsible for the care of their other children. For some parents, this can be a lifeline to everyday life that helps them cope, as one mother described: 'I had to get up and get breakfast on the table, get the children to school. There was no time to think, some days.' For others, the direct questions, confusion or changed behaviour of bereaved siblings can contribute to their own pain.

CHILDREN'S GRIEF – SIBLINGS

Before considering children's grief, it is necessary to understand something of their concept of death. This develops gradually as a child matures and is more dependent on cognitive development than age. Piaget and Cook (1952) identified four sequential stages through which thinking progresses:

1. The sensori-motor (infant) stage from birth to around two years, when only that which is visible continues to exist. Thus a child of this age will not be aware of the death but will react to any marked change in the behaviour of the main carer.

Figure 10.5 Siblings
Source: Reproduced by permission of Suzanne Thornton.

2. The pre-operational (pre-school) stage from 2–6 years, when a child believes that death is reversible and temporary, a departure or sleep. Children of this age have 'magical thinking' which may result in the belief that they caused the death. They are unable to grasp the finality of death for several weeks or months.
3. The concrete operational stage (school age) from 7–12 years, when thinking tools become available to the child. A child becomes less egocentric and experiences less magical thinking, being concerned with the actual rather than the hypothetical.
4. The formal operational stage (adolescence) when children are able to achieve a cognitive understanding of many concepts, including death.

As the next section indicates, these stages can be used as a framework within which to appreciate some of the ways in which children grieve. For further information, see Stewart and Dent (2005).

COMMON REACTIONS OF GRIEVING SIBLINGS

It is only natural that children react in some way to the death of their sibling. Like bereaved adults, they too experience similar feelings. Parents may see responses as troublesome, but it is important to consider the degree of intrusiveness created by the child's grief and how it affects everyday living. It is important to recognise that children will take cues from their parents.

Anger and aggression

'Why did Johnny have to die, anyway? If he hadn't died, then things would still be normal here' (child, no age given: Davies 1999, 52). 'Acting out' is common, when anger is displayed through arguing, showing off, disobedience and temper tantrums. It may also be due to the frustration of not knowing what to do with strong feelings, of wanting attention or disruption of usual family life. 'I get so mad sometimes because my brother had to die. Why him? Why? I get really mad when people ask me dumb questions about it all, and I try not to let mom and dad see how mad I am. But sometimes it just all comes out – just the smallest thing will set me off and I yell and scream and I just want to explode!' (13 year old: Davies 1999, 53).

Sadness and depression

'I miss my sister . . . We were really close . . . The things that I do . . . that we did together . . . it's not the same anymore. I try not to think about it . . . but I miss her. It's hard to be happy when I think of her and because I miss her. I just pretty much keep to myself now' (11 year old: Davies 1999, 54). Bowlby (1980) suggests that sadness is a normal and healthy response to any loss.

Usually, sad children are responsive to support and comfort from others, but if a child feels abandoned, unwanted and unloved, then depression can result. Indications of depression can appear as withdrawal from family activities, changes in eating or sleep activities, and/or difficulties at school. Whilst nothing alters the loss, acknowledging a child's grief, listening and showing love and attention can alleviate a child's pain.

Loneliness

'The worst thing is being lonely . . . You know other people have brothers and sisters . . . Just I don't have one now. You know, Christmas morning . . . being the only child . . . it's really lonely' (13 year old, nine years after her sister's death: Davies 1999, 58). For children who have had a close relationship with the dead sibling, this can be a difficult time. Encouraging children to play with their friends or find new friends may help as a temporary distraction in moments of family sadness.

Anxiety

This may arise from insecurity, when a child becomes clingy and unable to cope with real or imagined fears. Listening to the child, acknowledging fears and trying to overcome the anxieties may help.

Guilt

'I sometimes wish we hadn't argued so much . . . that I had told him that I like having him for a brother. But brothers argue . . . that's normal . . . isn't it?' (12 year old: Davies 1999, 60). This can be a common reaction in children after the death of a sibling, especially when it is unexpected. Again, listening and allowing expression of feelings can help.

LONGER-TERM EFFECTS

There are few long-term studies of bereaved siblings. However, Davies (1995, 1996) found that adults who had suffered sibling death in their childhood continued to have bouts of sadness for many years. Sibling grief is an individual journey and should not be expected to take a particular path or follow time limits. Grace Christ, an American psychologist, describes the concept of a 'cascade of events' (Christ 2000, 8–9). This is a process involving a number of events that may have a cumulative effect. 'Each stressful event may affect the child's self-esteem or self-confidence, which in turn shapes (and often distorts or exaggerates) the individual's perception of or response to subsequent events.' Going to a new school, leaving home, going to college, getting married and having children are examples which may trigger feelings about the deceased sibling. Children's capacity to think and use abstract concepts such as 'death' changes as they grow up, which means they may revisit their understanding of their sibling's death.

GRANDPARENTS

Just like parents, grandparents experience a wide range of strong emotions. Catherine's memory after Samuel's cot death at nine months was, 'I can remember the next day the milkman was coming and the paper was delivered and I thought, "Why were all these things still happening?" Because the world had stopped for us' (Stewart 2000, 336). Whilst grandparents are often seen as the supporters for the bereaved parents, the effect of their grandchild's death should never be underestimated.

Many grandparents describe having multiple griefs, which relate to their family roles. Gyulay (1975, 1,478) described this as 'triple-layered grief', where they have grief for themselves, for the parents and for their grandchild's loss of a future. Three years after her grandson Martin died, Elisabeth wrote: 'Grief took on a whole new meaning after Martin died, the double grief was almost unbearable – watching our own child and her husband. And feeling the loss of our grandson' (Stewart 2000, 208). She commented on the enormity of this grief, '. . . as a person who was usually in control of my public emotions I suddenly found I would weep in the most unexpected places and with the most unexpected people – this was difficult and hard to accept.'

Grandparents share the same range of feelings as parents and siblings, which includes shock, sadness and loss of hope. Amongst the limited number of

Figure 10.6 Grandparents
Source: Reproduced by permission of Suzanne Thornton.

studies of bereaved grandparents there is also evidence of the wide-ranging physical and behavioural changes, which can include fatigue, insomnia, loss of appetite, absent-mindedness and vivid dreams (Ponzetti & Johnson 1991, Stewart 2000). Professionals and information resources can help some grandparents recognise that these changes are linked to grief and not to the changes that come with ageing. Marie wrote after her granddaughter Ruby's unexpected death at nine days, 'I had previously been aware of the normal stages of grieving but in this book[4] I learned of some of the physical effects. I hadn't connected my loss of appetite or my inability to concentrate with my loss, nor did I think of the necessity to ensure that I should watch my own health' (Stewart 2000, 273).

So, how do grandparents cope? In Stewart's (2000) study, grandparents coped in various ways, which included helping, being with and listening to the parents, as well as acknowledging their own grief. Grandparents offered help to the parents, such as babysitting, phoning daily and organising the funeral tea. Benita, a grandmother, explained: 'There was a strong instinct to stay with them and if I left, to me, it would be like abandoning them. For all the pain it would cause we just had to see the whole thing through together' (Stewart 2000, 347). Many grandparents put their own grief second and the needs of parents and other grandchildren first until there was time to acknowledge their own loss. A grandmother said, 'I could share some feelings with my daughter and son-in-law, but often I felt I must be strong for them and hide my feelings as they were struggling.' Within families, grandparents often helped parents to create a continuing place for the grandchild in the family through talking about the child. Pip, whose daughter died, said, '. . . grandparents have a role in remembering to remember. It is the acknowledgment that is important to me' (Stewart 2000, 217–8).

This section has provided a glimpse of family members' grief after a child dies suddenly. The next section offers theoretical perspectives that can help professionals to identify how they might assist grieving family members.

PERSPECTIVES ON GRIEF – WHAT CAN THESE OFFER TO PRACTICE?

We often ask health professionals or undergraduate nurses who attend our workshops, 'What do you know about grief?' The overwhelming and immediate response is: 'Kubler-Ross and the stages of grief'. In 1969, the first edition of Elisabeth Kubler-Ross' *On Death and Dying* was published (Kubler-Ross 1969). As a single text, it has made an enormous contribution to raising public and professional awareness about bereavement. The interviews that she and her colleagues undertook with over 200 dying patients offer a description of

---

[4] Gerner (1990), a self-help book for grandparents.

how people often respond when they become aware that they have a terminal illness. She identified five stages of grieving:

- Denial and isolation – 'it can't be true.'
- Anger – 'why me?'.
- Bargaining – 'if I do this I will get better.'
- Depression – related to losses such as relationships, health and a future life.
- Acceptance – a time of withdrawal like '"the final rest before the long journey", as one patient phrased it' (Kubler-Ross 1969, 124).

Although it should be noted that her work is based on grieving for one's *own* death, not grief at another's death, the stages offer professionals a framework for understanding the complex thoughts and feelings associated with death. There are many other useful perspectives on grief which are not as widely accessed by professionals. So, in this section, we have included a selection of ideas, from health, sociology and psychology, which have informed our research, practice and teaching. This discussion acts as a series of 'information bytes' which offer insights about supporting bereaved families. The image we use for this section is a child's kaleidoscope, where the end can be turned around to combine the fragments of different coloured plastic into different patterns (Figure 10.7). These 'information bytes' can be combined in different ways to work with different people.

MODE OF DEATH – UNEXPECTED AND SUDDEN

The sudden death of a child is untimely and without warning. As Doka (1996, 11) noted, sudden death brings a range of challenges which 'include intensified grief, the shattering of a person's normal world and the existence of a series of concurrent crises and secondary losses'. Such losses can include loss of privacy with the involvement of the coronial system to investigate the death and

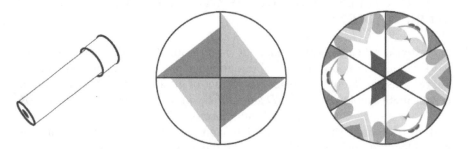

Figure 10.7 Kaleidoscope of practice
Source: Reproduced by permission of Suzanne Thornton.

loss of daily activities such as taking the dead child to school. The nature of sudden death, as Doka describes, can be associated with difficult grieving. Parkes (1972) explored the idea of determinants (risk factors) of grief outcome and identified the importance of the mode of death in terms of factors such as:

- 'Timeliness' in the expected order of life events.
- Opportunities to prepare for the death.
- Whether there was a need to hide feelings.

Many of these determinants occur with a child's sudden death. Similarly, grief following violent death, such as homicide, may affect family members' future relationships and provoke strong grief reactions, particularly when there is ongoing involvement of the criminal justice system when a case goes to trial several years after the death (e.g. Redmond 1996, Riches & Dawson 2000).

However, identifying risk factors for grief outcome does not mean that all people will experience responses such as anxiety, depression and physical illness (Wortman & Silver 2001). Evidence from a range of situations, which are not confined to sudden death of a child, indicates that grief is individual and that in many situations people find a way to adjust to death with support from family and friends (Parkes 2001).

BEREAVED PEOPLE ACTIVELY MAKING SENSE OF THEIR WORLD

The individuality of grief is described in recent sociological and psychological writing as people making sense of, or constructing meaning from, what is happening to them. This has been described as a new paradigm of grief (Neimeyer 2001). For example, Attig (2001, 34) proposed that grief is a 'transition from living in presence [of the deceased] to loving in absence', which involved people having to relearn their everyday world in every aspect such as:

- Physically, finding a way to continue to live in the physical space that was shared with the deceased or deciding to move house.
- Emotionally, feeling the pain of loss.
- Socially, managing responses from other people, either family members or others, who may not know how to acknowledge the loss.

This view is based on the premise that as individuals we construct the reality of our world based on our previous experiences, values and beliefs. It offers an explanation for the different meanings that can be held by different people about the same death (e.g. see Nadeau 2001). For example, Dean died aged eight years in a car accident. He has three older brothers in their twenties. Dean's death has a meaning for his mother, which is about the loss of her youngest child, who was an unexpected and much welcomed addition to their family. His father works overseas and has rarely seen Dean, which means that his loss includes grieving for a son that he did not know well. The question is how do parents grieve their loss and the different meanings it has for them?

Riches and Dawson (2000) reported findings from over 50 bereaved UK parents and siblings. Many of these deaths were sudden and included murder, suicide, accidental falls and air disaster. They concluded that: 'Bereaved people are active individuals, making choices as they deal with their experience of loss. Parents and siblings are not simply victims of circumstance' (p. 16). Instead, they use a combination of three resources to make sense of their experience:

- Personal: includes beliefs that might make sense of the death, learning from previous experiences and ability to acknowledge feelings.
- Social: includes roles, personal relationships and membership of groups which can provide support and a sense of identity.
- Cultural: includes norms such as beliefs and patterns of behaviour (e.g. relating to families, parental roles, grief and funerals – all of which provide a framework of an expected way to respond).

This is a reminder that whilst professionals are part of the social and cultural resources available to bereaved people, professionals cannot 'fix' another person's grief since this is also shaped by personal resources.

CULTURAL CONSTRUCTIONS OF GRIEF SHAPING PEOPLE'S EXPERIENCES

The importance of cultural constructions as a resource, and a constraint, for bereaved people should not be underestimated. The term 'culture' is commonly associated with ethnicity (e.g. Caucasian or Afro-Caribbean) and religion (e.g. Jewish or Hindu faith). Within the scope of this chapter we are unable to provide a discussion about the ways in which professionals might work with specific ethnic or religious groups. We suggest that whilst there are certain death practices and norms associated with a cultural group, many individuals within such groups have differing views. Consequently, there may be as much variation within a cultural group as between different cultural groups. We believe it is more effective to:

1. Ask bereaved people, 'What is appropriate for your beliefs with regard to . . .? [the funeral, post mortem, care of the child's body and so on]'.
2. Know how to access relevant resources and support people who are community leaders or skilled in working with a particular ethnic or religious group.

For the purposes of this discussion we have used 'culture' to indicate a group of people who have shared values and beliefs that determine everyday practices and activities. Thus a bereaved parent may live within a family culture, a workplace culture and the culture of the society or country within which they live. How does this help or hinder grief? We have selected three areas for comment.

GENDER

Do men and women grieve differently? There are differing interpretations. Some oft-cited studies indicate that maternal grief is more intense and long-lasting than paternal grief (e.g. Dyregrov & Matthiesen 1987, Lang & Gottlieb 1993). However, Finkbeiner's (1996) work with over 30 parents proposed that whilst the grief had similar depth, there were differences in the demonstration of feelings, which are largely determined by cultural expectations of gendered behaviour. Comments included in Rosenblatt's text describe this in different ways such as: 'Cause she's different and I'm different. And we're wired up differently . . . She's the kind that wants to be with somebody when she's feeling bad. I'm not. Just leave me alone' (Rosenblatt 2000, 146). This serves to remind us to avoid judgements; as one nurse wrote, 'I expected the father to be upset after his son was killed in a car crash. He said nothing, I was left feeling that he did not care, but later someone told me that was his way of coping.'

POPULAR AND PROFESSIONAL CULTURES OF GRIEF

Walter (1999) drew on the work of Wortman and Silver (1989) to describe the 'clinical lore' or the culture of health professionals. He proposed that normal grief was viewed as 'expressing your feelings, letting go and returning to emotional normality after a year or two' (p. 156) and abnormal grief was the opposite (of this). This view can shape what professionals say to people, such as 'you need to talk about your feelings'. Yet, not everyone wants to talk; as one mother said: 'I did not want to keep sifting over the entrails of my feelings with a load of strangers.' Just as there is a culture within which health professionals practice, so there is the overarching culture of British society, in which Walter proposed that 'popular guidelines' for grief exist. These include the notion of 'time-limited grief', which is apparent in comments such as: 'She is still crying and it is more than six months since he died.' Such a comment implies a norm that grief has aspects which should end within a certain time period. When such comments are made, bereaved family members may feel angry or hopeless that their grief is not being acknowledged; in effect their grief is being disenfranchised.

DISENFRANCHISED GRIEF

Disenfranchised grief occurs when there is a lack of support for a bereaved person because their bereavement is not valued or acknowledged (Doka 1989). The classic example is where parents who have had a miscarriage are told: 'Never mind, you can have another one.' This denies them the opportunity to be recognised publicly as grieving parents and represents the view that a miscarriage is commonplace. In many instances, fathers' or grandparents' grief may be disenfranchised when people ask: 'How is the mother of the child?' and never ask about how the father or grandparents are. Whether acknowledged by others or not, individuals continue to grieve. A well-known perspective is William Worden's work.

TASKS OF GRIEVING AND GRIEF WORK

Worden's (1991) classic text has been used widely by many health practitioners as a basis to plan their work with bereaved people. He proposed four tasks of grieving to:

- Accept the reality of the loss.
- Work through the pain of grief.
- Adjust to an environment in which the deceased is missing.
- Relocate the deceased emotionally and move on with life (pp. 10–16).

Implicit in Worden's tasks is the notion of concentrating on the loss in order to accept and then adjust, hence the importance of activities such as planning the funeral, which helps to make the death 'real'. However, working through the tasks of grieving does not necessarily mean continually concentrating on the death. A recent review concluded that there are some situations and people where avoidance, rather than confrontation, of the loss may have benefits (Stroebe 1992–3). Stroebe and Schut (1999, 2001) proposed the dual process model (DPM) based on research with Dutch widows and widowers, whereby grief involves two coping activities:

- Restoration-oriented coping concentrates on reorganising life within a world where roles and activities have changed (known as secondary losses). It includes altering daily routines such as no longer taking the deceased child to school, starting new activities and keeping busy in order to limit time and energy spent on loss-oriented coping. Mary Semel (McCracken & Semel 1998, 261) described how she tried to find a distracting activity after her child died in a car crash: 'I looked for things I could do that would bring relief, knowing full well it would be short lived, maybe lasting only an hour at a time. When I found something that worked, I indulged myself as much as I could. I thought of myself as finding stepping stones across a river of pain. Some of the things I tried were aerobics, swimming, yoga, tennis, writing and above all, good books.'

- Loss-oriented coping concentrates on the primary loss of the person and includes activities such as acknowledging feelings or creating a memory box. Marie described this: 'During the graveside ceremony, the rain was pouring down and I held this umbrella over the girls and me. This umbrella I will *never* use again but I have put it in a place I pass by most days, and I touch it and remember. I'm just leaving it there – that's "Ruby's umbrella"' (Stewart 2000, 273–4). As a model this offers an explanation of how people move back and forth between intense feelings and keeping going with everyday life. Professionals may find that it can offer insights to some family members about the ways in which they manage their grief. Equally, like other perspectives, it is not a universal explanation for the nature of grief.

GRIEF: ENDINGS OR CONTINUING BONDS?

Many professionals will be familiar with the stage/phase models which envisage grief as a trajectory from the time of death to a point of recovery (Parkes 1972), reorganisation (Bowlby 1980) or re-establishment (Rando 1986). As Walter (1999) points out, these writings have been interpreted as a prescription of how grief should be, rather than a description of how it is for many people. The consequence has been the development of expected norms such as the comment, 'Time heals; you will get over it', which many bereaved parents describe as insensitive since it can imply forgetting their child as opposed to finding a way of living with their death.

In the mid-1990s a range of research studies demonstrated a 'continuing bond' with the deceased, as opposed to an ending to the relationship, which was how the end points of the stage/phase grief models were often interpreted. Silverman and Nickman (1996) described this bond as 'the paradox of letting go and remaining involved' (p. 351) where there is a continuing sense of presence, memory or inner representation of the deceased (see also earlier discussion regarding Attig 2001). The implications for professionals are considerable, since the notion of continuing bonds emphasises the importance of enabling families (if they wish) to have tokens of remembrance, attend memorial services over many years, reminisce and talk about their dead child. However, rather than assuming that all people want to maintain a continuing bond, it is worth considering a study by McClowry et al. (1987) which involved the parents and siblings of children who died of cancer. Three patterns of grieving were identified:

- 'Filling the emptiness', which meant keeping busy and not focusing on the grief.
- 'Getting over it', where the death was accepted and life carried on.
- 'Keeping the connection', where family members sought to remember the child even whilst undertaking new activities.

This work, whilst nearly 20 years old, continues to provide a timely reminder of the diversity of ways in which people grieve.

SUMMARY

This section has provided 'information bytes' that we believe are useful in practice. As such, the 'bytes' need to be interpreted with an appreciation that:

- Perspectives are not absolute truths and cannot be generalised to all bereaved families.
- Different perspectives contribute to understanding the complexity of grief, like changing the focus of a camera to zoom in or out to look at different elements of the same picture.
- Research and practice illustrate the individuality of grief, hence one perspective may fit one person and not another.

The next section identifies strategies for practice which are underpinned by the experiences of family members and evidence from theoretical perspectives.

WORKING WITH BEREAVED FAMILIES

All professionals working with bereaved families have a range of skills and experience from their existing practice. These include: current expert discipline-specific knowledge, ability to communicate with others, empathy, working in multi-disciplinary teams and legislative or local policy requirements for documentation. These skills are invaluable when working with bereaved families. This section echoes some of the points in Chapter 1 and outlines strategies for practice during three time periods:

- At the time a child dies.
- In the first few weeks after the death.
- In the months and years after the death.

The diverse roles which readers of this book hold, ranging from a police officer to a Health Visitor, means that some information may not be applicable to some scopes of practice. For professionals involved in responding to unexpected child deaths, this chapter can be read in conjunction with Chapter 7.

In our 2004 text we proposed that professionals consider having three goals for their practice. These relate to the three time periods and are based on the experiences and perspectives of bereavement discussed in the previous sections:

1. Assisting family members to hear about and recognise the child's death at the time of death.

Practice includes telling about the death, offering information in terms of funerals or post mortems, listening to family members' shock and offering choices to see, touch and hold the child.

2. Assisting family members to find ways to cope with the losses that death brings in the weeks after the death.

   Practice includes listening to family members trying to make sense of what is happening and offering strategies to help them manage the secondary losses and stresses, e.g. changed routines or loss of privacy when media are involved.

3. Assisting family members to find ways to adjust to a new reality (in the months and years after the death).

   Practice includes listening to the ways in which families are making sense of the death within their own world view and helping them to find ways in which other bereaved people have responded.

So, what is the evidence available to determine best current practice with bereaved families? Studies report bereaved families experiencing different bereavement events, varying interventions and outcome measures with differing periods of follow-up, which precludes definitive statements about practice that can be applied to all people. In addition, Schut et al. (2001) questioned the assumption that 'bereavement interventions', such as counselling, are always beneficial. They concluded that:

1. Primary interventions aimed at all bereaved people showed no benefits for grief symptoms and outcomes, except possibly for children.
2. Secondary interventions for 'at-risk bereaved' showed marginal benefits in the short term.
3. Tertiary interventions for people experiencing complicated grief produced some beneficial and lasting results.

This supports Parkes' (2001) view that the majority of people grieve with the help of family and others without specialist interventions. Consequently, it appears that practice requires using core principles in order to respond to individuals' grief.

CORE PRINCIPLES FOR PRACTICE

We propose that professionals involved with bereaved families use some core principles to guide their practice. These are fundamental to practice in other situations and we have made only brief comments in relation to sudden death.

CARING provides an acronym (listed below) to help remember the principles but does not reflect the importance of particular activities. For example, 'getting in touch with ourselves' is central to being able to provide acknowledgement or recognition.

Careful listening
Acknowledgment
Recognising
Informing
Negotiating social support
Getting in touch with ourselves.

Careful listening takes many forms. Listening to family members is the central part of practice. The challenge for us, as professionals, is to learn to be quiet. What families say can help us to respond to their needs. One approach is to be willing to listen to the stories that people share. Stories can be a means by which many people make sense of what the bereavement means for them, their identity and their changed world. Stories occur when we link events together and help us understand the loss and change (Walter 1996). One father wrote, 'Each morning I wake up and wonder how I will continue breathing, and I do. I have to keep going over what happened, like a record going round and round, until I can get past the scratch that has torn across my life.' Stories can be short comments or lengthy narratives told to oneself, a journal or shared with others, such as family, friends and professionals.

Acknowledgment. After the death of their child, families emphasise the importance of having the death acknowledged. An opening introduction might be a short, 'I'm really sorry to hear about Mary's death. I don't know what to say. I am the police officer who went to the place of the car crash.' What counts is acknowledging the death, in contrast to making no comment or avoiding contact. One mother described her feelings: 'I felt so angry when the neighbours crossed the road rather than meet me face-to-face and my Health Visitor did not ring up until four weeks after his death.'

Recognising that family define who they are and what their needs are. This may include members who are not biologically related to the child, but have a significant place in the family. Professionals may need to suspend assumptions about who is a member of the family and avoid pre-judging their needs. For example, whilst a professional may feel that the family need to know what a post mortem involves, the parents might rather have the opportunity to sit with their dead child as part of accepting the reality, before hearing about the word 'post mortem'.

Informing includes making sure that families have information that is relevant and appropriate to the situation. This requires knowing about current and local practices and resources. 'What will happen next is . . .' 'You can organise a funeral after the coroner's investigation . . .' 'The people who will contact you are . . .'. The quote from the mother who described being in a fog highlights the need to repeat information at different time points since people in shock may be unable to concentrate or remember. The amount of information offered needs to be tempered to avoid overload yet be sufficient for families to have choices. This can mean encouraging them to take time before making decisions about the funeral: 'It can be all right to wait a few days; it doesn't have to be decided now.'

It is important to allow time to listen and talk about information and not to undertake the 'drop and run' approach, as one mother called it. After her son died, the general practitioner came to visit for an hour, talked to her about grief, left some information leaflets and told her where she could contact a self-help group. She felt the written information was dropped in without the chance for her to ask questions. This equally applies to children – it can seem that reading them a book about death and grief may be 'doing what is needed' but without the chance to ask questions in the days that follow, children can have that same feeling of being 'left hanging'. Similarly, it may be useful to remind families of the variable quality of resources on the Internet, which can create support or distress for some family members according to their needs and interests. Such resources include music for funerals, funeral service plans, online memorials, books of remembrance/condolence, chatrooms, online counselling, and parent and professional texts about grief (see Appendices 6 & 7).

Negotiating social support means ensuring that family members have access to social support from friends, family, self-help groups and statutory agencies. For example, 'Do you have anyone you would like to sit with you?' and 'Would you like to talk to another bereaved parent?' Family members can then choose how they use such support, if available. Schut (Gray 2005) provides an important reminder that the involvement of professionals can be seen as a sign by extended family and friends that their services and support are not needed, so they withdraw. One option, having first checked that this is what the parents want, is to hold a meeting with, or individually contact, key family members and friends to talk about how they can support each other and the parents. Key points for those who would like to offer help are the same as for professionals – listen, acknowledge, share ideas and offer practical help such as cooking, cleaning or looking after siblings. To help grandparents help the parents, Kolf (1995, 21–22) used the acronym of being a PAL, which is equally relevant for friends and other family members:

Presence is about physically being there with the parents.
Assistance is practical help.
Listening whenever needed to parents talking through their 'tapes of grief',
    where the same story or feelings are repeated again and again.

Getting in touch with or knowing oneself is a reminder of the obvious fact that working with bereaved families requires us, as professionals, to be alongside people in life-changing moments of distress. The experience inevitably touches each of us as a person and it can raise questions and strong feelings about 'What if it was my child?', 'What is the purpose of my life?' and 'How can life be so unfair?' Knowing and recognising these responses can enable us to listen to people's world views rather than imposing our own beliefs on their experience. As Riches and Dawson (2000, 184) noted, '. . . some of the land-scape the bereaved parent or sibling inhabits may seem familiar to us, and we may think the maps we already possess might help in guiding them through this territory. But it is their journey, not ours, that has to be travelled.' Respect for individuals means suspending judgements and expectations, which can be particularly difficult when a family member was involved in the events leading to the child's death, such as the carer for a child admitted with intentional physical injuries.

AROUND THE TIME OF DEATH

This time period covers moments such as attempts to resuscitate, telling about the death and planning the funeral. When a criminal investigation is undertaken for homicide, the funeral may be delayed. Space precludes discussion of points relevant to all the various ways in which children can die suddenly – where possible, we have highlighted some specific considerations.

TELLING OF THE DEATH

Families may have been absent, or present, when their child died. In any situation there is no easy way to tell families that their child is dead. Many parents remember the experience in vivid detail for many years. The aim has to be to tell them as soon as possible after the death in a clear, honest and compassionate manner. Lessons that professionals can learn from parents include the following:

- Being specific and using the word 'dead', not euphemisms of 'lost' or 'passed away'.
- Using the child's name: 'I am sorry to tell you that Mary is dead'.
- Recognising the unreality of this news and repeating the information as needed.
- Being able to answer questions about the circumstances of the death if parents were not present (e.g. who, what and when it happened).
- Considering the meanings that words have for parents. Lord (1997) noted that families may prefer 'car crash' in situations where it was the result of drink-driving, rather than 'road traffic accident', which implies an unintentional accident. Similarly, with homicide, has the child died or been 'killed' or 'murdered'?
- Planning for families' need to disbelieve the news and to see and touch their child. Mary Semel (McCracken & Semel 1998, 3–4) wrote about this when her son Allie died:

'We get out of the car and people in uniforms approach.
"Your son is deceased."
Deceased? I don't understand. What does this mean, deceased?
I gather myself. I have to get to Allie. I have to be with my son.
They try to restrain me. I insist. The blue car is wrapped around a tree.
Under a tarp, two slender bodies stretch side by side.'

TELLING CHILDREN ABOUT THE DEATH

Telling parents also means supporting them when they give the news to other
family members, including their surviving children. Informing children depends
on their developmental level and understanding of the concept of death.
Giving news of sudden death can be very difficult. Ideally, siblings should be
told by their parents, but if they are too overwhelmed then this responsibility
may fall to a professional. If possible, the news should be given in a quiet place.
To begin the conversation, a professional may prepare a child by saying they
have some bad news to tell them. Providing a brief but accurate description
of what happened may help to reinforce the reality.

Davies (1999, 42, adapted) suggests an acronym of CHILD to guide
professionals:

Consider the child's age, developmental level and capacity to understand
  thoughts and feelings.
Honesty. Telling the truth as completely as possible, though simply, is crucial,
  using the word 'death' so that the child is not confused. Only simple answers
  and explanations are needed, saying 'I don't know' when appropriate.
Encourage parents to **involve** children in family discussions and choices
  as much as possible. Even young children can be involved with the
  funeral by drawing a picture of their sibling, or writing their feelings and
  thoughts.
Listen. Allow children to talk of their feelings and thoughts rather then
  rushing in with reassurance and complicated information. Be attuned to
  magical thinking in younger children.
Do it over and over again. Remind parents that children may need to be
  told frequently about the death, especially as they develop and gain new
  understanding and insights.

Each child will react differently. Younger children, who have not fully understood the meaning of death, may show no visible sign of sadness and may
continue normally; others may attempt to gain some control by finding soli-
tude to let go of their feelings in private. It is important that parents are prepared to offer constant comfort to the child, reassure them that they are loved
and answer questions that may appear bald and direct, such as 'Can I have his
toys now he is dead?'

WHAT NEXT?

Amidst the shock and crisis that sudden death brings is inevitably the question, 'What happens next?' For many parents, the question is, 'Can I see or be with my child?' Professionals need to be able to indicate clearly what events will follow for the families and child and what choices they have to be with and see their child in the next few hours or days. For example, in the following situations:

- If an apparently well baby dies suddenly at home then this will require coronial investigation. What does this mean?
- If the child was murdered, what will the police do next? Who will be the police liaison person? What media coverage might there be?
- If the child was killed in a car crash, what happens next in terms of who was responsible?
- In a range of situations, will a post mortem be required? If so, what does this involve? Who does it? What information can it provide? Do parents have any choice about it? When will it be done and when will the findings be made known?
- If a baby dies soon after birth, for example because of an unexpected congenital abnormality, then their birth needs to be registered, often at the same time as registering the death. How is this done?
- After a death is registered there can be a funeral – how is this organised and what do families need to do?

Professionals will be aware of many of the answers to these specific questions according to the role that they hold. Relevant information in this text includes responding to unexpected deaths (Chapter 7), police role in unexpected deaths (Chapter 8) and paediatric post mortem (Chapter 9). Appendix 8 contains information on:

- registering births and deaths
- involvement of the coroner
- post mortems
- organising a funeral.

Families also need to know what social support is available to them from statutory and non-government agencies such as The Compassionate Friends and Victim Support. It is useful to offer families some, but not an overwhelming amount of information on grief and local support (see Appendix 12). The professional who then follows up with the family can discuss the options. Some people will appreciate the information, as one mother said, 'It seems odd but I read all the information they gave me the day she died. I needed to find out everything about grief and people and groups. It was my way of coping.' Equally, a father said, 'They gave us pamphlets and I never looked at them. It was the people who came to see us that got us through this.'

BEING WITH THEIR CHILD

Being with their child can take different forms for different families. It can include physical and spiritual care for the child as a member of the family. Some examples of this are included in Appendix 9, with a discussion of hand-prints and photographs in Appendix 10. These activities can help parents grasp that the death has occurred. Depending on the nature of the death, the opportunities which families want may or may not be available. For example, opportunities to wash their child will not initially be available during a homicide inquiry or prior to a post mortem. Many people have never seen a dead body before, therefore it is critical that a professional prepares bereaved family members for their child's appearance (e.g. colour, trauma to body parts and cold skin that is firm to touch if the body is stored in a mortuary) and stays with them when they first see their child.

COMMUNICATION AND REFERRAL

In the past few years, the number of voluntary services available to work with bereaved families, particularly bereaved children, has grown significantly. Therefore we would hope that that there is ongoing support for families. The Every Child Matters policy (HM Government 2003) identifies lead profession-als to co-ordinate a range of services involved with a child or family and we perceive the value of such a strategy after the death of a child in order to ensure an integrated response. For example, whichever professional informs the parents about the death needs to ensure that the parents know who will contact them in the forthcoming days and who they can contact.

All professionals involved with families need to ensure that the relevant documentation is completed to inform other agencies about the death. This underpins a multi-agency approach to child mortality and ensures that inappropriate reminders about the death are avoided, for example a hospital outpatient appointment being sent four weeks after a child died.

IN THE WEEKS AND MONTHS AFTER THE DEATH

The purpose of contact during this time is to assist family members to find ways to cope with the losses that death brings, leading on to finding ways to adjust to a new reality.

GETTING THROUGH EACH DAY

In the following weeks, many parents describe the struggle of getting through each day when they feel such pain, confusion and exhaustion. All family members experience the hourly shifting balance between loss-oriented coping (e.g. crying and feeling sad and purposeless) and restoration-oriented coping (e.g. doing the washing, moving house and taking the children to school). Marnie said: 'Three weeks on and I was crying and crying, Tom said nothing and the children were unsettled, clingy and quiet. Six weeks on I stopped crying all the time, I had periods when I could think straight and I decided to wallpaper the lounge. I did one wall, and then I sat down and howled. That was how it was. I got the energy to do a bit, think about other things and then suddenly I would be overwhelmed again.' As time goes on, some of the immediate emotional and physical responses diminish (e.g. tiredness or insomnia) and for many family members it is about feeling alone on their grieving journey as other family members respond differently to them.

The principles of the CARING acronym continue to be useful, in particular remembering to acknowledge the child. Marnie said sadly that, 'After three months no one asked me how I was feeling. I felt like I should be "over it" and what I really wanted was for people to say her name, and then I could talk about her.'

CONTRACT OF CARE

Any professional who provides ongoing support needs to have identified the purpose of visiting and we find it helps to establish a 'contract of care' with family members at the first follow-up visit. This includes explaining that:

- Bereavement support is finite, and ends when they no longer need it.
- The purpose of visits is for the professional to listen, assess needs, offer suggestions for coping, and ensure access to resources and referrals as needed.
- The frequency of visits may be weekly to start with and extend to monthly with additional telephone contact.
- Duration of visits is generally one hour to allow the parent and professional to concentrate and then have a respite.

The professional's focus is assessment of the situation based on the parents' description of events and their responses, combined with observation. A range of assessment tools are available (see Raphael 1984, Rando 1986, Worden 1991). We have included a tool in Appendix 11 which was evaluated with favourable comment from UK Health Visitors in a randomised trial (Dent 2002). The tool provides a framework with which to plan visits and organise information. It is based on the premise that death brings a range of stressors and that professionals can assist family members to use personal and social resources to help them adjust (see Riches & Dawson 2000). The framework is not a checklist but it alerts professionals to the needs that the family member identifies or is experiencing. It may take a number of visits to ask all of the questions in the framework. A case study is included in Appendix 11 to illustrate how the framework might be used.

HOW CAN PROFESSIONALS ASSIST FAMILIES TO COPE WITH THEIR CHILD'S DEATH?

Individual family members have to find their way of coping and living with their bereavement because no one else can do it. As we discussed in the first section of this chapter, grief involves feelings, physical responses and a cognitive reconstructing of how people see themselves and the world they live in. Professionals can encourage, support, suggest and in some instances refer for expert counselling. Along the way, there are a number of suggestions which may assist some people in coping. Three useful phrases in this process are:
'How?', 'I wonder if . . .' and 'How can I help?'

'How?'

The former enables us to find out about people's current experience – it is like an oil gauge. 'How are you feeling?' It is particularly important to start with the person you are addressing before extending to the rest of the family: 'How is your partner/daughter/mother feeling?' Many fathers comment that they are rarely asked how they feel or 'How are you doing?' Frequently, they hear the message that the mother's grief is recognised and that they are placed in a support role. 'How . . .?' is also a valuable tool to gauge coping strategies and issues of importance. For example, the answer to questions such as 'How has it been since you tried eating breakfast every day?' and 'How did it go on the first day back at work?' can mean that people have a chance to talk if they wish and help professionals identify resources that might be of use. This can lead on to the next phrase.

'I wonder if . . .'

The purpose of this phrase is to avoid assumptions about others' experiences and yet to be able to offer gently either new interpretations or strategies that might assist them. Instead of asking 'Have you tried . . .?', which requires a yes/no answer – or the normalising statement 'Grief generally means people are tired' – the use of 'I wonder if . . .' suggests that people can consider and then use or reject. It can be prefaced in an early meeting explaining the professional's role, as: 'One of the things I can offer is to make some suggestions when I wonder if they may help. You can then choose to use or leave them – just whatever feels best for you.' There is a range of ideas drawn from research, stories and practice, which may help adults at some time in their grief, listed in Box 10.1.

Finally, a more direct question can at times help family members identify how professionals can assist.

'How can I help?'

This phrase can enable the bereaved person to have both a sense of choice and control, rather than feeling passive with professionals taking a directive

Box 10.1 Strategies that bereaved family members may find useful[5]

Trying different coping strategies, such as

- Learning to balance physical activity and keeping busy with times of being quiet and sad.
- Stating to people when it would be good to see them or not see them.
- Setting small goals to be achieved before moving on to the next, like getting a meal ready, then going to the supermarket, and then going back to work.

Caring for self and others physically

Eating, resting and if possible, sleeping regularly. When this is hard to maintain, try using strategies such as a star chart, where a star is stuck on the chart for each meal that is eaten and for having gone to bed by an agreed time. When an agreed number of stars are achieved there is an agreed reward, such as an activity, book or meal out.

Gaining new meanings about grief, death and life

For some people this may include:

- Reading poetry, stories of other bereaved families and self-help texts on grief.
- Joining local bereavement groups or online chatrooms to hear from and talk with others who have had a similar event in their lives.
- Becoming involved in spiritual or community activities.
- Using creativity (such as gardening, drawing, poetry and fashion) as a means to express and explore feelings and ideas.
- Using images and metaphors of grief (such as waterfall, journey or pool).
- Trying a personal statement or mantra e.g. 'take each day at a time' and 'keep breathing'.
- Focusing on a soothing or meaningful photograph, view or piece of music.

Creating rituals

Christmas, Mothers' Day and Fathers' Day, birthdays, death days or other milestones, which might involve activities with other people. These can include planting a tree, having a cake, playing a piece of music, writing a poem, writing in a journal, lighting a candle, and releasing a balloon with a letter attached.

---

[5] In Stroebe and Schut's (2001) framework these strategies combine restoration and loss-oriented coping.

Creating personal and family mementoes

This might include making:

- A memory box with selected items from the child's life, such as scan photographs during pregnancy, birth and death certificates, items of clothing, photographs, favourite toys, drawings from siblings, and foot and hand prints.
- A personal Web page.
- A DVD with photographs, meaningful poems and music accompanied by reflections.

Making a public memorial

This might include writing in a memorial book, whether in a church, funeral parlour, on an online website, planting a tree, having a headstone or commemorative plaque made, creating a scholarship for a school, sponsoring research, and funding equipment for a playschool or a seat bench in a favourite spot.

role. It can also help them to analyse what is important to them. In many instances, the answer is, 'There is nothing you can do, but what helps is listening to me, because a lot of people do not want to hear about her death.'

HOW CAN PROFESSIONALS HELP SUPPORT BEREAVED CHILDREN?

We believe that professionals providing follow-up support have a key role in supporting parents to help their children. Key principles for professionals and family members are to:

- Be honest.
- Use words that can be understood.
- Be prepared to 'drip feed' information in a way that allows children to build up their understanding. Be prepared to answer questions that may seem blunt and direct, such as: 'Now he is dead, can I have his room?'

There is a wide range of resources now available for bereaved children that are suited to different ages and which include self-help groups, phone lines, texting, emails, videos, books and group and individual counselling. These can be of assistance to different children at different times. It is beyond the scope of this chapter to discuss these in detail. Resources are listed in Appendix 6, where a number of texts are listed, suited to different ages and deaths. For example, Crossley and Stokes (2001) produced a text for Winston's Wish, which is aimed at supporting a child who has been bereaved by suicide. They provide a strategy that could be used by children or adults after any death. Choose three small stones that can be held, looked at and handled regularly:

- A smooth pebble, to remind of everyday memories of [name], like their favourite food.
- A sharp rock, to remind of difficult times with [name] when we argued or they cried a lot.
- A polished gemstone, to remind of special, happy memories with [name], like the picnic at the sea last year.

Monroe and Kraus (2005) provide a useful overview for professionals in *Brief Interventions with Bereaved Children*. It includes chapters on family assessment; the role of schools and groups; and examples of working with children after suicide, traumatic death and witness to murder or accident. The Child Bereavement Network has produced a belief statement which can help guide practitioners (Appendix 12), and Willis (2005) describes the work of CBN further.

LIVING WITH BEREAVEMENT AS TIME PASSES

As time progresses, generally fewer professionals have contact with the family for reasons other than those associated with the death of their child, such as bereavement support. This can differ in circumstances where criminal justice investigations continue over a period of years.

DIFFICULT DEATHS AND COMPLICATED GRIEF

Many deaths described in this book are sudden or violent, which can make it hard for grievers to make sense of, or see any sense of meaning in, the death (Riches & Dawson 2000). Riches and Dawson proposed that such deaths were 'difficult' to grieve because of:

- The lack of support from others as a result of stigma, shame or uncertainty associated with the death.
- An inability to undertake everyday activities because of feelings of anger, confusion, frustration or a desire for revenge.

Hence, bereaved families are dislocated and their grief disenfranchised. How can professionals help? The core principles of listening, acknowledging, visiting and ensuring that there is someone in regular contact are vital. The role of the visiting professional may vary according to local areas and resources. For example, Ellison (2005) describes the role of the Family Services Liaison Office in the Metropolitan Police Services in updating families on the progress of criminal investigations. Professionals need to be aware that some family members may experience depression, post-traumatic stress disorder (PTSD) or complicated grief. It is beyond the scope of this chapter to discuss these (see Rando 1993, Figley 1996, Hindmarch 2000). However, we make brief mention of complicated grief, for which there is evidence from Schut et al. (2001) that referral for specialist interventions can improve outcomes. Rando defines complicated grief as:

- To deny, repress or avoid aspects of the loss, its pain and the full realisation of its implications for the mourner; and
- To hold onto and avoid relinquishing the lost loved one (Rando 1996, 142).

Prigerson (2005) concludes that complicated grief has a basis in attachment, and that it is characterised by disbelief, yearning and difficulty moving on, which differentiates it from both depression (characterised by sadness) and PTSD (characterised by avoidance, horror and fear). As she describes, 'those with complicated grief resemble vehicles inextricably stuck in the morass of mourning, wheels spinning, going over and over in their minds the events that led up to the death. . . . The road to recovery and readjustment has ended in a swamp' (p. 38). Her article offers sample questions to identify complicated grief, defined as evidence of symptoms for a minimum of six months, in the areas of:

- 'yearning/longing/heartache and four of the following:
- trouble accepting the death
- inability to trust others
- excessive bitterness or anger related to the death
- uneasy about moving on
- numbness/detachment
- feeling life is empty or meaningless without deceased
- bleak future
- agitated' (p. 39).

For the purposes of this chapter, which is a resource for professionals who provide support to families and who are not specialists in the field of grief, we encourage professionals to:

- Feel confident in their ability to provide support and acknowledgement to bereaved families.
- Talk with colleagues about their practice in order to confirm activities and decisions.
- Be mindful that many sudden deaths are difficult and to seek assistance if either they, or a family member or the person themselves, have a concern about the intensity and form of a person's grief over time, whether it might be depression, complicated grief or PTSD. See also Hindmarch (2000, 132–4), who provides an example on clarifying the meaning of suicidal statements and Figley (1996) for an overview of traumatic death treatment and resources.

ADJUSTING TO THE DEATH

Over time, many family members find ways, with the support of friends and family, to move beyond the swamp that Prigerson describes and to live with their child's sudden death. 'I think [we've changed to] sort of live life to the fullest, really enjoy things. We're probably more day-to-day people than we were before . . . The thing that we got, which we think is important . . . it's . . . just enjoy the intensity of life' (Rosenblatt 2000, 195). Mary said five years after Kirsty's death: 'I would never wish for this to have happened to me or anyone. It has changed how I see the world. I try and help others and I take a part of her with me wherever I go. It was one of the reasons that I went to train as a nurse.'

Many parents actively seek to remember their child at significant times, like the anniversaries of their birth and death, and significant milestones such as the age when they would have gone to school or university. Pip's comment about 'remembering to remember' (Stewart 2000, 274) is an important contribution which grandparents make, such as phoning on an anniversary or asking, 'I wonder what he would have looked like now? He would be 14 this year.' Other children as they grow up may ask, 'What happened when she died?' Telling the story or looking at photographs can be how families keep a continuing bond with their child. These occur within the family without the involvement of people in a professional role.

However, when professionals come into the lives of families months and years after a child's death and as time progresses, they may not initially know about the death and the importance it holds. This includes situations such as caring for a family in a subsequent pregnancy, or working with a family where another child becomes ill or a family member dies. Just as the ripple of bereavement goes out to touch the lives of different people, so the effect of a child's death goes on over time. The focus of this chapter is not on these situations, but Figure 10.2 is a useful reminder to professionals to be aware of such situations, which can challenge a family's adjustment to the death. The same strategies of listening, acknowledging and offering time and support are still relevant.

AND FINALLY, THE COST OF CARING FOR PROFESSIONALS

When a child dies, all professionals have a range of coping skills to deal with the emotional demands of working with families, but it is unrealistic to expect carers to handle such challenging demands through coping skills alone. We cannot bring a child back to life, which is what is most wanted, so we have to fall back on what little we have to offer. Caring is one of our most important resources; a way of being and a state of natural responsiveness to others. All of us, however skilled, have the potential to be affected when exposed to dying and death. Space limits a detailed discussion on caring for ourselves – for further information see Dent & Stewart (2004) – thus the acronym BALANCE offers some reminders about this:

Be aware of your own limitations.
Access support and supervision to meet *your* needs.
Look after yourself physically, emotionally and spiritually.
Advance your learning by reading widely and talking to others.
Notice any changes in sleep, eating and mood patterns and *take action*.
Cherish yourself – you are special!
Energise yourself by taking regular exercise.

CONCLUSION

The ideas we have proposed in this chapter do not offer a recipe for working with bereaved families. We encourage professionals to feel confident about using strategies and frameworks of grief, such as those we have outlined, as part of the toolkit of their existing practice in order to work with individuals' experiences of grief.

ACKNOWLEDGEMENTS AND DEDICATION

This chapter is dedicated to the families of children who have died suddenly. We acknowledge:

Families and colleagues with whom we have had the privilege to work and who have taught us so much.
Suzanne Thornton for her creative diagrams.

III Learning Lessons

11 Reviewing Child Deaths

MARTIN WARD PLATT

The publication of the Children Act 2004 and subsequent guidance in *Working Together to Safeguard Children* (HM Government 2004a, 2006b) set the scene for new processes for responding to and learning from childhood deaths. Evidence from the US and elsewhere suggests that formal review processes such as this may lead to the development of interventions to prevent future child deaths (Gellert et al. 1995, Onwuachi-Saunders et al. 1999, Durfee et al. 2002, Rimsza et al. 2002, Bunting & Reid 2005) in a process analogous to the lessons that are learnt in this country through, for example, the confidential enquiry into maternal deaths (CEMACH 2004).

Drawing on this experience, Local Safeguarding Children Boards (LSCBs) are expected to put in place procedures to review all childhood deaths in a systematic way. *Working Together* defined the LSCB functions in this respect as collecting and analysing information about each death with a view to identifying: (i) any case giving rise to the need for a review mentioned in regulation 5(1)(e); (ii) any matters of concern affecting the safety and welfare of children in the area of the authority; and (iii) any wider public-health or safety concerns arising from a particular death or from a pattern of deaths in that area. This chapter will discuss different historical approaches to child death reviews, then focus on the purpose, process and potential outcomes from the child death review process which is to be implemented in England and Wales.

EXISTING APPROACHES TO CHILD DEATH REVIEW TEAMS

There are many ways in which deaths can be reviewed, some of them very ancient. The coroner system in England, for instance, dates back to 1194; however, the system of coroner's inquests that we have at the start of the 21st century is only one possible way of establishing the circumstances leading to death. It is reserved for those that are sudden, unexpected, accidental or suspicious, or where there is no clear medical explanation. Coroners have wide discretion over the manner in which they undertake their functions, including

Unexpected Death in Childhood: A Handbook for Practitioners. Edited by P. Sidebotham and P. Fleming.
Copyright © 2007 by John Wiley & Sons, Ltd.

the possible use of a jury; a coroner and jury form a kind of death review team. At the time of writing, the system is about to be reformed extensively.

Another type of child death review is the Serious Case Review system (also know as a 'Part 8' enquiry under the Children Act 1989). This is used by Local Safeguarding Children Boards – and was formerly used by Area Child Protection Committees – for cases in which serious harm or death has befallen a child and abuse or neglect are known or suspected to be a factor in the death. The purpose of these serious case reviews is to:

- Establish whether there are lessons to be learnt from the case about the way in which local professionals and agencies work together to safeguard children.
- Identify clearly what those lessons are, how they will be acted upon, and what is expected to change as a result and as a consequence.
- Improve inter-agency working and better safeguard children.

The method for conducting this review is that a single person in each agency conducts interviews with the parties from their agency who had dealings with the case, scrutinises the relevant documentation and writes a report based on their findings: the management review. An independent chairperson then writes an overview report based on those from each agency. The process may require a large amount of work and take a long time: the Serious Case Review on Ian Huntley, who committed the Soham murders, ran to sixty pages (Kelly 2004). Serious Case Reviews are scrutinised by a Serious Case Review Committee with multi-agency membership, responsible to the Local Safeguarding Children Board. Details of the Serious Case Review process are set out in Chapter 8 of *Working Together* (HM Government 2006b) and are covered in Chapter 12 of this book. It is important to recognise that these reviews are not enquiries into how a child died or who is culpable and that holding a Serious Case Review does not negate the need for wider child death review processes.

Health-care organisations normally conduct reviews of serious clinical incidents, using a small panel of people with the relevant expertise under the clinical governance procedures that are defined by the organisation. These are referred to in various different ways, such as 'Critical Incident Review' or 'Formal Case Review'. They may use techniques such as root cause analysis to uncover the underlying system failures, if any, that led to the incident; and they are (or should be) conducted in a spirit of systems analysis and collective learning. They are the antithesis of the older 'name, shame and blame' culture that used to be the pervasive model, and are regarded as the best means for obtaining organisational learning and a more open culture of safety than used to exist. These teams have much in common with, and may even be identical to, the individual case discussions that are described later.

The confidential enquiry systems in the UK use either experts reviewing anonymised cases independently and subsequently collating their views (as in the maternal deaths enquiry), or bringing together a panel of relevant experts to scrutinise a series of cases (as in the Confidential Enquiry into Stillbirths and Deaths in Infancy, or CESDI). In this system, a panel is another kind of review team: it is highly objective because the institution, the patient and the professionals concerned are all unknown to the assessment panel; however, the very fact of the anonymity means that there can be no direct feedback of findings to the institution concerned. Findings may be aggregated and presented in reports that pick out themes. Confidential enquiry teams have something in common with the 'high-level' child death review teams that are discussed later.

It can therefore be seen that the scrutiny of child deaths by teams of people is not a new concept. The vision of *Working Together* is that the process will be mandatory, formalised and to some extent unified.

CHILD DEATH REVIEW IN THE UNITED STATES

Most of the recent work specifically on child death review (CDR, also some-times referred to as child fatality review, CFR) has taken place in the US. The early systems were set up in Los Angeles, North Carolina and Oregon in 1978, with the specific remit of trying to identify fatalities that might have been linked to child abuse. Over the next decade or more the practice spread across many states and was given further impetus by the publication of an influential study from Missouri into the under-ascertainment of abuse as a factor in child death (Ewigman et al. 1993). Subsequently, the focus was predominantly on child abuse and preventable accidents, but in recent years states have been encouraged to undertake reviews of all child deaths. Further details, including a history of child death reviews and the various models used, can be found at www.childdeathreview.org, a site maintained by the Michigan Public Health Institute.

For the most part, the review process in the US is undertaken by an expert panel using written material collated from all the relevant agencies. Because of the diverse methods for case review that have developed *ad hoc* across the US, the American Academy of Pediatrics (AAP) has published a set of recom-mendations relating to the investigation of child deaths (Kairys et al. 1999). The AAP gives the following rationale for these reviews:

- quality assurance of death investigation at local levels
- enhanced inter-agency co-operation
- improved allocation of limited resources
- better epidemiologic data on the causes of death
- improved accuracy of death certificates.

These may now be seen as rather too narrow a view from a UK perspective. However, in the US, these reviews have led to major public awareness cam-paigns related to child safety in the home, in cars and in public facilities, for which there is an increasing body of evidence of effectiveness (Arizona Child Fatality Review Team 1999, Onwuachi-Saunders et al. 1999).

THE CESDI/SUDI STUDY AND THE KENNEDY REPORT

In the study of sudden unexpected death in infancy, run by the Confidential Enquiry into Stillbirth and Death in Infancy (CESDI: the CESDI/SUDI study), there was a stage of local case review that drew on the persons actually involved in the care of the child, as well as a subsequent anonymised confidential enquiry panel (Fleming et al. 2000). This local review panel provided the model promoted in the Kennedy report recommendations (Royal College of Pathologists & Royal College of Paediatrics and Child Health 2004) and is the basis of the 'low level' (individual case discussion) model for child death review discussed later.

However, it is important to realise how the world has changed in the decade or so since the CESDI/SUDI study. In particular, health-care institutions in the UK have developed sophisticated risk management systems, central to which is a recognition that the 'name, shame and blame' culture is the antithesis to effective risk management; and that an open, honest and transparent review of untoward incidents (including deaths), that is based on individual and organisational learning, is the best way to enable incidents to be analysed and learned from. Confidential enquiries, by contrast, were born of a fear of litigation that was part of the climate of professional discomfort of open discussion of incidents. This situation was commonplace in the 1980s and early 1990s. There may still be a place for confidential enquiry, especially since it can provide complete impartiality. However, the modern view is that effective local-learning can only take place in a climate of openness; and the persons best placed to contribute to, and learn from, a case review are those who actually participated in the care of the person who died. Indeed, the educational value of participating in an enquiry panel – even a confidential one – has been shown to be immense (Rankin et al. 2006).

For the purpose of reviewing unexpected child deaths, either the Kennedy model, or that of formal case review within a clinical governance framework, is arguably the most fit for purpose. However, the Kennedy model cannot be used exactly as it stands, since it was developed for the review of sudden unexpected deaths in infancy: it requires considerable modification in terms of its composition if it is to encompass the diversity of deaths in older children.

LEVELS OF CHILD DEATH REVIEW

In a 'low-level' review or individual case discussion, the participants are those with direct knowledge of the child and family, and the events surrounding the death. In contrast, in a 'high-level' review, or child death overview panel, the panel consists of a team without direct knowledge of the child, the family or the incident: this enables them to take a more objective view of individual case discussions, synthesise the emerging themes, sanction as appropriate any recommendations, and make recommendations of their own. In using the term 'child death review team' it is therefore important to be clear about the level at which a review team is functioning and the remits of the low-level and high-level teams respectively. In the sections following, the concepts of 'low-level' and 'high-level' review teams are enlarged upon, focusing on their remits and composition.

LOW-LEVEL REVIEW (INDIVIDUAL CASE DISCUSSIONS)

Low-level child death review is, essentially, the process of individual case discussion that is referred to in paragraph 7.43 of *Working Together* (HM Government 2006b), the review process referred to in Kennedy (Royal College of Pathologists & Royal College of Paediatrics and Child Health 2004, Section 8), and that of formal case review within a health service clinical governance framework. It has the following purposes:

- share oral information not captured in written records
- provide a 'safe' environment for participants to speak frankly
- analyse all of the circumstances
- agree the most likely causal and contributory factors
- detect any system errors
- examine the role of any agencies with responsibility for the child
- identify lessons to be learnt
- agree steps in relation to child protection if necessary
- plan appropriate support for the family.

The process of carrying out an individual case discussion following an unexpected death is outlined in Chapter 7 and a proforma is provided in Appendix 13. This particular model has been developed for the purposes of responding to a sudden unexpected death in infancy. Extending the same principles to unexpected deaths in older children, or to those deaths that were perhaps expected deaths, may require some modification of the basic format. Nevertheless, the same principles should hold, that as well as clarifying the cause or causes of death, these reviews are able to look at wider aspects of the circumstances surrounding the death and factors that may have contributed; to address the ongoing needs of the family; and to provide support to the professionals involved.

Which deaths should be reviewed? Those that are sudden, those that are unexpected and those that are 'unnatural' – broadly the same classes of death that would be the subject of a coroner's inquiry – are the most obvious candidates for review. This is clear from the North American experience, and it is also the intention of *Working Together*. 'Accidents' are rarely so random and unavoidable that no lessons can be learnt from them; it has been suggested that the very term be abandoned (Davis & Pless 2001). Sudden infant deaths also come under this heading.

However, low level CDR should arguably take place for all deaths, irrespective of their apparent inevitability or the severity of the medical condition that gave rise to them. This is because there are always quality issues to be examined, even in the most natural and unpreventable deaths. Deaths of children who die from malignant diseases, other predictably lethal diseases and congenital anomalies, and deaths in babies who never leave hospital (mostly, but not exclusively, premature babies) all benefit from review. There will always be questions about the extent to which family support needs were met, the quality of terminal care and aspects of symptom management. There are decisions to be taken in relation to supporting the family after the death. And the teams best placed to carry out CDR for such children are those who looked after them; they are the persons with the necessary specialist expertise to do this and the ones who will be providing continuing support for the family.

ADMINISTRATIVE SUPPORT FOR CDR

The chairperson (see below) should not be responsible for setting up either a low-level or a high-level CDR meeting. This administrative task is nonetheless crucial and the choice of the people who undertake it will be an important factor in the success or failure of the CDR process. The quality and effectiveness of the meeting will depend to some extent on the amount of written documentation that can be made available to the team, because it is never possible to bring together all of the professionals who could possibly contribute verbally, and their written materials have to be the substitute.

The timing of an individual case discussion is important. It should be held as soon as possible after the death, as the further away from events you go, the more likely it is that information will be lost or critical issues neglected. This needs to be balanced against the requirements of any ongoing investigation to ensure that all relevant information, including the results of any post-mortem investigations, are known to the team. For SUDI cases, the case discussion will normally take place two to three months after the death. As soon as possible after the death, a date should be set after discussion with the key professionals involved, including the police and coroner, to ensure that the process will complement rather than conflict with any coronial inquiry or police investigation.

Where death has occurred in hospital, or the child is under a clinical team, the organisation of the review can most sensibly be undertaken by that team. However, when a child dies suddenly and unexpectedly – in a car accident or drowning in a river, for instance – there may be no obvious person to take on the task of organising a multi-agency, multi-disciplinary case review. Under these circumstances, a new system will have to be developed whereby notification of the death activates an administrative system to gather the relevant documentation together, and organise for those involved with the child and the events leading to the death to come together for a CDR. In this situation, the rapid ascertainment of the death is a major challenge (as covered in Chapter 7). Once ascertained, a review group will need to be convened to discuss the death. Because there will frequently be no prior involvement of any particular agency, other than school, the low-level review team will need to consist of those who were involved at the scene of any fatal accident, as well as those with some responsibility for, or knowledge of, the place where the accident took place. The natural body to organise the formation of this group is the high-level team, as will be discussed later; but this will require the services of a knowledgeable administrator.

In preparation for the case discussion, the administrator should inform all professionals involved, advising them of the timing and venue, and of the purposes of the review. As many records as possible, or copies of them, should be collated. This should include both hospital and primary care health records, any Social Services records pertinent to the case, police records and those of other agencies. It is neither appropriate nor necessary for all of these records to be made available to all professionals involved, but someone from each agency should take responsibility for collating and reporting on their own agency's records. To gain maximum value from the meeting, it is very helpful for a chronology of events to be drawn up, though this sometimes emerges from the general practice record. One professional should take responsibility for informing the family of the review and seeking their views, including any information they would want to make known to the review team and any questions they might want to ask.

Depending on the circumstances of the death, the relevant documentation might include any or all of the following:

- GP records.
- Ambulance and/or paramedic records – and perhaps any recordings made of a 999 phone call, especially if instructions for resuscitation were given.
- Accident & Emergency records – medical, triage and nursing (if these are separate).
- Other hospital records of the child.
- Hospital records of the mother (especially obstetric notes, especially important for infant deaths).
- Health Visitor records, for pre-school children.
- Personal child health record book, for pre-school children.
- Copies of any written statements that amplify the record of events, subsequently made by professionals in any agency or discipline.

- An account of the scene of the death, with photographs or video recordings if these were made by the police.
- Information from interviews given to the police.
- A copy of the autopsy report, or a verbal presentation of its contents.

There may also be relevant information from the police relating to the parents, but it is generally most appropriate that this should be given orally at the meeting. An important example might be calls to the house for incidents of alleged, or actual, domestic violence, which are highly relevant to infant deaths. Any relevant Social Services records are important and it is one of the roles of the social worker to bring such information to the review. There may be records from other agencies such as Fire and Rescue, Mountain Rescue, helicopter crews or lifeboats, depending on the circumstances of the death.

The individual case discussion itself will normally take between one and one and a half hours. To start with, every member should introduce themselves and outline their role in relation to the death. The chairperson should set out the purposes of the case discussion and establish ground rules (Box 11.1). The most important 'rule' is that this review meeting is a private and confidential professionals' meeting, with a 'public' outcome that is confined to these areas:

- A brief factual resume of the sequence of events. This can easily be constructed from the chronology and may be augmented by any other relevant oral information.
- A list of the issues identified.
- A list of learning points, action points and general recommendations.
- If a proforma is used, this may also form part of the output of the review.

One person should describe briefly the chronology and circumstances leading to death; other participants may then add any other relevant information. Information is shared on the outcome of any investigations, including the history and examination, autopsy, scene investigation and any police investigation. A discussion may follow in order to clarify the cause or causes of death and any con-

---

Box 11.1 Ground rules for an individual case discussion

- Respect for the process – participants should agree how they will conduct the review, including timekeeping, taking notes and the process for reaching agreement.
- Respect for each person present – every professional has an important contribution to make and should be enabled to share their views openly and honestly.
- Information shared in the meeting will not be discussed outside of the meeting without the agreement of all present, and only factual information, not opinions or discussions, will be recorded in the 'public' output.

tributory factors. Once the circumstances of death have been reviewed, attention should then turn to any support needs of the family and finally, a chance for individual professionals to share any concerns they may have for themselves or about the process. Any actions or recommendations coming from the review should be agreed by all participants and written down before the close of the meeting. Throughout this process, the chairperson should bear in mind the various purposes of the case discussion as outlined above.

In some situations, information shared at the individual case discussion may indicate that maltreatment played a role in relation to the death, or there were issues around parental care which, whilst not directly leading to the death, nevertheless may have implications for siblings or for future children. In most circumstances, providing there has been an appropriate 'rapid response' to the child's death, any concerns will have been identified at an earlier stage, but there will inevitably be some cases where it is only once the full picture is brought together that specific issues come to light. These issues should always be taken seriously and should be addressed directly by the chairperson. Where such issues are identified, consideration should be given as to whether there is a need for a Section 47 child-protection investigation, a criminal investigation, or a Serious Case Review. The participants of the review should agree how these concerns will be addressed and who is responsible for initiating any of the agreed processes.

Providing a 'safe' environment

The importance of this feature cannot be over-emphasised. In the wake of a death, there are many professionals who feel upset and distressed. Some feel guilty, usually in a rather poorly defined way, from the heart rather than the head. Some feel that if only they had been a bit more observant, obsessional or vigilant, the event might not have occurred. These negative thoughts gnaw away at conscientious professionals in the days and weeks following a death and can become destructive of self-esteem and capability. Being able to share the pain, recognising that others feel similarly, and hearing a consistent message from respected peers that doing your best is all you can do, is part of achieving personal resolution of distress. For this reason also, it is vital that case reviews are conducted in a positive, supportive and learning mode, and not in a negative, blaming and destructive atmosphere. Furthermore, if any of the participants do not feel safe and comfortable with the group, they may not share important information, which would undermine the fundamental rationale of the panel.

Detect any system errors in the provision of care and/or surveillance

This is a crucial part of the process, because it recognises explicitly that individual workers operate within a complex system of relationships, and it is commonly the failings of systems that lead to the tragedy. What appear on the surface to be errors made by individuals are very frequently errors that arise because of system design, unexpected circumstances or the existence of rules or procedures that interfere with the proper discharge of people's duties rather than assisting them – and therefore the procedures are not followed or the rules not obeyed. A detailed review will often uncover lapses and slips (the phone call that was forgotten, the email discarded, the piece of paper lost) that are part of the human condition, yet often better design of systems, the provision of better communications devices, or the creation of more effective barriers, can decrease the impact of these human errors.

Examine the role of any agencies with direct or indirect responsibility for the child

This needs to be done systematically, ideally with a proforma (see later) so that there is a consistent approach. An agency is usually thought of as being Social Services, Education, Probation Service or 'Health'; but for the purposes of enquiring into deaths a much broader view must be taken. An agency, or agent, could be a family or a parent; it could be a commercial enterprise; it could be an emergency service. Children at school, or on a school trip, for example, are the direct responsibility of Education. However, the same child might be on a Social Services case load, and therefore indirectly be the responsibility of Social Services. While at home, a child will mostly be the direct responsibility of parents, or perhaps some other adult. If a child is truanting from school, he or she is no longer the direct responsibility of any agent or agency, but remains the indirect responsibility of Education until the end of the school day. Depending on the circumstances of a death, it will usually be possible to define each agency or agent with either direct or indirect responsibility for the child, and hence to evaluate the respective contributions of each agent or agency to the death itself, or in relation to the possible prevention of the death.

THE COMPOSITION OF THE REVIEW TEAM

It follows that the composition of a low-level CDR team, like the documentation, will be specific to the circumstances of the death. Although this has already been emphasised, it bears repeating that if a CDR is to be enhanced by the sharing of relevant oral information, it follows that a CDR panel cannot consist only of senior officials who were not involved with the family. It has to consist of those who had that contact, and these people will also be those with the strongest interest in learning from the events. A number of features will help to determine who should come together for the CDR meeting:

- Age of the child (e.g. Health Visitor for pre-school child, class teacher for primary school child).

Box 11.2 Example of participants in an infant death review

Chair

Child Protection	Pathologist
Nurse	Police Officer
Paediatrician	Ambulance Paramedic
'Designated' Doctor	Social Worker
Health Visitor	Lay Person
GP	

Box 11.3 Example of participants in a child death review, where the child has been in a fatal traffic accident

Chair

Paediatrician	Police Officer
Ambulance Crewman	Fire and Rescue
A&E Doctors	Class Teacher
A&E Nurse	Lay Person
GP	

- Stage (e.g. secondary school: the head of year may be appropriate).
- Circumstances (e.g. police, for those cases reported to the coroner; designated child protection doctor and nurse, for sudden infant death).
- Health (e.g. hospital staff, if the child attended for a current illness, or had attempts at resuscitation in the Accident and Emergency Department, or received end-of-life care there).
- Agency involvement (e.g. Social Services, Education).

This list is not exhaustive. The range of possible circumstances is huge, but identifying appropriate persons to come together for the child death review meeting is relatively straightforward once the agencies involved with the child have been identified (Boxes 11.2 and 11.3). The roles of some of the possible attendees are discussed below.

Conversely, because many child deaths occur in hospital, the health service clinical governance structures can be used to ensure that CDRs take place for any child dying there. For these, it is not too difficult to create and administer a system for the deaths to be scrutinised by the appropriate people, and for a report to be produced and passed on to the high-level team.

Chairing an individual case discussion

The chairpeople have a crucial part to play in the CDR process. They are required to understand the nature of the process of the review group. They have to bear in mind, and articulate to the participants, that it is a profession-als' meeting, that there will not be any detailed minutes (to encourage full and frank discussion), and that the written output will consist only of a summary of the facts, a list of the issues highlighted by the group, a list of lessons to be learnt (if any), and any recommendations that could be considered by the partner agencies represented on the group (via the high-level review team). It would be for the chairperson to produce this output and to ensure that all parties were happy with it before sending it to its various destinations – which will include the participants themselves (for insertion into relevant case files), the coroner, and the high-level review team.

There is no obvious reason why the chairpeople should be from any particu-lar professional background. Their personal attributes, such as the ability to hold the group together, manage distress among the members and keep the focus on learning rather than scapegoating, would be more important than their qualifications or their profession. Where case discussions happen in hos-pital, Trusts may already have a number of people who could take on this role, as they will be used to undertaking formal case reviews for other clinical inci-dents. For deaths with no health service involvement, the Serious Case Review committee of the LSCB might organise a pool of such chairpeople (and their training); or this could be a remit of the high-level child death review team as discussed later in this chapter. Another effective pool of chairpeople for low-level CDRs would be the members of the high-level review team, as discussed later in this chapter.

The pathologist

Pathologists have many calls on their time and the pathologist(s) who under-took the autopsy may not be able to come to every case discussion; further-more, not all children who die have an autopsy. A paediatric pathologist will conduct many of the autopsies for deaths in infants, often in conjunction with a forensic pathologist, but autopsies on some older children will be undertaken by an adult-trained or forensic pathologist. While the presence of the patholo-gist at a case discussion is always helpful, the key item that the team needs to have is the result of the autopsy. The written autopsy report, when commis-sioned by the coroner, belongs to the coroner and can only be released with their permission. Nevertheless, the main autopsy findings (rather than the full report) should be available to the review panel. It is satisfactory either for the pathologist, if present, to share the autopsy findings orally, or for someone else – often a paediatrician – to present them after having a conversation with the pathologist. It is possible that when the pathologist can attend the meeting, he or she may even defer their final report until after the meeting, since the way pathological findings are interpreted may be influenced by hearing the views of the participants and other material presented at the meeting. Where a child has died at the scene of a road traffic accident, the pathologist's findings will seldom add much to the deliberations of the panel but where, for example, a child has presented as a sudden unexpected death in infancy, the pathologist's findings may be very important.

Medical (paediatric) input

The medical input to an individual case discussion will also vary according to the circumstances. In some situations it is obvious: if the child died in hospital, the paediatrician involved in that child's care should be central to the review. But there may also be paediatric intensivists or other specialists involved, as well as a general paediatrician; their input may also be important. And although this is easily forgotten, not all children under 18 are looked after by a paediatrician: for instance, if a woman aged 16 years dies shortly after giving birth, the obstetricians would be her main medical carers, and there may be no reason for paediatric involvement. Although she will be subject to a confidential enquiry into her maternal death, there will also be important issues that could usefully be discussed as part of a CDR. Similar situations will arise with the 17-year-old victims of road traffic accidents who die in adult intensive care units, having been treated by adult specialists.

In relation to sudden unexpected deaths in infants, it will generally be sensible to involve the named or designated paediatricians for child protection, as issues related to the safeguarding of other children, or the possibility of the death having occurred unnaturally, should always be considered.

For reviews convened on children dying suddenly and unexpectedly outside of hospital, where no hospital specialist, paediatrician or even GP has had contact with the child, there is nevertheless a good case for having a paediatrician present at the review, for two reasons. Firstly, if there is not a pathologist present, a paediatrician would be the most logical person with whom the pathologist might discuss the findings of the autopsy. Secondly, there may be issues relating to aspects of community child health: for instance, the issue might arise that the child was not in contact with health services, but perhaps should have been. In this situation, the best choice of paediatrician would be the community paediatrician looking after children in the area in which the deceased child lived.

General practitioner

GPs tend to know their youngest children and their families better than the older children, who may seldom if ever have contact with the practice. So once again, the value of involving a GP will depend on the circumstances of the death. However, the GP ought always to be invited to participate, whether or not there appears to have been much contact with the child. He or she may still have important insights into members of the close or extended family that are highly relevant in relation to contributory factors to the death. Participating in case discussions, one quickly learns never to second-guess or underestimate the information or contribution that any member of the group may disclose.

School teacher

Children of primary school age have, in each year, one teacher to whom they relate for all aspects of teaching. This teacher is the person who, outside of the family itself, knows the child best. It is therefore potentially of great benefit to involve the class teacher in any individual case discussion on a child of primary school age. Such a person is invaluable for giving relatively objective insights into the child's personality and temperament, behaviour and intellectual ability.

For children in secondary education, it is less obvious that anyone at school necessarily has a sufficiently close relationship with them to be able to contribute to the case discussion. However, for some children there may have been a more intense level of contact, or there may be a close relationship between the child and someone in a pastoral care role, or the head of year, or some particular teacher with whom the child developed a special bond of trust or confidence. It will always be worth making the relevant enquiries, even if it turns out that they draw a blank.

Nurses, health visitors and midwives

Occasionally, a school nurse will have had a great deal to do with a child, but for children dying in hospital it is usually nurses on paediatric intensive care units, Accident and Emergency Departments, and on paediatric wards, who have been in contact with them before they die. Many nurses tend to be involved even if the admission was short or the child died in the Emergency Department, so there has to be some selection or choice as to who might best come to a case discussion. There is no reason to exclude anyone who feels they want to be there or has something to contribute. Shift patterns and other constraints prevent the review being dominated by large numbers of nurses.

For children who are pre-school, a key professional is the Health Visitor; and this person is most important of all for infant deaths, as regular contact with families is the norm in the first postnatal year. A case discussion on an infant dying suddenly and unexpectedly should arguably not go ahead if the Health Visitor cannot be there. For very young infants, it may be the community midwife who has had most contact with the family. He or she will have valuable information about the pregnancy, the mother's physical and psychological health, and the immediate needs of the family.

Police

The police have a variety of different roles in relation to child deaths. They will almost always be involved directly in fatal road traffic accidents and in the immediate management of sudden unexpected deaths in infancy. They will also invariably be involved in cases of suspected suicide or homicide and through the coroner's officer system, they are aware of all deaths reported to the coroner. Depending on their role in relation to the death in question, they will have different contributions to the CDR process. Involvement of the police in a case is not a reason for avoiding having a case discussion, but where a CDR is contemplated on a child whose death is being investigated by the police it may be sensible to involve the police at an early stage in the process of setting up the review so that it does not impede any forensic investigations. In particular, the police and coroner or coroner's officer will need to consider the status of any information shared at the meeting and any notes made. These potentially constitute disclosable information and with this in mind, in some situations it may be appropriate for the case discussion to go ahead without a police officer or coroner's officer present; in any event this should be discussed and agreed with all parties. Case discussions in situations where there are forensic dimensions are discussed later.

Lay input

A lay person can be very helpful indeed in seeing events differently to the professionals and challenging some of the professionals' assumptions. There does not have to be a discrete pool of lay persons formed for the purpose of CDR work; where a case discussion takes place where police were not involved, for example, a police officer will often have exactly the lay perspective that the review group needs. The same will occur with other persons who may be 'professional' in one context or for one kind of group, but who are effectively 'lay' in a different context.

Another possible means of enlisting a lay person is to use members of the high-level review team. It has already been pointed out that such people would also be useful in chairing the individual case discussion. In either role, this has the twin advantage of providing a lay perspective for the review and of contributing to the ongoing training and expertise of the members of the high-level review group. This will be covered more fully when discussing the high-level review team later in this chapter.

It would be tempting, if there was a lay person in the chair, to regard this as an adequate alternative to having a lay person as a member of the group. This combined role might work quite well under some circumstances, but the chairperson already has plenty of things to think about and it might be argued that the role of a lay person would best be discharged if they were part of the group rather than its chairperson.

Coroner

In any locality, there needs to be collaboration between those organising CDRs and the coroner. It is courteous to notify the coroner of the date of the review meeting. This enables the coroner either to join the meeting should they wish, or to send a coroner's officer if they prefer. In practice, many coroners may feel it would be inappropriate to be involved in this way, but it remains important to keep the coroner informed about the process in relation to the case, and it also means that the coroner can expect the written output from the review a short time after it takes place.

The bereaved family

We must not forget that the bereaved family is central to the purpose of the review. They need as full an explanation of the death as it is possible to provide, and both adults and siblings may need continuing help and support to come to terms with their loss. They need to have the reassurance that the death is being taken seriously and that any possible lessons are being learnt. This applies to all deaths, including those that are expected or even planned for, since palliative care also needs examination with the aim of continuously improving it.

The question is frequently asked as to whether the family should be participants in CDR. Apart from the fact of the distress that the process would potentially cause, it is important to bear in mind that the review process is essentially for professionals and should be conducted as dispassionately as possible; furthermore, there is always the possibility that child protection concerns might lurk within the case and full and frank exploration of these is unlikely to be facilitated by the presence of the parents. The case discussion should therefore be regarded as a professionals' meeting to which parents are not invited, but as indicated above, careful thought must be given as to how to involve the family, to seek their views and to feed back information to them following the review.

IS LOW-LEVEL REVIEW EVER INAPPROPRIATE?

There are some deaths for which a review might not, on the face of it, be appropriate. Where there is an active police investigation in relation to an alleged murder or manslaughter, the case may be regarded as *sub judice*, and a review might not be considered possible until any criminal proceedings have run their course. However, I have had experience both of the police themselves organising a meeting of all the relevant professionals a short time after the death, and of the police finding value in a case discussion held a short time after the death, in which the discussions in relation to the events leading up to the death were considered helpful and important in the context of the investigation. It is, therefore, possible that where there is close trust and collaboration between agencies, there will be very few instances when an individual case discussion will be inappropriate or inadvisable. These might be confined to certain circumstances, such as when a child disappears and the body is discovered only several years later, where the case involves an unidentified dead child or when the final events in a child's life take place outside of the UK.

There is often confusion about the status of any recommendations made at an individual case discussion. There are essentially two levels of recommendations arising from these reviews: recommendations and actions relating directly to the case, for example a need to provide counselling for affected siblings, or to support the family in applying for rehousing; and wider recommendations based on the analysis of contributory factors or system failures, for example where a case identifies a particular risk that might be prevalent in a community, such as a traffic black spot. Recommendations can be contentious and even inappropriate if they relate to an agency not represented by the persons present and strong chairing is sometimes needed to avoid this. The recommendations will be fed to the high-level review team and then to the LSCB, which in principle will have the clout to ensure that the findings are actioned in the relevant agency. While any recommendations emerging from a case discussion will necessarily be of a provisional nature, pending consideration at the higher level, once sanctioned by a high-level team they will have considerable force, as discussed later.

HIGH-LEVEL CHILD DEATH REVIEW

The purpose of a high-level child death review is quite different to that of an individual case discussion and its composition has to reflect the strategic nature of its function, together with its need to influence the policies of different agencies, either directly or through the LSCB. Some of the purposes will be:

1. Obtaining assurance that appropriate individual case discussions have taken place.
2. Scrutinising the recommendations from individual case discussions and passing these on to the relevant agencies if approved.
3. Analysing any common themes arising from the individual case discussions.
4. Synthesising, from time to time, recommendations based on the themes identified in scrutiny of the deaths.
5. Recommending a Serious Case (Part 8) Review, especially when this is a recommendation from an individual case discussion.
6. Producing an annual report relating to the area(s) they cover, for presentation to the relevant LSCBs.

In order to cover a population of at least 500,000, it is likely that several adjacent LSCBs will wish to create a joint review team. Such a team will need a permanent core membership but will also need to be constituted with the flexibility to bring in extra expertise *ad hoc* depending on the cases under discussion. The review team will need to relate in a 'horizontal' fashion to the Serious Case Review committees in each LSCB area, but will also be responsible for reporting 'vertically' to each of the LSCBs it serves (Box 11.4).

The core membership of the review team will have to reflect those agencies and authorities most likely to be involved with the majority of the cases: Health, Police, Social Services, Fire and Rescue, Education and Ambulance (Box 11.5). Where, for example, three LSCBs decide to share the high-level review activity, it may be found that a senior Social Services manager comes from one area, someone from the education department of the local authority

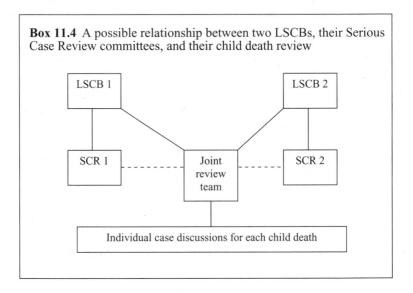

Box 11.4 A possible relationship between two LSCBs, their Serious Case Review committees, and their child death review

---

Box 11.5 Example of agency membership of a high-level review team

	Chair	
Health:		Police
Public Health		Ambulance
Nurse		Fire and Rescue
Paediatrician		Social Services
Pathologist		Education
GP		Lay Person

from another area, and someone from a Health Trust (perhaps a designated doctor and/or public health consultant) from a third. A single police force might cover all three LSCBs and the same might apply to Fire and Rescue, and ambulance. Specialist input from highways or other local authority or borough departments might be required *ad hoc*. More than one medical person might be appropriate, as might some nursing input.

The high-level child death review team (CDRT) will need to avoid the temptation to undertake reviews in a 'low-level' style, since, being armed with only the relevant documentation but unable to hear the verbatim input from the front-line professionals involved in the case, a high-level team would be unable to achieve the same insights into local processes as a low-level one can, and could never negotiate the continuing support for the bereft family. It is for the high-level team to stand back from the low-level process and consider recommendations and themes. In order to achieve this, some thought will need to be given to the type of education and training that both chairpersons and members of CDRTs might need. It may be particularly useful to consider that a core function for members of the high-level CDRT might be to chair individual case discussions. This would especially apply to those reviews without a 'natural' chairperson, such as reviews on children dying suddenly and unexpectedly (since other deaths, especially 'planned' and hospital ones, will usually have a medical focus and a local system that will provide a chairperson, as discussed previously). This would have the advantage of giving the members of the CDRT a valuable experience of the power of the individual case discussions, knowledge (and some ownership) of the recommendations, quality assurance for the CDR process, and clear linkage between the two levels of the process.

Recommendations from a high-level review team should be taken very seriously by the relevant agencies, since this is the engine by which the lessons learnt from the CDR process can influence policies and procedures and drive organisational change. Participants in high-level teams have a duty to feed any recommendations into the management structures of their own organisations, and those bodies will need to give the recommendations appropriate scrutiny. Ultimately, it will be for the LSCB to decide how it wishes to manage this process and to evaluate the extent to which changes have been made.

In setting up a CDRT, careful consideration should be given as to the possible outputs from the team and how these will be used. Close links should be established with local children and young people's strategic partnerships and with other bodies that may be involved in local planning. Recommendations should be kept to a minimum and should have a strong public-health focus on prevention of future deaths. Although it is not the role of the CDRT to carry out all actions arising from such recommendations, they should bear in mind the need for other bodies to translate these recommendations into Specific, Measurable, Achievable, Realistic and Time-bound action plans. A focus on appropriate outputs from the review will help to clarify the process by which deaths are reviewed, which in turn will clarify the information required by the review team.

RUNNING A CHILD DEATH REVIEW TEAM

A number of stages are required in the process of child death review, from the initial ascertainment of the death through to the high-level review by the CDRT.

Ascertainment of child deaths

That there needs to be a robust system of notification of all deaths to the team and a central point for notification is self-evident; what is less obvious is how difficult it can be to create such a system. This is because up to 40% of infant deaths, and a substantial proportion of deaths in older children, take place outside the locality in which the child lived, or the LSCB area in which the death is scrutinised. It is not sufficient to relate to one or two local coroners: in effect, a wide geographical area has to be covered if all the deaths relevant to an LSCB area are to be ascertained. In order to ensure timely and complete notification of all deaths, multiple sources of notification will almost certainly be required. The sources of data and the geographical areas will necessarily overlap with other adjacent LSCBs, resulting both in duplication of effort on the one hand and a high likelihood of missing some deaths on the other.

Nor is it possible to rely on the central collection of death information from the Office of National Statistics, if the purpose is to ascertain deaths rapidly, because ONS data are only collated annually. ONS data are extremely useful for verifying and auditing the effectiveness of local coverage, but they cannot be used for primary ascertainment of deaths in a timely fashion. Although coroners may be able to notify the CDRT of each death referred to them at an early stage and may be able to pass on a basic report if one is prepared by their officer, it must be remembered that the coroner involved with the death is the coroner for the locality where the death occurred, not the area where the child lived (except for children dying abroad). Primary Care Trusts ultimately know about many of the deaths, but not necessarily in a particularly timely fashion and not necessarily very efficiently for older children. There are always gaps, especially with infants dying before discharge from hospital, older teenagers and children dying abroad or out of the PCT area.

Our own experience in the north of England has been that centralised ascertainment, using the CEMACH office with its pre-existing network of hospital Emergency Departments, mortuaries, individual paediatricians, police units and Social Services, has proved both effective and efficient. Duplication of systems is avoided and the expertise both in ascertaining the deaths and ensuring that the core dataset and other crucial documentation is collected rapidly (see below) is maintained.

Data gathering

There are two levels of information required for each child death. The first includes identifiers (name, gender, date of birth, address and postcode); demographics (ethnicity, date and place of death); the 'cause' of death as certified, if this has taken place; an indication of the professionals involved; whether the case was referred to the coroner; and whether an autopsy was held. All of this is captured on the core dataset proforma developed by CEMACH and adopted by the DCSF for general use. The skill lies in knowing to whom the proforma should be sent for completion – sometimes to a hospital doctor and sometimes to the general practitioner.

Further documents will then be needed to inform the child death review process, which is the second level of information required. The variety and nature of the documents have already been described. The key to this phase of information ascertainment is to obtain a copy of the general practice records, since these contain details of the child's other health contacts, if any, which enable these records to be obtained quickly and efficiently. It is then possible to convene a local case discussion.

Once a local case discussion has taken place, the CDRT can be provided with the written output from that discussion. The form of this has been discussed earlier in the chapter, as has the use of the proforma developed by CEMACH for use in confidential enquiry meetings, reproduced in Appendix 14 and based on similar proformas developed and used in the US. The amount and nature of information that the CDRT needs will depend on the nature of the death (Box 11.6). What cannot be stressed too much is that the CDRT must avoid getting bogged down in the details of individual deaths, or trying to repeat the local case discussion. If the CDRT has reason to be concerned about the quality of or conclusions from an individual local case discussion, this important view will need to inform the process of continual quality improvement for the local processes.

Material coming to each CDRT meeting must be handled in accordance with the usual standards for information governance, bearing in mind that although these are named-person data, the subject is dead; and that there may be confidential third-party information contained in the material. All team

---

Box 11.6 Information required by a high-level child death review team

- The core data set.
- The factual account from the local case discussion, together with the list of issues, learning points and recommendations.
- The proforma, if one was used, which captures the involvement and contribution of different agencies and grades the 'avoidability' of the death.

members should arrive at the meeting having had time to read the papers and familiarise themselves with the cases to be discussed. The chair and administrator must therefore ensure that systems are in place for secure and timely distribution of the information, and that it is shredded or subjected to other confidential destruction after the meeting. There will need to be arrangements for the secure storage of 'top copy' documents centrally. This should be the responsibility of one of the LSCBs sharing the administration of the CDRT.

Evaluating the deaths

The focus of the CDRT meetings should be on analysing the information provided, with a view to identifying any case giving rise to the need for a Serious Case Review, any matters of concern affecting the safety and welfare of children in the area of the authority, and any wider public-health or safety concerns arising from a particular death or from a pattern of deaths in that area (HM Government 2006b). This can be achieved primarily by reference to the summaries or proformas referred to above. If the local case discussions are working well, there should rarely be a need for some other form of additional in-depth review, unless a Serious Case Review is proposed. By the time a CDRT considers a case, there will probably have been an inquest under the jurisdiction of the coroner.

Any CDRT meeting will be likely to give different levels of consideration to the various different cases. Given the long-standing structures and culture for the close and critical local examination of neonatal deaths, this is an area where the CDRT will need simply to have assurance that the correct processes of local scrutiny are in place and functioning. In contrast, where local case discussions have identified significant contributory factors, or where the death has been judged locally as avoidable or potentially avoidable, the CDRT will give the death the closest scrutiny. It will concentrate on any contributory factors in the different domains (Box 11.7, Appendix 15) including extrinsic or environmental factors, personal or intrinsic factors, agencies or agents directly or indirectly involved with the child or family and the medical care provided. This is where having the chair of the local case discussion as part of the CDRT, or invited to the meeting to discuss the case, will be especially valuable.

The CDRT will wish to provide its own summary and judgement. The final part of the process is then to decide whether, based on findings either from individual deaths or from the overall pattern of deaths, any recommendations should be made to the Local Safeguarding Children Board, constituent agencies, or any other bodies that may be able to influence change. One of the key issues here is interpreting the concept of 'avoidable' or 'preventable' deaths (Box 11.8). Durfee et al. (2002) define a preventable death as 'one in which, with retrospective analysis, the review team determines that a reasonable

Box 11.7 Assessment of contributory factors

A. Environmental (extrinsic) factors

Consider environmental factors extrinsic to the child that may have had a bearing on the events leading up to the death and the strength of their contribution. Consider the weather, housing or environment, health and safety issues, hazards, exposures and so on.

0=not relevant at all

1=probably a minor factor among the events leading up to the death

2=probably a significant factor among the events leading up to the death

3=probably a major factor, but one of several others impacting on the death

4=directly and overwhelmingly important factor in the death.

B. Personal (intrinsic) factors

Consider factors intrinsic to the child that may have had a bearing on the events leading up to the death and the strength of their contribution (e.g. any impairment or disability, ill health, mental illness or behavioural problems, use of drugs or alcohol).

0=not relevant at all

1=probably a minor factor among the events leading up to the death

2=probably a significant factor among the events leading up to the death

3=probably a major factor, but one of several others impacting on the death

4=directly and overwhelmingly important factor in the death.

C. Agencies or agents _directly_ involved in supervising or providing services for the child

Consider any agencies directly supervising the child or providing services at the time of the death or incident leading to death (e.g. parents, other family members, other carers, health, Social Services and education). For each agency directly involved, consider the identification or awareness of any hazard or risk, or lack of this, and the appropriateness of the agencies' handling of the child in terms of timely involvement of other agencies, emergency services, or provision of appropriate care.

0=not relevant at all

1=responsible for a minor or background factor relating to the death

2=responsible for a significant factor relating to the death

3=responsible for one of several important factors impacting on the death

4=responsible for a single important factor relating to the death.

D. Agencies or agents *indirectly* involved, but not actively supervising or providing for the child

Consider any other agencies involved with the child or family, but not directly supervising the child at the time of the death or incident leading to death, or any agency that was not, but could have been involved with the child or family. Consider the potential for any such agency to have made an impact in preventing the death.

0=not relevant at all

1=may have removed a minor or background factor relating to the death

2=may have removed a significant factor relating to the death

3=may have removed one of several important factors impacting on the death

4=had the potential to remove a single important factor or more than one of several important factors impacting on the death.

E. Medical care

Consider any medical care provided to the child prior to the death, or medical care that could have been provided but wasn't. For example, consider whether there was any evidence of failure to recognise the severity of illness of the child outside hospital or within a hospital environment; any evidence of failure to prioritise the management of the child; any adverse events that affected care.

0=not relevant at all

1=probably a minor factor among the events leading up to the death

2=probably a significant factor among the events leading up to the death

3=probably a major factor, but one of several others impacting on the death

4=directly and overwhelmingly important factor in the death.

intervention (e.g. medical, educational, social, legal and psychological) might have prevented the death. Reasonable is defined by taking into consideration the conditions, circumstances or resources available.' This is a useful approach as, in one sense, every death is potentially avoidable but not every death could be prevented given our current knowledge and resources.

CHAIRING THE MEETINGS

The choice of chair for a multi-disciplinary, multi-agency high-level review team is not obvious. The chair could rotate between the existing chairpersons of the SCR committees on an annual basis, but that would impose a substantial workload on the person selected. Looking more widely, there is no particular

---

Box 11.8 Assessment of avoidability

1. Avoidable:
   a) where there were identifiable failures in the child's direct care by any agency, including parents, with direct responsibility for the child
   b) where there were latent, organisational or other indirect failure(s) within one or more agency, including parents, with direct or indirect responsibility for the child
   c) where there was a failure of design, installation or inadequate maintenance by agencies with responsibility for public safety.
2. Potentially avoidable:
   a) at a higher level than the agencies, with direct or indirect responsibility for the child (e.g. political or social structures, terrorism and crime)
   b) where no agency, including parents, was involved with the child
   c) where intrinsic factors were the principal factors leading to the death
   d) where there were potentially modifiable factors extrinsic to the child
   e) where the causal pathway leading to the death was potentially amenable to intervention.
3. Unavoidable:
   a) death caused by unmodifiable or unpredictable factors extrinsic to the child
   b) death due to undiagnosed, asymptomatic conditions presenting with a lethal event
   c) planned palliation for unpreventable, incurable disease or anomaly.

---

background that is more or less suitable. It would be possible even to rotate the chairperson function among the members of the group, provided that there was a clear remit for the chairperson, and well-thought-out terms of reference for the group. Good chairing could come from the police, from Social Services or from any of the disciplines represented on an LSCB Serious Case Review committee. It is important, however, that whoever chairs the review team is independent in the sense that they do not hold direct line-management responsibility for front-line practitioners providing services to families. This will enable a degree of objectivity that may not be possible in those responsible for service provision.

THE RELATIONSHIP BETWEEN CDR AND SERIOUS CASE REVIEW

Should a child death review not take place if there is going to be a Serious Case Review? Since SCRs are commissioned by SCR committees and CDRs on sudden unexpected child deaths will usually be organised by a high-level review team, there is a clear possibility for tension between the two processes and a strong temptation to choose one process over the other to avoid 'duplication'. But will this always amount to duplication? Sometimes this view may be appropriate but it is worth considering the different time scales and functions of SCR and CDR before assuming that a Serious Case Review could entirely replace a child death review. For example:

- Serious Case Reviews have a specific remit in relation to identifying lessons to be learned about the way in which local professionals and organisations work together to safeguard and promote the welfare of children (HM Government 2006b); they do not have the scope to address wider issues, including aspects of care following a death, or identifying wider factors that may have contributed.
- Management reviews in health that feed into the SCR process seldom include any critique of medical management in hospital in relation to a child's death. However, the clinicians involved at the receiving hospital have an obligation to scrutinise every child death, and a CDR does this.
- CDRs allow participants to share with one another their oral information. SCRs cannot do this.
- There may need to be plans for the support and care of the bereft family. That is a specific purpose of CDRs but is not in either the timescale or remit of SCRs.
- Information from CDRs, like that from Kennedy reviews, goes forward to the coroner, who generally finds this information helpful. SCRs often take place after an inquest.
- The Kennedy protocol assumes that SUDI reviews will always take place (Royal College of Pathologists & Royal College of Paediatrics and Child Health 2004); there is no exception for SCRs.
- *Working Together* (HM Government 2006b) also assumes that CDRs will take place routinely, in 7.43 (Box 11.9).

If these differences between SCRs and CDRs are acknowledged, it follows that the CDR process ought to take place whether or not an SCR is commissioned. It will also sometimes happen that a CDR will turn up facts that result in a recommendation for a Serious Case Review.

OUTPUTS FROM THE CHILD DEATH REVIEW PROCESS

As indicated above, child death review processes have the potential to influence local plans for children, young people and families. There need to be strong links between child death review teams, the Local Safeguarding Children Board and other bodies working in a local area to facilitate action in this regard. The LSCB should be provided with an annual report summarising the findings of the CDRT and this should be made available to all constituent

Box 11.9 *Working Together*, paragraph 7.43

'A case discussion meeting should be held as soon as the final post-mortem result is available. The timing of this discussion varies according to the circumstances of the death. This may range from immediately after the post-mortem to 8–12 weeks after the death. The type of professionals involved in this meeting depends on the age of the child. The meeting should include those who knew the child and family, and those involved in investigating the death – i.e. the GP, Health Visitor or school nurse, paediatrician(s), pathologist, senior investigating police officers and, where appropriate, social workers' (HM Government 2006b).

Source: Crown copyright material is reproduced with the permission of the Controller of HMSO and Queen's Printer for Scotland.

agencies and to the public. The teams can also have a major impact on public opinion and action and a well-thought-through media strategy can help to influence change locally. Perhaps the greatest potential value, though, is in influencing regional and national initiatives where lessons learnt could have a much wider impact on children's well being. In order for this to happen, there needs to be a system for regional and national collation of the data collected, to identify trends and variations in patterns of death. The proposed national core dataset will facilitate this and provide the potential for future research and development.

SUMMARY

Child death reviews have enormous potential to drive improvements in professional practice, public health and environmental safety. They have to function at two levels – at a low level, involving those professionals directly concerned with the child or the death, and at a high level, that can integrate the findings of low-level reviews, scrutinise their recommendations and present a detailed analysis to the LSCBs to which they are accountable. Properly conducted and embedded within the safeguarding framework, they will become valued by the participants, the agencies to which they belong and the parents of the children who die. They will enhance participants' learning and provide professional support. Once they are firmly established, people will wonder how we ever got on without them.

12 Serious Case Reviews

PAUL TUDOR
PETER SIDEBOTHAM

INTRODUCTION

A Serious Case Review (Chapter 8 review/Part 8 review) is the process by which a Local Safeguarding Children Board (LSCB, formerly an Area Child Protection Committee) carries out an inquiry into the death of a child when abuse or neglect are known or suspected to be a factor in the death, in order to identify lessons to be learned about the way in which local professionals and organisations work together to safeguard and promote the welfare of children (HM Government 2006b). It is estimated that possibly up to 200 Serious Case Reviews are undertaken each year and they are all submitted to the Commission for Social Care Inspection (CSCI) regionally (in future to OFSTED) and to the Department for Children, Schools and Families (DCSF) nationally. No precise figures are published and indeed, in a Commons statement on 21 March 2001 the then Minister for Health, John Hutton, stated: 'Information is not collected on the number of case reviews that have been carried out in accordance with Chapter 8.' Therefore the figure of 200 is an estimate based on good sources.

Of the approximately 200 reviews, about half relate to actual child deaths as a result of abuse and neglect at the hands of their carers. This figure of 100 correlates to the long-held publicity of the NSPCC that 'two children die per week as a result of child abuse and neglect'. The other 100-plus Serious Case Reviews comprise 'near misses', 'child deaths in other significant circumstances' and 'serious breakdowns of multi-agency working together'.

HISTORICAL CONTEXT AND LITERATURE SURVEY

Within the UK, there is a long and noteworthy tradition of deaths from abuse being reviewed and having a major impact on legislation, government guidance and social policy. It is worth making a passing reference to the formation of the NSPCC in 1889 (i.e. it was federated into a national organisation following the inception of local societies); the first Act of Parliament

Unexpected Death in Childhood: A Handbook for Practitioners. Edited by P. Sidebotham and P. Fleming.
Copyright © 2007 by John Wiley & Sons, Ltd.

passed to prevent cruelty to children, also in 1889, known as the Children's Charter; and the Children and Young Person Act of 1933, the first schedule of which identifies a wide range of offences against children, which have become known as Schedule One offences (the significance of this guidance was that offenders under this Act, often referred to as Schedule One offenders, could not have their convictions spent as most other offences under the Rehabilitation of Offenders Act).

The first case that attracted major public interest – indeed, an outcry – was that of Dennis O'Neill (1944). He was killed by his foster father and the resulting enquiries (Monkton Enquiry and Curtis Committee) impacted significantly on the 1948 Children Act, with its focus on boarding-out regulations. For a most poignant and insightful account of the family history, and reflections on the case *vis a vis* professional practice, see the book written by Dennis O'Neill's older brother, Tom O'Neill, who became a residential social worker (O'Neill 1981). The enquiry into the death of Maria Colwell in 1974 (Howells & Colwell 1974) attracted huge public and media interest and, arising directly from the enquiry, formal systems of case conferences and registers to be operated in every local authority were introduced in a DHSS memorandum.

Through the 1970s and early 1980s a cohort of children were the subject of inquiries following their violent deaths (Darryn Clark, Karen Spencer, Lester Chapman, Lisa Godfrey and Steven Meurs, among others) and the DHSS produced a small booklet, *Child Abuse: Study of enquiry reports 1973–1981* (Department of Health and Social Security 1982). Using evidence from 19 inquiries (including that of Maria Colwell), this gave an interesting and helpful analysis under the headings of Agency Function, Professional Practice and Context.

Sadly, the trend of child deaths followed by large-scale inquiries using panels of experts continued through the 1980s, by which time the phrase 'child abuse' had been introduced in order to cover the full range of abuse (ie. sexual and emotional, not just physical abuse and neglect as the earlier phrases of battered baby syndrome and non-accidental injury had implied). The cohort of the 1980s included Jasmine Beckford, Kimberley Carlisle, Tyra Henry, Heidi Koseda and Doreen Aston, and again the Department of Health undertook the same exercise as they had 10 years earlier, i.e. *Child Abuse: A study of enquiry reports 1980–1989* (Department of Health 1991).

During the 1990s there was a move away from the large-scale inquisitorial style of inquiry and under the 1991 *Working Together* guidance, Serious Case Reviews organised and run by local Area Child Protection Committees became the norm. Whilst this development was desirable from the perspective of the practitioners and the families involved, there has not been an adequate system of disseminating the lessons and thus the impact of the findings of these reviews has been reduced. However, two significant studies have collated material from a number of Serious Case Reviews, analysing cases, drawing themes and highlighting many issues of professional practice applicable to all agencies (Reder et al. 1993, Reder & Duncan 1999).

Finally, the death of Victoria Climbié in 2000 and the subsequent inquiry chaired by Lord Laming (Cm 5730 2003) has had a major impact on UK child protection practice, leading to the government's response of a Green Paper, *Every Child Matters* (HM Government 2003); the 2004 Children Act (HM Government 2004a); and a significant reorganisation of Children's Services with a new edition of *Working Together* (HM Government 2006b). What were formerly Area Child Protection Committees have now been reconstituted on a statutory basis as Local Safeguarding Children Boards.

THE CONTEXT OF SERIOUS CASE REVIEWS WITHIN ALL CHILD DEATHS

With the inception of the philosophy of safeguarding rather than protection, the new Local Safeguarding Children Boards have now been charged with the responsibility of establishing processes for responding to unexpected child deaths and for evaluating and reviewing all child deaths. These LSCB functions are described in detail in Chapters 7 and 11. The *Working Together* guidance (HM Government 2006b) makes it very clear that at any time in the work of the child death review panel and/or the operation of the rapid response teams, a referral for a Serious Case Review may be made (Figure 12.1). Thus, if at any stage in the rapid response, suspicions of abuse or neglect become apparent, a formal Section 47 strategy meeting will be held and a child

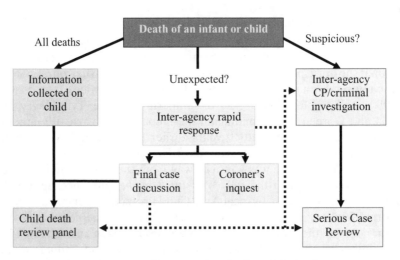

Figure 12.1 Processes for responding to and reviewing child deaths
Source: Reproduced by permission of University of Warwick.

protection investigation initiated; the case will be notified to the LSCB and consideration given as to whether or not to hold a Serious Case Review. Similarly, if during the process of a child death review, concerns of a child protection nature, or issues around inter-agency working to protect children emerge, the case will be notified to the LSCB for consideration of a Serious Case Review. It is important to recognise that the holding of a Serious Case Review does not negate the child death review process as described in Chapter 11, the two being different and complementary processes with differing remits and outcomes.

THE PROCESS

The purpose of Serious Case Reviews is explained in paragraph 8.3 of *Working Together to Safeguard Children* (HM Government 2006b) as to:

- establish whether there are lessons to be learned from the case about the way in which local professionals and organisations work together to safeguard and promote the welfare of children
- identify clearly what those lessons are, how they will be acted upon, and what is expected to change as a result; and
- consequentially, improve inter-agency working and better safeguard and promote the welfare of children.

The criteria for invoking a Serious Case Review are two-fold: 'When a child dies, and abuse or neglect are known or suspected to be a factor in the death . . . the LSCB should always conduct a Serious Case Review into the involvement with the child and family of organisations and professionals . . .' (para. 8.2).

Secondly, the LSCB should always consider whether a Serious Case Review should be conducted in the following circumstances:

- where a child sustains a potentially life-threatening injury or serious and permanent impairment of health and development through abuse or neglect, or
- has been subjected to particularly serious sexual abuse, or
- their parent has been murdered and a homicide review is being initiated, or
- the child has been killed by a parent with a mental illness, or
- the case gives rise to concerns about inter-agency working to protect children from harm (para 8.2).

Additionally, 'any professional may refer such a case to the LSCB if it is believed that there are important lessons for inter-agency working to be learned from the case. In addition, the Secretary of State for the Department of Education and Skills has powers to demand an inquiry to be held under the Inquiries Act 2005' (para. 8.8).

SERIOUS CASE REVIEW SUBCOMMITTEES

Most LSCBs have established or are establishing a specific subcommittee to undertake all Serious Case Reviews. Upon notification of a child death as a result of abuse or neglect, or upon referral from any agency, there needs to be urgent liaison between the chairperson of the LSCB and the chairperson of the Serious Case Review subcommittee to confirm the decision to proceed or not. Ultimately, it is the decision of the chairperson of the board but no doubt they will be greatly influenced by the recommendation of the Serious Case Review subcommittee and its chairperson.

In our experience, the majority of Serious Case Review subcommittees are standing committees and we would advocate this; when there is not a Serious Case Review being currently undertaken, the committee still has important work in auditing the progress of action plans from previous Serious Case Reviews and analysing and disseminating the lessons from nationally reported reviews. Some Local Safeguarding Children Boards still retain the structure of an *ad hoc* Serious Case Review subcommittee, which is only called into action when a Serious Case Review is initiated.

SCOPING EXERCISE

Once the decision has been made to proceed with a Serious Case Review, a scoping exercise takes place and this covers such issues as:

- the appointment of the independent author for the overview report
- the use of outside experts
- over what time period events should be reviewed, i.e. how far back and how wide (e.g. extended family)
- links with parallel inquiries (e.g. homicide review, suicide review, serious incident review [Health, Youth Justice Board])
- links with the coroner and the Crown Prosecution Service
- the timetable of the review process (i.e. a series of meetings and targeting the presentation to the LSCB)
- managing any public/media interest.

FAMILY PARTICIPATION

There has been a fascinating development between the 1999 and 2006 editions of *Working Together*. In the 1999 guidance, as part of the scoping exercise, the phrase appeared: 'Should family members be invited to contribute to the review?'

The 2006 guidance has the phrase: 'How should family members contribute to the review and who should be responsible for facilitating their involvement?'

So, the previous open question has now been turned into a presumption that family members will invariably be invited to participate, though, of course,

Box 12.1 An example of a scoping exercise

A six-week-old baby girl was admitted to the Emergency Department with severe head injuries. The explanation provided by the mother was that the baby had fallen out of her car seat while she was being carried up a flight of stairs to the family home. At the time of this incident, the baby's name was on the Child Protection Register under the categories of neglect and emotional abuse. This was as a consequence of concerns over her mother's mental health and her father's misuse of alcohol and possible drug misuse.

A panel was convened for the Serious Case Review, with representatives from Social Services, health (designated doctor and nurse), education and police. An independent chair for the panel was appointed.

Terms of reference were drawn up according to Chapter 8 of *Working Together*:

- The time period over which *events* were to be reviewed was set to span the point of initial referral during pregnancy through to the strategy meeting following the incident.
- The time period over which the *family history and background information* should be researched was established as being from the point of first significant involvement with one or both of the parents by the agency or service concerned. Some specific aspects were identified that required detailed review, including the mother's mental-health issues, the paternal history of substance misuse, issues around housing provision and safety standards, and the support and advice offered to the parents during the pregnancy and after delivery.
- The agencies that needed to contribute a management review or report of their involvement were identified and included:
  - education
  - police
  - probation
  - Social Services
  - the Primary Care Trust
  - the Hospital Trust
  - county council legal services
  - community alcohol service
  - community drugs service
  - the council housing department
- A process was established for informing and involving the family, including inviting the family to contribute to the review and setting a process for informing them of the outcome of the review.
- Consideration was given as to the timing of the review in relation to any criminal investigation and the coroner's processes.
- An initial press statement was agreed and plans established to deal with any media interest.
- The review panel confirmed that it wished staff involved in the case to be kept informed of findings and outcomes. Arrangements were made

> for feeding back and disseminating the findings of the overview report and individual management reviews.
> - The scope of the individual management reviews was to include:
>   - full information on the subject child
>   - full information on the siblings
>   - full information on the parents from the date of antenatal care of the first child.
> - Management reviews were to be submitted within five weeks.
> - A draft overview report was to be prepared within 10 weeks.
> - An extraordinary meeting of the LSCB would be convened in 16 weeks to consider the Serious Case Review.
> - A series of panel meeting dates were set.

participation does not necessarily mean attendance. Family members can be offered other mediums such as a tape or writing to the panel. Even convictions following the death of the child should not preclude the parents from being given the opportunity to participate. Moreover, the Serious Case Review panel members should not make assumptions that family members would be too distressed or too emotionally involved to make a meaningful contribution to 'lessons to be learned'. There is an increasing body of evidence of very productive engagement with families. At the very least, they should be informed that the Serious Case Review process is taking place, even if they do not wish to participate, and they should be offered the opportunity for feedback at the end of the process.

It has been a privilege to experience a number of very poignant and powerful situations – interviewing mothers in prison following their convictions for neglect; interviewing a father after his wife had left with their child and her new partner had killed the child; and interviewing a mother whose husband hanged their two boys during his first overnight staying contact (this followed an acrimonious legal custody and contact process). These have all made extremely helpful and insightful contributions to the Serious Case Review.

INDIVIDUAL MANAGEMENT REVIEWS

Upon completion of the scoping exercise, letters will be sent to all the constituent agencies of the LSCB plus other external services that have been identified as having had some involvement with the child or family. These letters will set out the terms of reference based on the scoping meeting (see above) and will ask for management reviews. From experience, it is very valuable for the request for management reviews to be prescriptive in its format, which should follow the template offered following paragraph 8.27 in *Working Together* and reproduced in Box 12.2.

Box 12.2 Individual management reviews (reproduced with permission from HM Government 2006b)

Source: Crown copyright material is reproduced with the permission of the Controller of HMSO and Queen's Printer for Scotland.

Management reviews

What was our involvement with this child and family?

Construct a comprehensive chronology of involvement by the organisation and/or professional(s) in contact with the child and family over the period of time set out in the review's terms of reference. Briefly summarise decisions reached, the services offered and/or provided to the child(ren) and family, and other action taken.

Analysis of involvement

Consider the events that occurred, the decisions made, and the actions taken or not taken. Where judgements were made, or actions taken, which indicate that practice or management could be improved, try to get an understanding not only of what happened but why. Consider the following specifically:

- Were practitioners sensitive to the needs of the children in their work, knowledgeable about potential indicators of abuse or neglect, and about what to do if they had concerns about a child?
- Did the organisation have in place policies and procedures for safeguarding and promoting the welfare of children and acting on concerns about their welfare?
- What were the key relevant points/opportunities for assessment and decision-making in this case in relation to the child and family?
- Do assessments and decisions appear to have been reached in an informed and professional way?
- Did actions accord with assessments and decisions made? Were appropriate services offered/provided, or relevant inquiries made, in the light of assessments?
- Where relevant, were appropriate child protection or care plans in place, and child protection and/or looked after reviewing processes complied with?
- When, and in what way, were the child(ren)'s wishes and feelings ascertained and taken account of when making revisions about children's services? Was this information recorded?
- Was practice sensitive to the racial, cultural, linguistic and religious identity of the child and family?
- Were more senior managers or other organisations and professionals involved at points where they should have been?

- Was the work in this case consistent with each organisation's and the LSCBs' policy and procedures for safeguarding and promoting the welfare of children, and with wider professional standards?

What do we learn from this case?

- Are there lessons from this case for the way in which this organisation works to safeguard and promote the welfare of children?
- Is there good practice to highlight, as well as ways in which practice can be improved?
- Are there implications for ways of working, training (single- and inter-agency), management and supervision, working in partnership with other organisations, and resources?

Recommendations for action

- What action should be taken, by whom and when?
- What outcomes should these actions bring and how will the organisation evaluate whether they have been achieved?

As can be seen, the management review will be expected to contain a chronology of the agency's involvement. All the individual chronologies are subsequently merged into an integrated chronology. If the request is very clear, with a template of the chronology, the use of an appropriate spreadsheet, precise instructions regarding the designation of family members (e.g. initials) and of professionals (e.g. HV1, HV2, SW1, SW2), then the integration can be effected electronically and very smoothly. From bitter experience, if the instructions are not precise and/or are not adhered to, then the integration can be a very long and tedious 'cut and paste' process. An example of a chronology template is given in Figure 12.2.

Once it is known that a Serious Case Review is to be undertaken, each organisation will need to secure the case records to guard against loss or interference. A senior officer will be appointed to write the management review and this task will include reading and analysing the records and interviewing staff involved, including managers.

We are very mindful that this is a potentially large task including, for example, many years of Social Services' involvement and multiple health interventions. Therefore, inevitably, there tends to be a focus and emphasis on the chronology, i.e. the diary of who did what and when. However, it is in fact the analysis that is key to this process. The 10 bullet points are a very helpful trigger to the author to address and assess the information they have gathered. Similarly, in the third section, entitled 'What do we learn from this case?' the author needs to highlight the issues that are raised there. From experience and

Date	Family member	Agency/ source	Episode/event	Outcome/action/ communication	Notes
Column formatted to standard date format.	Use agreed abbreviations/ initials.	Source of the information	Brief description. NB: all cells formatted to wrap text, therefore not limited to how much can be entered.	Any action taken and by whom; include any responses by other agencies	e.g. links to body of report/policy or procedures, cross referencing to files, case notes etc.
22/4/06	HM	Health	Home visit to review progress.	HV1 noted poor maternal bonding with child and flat effect; discussed with line manager.	See page 10 of review report.
27/4/06	GM	Health	Attended for repeat prescription of methadone.	Prescription issued, noted in GP record.	No indication from notes of actual compliance.

Figure 12.2 Chronology template

from much of the literature, we would want to emphasise supervision and support. We are also very keen that we learn from good practice and successes, not only highlighting shortcomings.

STAFF CARE

Inevitably, it is a very stressful time for the staff in all of the organisations when a child on their caseload has died or suffered serious injuries, or when there has been a death or serious incident in other circumstances. It is therefore essential that those involved in the Serious Case Review process, whether internally at management-review level or externally at LSCB level, are very sensitive to the feelings and needs of the staff. Before the staff are interviewed, they need to know the terms of reference, the purpose, the process and the time scale of the review. As their case records have been secured elsewhere, they will need access to the records prior to an interview. Interviews should be set up in advance by appointment and take place in a decent venue with hospitality and privacy. Each organisation needs to have a policy on the interviewee having a supporter – a friend, a colleague, conceivably a trade union representative or a legal advisor. Interview notes must be prepared and shared with the interviewee prior to the management report being written so that accuracy can be checked.

'Serious Case Reviews are not part of any disciplinary process . . . but information that emerges . . . may indicate that disciplinary action should be taken under established procedures . . . in some cases disciplinary action may be needed urgently to safeguard and promote the welfare of other children' (HM Government 2006b, para. 8.24). Organisations should also consider whether staff involved need extra professional or personal support and/or to be referred for counselling.

THE OVERVIEW REPORT

It is envisaged that the production of management reviews will take a minimum of six weeks; eventually they are presented to the Serious Case Review panel, which then commences a series of meetings, partly to identify further enquiries and to resolve any inconsistencies, partly to debate and analyse the information, and also perhaps to meet family members. There is a strong argument in favour of undertaking a consultation exercise by distributing relevant sections of the draft to the relevant agencies, giving them an opportunity to check for accuracy and to comment on interpretations.

The objective of this stage of the process is to prepare and agree (through a number of drafts) the overview report, which is to be presented to the LSCB. Again, there is a template for the overview report in *Working Together* (Box 12.3).

Again, as we suggested in relation to management reviews, there is a danger that too much attention is given to the facts whereas the essential purpose is to produce an analysis which leads to the conclusions and the lessons to be learned. In making a series of recommendations, the panel in general and the overview author in particular must ensure that the recommendations are SMART, i.e. specific, measurable, achievable, realistic and timely.

An example of recommendations relating to the chronic and 'stuck' nature of long-term neglect cases was as follows:

Social and housing services

1. To conduct a specific, live (i.e. home visit) audit and review in cases of neglect open over six months; this will focus on the environmental domain of the assessment framework, and will include hygiene, finances, the children's bedrooms, clothing and so on.
2. To undertake an independent audit and review as per recommendation 1 above in all cases of neglect open over 12 months. The independence would come from a senior or possibly a different social worker.

These were accepted by the LSCB and it is known that they have been implemented successfully by Social and Housing Services.

An example of a non-specific recommendation would be: 'Doctors should receive child-protection training.'

An example of a recommendation that would be impossible to measure would be: 'Hospital records for babies and children must contain all relevant information.'

Box 12.3 Overview report

Source: Crown copyright material is reproduced with the permission of the Controller of HMSO and Queen's Printer for Scotland.

Introduction

- Summarise the circumstances that led to a review being undertaken in this case.
- State terms of reference of review.
- List contributors to review and the nature of their contributions (for example, management review by LA and report from adult mental health service). List review panel members and author of overview report.

The Facts

- Prepare a genogram showing membership of family, extended family and household.
- Compile an integrated chronology of involvement with the child and family on the part of all relevant organisations, professionals and others who have contributed to the review process. Note specifically in the chronology each occasion on which the child was seen and the child's wishes and feelings sought or expressed.
- Prepare an overview which summarises what relevant information was known to the agencies and professionals involved, about the parents/carers, any perpetrator and the home circumstances of the children.

Analysis

This part of the overview should look at how and why events occurred, decisions were made and actions taken or not. This is the part of the report in which reviewers can consider, with the benefit of hindsight, whether different decisions or actions may have led to an alternative course of events. The analysis section is also where any examples of good practice should be highlighted.

Conclusions and recommendations

This part of the report should summarise what, in the opinion of the review panel, are the lessons to be drawn from the case and how those lessons should be translated into recommendations for action. Recommendations should include, but should not simply be limited to, the recommendations made in individual reports from each organisation. Recommendations should be few in number, focused and specific, and capable of being implemented. If there are lessons for national, as well as local, policy and practice these should also be highlighted.

An example of a recommendation that is unrealistic might be: 'The Assistant Director of Social Services should ensure that all referrals for Family Support receive a response within 24 hours.'

Taken from *Safeguarding Through Audit* (Handley & Green 2004).

If the recommendations are SMART they can easily be converted into an action plan, an example of which is reproduced in Figure 12.3.

Some of the recommendations will be multi-disciplinary, e.g. Local Safeguarding Children Board procedures or training; others will be agency-specific and it is the responsibility of the LSCB through its subcommittees to audit the plans until they can be signed off.

The overview report is presented to the Local Safeguarding Children Board as an agenda item in an ordinary meeting, or sometimes an extraordinary meeting is scheduled specifically to receive the report. The LSCB may not accept the report and may ask for further work to be done. However, assuming that the report is accepted and signed off by the chairperson of the LSCB, consideration will then have to be given to publication of the whole report or only an executive summary; many LSCBs are now placing these overview reports on their websites. Consideration will also need to be given to debrief-

Recommendation	Agency(cies) responsible	Action to be taken to implement recommendation	Date for completion
The recommendation comes from the overview panel and should be as specific as possible.	Identify which agency(cies) are responsible, and where possible the person within that agency who should take responsibility for ensuring the recommendation is carried out.	All action points need to be specific and measurable and should relate to specific dates for completion. Individual agencies may need to further develop the action plan, with specific steps to be taken to achieve each point.	
1. The LSCB explores with partner agencies the development of an inter-agency protocol relating to the identification and management of cases where self-harming behaviour by a child or young person has been identified as a problem.	WSCB chairperson to convene group.	Group to review current guidance, extend to involve education, primary care. Develop inter-agency protocol to be held in single-agency procedures. New procedures to be notified to LSCB.	November 2006 April 2007
2. There should be a comprehensive review of record keeping, filing and storage in the Midwifery Service in relation to child protection and in situations where other child welfare concerns are raised. This review is to be undertaken with the support of Primary Care Trust Child Protection Teams.	Health: Midwifery manager. Designated nurse for child protection.	Review of Midwifery record-keeping, filing and storage in relation to child protection and child welfare concerns. Guidance and support to be given by Child Protection Teams. Report to LSCB on progress achieved.	December 2006

Figure 12.3 Template for recommendations

ing and feeding back to staff and family members, plus dissemination of the key findings and the lessons to be learned – perhaps via a newsletter, training programmes and so on. Copies of the overview report, the action plan and the individual management reviews are sent to OFSTED and the DCSF.

'At least as much effort should be spent on acting upon recommendations as on conducting the review' (HM Government 2006b, para. 8.34),

A summary of the process is contained in Figure 12.4.

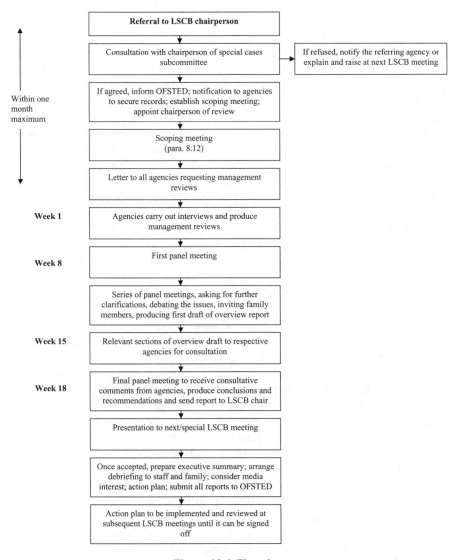

Figure 12.4 Flowchart

ISSUES ARISING FROM SERIOUS CASE REVIEWS

The following two subsections arise from findings in previous Serious Case Reviews, some from the lead author's cohort, some from literature and others from nationally-reported reviews. They are offered in the spirit of learning from these cases.

FAMILY CHARACTERISTICS

Whilst family characteristics in fatal abuse cases have been reviewed elsewhere, a few specific issues are worth highlighting because of the implications for Serious Case Review processes. Published literature confirms a high correlation between child abuse/neglect and domestic violence – 'recurrent violence between partners was reported in at least half of the cases' (Reder et al. 1993); 62% in *Learning from Past Experience* (Sinclair & Bullock 2002); and 60% in the cohort of Serious Case Reviews chaired by the lead author. A more recent perspective of 'couple fighting', i.e. where each partner is equally a perpetrator and a victim, suggests that the children are even more at risk as the couple are oblivious to the safety of the children. It is therefore essential that consideration is given to whether domestic violence played a role and how professionals responded to any such violence.

Reder reports: 'the cases indicated a significant association between fatal child abuse and mental health problems in the caretakers' (Reder & Duncan 1999). Falkov reports: 'clear evidence of psychiatric morbidity in one or both of the child's caretakers in at least 32% of the cases' (Falkov 1995). Significant mental health or depression is reported in 60% of the lead author's cohort. Other frequently reported circumstances include substance misuse (both alcohol and drugs) and parents having experienced a deprived, neglectful or even abusive background themselves. It is important to consider the health (including mental health) records of the parents/carers. Confidentiality needs to be respected but such information can be disclosed for a Serious Case Review as it is in the public interest to do so.

In the lead author's cohort there was only evidence of stability in the family relationships in 5 out of 20 cases, i.e. 75% were characterised by frequent separations, the children being moved between relatives and so on. The family itself may be the only accurate source of information on family relationships and consideration should be given to exploring this with the family.

Another feature which has appeared quite frequently is that of a significant lack of antenatal care (or indeed none) and/or concealed pregnancies (several instances, both in the national literature and in the lead author's cohort). Furthermore, elements of deceit must be acknowledged, e.g. one of the concealed pregnancies was the woman's eighth pregnancy, while all six of her previous children were being looked after by relatives or had been adopted (plus a stillbirth). In another case it was the woman's fourth pregnancy and when she arrived at hospital she professed shock and surprise, claiming that she did not know she was pregnant, and yet she had disclosed it to a third party a few days earlier. Other aspects of deceit manifest themselves as giving false explanations of injuries, breaching bail conditions (in several examples the perpetrator of the abuse should not even have been at the scene, according to bail conditions) and giving aliases/false names to avoid checks showing up previous information.

A failure to engage with the services becomes very apparent in retrospect, i.e. sequences of failed appointments at clinics and schools, no reply home visits by social workers even when made by appointment; these need to be charted and shared across agencies at the time in order to appreciate their significance.

SOME PROFESSIONAL AND PRACTICE ISSUES

Writing in the wake of the Jasmine Beckford inquiry, Dingwall asks the question: 'What stops people acquiring and using relevant information?' (Dingwall 1986). He answers his own question by pointing out that the necessary information was not available at an appropriate time and in a useable form; he analyses four types of information:

- that which is completely unknown
- that which is known but not fully appreciated
- that which is known but not fully assembled
- that which is available to be known but does not fit current modes of understanding.

In Section 4.2 of the 1991 *Study of Enquiry Reports* (Department of Health 1991) there is a focus on what might be characterised as 'the information is there, but . . .' Using this framework, the information is there, but . . .

1. The source is not valued. Referrals from neighbours or relatives, which are anonymous and are attributed to be malicious and therefore downgraded. **Malice is a motive; it does not measure the truth or accuracy of the referral information.**

Case example A – Source not valued

Young parents were going through an acrimonious separation with a view to divorce. Their two-month-old baby sustained head injuries, which the mother explained as an accident, i.e. the child slipped out of the pram as she was negotiating steps up to the flat. The father made a referral to Social Services, stating that he did not believe this explanation. The danger was that the possible motive of the referral distracted professionals from the analysis of risk contained in his information, i.e. that the injuries were in fact non-accidental.

---

2. New information is not let into the established mode or not distinguished from the flood. In long-term neglect cases with months or even years of involvement from many different agencies and services, referrals and new information which meet the Section 47 threshold are often regarded as 'more of the same' and filed/regarded as 'routine'. This reinforces the Lord Laming recommendations in the Victoria Climbié inquiry about how crucial it is to have chronologies up to date and easily accessible.
These are stories, not episodes.

Case example B – Not letting it into the established mode

The name of a child aged two was placed on the Child Protection Register under the category of neglect and therefore the focus of all the professional intervention was on neglect. As the risks had apparently reduced, the child's name was de-registered at the first review conference. In fact, the child had sustained some bruises, which were attributed to accidental falling and poor parenting. There injuries continued post-registration until the child was presented to hospital with multiple and life-threatening injuries, including current and old fractures. The original bruises should have been perceived and investigated on their own merit, and not categorised within a narrow neglect 'silo'.

---

3. There is still a lack of an appropriate and necessary focus on the child. Adult services (psychiatry, psychology and substance misuse teams) and general practitioners are still reluctant to share information, which may impact on the safety of a child, under the umbrella of patient confidentiality (i.e. the adult's/parent's confidentiality). The new edition of *Working Together to Safeguard Children* (HM Government 2006b) has taken account of the Bischard inquiry recommendations following the Soham tragedy, with its focus on information sharing and the paramountcy principle of child protection.
4. There is often a lack of rigorous assessment. This is described in detail in the Peter Reder literature (Reder et al. 1993, Reder & Duncan 1999) and is evident in the lead author's cohort; in over 50% of the Serious Case Reviews there had not been a rigorous assessment, which means that vital analysis is missing.
The best indicator of dangerousness is past evidence.
5. Too much weight has been given to the children's wishes and insufficient weight has been given to the children's best interests.

Case example C – Wishes/best interests

Two boys aged nine and six were residing with their mother, who had separated from their father on the grounds of domestic violence and intimidation. The father was having limited daytime contact but made an application to the court for staying contact. A Family Court Welfare Officer report (following an assessment) recommended that this should not be granted even though the boys had expressed a wish to do so to their mother's lawyer. A proposal took place outside of the court to which the judge gave his agreement, i.e. that the boys should have overnight contact, and on the first evening the father hanged both boys. Too much credence had been given to their wishes and insufficient credence to their best interests.

---

6. There is intra-agency communication breakdown, not only inter-agency communication failures, which are invariably reported. A notable example of intra-agency communication problems is that of uniformed and beat police officers not adequately processing domestic violence incidents by reporting/referring to their family protection units and thus links with the Child Protection Register and/or Social Services being missed.

Case example D – Intra-agency communication breakdown

A young child was living in a home environment frequented by several adults. Uniformed police were frequently called out to incidents of fighting, intimidation, damage to property and 'disturbance of the peace'. However, they did not identify the possible impact on the baby of this broader perspective of domestic violence and therefore did not liaise with their family protection unit colleagues, up to the point of the baby dying of multiple injuries aged eight months.

---

7. The use of language distracts colleagues. If a doctor or nurse describes an injury as 'minor', other professionals are likely to downgrade it. However, a minor manifestation, e.g. a small laceration, may be extremely suspicious and risky in its causation in particular circumstances and therefore, in fact, may need to attract a high-level response. Similarly, what was a child protection plan in a departing authority may be interpreted as a family support plan in a receiving authority and, in so doing, attract a very different level of intervention.

Case example E – Differing interpretations

A young child was placed on the Child Protection Register following a fatal assault on a sibling. One element of the Child Protection Plan was that she would reside with her grandmother in another authority whilst her mother undertook an assessment. At the receiving-in conference in the new authority, it was determined that as there were no identified risks in this new area, the child's name would not be placed on the Child Protection Register, i.e. there was an inconsistency between the two authorities. Moreover, no social work intervention was offered. When the mother subsequently came to live with her own mother in the second authority and went on to have another baby, no risks were perceived until that child died at the age of 11 weeks. The precise cause of death was unascertainable but starvation was likely to be a contributory factor as the baby had not been fed for more than 15 hours prior to admission.

IN CONCLUSION

Serious Case Reviews have over the years had a major impact on child protection practice in the UK. Alongside the other child death review practices described in this book, Serious Case Reviews remain an important statutory role of Local Safeguarding Children Boards. In order for them to be truly worthwhile, however, they need to have a clear focus with defined terms of reference, a focused scoping exercise, full and frank sharing of information by all agencies, and careful analysis of the data. Too often Serious Case Reviews have been accused of repeating the same conclusions, or of suggesting unrealistic or vague recommendations that do not achieve change. To move beyond this we would suggest that a lot more emphasis needs to be placed on doing these reviews well. In particular, on moving beyond simply creating a chronology and recognising failings, to analysing the findings and translating these into specific, measurable and achievable recommendations that are then backed up by well-thought-through and monitored action plans.

It is also important that the findings from Serious Case Reviews should feed into the overall child death review processes and that findings from across the country are collated. It is therefore encouraging to see a revitalisation of the early studies which collated and published thematic findings. To date, there has been an inadequate use made of the wealth of case material contained in literally hundreds or even thousands of Serious Case Reviews. The dissemination of the lessons has tended to be somewhat haphazard, i.e. some are in the public domain but many are not. It is perhaps even more regrettable that regional offices of the Commission for Social Care Inspection (CSCI) have not taken this initiative at a more local level. Within Local Safeguarding Children Board

areas there are various initiatives at dissemination, such as briefings and training programmes, and, indeed, as stated earlier, some Local Safeguarding Children Boards put the executive summaries on their website.

It is extremely important that the lessons from the many Serious Case
Reviews are learned locally, regionally and nationally, and not only the high-
profile cases such as that of Victoria Climbié. We owe it to all children at risk
of abuse and neglect 'to improve child protection procedures and practices'
by learning the lessons from those children who have been fatally abused.

Appendix 1 Emergency Department Flow Chart and Checklist

Source: Reproduced by permission of University of Warwick.

Unexpected Death in Childhood: A Handbook for Practitioners. Edited by P. Sidebotham and P. Fleming.
Copyright © 2007 by John Wiley & Sons, Ltd.

Baby/child found lifeless – ambulance called by 999
Ambulance informs Emergency Department

Emergency Dept triage nurse receiv ing call, notes time and notifies:
- Senior Emergency Dept resuscitation team – prepares equipment and drugs
- Paediatric registrar – informs consultant
- Nurse allocated for parents (experienced, trained)
- *Ward clerk orders child and par ent medical records from store, for immediate delivery*

Ambulance arrives at Emergency Department

Emergency Department resuscitation room
- Attempt resuscitation
- Preliminary history
- Preliminary examination
- Obtain laboratory specimens
- Rectal temperature and time
- Most senior doctor discusses with team and parents prior to stopping resuscitation

Parents
- Greet at door
- Quiet room
- Offer to view resuscitation accompanied
- Offer chaplain

Emergency Department following resuscitation
- Senior paediatrician declares dead and notifies police/coroner
- If coroner agrees, may wipe face, remove ET tube (after visualisation) and IV cannulae
- Complete paediatric examination (Appendix 3)
- Clothing removal must follow police protocol
- Put on clean nappy; wrap in hospital baby blanket

Parents
- Carry baby into room in arms as a baby
- Refer to baby by name
- Give baby to parents to hold but supervise at all times

Parents interviewed by paediatrician and police to obtain full history
Consider health and child protection needs of family

Complete documentation
Complete notification (checklist)

Caring for the family
- Mementoes and photos
- Procedural information
- Bereavement support

Multi-agency strategy discussion

Staff debrief

Parents return home; arrangements for home visit

Sudden unexpected death in infancy – checklist

Child's details (addressograph label)
NAME:
DOB:
Address:

Name of paediatrician:
Name of staff member supporting parent(s):
Name of police officer in charge:

ACTION	Y/N/NA*	DATE	TIME	ACTIONED BY
Consultant paediatrician called				
Police child protection team informed; Name:				
Coroner's officer informed; Name:				
Specialist paediatrician called; Name:				
Initial history taken and recorded				
Soiled or wet nappy bagged, labelled and stored				
Sites of vascular access during resuscutation documented				
Detailed physical examination of child				
Body map/diagrams				
Photographs				
Samples taken sent for examination; Details:				
Social Services enquiries made				

GP informed			
HV informed			
Hospital chaplain or other religious leader contacted if appropriate			
Child Health Computer and hospital PAS system informed			
Mementoes taken for parents			
Hair			
Footprint			
Handprint			
Photograph			
FSID pack and contact details given to parents			

* Y – yes, N – no, NA – not applicable

Appendix 2 History Proforma

Source: Reproduced by permission of University of Warwick.

1. Identification data

Name of child   Sex M/F

                                                   Ethnicity

Date of birth   Date of death

Address

Postcode

Name of father (+ address if different from child)   DOB

Name of mother (+ address if different from child)   DOB

Name of partner (if relevant + address)   DOB

GP name & address

Consultant

SUDI consultant

Police officer/senior investigating officer

Social worker

Coroner/coroner's officer

Other professionals

Unexpected Death in Childhood: A Handbook for Practitioners. Edited by P. Sidebotham and P. Fleming.
Copyright © 2007 by John Wiley & Sons, Ltd.

2. Details of transport of child to hospital

Place of death: home address as above/another location (specify)/DGH (specify)

Time found   Time arrived in A&E

Resuscitation carried out?   Y/N   Where?: at scene of death/Ambulance/A&E

By whom: carers/GP/ambulance crew/hosp staff/others (specify)

Confirmation of death   Date   Time   Location   By whom?

3. History

Taken in A&E by   Taken at home visit by

History given by

Relationship to child

Events surrounding death

Note: who found the child, where and when; appearance of the child when
    found?
Who called emergency services?
When child was last seen alive and by whom?
Details of any resuscitation at home, by ambulance crew and in hospital.
For accidental/traumatic deaths, details of circumstances around the death;
    witnesses.

Detailed narrative account of last 24–48 hrs

To include details of all activities and carers during last 24–48 hours.
Any alcohol or drugs consumed by child or carers.
For SUDI, include details of last sleep including where and how put down,
    where and how found, any changes; details of feeding and care given.
Details of when last seen by a doctor or other professional.
Further details of previous 2–4 weeks, including child's health, any changes to
    routine.

Family history

Details of all family and household members including names; dates of birth;
    health, any previous or current illnesses including mental health; any medi-
    cations; occupation.
Maternal parity and obstetric history.

Parental relationships.
Children, including children by previous partners.
Household composition.
Any previous childhood deaths in the family.

Past medical history

Of the child, to include pregnancy and delivery; perinatal history; feeding; growth and development.
Health and any previous or current illnesses; hospital admissions; any medication.
Routine checks and immunisations.
Systems review.
Behavioural and educational history where appropriate.

Social history

Type and nature of housing; any major life events.
Any travel abroad.
Wider family support networks.

Any other relevant history

May vary according to the age of the child, nature of the death.

Information retrieved from records

Hospital, GP, Health Visitor, midwife, NHS direct, etc. (include family-held records such as Health Visitor red book).
Ambulance crew.
Social Services, databases, case records, Child Protection Register.
Police – intelligence, assist, PNC, domestic violence, etc.

Appendix 3 Physical Examination Proforma

Source: Reproduced by permission of University of Warwick.

To be carried out by consultant paediatrician and CPT supervisor/manager – CSI to be utilised for photographs, etc. where relevant.

Physical examination carried out by:

- Rectal temp (low reading thermometer) _____
  Date/time _____ and interval from death _____
- Full growth measurements   Centile
  length   _____   _____
  head circumference   _____   _____
  weight   _____   _____
- Retinal examination
- State of nutrition and hygiene
- Marks, livido, bruises or evidence of injury – to include any medical puncture sites and failed attempts: **(Should also be drawn on body chart overleaf)**
  NB: Check genitalia and back.
       Check mouth: is the fraenum of lips/tongue intact?
- *Further details, observations and comments*
- List all drugs given at hospital and any interventions carried out at resuscitation.
- Document direct observation of position of endotracheal tube prior to removal.

Date, time
Signature(s)

Unexpected Death in Childhood: A Handbook for Practitioners. Edited by P. Sidebotham and P. Fleming.
Copyright © 2007 by John Wiley & Sons, Ltd.

Appendix 4 Laboratory Investigations

Source: Reproduced by permission of The Royal College of Pathologists and The Royal College of Paediatrics and Child Health.

After death is confirmed, the body is under the jurisdiction of the coroner. Complex investigations should be discussed with the coroner first.

Blood samples should be taken from a venous or arterial site (e.g. femoral vein) – cardiac puncture should be avoided as this may cause damage to the intrathoracic structures and make post-mortem findings difficult to interpret. If the post mortem is to be conducted within 24 hours it may be best for the samples to be taken by the pathologist.

Sample	Send to:	Handling	Test
Blood (Serum) 0.5 ml	Clinical Chemistry	Normal	Urea and electrolytes
Blood (Serum) 1 ml	Clinical Chemistry	Spin, store serum at −20 °C	Toxicology
Blood (Lithium heparin) 1 ml	Clinical Chemistry	Spin, store plasma at −20 °C	Inherited metabolic disease
Blood (Fluoride) 1 ml	Clinical Chemistry	Spin, store plasma at −20 °C	3OH butyrate, sugar, FFA, lactate
Blood EDTA 0.5 mls	Haematology	Normal	FBC
Blood cultures – aerobic and anaerobic 1 ml	Microbiology	If insufficient blood, aerobic only	Culture and sensitivity
Blood from syringe onto Guthrie card	Clinical Chemistry	Normal (fill in card – **do not put into plastic bag**)	Inherited metabolic diseases

Unexpected Death in Childhood: A Handbook for Practitioners. Edited by P. Sidebotham and P. Fleming.
Copyright © 2007 by John Wiley & Sons, Ltd.

Blood (Lithium Heparin) 5 ml	Cytogenetics	Normal – keep unseparated	Chromosomes (if dysmorphic)
CSF (a few drops)	Microbiology	Normal	Microscopy, culture and sensitivity
CSF 0.5 ml	Clinical Chemistry	Store at –20 °C	Inherited metabolic diseases
Swabs	Microbiology	Normal	Culture and sensitivity
Urine (if available)	Clinical Chemistry	Obtain on filter paper by squeezing nappy. Spin, store supernatant –20 °C	Toxicology, inherited metabolic diseases
Urine (few drops, if above sample taken)	Microbiology	Normal	Microscopy, culture and sensitivity

Total Blood Samples:

Clotted blood	1.5–2 ml
Lithium heparin	1 ml
Fluoride	1 ml
EDTA	0.5 ml
Blood culture	1 ml

in practice, difficulties with obtaining samples may necessitate smaller samples.

NB: Optimal microbiological and virological investigation after SUDI is currently the subject of a review by the Health Protection Agency, which will aim to produce definitive, evidence-based recommendations within the near future. The current recommendations should be seen as an interim minimum standard.

1a. Additional samples to be considered after discussion with consultant paediatrician.
   1. Skin biopsy for fibroblast culture.
   2. Muscle biopsy if history is suggestive of mitochondrial disorder.

1b. Forensic considerations
- Ensure you have the permission of the coroner to take samples.
- Document all samples taken, label and ensure an unbroken 'chain of evidence'.
- This may mean handing samples to a police office directly, or having the laboratory technician sign on receiving them in the laboratory.
- Samples given to police or coroner's officer must be signed for.
- Record the site from which all samples were taken.

Appendix 5 Scene Examination Proforma

Source: Reproduced by permission of University of Warwick.

Child's name _____

Date of birth _____ **Date of death** _____

Address _____

Date of scene visit _____

Persons present _____

Room

Note: size; orientation (compass); contents; 'clutter'; ventilation – windows and doors (open or shut); heating – (including times switched on/off); measure drawer temperature __ __ __ __ __ __ __ °C.

Sleep environment

Note: location, position of bed/cot in relation to other objects in room; mattress, bedding, objects.

Unexpected Death in Childhood: A Handbook for Practitioners. Edited by P. Sidebotham and P. Fleming.
Copyright © 2007 by John Wiley & Sons, Ltd.

Position of baby

When put down; when found

- **Any evidence of over-wrapping or over-heating?**   **Yes/No**
- **Any restriction to ventilation or breathing?**   **Yes/No**
- **Any risk of smothering?**   **Yes/No**
- **Any potential hazards?**   **Yes/No**
- **Any evidence of neglectful care?**   **Yes/No**

Diagram of scene

Note: north/south orientation; room measurements; location of doors, windows, heating; any furniture and objects in the room.

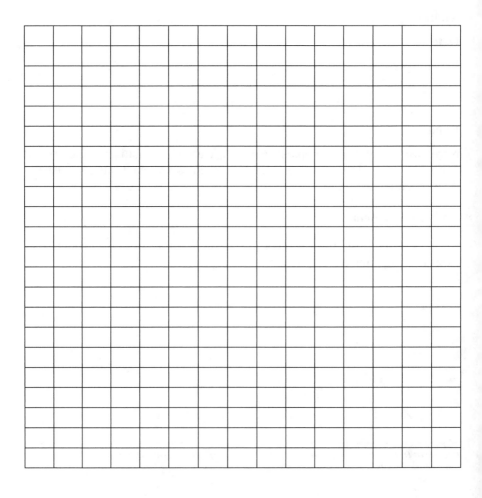

Appendix 6 Resources for Bereaved Adults (Parents, Family Members, Friends)

Source: Reproduced by permission of Dent and Stewart.

There are now a wealth of organisations offering information, support groups, online resources and telephone helplines. Many of these provide resources for bereaved adult family members, bereaved children and the professionals working with families – hence we have listed them under headings of child bereavement in general and then specific categories.

Rather than list a range of texts and leaflets we have listed organisations which have resource lists, libraries of books and videos, links to websites and book reviews – predominantly in the UK, which then link to international organisations and a few from overseas.

[NB Every attempt has been made to ensure that information is accurate at the time of going to press. However, given the changing nature of groups and organisations it is likely that some addresses will have altered and new websites developed during the time that this book is published.]

CHILD BEREAVEMENT IN GENERAL

Alder Centre

Royal Liverpool Children's NHS Trust
Alder Hey, Eaton Road, Liverpool L12 2AP
Tel: 0151 252 9759
Provides information and support after death of a child for any reason.

Alliance of Grandparents, A Support in Tragedy

www.agast.org
Provides support and information for bereaved grandparents.

Unexpected Death in Childhood: A Handbook for Practitioners. Edited by P. Sidebotham and P. Fleming.
Copyright © 2007 by John Wiley & Sons, Ltd.

Centering Corporation

www.centering.org
Has an extensive range of books for sale, based in the US, also offers links to other grief sites.

Bereaved Parents USA

www.bereavedparentsusa.org
Provides monthly meetings, newsletters open to parents, siblings and grandparents.

Child Bereavement Trust

Aston House
West Wycombe, High Wycombe, Buckinghamshire HP14 3AG
Tel: 01494 446648 for general inquiries
Information and support line: 0845 357 1000
www.childbereavement.org.uk
Provides support for families after the death of a child and education for professionals.

Child Death Help-line

Great Ormond Street Hospital, London
And at Alder Hey Hospital, Liverpool
Freephone for both: 0800 282 986 (7pm–10pm each evening; and 10am–1pm Monday, Tuesday, Thursday and Friday; 10am–4pm Wednesday)
www.ich.ucl.ac.uk
www.childdeathhelpline.org.uk
Provides support from trained volunteers to anyone affected by the death of a child, from whatever cause.

Childhood Bereavement Network

National Children's Bureau, 8 Wakeley Street, London EC1V 7QE
Tel: 020 7843 6309
www.childhoodbereavementnetwork.org.uk
This organisation acts as an 'umbrella' linking individuals and agencies working with bereaved children and their families. It provides a list of services and information relevant to bereaved children throughout the UK.

Childline

Studd Street, London N1 0QW
Tel: 0207 239 1000

For Children: Freepost, NATN 1111 London E1 6BR
Tel: 0800 1111 (24 hour help-line)
www.childline.org.uk
Provides support to any child or young person including bereaved children.

The Compassionate Friends

53 North Street, Bristol BS3 1EN
Tel: 0845 123 2304 (help-line); 0845 120 3785 (enquiries)
www.tcf.org.uk
Provides support and information for families whose child has died for any reason and at any age.

Cruse Bereavement Care

PO Box 800, Richmond, Surrey TW9 1RG
Tel: 0208 939 9530; help-line: 0844 477 9400
www.crusebereavementcare.org.uk
Cruse offers support to anyone who has been bereaved. There are particular resources for schools and children (the Youth Involvement Project www.rd4u.org.uk – young people can telephone free on 0808 808 1677, Wednesdays 4pm–7pm or leave a message at any time).

Grief Recovery Online for all Bereaved

www.groww.com
Provides chatrooms, information, inspirational pages, memorial pages and links to other sites.

Growth House

www.growthhouse.org/death.html
Offers online support, chatroom, forum for professionals, resources and links to other sites.

SPECIFIC SITUATIONS OF DEATH

ACCIDENTS INCLUDING ROAD TRAFFIC CRASHES

Brake Care

PO Box 548, Huddersfield HD1 2XZ
Tel: 01484 559 909
www.brake.org.uk
Provides support and information for those bereaved by a road crash.

Campaign Against Drinking and Driving

PO Box 62, Brighouse, West Yorkshire HD6 3YY
Tel: 0845 123 5541
www.cadd.org.uk
Provides support and information for those bereaved by a road crash.

Road Peace

PO Box 2579, London NW10 3PW
Tel: 0208 838 5102; help-line: 0845 4500 355
www.roadpeace.org
Provides support and information for those bereaved by a road crash.

PERINATAL AND INFANT DEATHS

Bliss

9 Holyrood Street, London SE1 2EL
Tel: 0207 378 1122
Help-line Tel: 0500 618140 (9.30am–5.30pm Mondays to Fridays)
www.bliss.org.uk
Provides support to families whose children live and/or die in neonatal intensive care units.

Foundation for the Study of Infant Deaths (FSID)

Artillery House, 11–19 Artillery Row, London SW1P 1RT
Tel: 0207 222 8001
Help-line 0207 233 2090 (9am–11pm Mondays to Fridays, 6pm–11pm Saturday and Sunday).
www.sids.org.uk
Provides support and information for parents and professionals.

SANDS (Stillbirth and Neonatal Death Society)

28 Portland Place, London W1B 1LY
Tel: 0207 436 7940; help-line: 0207 436 5881
www.uk-sands.org
Provides support and information for families and professionals after the death of a baby during late pregnancy or around birth.

Scottish Cot Death Trust

Royal Hospital, Yorkhill, Glasgow G3 8SJ
Tel: 0141 357 3946
www.sidscotland.org.uk
Provides support and information for bereaved families and professionals.

TAMBA (Twins & Multiple Births Association)

2 The Willows, Gardner Road, Guildford GU1 4PG
Tel: 0870 770 3305
www.tamba.org.uk
Provides support and information for families experiencing a multiple birth
and this includes where one or more of the children dies.

VOLUNTEER OR PROFESSIONAL
COUNSELLING RESOURCES

British Association of Counselling

BACP House, 15 St John's Business Park, Lutterworth LE17 4HB
Information line: 0870 443 5252
www.bacp.co.uk
Provides a list of approved counsellors in local areas.

Samaritans

PO Box 9090, Stirling FK8 2SA
Help-line: 08457 90 90 90 for bereavement support
www.samaritans.org.uk
Provides local branches and a 24 hour help-line, staffed by trained volunteers,
available for anyone in need whether as a result of bereavement or any other
life events.

INFECTION – MENINGITIS

Meningitis Research Foundation

Midland Way, Thornbury, Bristol BS35 2BS
24 hour help-line 080 880 03344
www.meningitis.org
Provides support to families whose child has died from meningitis.

National Meningitis Trust

Fern House, Bath Road, Stroud GL5 3TJ
General enquiries: 01453 768000
Help-line: 0345 7538118
Provides support to families whose child has died from meningitis.

SUICIDE

Survivors of Bereavement by Suicide (SOBS)

The Flamsteed Centre, Albert Street, Ilkeston, Derbyshire DE7 5GU
Tel: 0115 944 1117; help-line: 0870 241 3337
www.uk-sobs.org.uk
Provides support and information to those who have experienced suicide.

TRAUMA INCLUDING HOMICIDE

Mothers Against Drink Driving

www.madd.org
Based in the US, it provides information and support.

Parents of Murdered Children

www.pomc.com
Offers online support, group meetings, education and legal information.

Support After Murder and Manslaughter

Cranmer House
39 Brixton Road, London SW9 6DZ
Tel: 020 7735 3838
www.samm.org.uk
This organisation works with the Home Office and Victim Support to offer
training and support on the effects of murder and manslaughter for family and
friends.

Victim Support

Cranmer House, 39 Brixton Road, London SW9 6DZ
Tel: 0207 735 9166
www.victimsupport.com – redirects to Scotland, England, Wales and Republic
of Ireland sites.
Offers support to people who have experienced the effects of crime.

Appendix 7 Resources for Professionals

Source: Reproduced by permission of Dent and Stewart.

See the resources listed in Appendix 6 for family members. Many of these are relevant to professionals and have:

- information leaflets
- education sessions
- booklists.

RELEVANT JOURNALS INCLUDE

- *Journal of Omega, Death and Dying*
- *Mortality*
- *Bereavement Care* (sample articles available from www.crusebereavement-care.org.uk/ber_care.htm)

TEXTS

Many of the references we have used provide valuable resources for professionals. Others include:

Corr, C. & Balk, D. (1996) *Handbook of adolescent death and bereavement.* USA: Springer.

Lindsey, B. & Elsegood, J. (Eds.) (1996) *Working with children in loss and grief.* London: Bailliere Tindall.

Martin, T. & Doka, K. (1999) *Men don't cry – women do: Transcending gender stereotypes of grief.* London: Routledge.

Parkes, C. M., Launganui, P. & Young, B. (Eds.) (1997) *Death and bereavement across cultures.* London: Routledge.

Tschudin, V. (1996) *Counselling for loss and bereavement.* London: Balliere Tindall.

Unexpected Death in Childhood: A Handbook for Practitioners. Edited by P. Sidebotham and P. Fleming.
Copyright © 2007 by John Wiley & Sons, Ltd.

Walsh, F. & McGoldrick, M. (Eds.) (2004) *Living beyond loss: Death in the family*. USA: WW Norton.

Williams, M. (1996) 'An annotated resource list on traumatic loss.' In Doka, K. (Ed.) *Living with grief after sudden loss* (pp. 229–46). Taylor & Francis: Philadelphia.

Worden, W. (2001) *Grief counselling and grief therapy*. USA: Springer Publishing Co.

Wright, B. (1996) *Sudden death: A research base for practice* (2nd ed.). Edinburgh: Churchill Livingstone.

WEBSITES/ORGANISATIONS

Association for Death and Counselling

www.adec.org

Offers newsletter, conferences, publications and education that may be of use to health professionals.

Bereavement Research Forum

Secretary: Barbara James

The Rowans, Purbrook Heath Road, Waterlooville, Hants PO7 5RU

Tel: 023 9225 0001

email: barbara.james@rowanshospice.co.uk

The forum is a membership organisation offering three symposia yearly on different aspects of bereavement research. A conference is held bi-annually. There are opportunities for members to network, to learn about research and to discuss and be supported in their current or intended research.

Appendix 8 Practical Information for Families

Source: Reproduced by permission of Dent and Stewart.

This appendix provides an overview of the type of information which professionals may need to discuss with families. The nature and extent of such discussion will depend on the professional's role, the family's needs and the timing of contact with the family.

REGISTERING BIRTHS AND DEATHS

The Birth and Deaths Registration Act (1953) requires all births and deaths to be registered. There are varying requirements in Scotland and Northern Ireland.

The website www.statistics.gov.uk/registration provides details about the processes of registration in all countries in the United Kingdom. It enables people to search for their local office of the registrar of births, deaths and marriages. Details are also available in the local telephone directory. Written information is also provided in many of the booklets from self-help groups. Professionals need to make sure that families have time to ask questions about the processes of registration. Once registered, a birth or death certificate is issued and further copies can be obtained for a fee.

KEY POINTS

Birth

- After birth the health authority or hospital notifies the registrar of the birth.
- The birth must be registered by the mother and/or father (depending on whether they were married at the time of birth or conception) within 42 days of birth.
- Births can be registered in hospitals or at a local register office.

Unexpected Death in Childhood: A Handbook for Practitioners. Edited by P. Sidebotham and P. Fleming. Copyright © 2007 by John Wiley & Sons, Ltd.

Death

- Deaths must be registered within five days of the death unless there is a coronial investigation (see below).
- Deaths can be registered by relatives or someone present at the death – it does not have to be the parents of the child.
- Registration requires taking the medical certificate of cause of death to the local register office, unless a coroner is involved in which case the death cannot be registered until the coroner has completed their investigation.

INVOLVEMENT OF THE CORONER IN SUDDEN DEATHS

Under the Coroners Act (1988) certain deaths must be notified to the coroner before they can be registered. This includes deaths that are of unknown cause, sudden, unnatural or violent. The coroner is responsible to decide if further investigation is required. Investigations may include: post mortem; coroner's officer collecting further information by interviewing families and other witnesses; and/or criminal investigation in situations of likely homicide.

The coroner may decide that no further investigation is needed and a cause of death is confirmed, in which case the death can be registered. Alternatively there may be an inquest, in which case a cremation certificate or burial order may be issued by the coroner to enable the funeral to proceed, unless there are delays such as requiring further forensic tests in a criminal investigation.

Once the coroner informs the registrar about the cause of death, the death can be registered and a death certificate issued.

The Department of Health (DoH) funds a booklet produced by Victims' Voice, which is entitled *When sudden death occurs: Coroner and inquests*. This provides information for families about:

- the role of the coroner and coroner's officer
- the requirements for coroners to inquire into deaths
- post mortems, including return of organs to the body
- the purpose of the inquest
- the issue of a death certificate
- the timing of the funeral.

The rights of next-of-kin are noted, including:

- being told in advance of the date, time and place of the post mortem and the inquest
- having their choice of medical representative attending the post mortem
- being able to question witnesses at the inquest.

The booklet is available free:

- via the DoH website www.dh.gov.uk using the search term 'coroner'
- by accessing a link to the document at www.nnuh.nhs.uk/docs%5 Cleaflets%5C90.pdf
- by emailing Victims Voice at mailto:vv@coroner-info.org.uk
- on request from Victims' Voice at PO Box 110, Chippenham SN14 7BQ

POST MORTEMS

In sudden deaths where the cause of death is not known, such as cot death, the coroner requires a post mortem. In other situations, such as a known congenital abnormality, a post mortem is not always required but may provide information that helps understand the death or plan for future pregnancies.

The Department of Health website provides materials about families and post-mortems which include:

- a code for practice
- an information booklet for families [A simple guide to post-mortem examination procedure (29770/A)]
- consent forms.

These are available from www/dh.gov.uk/policy and/or by searching the DoH website www.dh.gov.uk using the search term 'post-mortem'.

The information booklet for families answers questions, in plain English, such as:

- who carries out post mortems?
- what is involved?
- when are the findings available?
- what about organ retention for diagnosis or, with permission of next of kin, for research?
- what are the options for full and partial post mortem?

Professionals talking with families about the information in this booklet need to take time to explain:

- who will undertake the post mortem (name of the pathologist)
- the possible value of information obtained from the post mortem
- the details of a post-mortem procedure including that a full post mortem generally has two incisions (back of the head and length of the breastbone), which are sutured after organs and tissues are returned (unless some samples are needed for further investigation) and then covered with a dressing
- where and when the post mortem will be done and when the child's body will be released
- who will contact the family and explain the post mortem to them.

ORGANISING A FUNERAL

Funeral directors can help families organise funerals. In some instances they will charge a minimal, or no, fee for the cost of a baby or young child's funeral. Costs vary among funeral directors, who are listed both in the local telephone directory and on websites such as those listed at the end of this appendix. For families on income support, it is possible to claim for costs directly from the Department of Social Services.

It can be helpful to reassure families that they can take the time to plan the funeral and that decisions do not have to be made in the first couple of days unless they wish for the funeral to occur immediately after the post mortem and release of the body.

Considerations that professionals may find appropriate to discuss with families include the following areas:

Burial or cremation? This generally depends on personal and religious beliefs. Other factors include whether the family:

- have a family burial plot
- want a place to visit which has a headstone, which requires burial
- feel that having a baby or child buried in a children's area of the cemetery is appropriate
- would prefer cremation and a commemorative plaque
- are able to afford the costs of a burial plot
- are concerned that there may be few ashes after cremation of a baby or young child.

Where will the service be held? The options include church, crematorium or funeral parlour.

What about travel for the child to the funeral? The family may wish to take the child in a casket in their own car and to carry them into the location of the service.

Open or closed casket? Depending on whether the child has any visible injuries and their general appearance after death, some families wish to keep the casket open until the end of the funeral service.

What type of service? Increasingly families are choosing a civil funeral as an alternative to services associated with a particular religion. Funeral directors can advise about funeral celebrants and ministers of religion. Alternatively, a family friend might conduct the service. Other decisions include whether to:

- make the service public or private for the family
- include other children at the funeral, in which case a family member can help parents take care of them
- accept flowers from friends and family at the funeral or ask for money to be given to a charity

- have a tribute book for people at the funeral to sign
- include in the service music, readings,[1] letters from family members
- have meaningful items in the room where the service is held such as: candles, flower arrangements with a particular theme associated with the child, toys, items that the child used, photographs in a collage or projected images during the funeral
- have opportunities for family and friends to put things in the casket such as toys, letters, drawings
- have a long or short service, particularly if children are attending
- end the service in a particular way (e.g. at a cremation does the casket remain or does it move behind the curtains? Is a symbolic ending such as releasing balloons planned?)
- audiotape or videotape the funeral service
- hold a funeral tea afterwards, and where this might be held and organised.

RESOURCES REGARDING CREMATION, BURIAL AND FUNERALS

Various ideas for cremation, burials and funerals are provided in leaflets available from bereavement organisations and in self-help texts.

CREMATION

Some information is available from The Cremation Society of Great Britain regarding provisions of facilities, respectful disposal and Catholics choosing cremation at www.srgw.demon.co.uk.

FUNERALS

Specific texts exist to aid planning a funeral (e.g. Nicola Daly (2005) *Sasha's legacy: A guide to funerals for babies*. Wellington, NZ: Steele Roberts). There are texts which include inspirational and memorial statements that might be used at a funeral or subsequent memorial service (e.g. Pinky Agnew (2006) *lifesongs: Readings for milestones*. Auckland, NZ: Random House). There are also websites which include compilations of music for when a child has died such as www.beforetheirtime.org.

Information is available about funerals, grief, books of condolence, bereavement organisations, and lists of local directors from:

---

[1]It is worth considering these choices carefully since they are forever associated with the funeral. For example, a favourite nursery rhyme of story which other siblings want to hear in the future may have very painful memories.

- National Association of Funeral Directors www.nafd.org.uk
- UK Funeral Guide and Directory of All Funeral Directors www.uk-funerals.co.uk
- National Society of Allied and Independent Funeral Director Services www.saif.org.uk

Appendix 9 Opportunities to Be with Their Child

Source: Reproduced by permission of Dent and Stewart.

Many families do not realise that they can spend time with their dead child. Depending on the circumstances, this may be in a hospital Emergency Department, in a mortuary, at a funeral parlour or at home. These examples may provide ideas for families about ways to be with their child.

Sitting with and touching their child. Consider where possible: a private and quiet location; having a professional to be with the family; avoiding interruptions; removing equipment such as intravenous cannulae (unless these are required to remain for a post mortem); and covering injuries to allow family members the choice of whether to look.

Washing and dressing their child. Make sure that parents know what opportunities can exist for this, whether in a hospital setting, at a funeral directors or at home. Generally if the child goes to the family home, then transport can be organised by the funeral director. If parents wish to take the child in their own vehicle this needs to be checked with local policies and, in case of an accident en route, a note needs to be attached to the child indicating that they are dead and being taken home.

Meaningful rituals for the dead child which reflect the family's personal and spiritual beliefs. If these need to occur at the scene of death or in a mortuary then consider who needs to attend, the size of the location required and particular requirements for the ritual. For many families, such rituals are about creating mementoes of their child.

Creating mementoes of their child. Examples of such mementos include photographs of the child, hand/foot/kiss prints of ink on paper or plaster casts of hand or foot, locks of hair, nail clippings, a video of visitors to see the child, a journal in which visitors write and the child's belongings such as the clothes that they died wearing. Considerations include: ensuring that family members request and consent to having mementoes. There are some families who may feel that a photograph is inappropriate or a spiritual violation. In some instances, families may want photographs taken and then held in the child's

Unexpected Death in Childhood: A Handbook for Practitioners. Edited by P. Sidebotham and P. Fleming.
Copyright © 2007 by John Wiley & Sons, Ltd.

file until such time as they wish to have them. See Appendix 10 for factors relevant to photographs and prints.

Going with their child to the mortuary or funeral directors. Consider what family or local support is available to take the parents and other siblings to the mortuary or funeral directors and then return them home.

Visiting their child. Ensure that families know:

- when, where and how they can visit their child, whether in a mortuary or at a funeral directors' parlour
- the time of any post mortem and when the child's body will be released for a funeral.

Appendix 10 Creating Footprints, Photographs and Mementoes

Source: Reproduced by permission of Dent and Stewart.

PRINTS OF HANDS, FEET AND MOUTH

Considerations include the following:

- **How** the print is taken. Is it an inkpad which requires subsequent cleaning of the skin with an alcohol wipe and may leave dark smudges, or is it a wipe with a sensitised label for an imprint?
- **One or two?** In general, it is worth taking a pair of prints and putting these facing each other on a card.
- **Card for the print.** Many hospitals and some funeral directors have presentation cards specifically for use with hand and footprints.
- **Making a clear print.** This requires a steady hand to press the hand or foot on the card without moving and smudging. With older children, it can be useful to have two people, one to take the weight of the arm or leg whilst the other places the hand or foot on the card.
- **Who does it?** Sometimes family members want to make the prints.
- **Mouth (or kiss) print.** These can be created with the use of lipstick.
- **Storage of prints.** For future use the images on a card can be scanned into a computer.
- **Allowing time to dry.** This is particularly important if an inkpad or thick lipstick is used. Sometimes a coat of lacquer can help to protect a lipstick image on the card.

PHOTOGRAPHS

Considerations include the following:

- **Who takes the photograph?** This might be family members (who may also want to be in the photograph), friends or a professional photographer.

Unexpected Death in Childhood: A Handbook for Practitioners. Edited by P. Sidebotham and P. Fleming.
Copyright © 2007 by John Wiley & Sons, Ltd.

Factors to consider are costs, skills of the photographer and the need for good quality photographs, which in the case of a newly-born baby may be very important.

- **What type of photograph?** Digital photography has tended to supersede discussion about risks of polaroid cameras, where the image may fade over time. Consider the pixel capabilities of any camera in order to maximise image quality for any future use. Print film can produce multiple sets with images stored on CD.
- **What and who is in the photograph?** This requires consideration of:
  - whether it is to be a solo photograph with the child or with different family members in groups looking at/touching/holding the child
  - use of a flashlight, which may improve detail but will create harsher images
  - choice of clothes that the child is wearing
  - focus on a particular part of the child if there has been damage in a crash or accident
  - choice of background for the photographs – try to avoid a busy background (floral curtains) or a clinical setting (with white walls).
- **How many photographs?** The answer from most families is – many. Take plenty and have the video running for long periods of time. Then even if there is an equipment failure, there are still plenty of photographs to choose from.
- **Where to print the photographs?** For frequent viewing, consider quality of paper and of printer, which may mean having selected images produced by a film shop.
- **Where to store?** Keeping multiple copies on CD, in print and in different locations can avoid damage or loss with burglary or fire.

CLOTHES

The smell and touch of the clothes in which the child died may be very important to families. It is important to ask families before assuming that they will not want to keep damaged clothes or that they would want to have them returned clean and washed.

MEMORABILIA

Evidence of the life and death of the child may be an important part of families' grieving and might be included in a memory box. Professionals can help families by offering them copies of available items such as identity bracelets and health and birth records. These items may be particularly important when a baby has died, since the family has had little opportunity to gather items over time like toys, photographs, letters, cards.

Families may also appreciate professionals offering suggestions about memorabilia that could be important in the future. This might include:

- birth and sympathy cards
- copies of birth and death notices in the newspaper
- a sympathy book for people who visit the family or attend the funeral to write in
- dried flowers from the funeral
- a videotape of the funeral
- letters and drawings from siblings about the child
- the family keeping a diary of their experience.

Appendix 11 A Framework to Guide Visiting

Source: Reproduced by permission of Dent and Stewart.

The questions in the assessment tool are derived from the current bereavement theories described in the first part of Chapter 10. The key areas are:

- Emotional and physical response to bereavement, and people's need to understand and be prepared for these (Parkes 1972, Bowlby 1980, Worden 1991).
- The shifts that can occur between loss-oriented and restoration-oriented coping, so that people can understand balancing their need to be sad and cry with activities such as doing the washing or going for a walk (Stroebe & Schut 2001).
- The continuing bonds which many people seek to develop with their dead child (e.g. Klass et al. 1996).
- The factors such as past loss and present physical and mental health which can contribute to or diminish the resources that people have to cope with stress (e.g. Parkes 1972).

The assessment tool was first published in Dent and Stewart (2004). It is not copyrighted and may be freely copied and used. We would appreciate acknowledgement of the source: Dent, A. & Stewart, A. (2004). *Sudden death in childhood: Support for the bereaved family*. Edinburgh: Butterworth Heinemann.

BEREAVEMENT ASSESSMENT TOOL

The questions are framed towards parent(s). These can be adapted to suit other family members. **It is not necessary to ask all questions at the first visit**, they can be included at future visits. What is more important is identifying what the parent(s) see(s) as most stressful at any given visit and working with these issues. A case study at the end of the appendix indicates how the framework can guide visits.

Unexpected Death in Childhood: A Handbook for Practitioners. Edited by P. Sidebotham and P. Fleming. Copyright © 2007 by John Wiley & Sons, Ltd.

About the death

How were the parents told of the death? Were they present at the death? Did the hospital staff give good care before the death? Were the parents kept fully informed as to what was happening? Were the parents satisfied with the Emergency Services? Were they satisfied with any care given by religious leaders in hospital?

After the death

Were the parents able to stay with their child for as long as they wanted? Were they given the opportunity of holding/washing/dressing their child? Were they given any tokens of remembrance, e.g. photographs, hand and footprints, locks of hair? Did their other children have the opportunity of seeing the dead child and saying goodbye in an unhurried way?

Post mortem and coroner (if applicable)

How did the parents feel about their contact with the coroner's officer? Were the findings of the post mortem/coroner's investigation explained clearly? Do they have any outstanding questions?

Information and follow-up

Have the parents been given any information by health professionals/ others about: grief, the cause of death, registering the death, arranging the funeral, mutual help groups? If appropriate, were the parents given a follow-up appointment to see a doctor at the hospital to talk of the death?

The funeral

Was (is) the funeral director/spiritual leader helpful? If there are other children, did they/will they attend the funeral? How do (did) the parents feel about the funeral?

The media

Has the media caused any problems for the family?

Relationships with members of the close family

Parents

> Are the parents able to talk together about the death? Are they finding they have different feelings at different times from each other? Are they able to be close to each other during this time?

Grandparents

> Are the grandparents able to talk about the death with the parents? Do they have different attitudes to the death? Are the grandparents able to help support the parents/other children? Do the grandparents need support or information?

Other children

> What do the children know about the death? Do the parents have difficulty in talking with them? Are the parents able to share their emotions with their children? Have they involved them in activities/rituals to mark the death of the child?

Support from friends, neighbours and other family members

> What support is available from other family members, friends and neighbours? Do the parents feel they have sufficient support? Do friends and others outside of the close family avoid them? Do the parents feel isolated and let down by them?

Practical difficulties

> Are there any practical problems which are causing difficulty for the parents at the present? What would help the parents?

Schools and community groups (where appropriate)

> Do the schools/playgroups of other siblings know about the death? Are the parents able to talk to the other children's teachers/play-leaders about the death? Do other parents at school/playgroup talk with, or avoid, the parents?

Health

Do the parents usually have good health? Has their appetite, sleeping or energy level been affected after the death? Has either of the parents suffered from depression in the past?

Past Losses

Has the mother had a miscarriage, termination or stillbirth in the past? If so, are there still painful memories? Have the parents experienced deaths of close family members or friends recently, some time ago, or as a child? Do these deaths still cause pain? Have there been other recent changes in the family such as divorce, redundancy?

Spiritual beliefs

Do the parents believe in God/a higher being/spiritual meaning of life? Do they feel angry with God? Do they wonder where their child is now? Would they like to talk to a priest/vicar/spiritual leader/someone else about the death? What meaning has the death for each member of the family?

Do the parents have any particular fears at the present?

Are there any other areas of concern for the parents?

What do parents perceive as the strengths of the family?

What do parents perceive as the needs of the family?

CASE STUDY USING FRAMEWORK FOR ASSESSMENT OF STRESSORS

Debbie Jones is a single mother living with her three children, Johnny (4), Kate (6) and Merrilyn (8). She and her husband divorced 18 months ago; her husband has remarried and is living in Spain. Since the divorce his parents have had no contact with the children and the father has returned once to see the children. Debbie's parents live nearby and see the children regularly. Debbie works part-time as a receptionist at a local vet's surgery. Johnny was killed by a passing car a week ago. Sarah, their Health Visitor, who had known the family for several years, heard by chance of Johnny's death. She immediately telephoned Debbie to arrange a visit, the day before the funeral.

Sarah continued to visit but her visits became less frequent as Debbie found ways to live with grief. Sarah visited just before the first anniversary and helped Debbie to plan a special day for the family.

Visit[1]	Stresses identified by Debbie	Suggested action
1	Should girls go to funeral? Grandmother against it. Father coming to funeral – how will Debbie cope?	Suggest that children can choose to go to funeral after explanations. Discuss with grandmother. Talk of anxieties re husband coming.
2	Debbie feels angry towards husband and guilty about the cause of Johnny's death.	Allow Debbie to talk of her feelings. Acknowledge and listen.
3	Girls more demanding and difficult to control in public situations. They scream and cry. Debbie finding work a huge strain.	Suggest routine for girls and time to talk about Johnny together. Speak to their teachers. Suggest that Debbie stops work for a few weeks in order to have time for herself and the family.
4	Debbie constantly crying, not eating and sleeping badly. Not working so has more time to sit and think.	Suggest looking at photographs of Johnny and family. Discuss the importance of trying to eat regularly and consider whether activities such as daily exercise and an evening warm milk drink might help break the cycle of insomnia or whether she wants a short course of night sedatives. Suggest Debbie joins the local Compassionate Friends group.

[1] The timing of visits will vary according to family needs and staff resources; the goal would be to have 3 visits within 4 weeks of the death.

5	Mother not acknowledging Debbie's pain and taking over in the house, which the other children resent. Kate sleeping with Debbie every night.	Suggest that Debbie and mother talk together and that Debbie explain how she is feeling and why she wants to talk about Johnny. Explain that Kate may be frightened of sleeping on her own and that she may need reassurance and time with Debbie. Continue to talk of Johnny and suggest that Debbie share her memories and some of her feelings with her husband and the girls.
6	Debbie continues to feel guilty about Johnny's death and angry with the driver.	Allow Debbie to talk about her feelings. Check on how she and the other family members are sleeping and eating. Talk about the effects of grief in terms of tiredness, confusion.
7	Feels The Compassionate Friends group is helping. Sleeping and eating better. Less stressed and tense.	Acknowledge progress. Suggest that next visit is in a few weeks, but available if needed.
8	Debbie feels she has 'good and bad days but [is] coping better'.	Praise progress and comment on how it was when first met her, discuss visiting in 1 month.

Appendix 12 Child Bereavement Network Belief Statement

Source: This statement was published in Dent & Stewart 2004, Sudden death in childhood: support for the bereaved family, pp 217–219. Copyright Elsevier.

We believe that all children have the right to information, guidance and support to enable them to manage the impact of death on their lives.

Further, in line with the Children Act 1989 and the Children (Scotland) Act 1995, we believe that any information, guidance and support offered to children should:

- acknowledge the child's grief and experience of loss as a result of death
- be responsive to the child's needs, views and opinions
- respect the child's family and immediate social situation and the culture, language, beliefs and religious background
- seek to promote self-esteem and self-confidence and develop communication, decision-making and other life skills
- be viewed as part of a continuous learning process for the child, contributing to the development of the child's knowledge and understanding as they grow into adulthood
- aim wherever possible, appropriate and feasible, to involve family members, other care givers and any professionals working with the individual child in a wider social context.

Such information should be:

- provided by people who have had appropriate training and who are adequately supported
- provided in an appropriately supportive, safe and non-discriminatory context
- regularly monitored, evaluated and reviewed.

Unexpected Death in Childhood: A Handbook for Practitioners. Edited by P. Sidebotham and P. Fleming.
Copyright © 2007 by John Wiley & Sons, Ltd.

Appendix 13 Local Case Discussion Proforma

Source: Reproduced by permission of The Royal College of Pathologists and The Royal College of Paediatrics and Child Health.

Date of LCD meeting _____ **Place of LCD meeting** _____

Name _____ *Date of birth* _____

Hospital _____ **Date of death** _____

Hospital unit number _____ **Place of post mortem** _____

Paediatrician _____ **Pathologist** _____

GP _____ **HV** _____

Child protection officer _____

Others present at LCD meeting _____

_____

_____

Not at LCD meeting but include in circulation of report: _____

_____

Review of case management: any issues identified

_____

_____

_____

Review of ongoing support needs identified

_____

_____

_____

Unexpected Death in Childhood: A Handbook for Practitioners. Edited by P. Sidebotham and P. Fleming.
Copyright © 2007 by John Wiley & Sons, Ltd.

Avon Clinico-Pathological Classification System						
Classification →	0	IA	IB	IIA	IIB	III
Criteria ↓	Criteria not collected	No factors identified	Notable factors	Possible contributory	Probable contributory	Explained
History						
Social						
Infant medical						
Family medical						
Final events						
Examination						
External examination of child						
Death-Scene Examination						
Observation						
Pathology						
Radiology						
Toxicology						
Micro/virology						
Gross pathology/histology						
Biochemistry/metabolic						
Other investigations						
Other criteria						
Abuse/neglect						
Specify …						
Overall Classification*						

* Equivalent to the highest classification in the grid

Brief explanation of specific notable/contributory or explanatory factors

_____

_____

_____

Appendix 14 Child Death Review Core Dataset

Based on and used with permission of CEMACH.

A. DEMOGRAPHIC AND DEATH CERTIFICATE INFORMATION

Please complete for all child deaths and attach a copy of death certificate.

1. **Unique identifier**
2. **NHS no.** 10 digits
3. **Surname**
4. **First name/s**
5. **Sex** m/f/unknown

6. **Postcode**
7. **Residential address**
8. **Date of death** dd/mm/yy
9. **Date of birth** dd/mm/yy
   If date of birth or date of death not known: estimated age yy

10. **Location of death** acute hospital (children's ward/adult ward/A&E/ NICU/PICU/ICU/other – free text) or mental health inpatient unit/learning disability inpatient unit or community (home of normal residence/transit/ residential care/hospice/public place/school/other – free text)

11. **Ethnic group** white/black African/black Caribbean/black other/Indian/ Pakistani/Bangladeshi/Chinese/mixed – specify/other _____

12. **Death certification**

Obtain directly from death certificate

12a. **Registration no.**
12b. **Place of death**
12c. **Cause of death I (a)**
12d. **Cause of death I (b)**
12e. **Cause of death I (c)**
12f. **Cause of death II**

Unexpected Death in Childhood: A Handbook for Practitioners. Edited by P. Sidebotham and P. Fleming.
Copyright © 2007 by John Wiley & Sons, Ltd.

B. PREVIOUS MEDICAL/DEVELOPMENTAL HISTORY

Please complete for all child deaths

13. Birth history

13a. Birth weight _____ kg
13b. Gestational age at birth _____ weeks
13c. Multiple birth yes/no/unknown
13d. Mother's DOB dd/mm/yy
If date of birth not known: estimated age yy

14. Did the child have any medical conditions at the time of death?

Describe each condition

15. Did the child have a previous history of any medical conditions?

Describe each condition

16. Did the child have developmental delay, impairment or disability?

Describe each condition

17. Was the child subject of a statement of special educational need? yes/no/unknown

18. What regular medication was prescribed (prior to the immediate terminal events)?

Specify which medications and dosages

19. Did the child have any surgery within the last 28 days? yes/no/unknown

If yes:

19a. What was the most recent operation? intra-cranial/intra-thoracic/intra-abdominal/other

20. Prior to the death, was the child in hospital (including mental health in-patient care) for more than three months or continually from birth? yes/no/unknown

21. What was the mode of death? death while receiving full active treatment, including CPR/death during limited treatment and no escalation, with no CPR/death following active withdrawal of treatment/brain-stem death

C. SOCIAL CIRCUMSTANCES OF CHILD

Please complete for all child deaths

22. Was the child usually living:

With two parents (married)
With two parents (cohabiting)
With a lone parent
With grandparents
With other relatives (not parents or
    grandparents), specify
With foster carers

In a residential children's home
In a secure unit
In a young offenders institution
Other, specify

23. Was the child on the child protection register? yes/no/unknown

23a. Category of abuse neglect/physical injury/sexual abuse/emotional abuse/
multiple categories/other
23b. Was this a re-registration? yes/no/unknown

24. Was the child looked after by the local authority? yes/no/unknown

25. Was the child subject to any legal order yes/no/unknown

25a. Type of legal order care order/anti-social behaviour order/parental
responsibility order/residence order/contact order/other court order, specify

––––––––––––––––––––

D. CIRCUMSTANCES OF DEATH – NON-NATURAL

Please complete for all child deaths as relevant

26. Did any of the following events precede the child's death?

Road traffic accident – complete 27 and proceed to Section E

Drowning – complete 28 and proceed to Section E

Fire/burns – complete 29 and proceed to Section E

Fall – complete 30 and proceed to Section E

Poisoning – complete 31 and proceed to Section E

Other accident, e.g. bite or sting, suffocation, sports injury, specify
––––––––––––––– and proceed to Section E

Substance misuse – complete 32 and proceed to Section E

Apparent homicide – complete 33 and proceed to Section E

Apparent suicide – complete 34 and proceed to Section E

Sudden unexpected death in infancy – complete 35 and proceed to Section E

None of the above – proceed to Section E

27. Circumstances – RTA

First 8 items can be obtained from STATS 19 form

27a. Date of incident dd/mm/yy
27b. Time of day hh/mm
27c. Type of vehicle pedal cycle/moped/motor cycle . . . taxi/car etc
27d. Casualty class driver or rider/vehicle or pillion passenger/pedestrian

If passenger:

27e. Passenger position front-seat passenger/rear-seat passenger

If pedestrian:

27f. Pedestrian location in carriageway/on footway etc

If motor vehicle (incl. taxi, minubus etc):

27g. Age of driver yy
27h. Breath test n/a/positive/negative/not requested etc
27i. Did vehicle have restraints? yes/no/unknown
27j. Were restraints used? yes/no/unknown
27k. Did vehicle have airbags? yes/no/unknown
27l. Did airbags deploy? yes/no/unknown
27m. Was airbag switched on? yes/no/unknown

If pedal cycle, moped or motor cycle:

27n. Was a helmet worn? yes/no/unknown

28. Circumstances – drowning

28a. Type of drowning bath/garden pond/swimming pool (domestic/private/municipal)/river, lake, canal/sea/other

For pool drownings:

28b. Was the swimming pool secured (fenced)? yes/no/unknown

29. Circumstances – fire/burns

29a. Type of fire/burn fire/chemical/hot liquid/electrical/other

If fire:

29b. Location of fire residential accommodation/main trade or business/
mobile – specify/other – specify
29c. Was a fire/smoke alarm present? yes/no/unknown
29d. Was fire/smoke alarm functional? yes/no/unknown

30. Circumstances – fall

30a. Type of fall fall on same level/fall on or from stairs/fall on or from ladder
or stepladder/fall from building or structure/other fall from one level to
another/unspecified fall

31. Circumstances – poisoning

31a. Type of substance solid/liquid/gas – specify/unspecified

32. Circumstances – substance misuse

32a. Was the child known to substance misuse services? yes/no/unknown
32b. Was the child known to be currently using:

Heroin	Amphetamines (excluding ecstasy)
Methadone	Cocaine (excluding crack)
Other opiates	Crack
Benzodiazepines	Hallucinogens
Ecstasy	Major tranquilisers
Cannabis	Anti-depressants
Solvents	Alcohol
Barbiturates	Other, specify _____

33. Circumstances – apparent homicide

33a. Method

Strangulation, asphyxiation or drowning	Hitting or kicking
Sharp instrument	Fire
Blunt instrument	Other, specify _____
Shooting	Not known

34. Circumstances – apparent suicide

34a. Method *(If more than one, give direct cause)*

Self-poisoning
Carbon monoxide poisoning
Hanging/strangulation
Drowning
Firearms
Cutting or stabbing
Jumping from a height
Jumping/lying before a train
Jumping/lying before a road vehicle
Suffocation
Burning

Electrocution
Other, specify _____
Not known

35. Circumstances – SUDI

35a. In what position was the child put to sleep? back/side/front/unknown

E. OTHER RELEVANT INFORMATION

Please complete for all child deaths

36. Please document any further information you think is relevant to the child's death

F. PROCESSING OF DEATH

Please complete for all child deaths

37. Who originally certified the death? doctor/coroner/uncertified

For doctor's cases only:

38. Where was the death certified? hospital (children's ward/adult ward/A&E/ NICU/PICU/ICU/other – free text) or community (home of normal residence/ transit/residential care/hospice/public place/school/other – free text)

39. Was the coroner consulted? yes/no/unknown

40. Were further investigations done? yes/no/unknown

40a. What further investigations were undertaken by the coroner? PM only/ inquest with PM/inquest without PM

41. Was a pathologist's post mortem done, i.e. without consultation with the coroner?

41a. Was a paediatric pathologist involved in conducting the post mortem? yes/no/unknown

42. Who gave final certification of death? doctor/coroner/uncertified

43. Is a police investigation in progress? yes/no/unknown

44. Was this death subject to statutory enquiry? yes/no/unknown

44a. Which statutory enquiry? Serious Case Review/Kennedy/prison or armed service

45. Was this case subject to local case review? yes/no/unknown

G. DETAILS OF PERSON COMPLETING FORM

46. Name

47. Job title

48. Profession

Appendix 15 CDRT Proforma for Analysis

Martin Ward Platt, used with permission of Confidential Enquiry into Maternal and Child Health (CEMCH).

A. The location of the death or incident immediately leading up to the death
Note where the child died/became unwell/was injured (domestic environment, educational establishment, health facility, other).

B. Environmental (extrinsic) factors
Consider environmental factors extrinsic to the child that may have had a bearing on the events leading up to death and the strength of their contribution. Consider the weather, housing or environment, health and safety issues, hazards, exposures etc.
0 = not relevant at all
1 = probably a minor factor among the events leading up to the death
2 = probably a significant factor among the events leading up to the death
3 = probably a major factor, but one of several others impacting on the death
4 = directly and overwhelmingly important factor in the death.

C. Personal (intrinsic) factors
Consider factors intrinsic to the child that may have had a bearing on the events leading up to death and the strength of their contribution (e.g. any impairment or disability, ill health, mental illness or behavioural problems, use of drugs or alcohol).
0 = not relevant at all
1 = probably a minor factor among the events leading up to the death
2 = probably a significant factor among the events leading up to the death
3 = probably a major factor, but one of several others impacting on the death
4 = directly and overwhelmingly important factor in the death.

Unexpected Death in Childhood: A Handbook for Practitioners. Edited by P. Sidebotham and P. Fleming.
Copyright © 2007 by John Wiley & Sons, Ltd.

D. Agencies or agents *directly* involved in supervising or providing services for the child

Consider any agencies directly supervising the child or providing services at the time of the death or incident leading to death (e.g. parents, other family members, other carers, health, Social Services, education). For each agency directly involved, consider the identification or awareness of any hazard or risk, or lack of this; and the appropriateness of the agencies' handling of the child in terms of timely involvement of other agencies or emergency services, or provision of appropriate care.

0 = not relevant at all
1 = responsible for a minor or background factor relating to the death
2 = responsible for a significant factor relating to the death
3 = responsible for one of several important factors impacting on the death
4 = responsible for a single important factor relating to the death.

E. Agencies or agents *indirectly* involved, but not actively supervising or providing for the child

Consider any other agencies involved with the child or family, but not directly supervising the child at the time of the death or incident leading to death, or any agency that was not, but could have been involved with the child or family. Consider the potential for any such agency to have made an impact in preventing the death.

0 = not relevant at all
1 = may have removed a minor or background factor relating to the death
2 = may have removed a significant factor relating to the death
3 = may have removed one of several important factors impacting on the death
4 = had the potential to remove a single important factor or more than one of several important factors impacting on the death.

F. Medical care

Consider any medical care provided to the child prior to the death, or medical care that could have been provided but wasn't. For example, consider whether there was any evidence of failure to recognise the severity of illness of the child outside hospital or within a hospital environment; any evidence of failure to prioritise the management of the child; any adverse events that affected care.

0 = not relevant at all
1 = probably a minor factor among the events leading up to the death
2 = probably a significant factor among the events leading up to the death
3 = probably a major factor, but one of several others impacting on the death
4 = directly and overwhelmingly important factor in the death.

G. Avoidability

Considering the responses to all the above issues, apply the highest classification from any of the categories:

1. Avoidable
   a) where there were identifiable failures in the child's direct care by any agency, including parents, with direct responsibility for the child
   b) where there were latent, organisational or other indirect failure(s) within one or more agency, including parents, with direct or indirect responsibility for the child
   c) where there was a failure of design, installation, or inadequate maintenance by agencies with responsibility for public safety.

2. Potentially avoidable
   a) at a higher level than the agencies with direct or indirect responsibility for the child (e.g. political or social structures, terrorism, crime)
   b) where no agency, including parents, was involved with the child
   c) where intrinsic factors were the principal factors leading to the death
   d) where there were potentially modifiable factors extrinsic to the child
   e) where the causal pathway leading to the death was potentially amenable to intervention.

3. Unavoidable
   a) death caused by unmodifiable or unpredictable factors extrinsic to the child
   b) death due to undiagnosed, asymptomatic conditions presenting with a lethal event
   c) planned palliation for unpreventable, incurable disease or anomaly.

Appendix 16 Tools for Developing a Child Death Review Team

Source: Reproduced by permission of the National Center for Child Death Review.

These two audit tools are based on material from the US Center for Child Death Review (www.childdeathreview.org) and used with kind permission. We have adapted the tools in their manual to make them appropriate to the UK situation. They can be used by developing child death review teams to help establish the focus, remit and structure of the teams. The US Center website contains a wealth of resources to support child death review processes and is well worth a visit.

Establishing a Child Death Review Team

Audit Tool 1

This audit tool has been developed to:

- identify the population base
- explore understanding of the purposes of the child death overview panel
- identify key players
- identify the processes by which you can establish a child death review team.

1. Define the geographic area that the child death overview panel will cover (particularly in relation to local authority, PCT and police boundaries):

   a. local authority/ies
   b. Primary Care Trust(s)
   c. police force(s)
   d. strategic health authority/ies
   e. hospitals.

Unexpected Death in Childhood: A Handbook for Practitioners. Edited by P. Sidebotham and P. Fleming.
Copyright © 2007 by John Wiley & Sons, Ltd.

2. What is the racial and ethnic makeup of your community? What do you know about patterns of deprivation and urban/rural mix?

- NB: Useful information can be obtained from http://neighbourhood. statistics.gov.uk

3. Define the population of your child death overview panel area:

   a. what is the total population in your identified community?
   b. how many children are under age 18?
   c. how many children are under age 5?
   d. annual birth rate?

4. Do you know how many children (0–18) died in the past calendar year of all causes? Consider where you might get this information

Age	Number

   a. <28 days (excluding stillbirths)
   b. 28 days to <1 year
   c. 1–4
   d. 5–9
   e. 10–14
   f. 15–18

5. What information (if any) do you currently have about causes of child death in your area?

6. Which agencies currently collect data on child deaths? How could you access this information? Consider public health, PCT, hospital records, registrar of births, deaths and marriages, coroner, police, Social Services and others.

7. Do any of the following types of review currently take place in your area?

   a. local case discussion for SUDI (following joint-agency rapid response)
   b. local case discussion for other SUDC
   c. infant mortality review
   d. hospital mortality review
   e. any other reviews.

8. What structures or processes are in place for Serious Case Reviews? (e.g. is there a standing sub-committee or is a panel convened *ad hoc*; are there terms of reference?)

9. Consider which professionals or agencies you might want to involve in developing or running your child death review team. Should they be core or co-opted members? Can you identify named leads?

Agency	Involve in planning?	Involve in child death review team?
Public health		
Child health		
Hospital medical and nursing staff		
Midwifery		
Primary care		
Children's Social Work Services		
Police child protection team		
Other police representatives		
Community representatives		
Parent representatives		
Coroner		
Registrar		
Education		
Ambulance/paramedic services		
Pathologists		
CAMHS		
Adult mental health		

10. Can you identify any specific factors which may help to establish child death review processes in your LSCB? (This may be individual 'champions'; resources available; structures already in place . . .)

11. Can you identify any barriers to implementation that you have encountered? If so, how might you address these barriers?

Establishing a Child Death Review Team

Audit Tool 2

This tool can provide a focus for developing your child death review team. You can use this tool to guide an initial planning meeting of your team, or to prompt discussions amongst key players. This may take more than one meeting to finalise.

1. Purpose – can you agree the key purposes, functions and tasks for your child death review team?
   Consider: prevention of child deaths; identification of fatalities resulting from abuse and neglect; improvements in inter-agency working; education of public and of professionals working with children.

2. Which deaths does/will your team review?
Consider: age range (maximum and minimum); categories of death (all deaths; unexpected deaths; unexplained deaths; suspicious deaths); deaths from certain causes – which causes?

3. What will be your geographical boundaries?
Consider: this in relation to boundaries of the different agencies involved. How will you deal with cross-boundary deaths and non-co-terminosity?

4. Membership
a. who does/should the core membership include and at what level should agencies/partners be represented in order for your child death review team to discharge its responsibilities effectively?
b. what type of professional/expert advice does your child death overview panel require and how is this to be provided?

Prompts:

Public health
Child health
Hospital medical and nursing staff
Midwifery
Primary care
Children's Social Work Services
Police child protection team
Other police representatives
Community representatives
Parent representatives
Coroner
Registrar
Education
Ambulance/paramedic services
Pathologists
CAMHS
Adult mental health

5. Do you have any form of agreement with individual agencies for their involvement in the child death review team? If so, what does this cover (accountability, funding, commitment, authority)? If not, can you set local agreements?

6. How will the team measure its effectiveness?
a. what outcomes have you identified for your child death review team?

    b. how will these be measured?

    c. what information will the team collect in order to measure its effectiveness?

7. What arrangements will you have in place for chairing the team? (Who will chair; how will this be decided; lines of accountability?)

8. What arrangements will you have in place for administration? (Who will be responsible for administration, % fte, which agency, job description and person specification?)

9. What systems can you put in place for notification of child deaths?
   Consider: who should be responsible; multiple sources of notification; are there any automatic systems that can build on current systems (e.g. the child health computer; registrar of BD&M); where should they be notified to?

10. What systems can you put in place for data collection?
    Consider: do you want to use a data collection form; will you collect agency records; who will collect and compile this information; how does the data you collect relate to your identified purposes and outputs?

11. What systems will you put in place for recording and storing data?
    Consider: any databases you could use; who will maintain this; how can you ensure security?

12. How will you address issues of confidentiality and information sharing?
    Consider: can you establish a memorandum of agreement; anonymising records, reports etc?

13. What systems will you use for evaluating the deaths?
    Some suggestions are provided in Chapter 11, but you may wish to consider developing your own models. These systems should be related to the agreed purposes and outcomes of the child death review team. Different systems may be needed for different types of review/different categories of death.

14. How will you run your team meetings?
    Consider: frequency and length of meetings; preparation – what information is sent out in advance; minute taking, etc.

15. How do you envisage the child death review team relating to other bodies, including the LSCB; strategic health authority; children & young people's partnership; individual agencies?
    Consider: outputs from the team; notes of meetings; annual reports.

16. Training

Consider: what training will be required by your team and how you will access this.

Having worked through this audit process, we recommend you set an action plan and timeline with specific, measurable outcomes and identified personnel. A template is provided below, but you may want to design your own.

Task	Date for completion	Person(s) responsible	Evidence of achievement

References

ABRAMSON, H. (1944) Accidental mechanical suffocation in infants. *Journal of Pediatrics*, **25**, pp. 404–13.

ACKERMAN, M. J., SIU, B. L., STURNER, W. Q., TESTER, D. J., VALDIVIA, C. R., MAKIELSKI, J. C. & TOWBIN, J. A. (2001) Postmortem molecular analysis of SCN5A defects in sudden infant death syndrome. *Jama*, **286**, pp. 2264–9.

ADAIR, S. M., MILANO, M., LORENZO, I. & RUSSELL, C. (1995) Effects of current and former pacifier use on the dentition of 24- to 59-month-old children. *Pediatr Dent*, **17**, pp. 437–44.

ADAMSON, P. S., MICKLEWRIGHT, J. & WRIGHT, A. (2000) *A league table of child deaths by injury in rich nations*, Florence, UNICEF Innocenti Research Centre.

ALTMANN, A. & NOLAN, T. (1995) Non-intentional asphyxiation deaths due to upper airway interference in children 0 to 14 years. *Inj Prev*, **1**, pp. 76–80.

AMERICAN ACADEMY OF PEDIATRICS (2005) The changing concept of sudden infant death syndrome: diagnostic coding shifts, controversies regarding the sleeping environment, and new variables to consider in reducing risk. *Pediatrics*, **116**, pp. 1245–55.

AMPOFO-BOATENG, K. & THOMSON, J. A. (1991) Children's perception of safety and danger on the road. *Br J Psychol*, **82** (Pt 4), pp. 487–505.

ANDERSON, G. C. (1991) Current knowledge about skin-to-skin (kangaroo) care for preterm infants. *J Perinatol*, **11**, pp. 216–26.

ANON (1961) Prone or Supine? *BMJ*, **1304**.

ANON (2000) *Community approach to road safety education* (No. 03). London, Department of Transport.

ARENA, J. M. (1959) Safety closure caps; safety measure for prevention of accidental drug poisoning in children. *J Am Med Assoc*, **169**, pp. 1187–8.

ARIZONA CHILD FATALITY REVIEW TEAM (1999) Sixth annual report. Phoenix, Arizona, Arizona Department of Health Services.

ARNESTAD, M., CROTTI, L., ROGNUM, T. O., INSOLIA, R., PEDRAZZINI, M., FERRANDI, C., VEGE, A., WANG, D. W., RHODES, T. E., GEORGE, A. L., JR. & SCHWARTZ, P. J. (2007) Prevalence of long-QT syndrome gene variants in sudden infant death syndrome. *Circulation*, **115**, pp. 361–7.

ASHER, K. N., RIVARA, F. P., FELIX, D., VANCE, L. & DUNNE, R. (1995) Water safety training as a potential means of reducing risk of young children's drowning. *Inj Prev*, **1**, pp. 228–33.

ASSOCIATION OF CHIEF POLICE OFFICERS (2002) *Guidelines for the investigation of infant deaths*. London, ACPO.

ASSOCIATION OF CHIEF POLICE OFFICERS (2004) *Radiology in child abuse investigations – A good practice guide for investigators*. London, ACPO.

ASSOCIATION OF CHIEF POLICE OFFICERS (2005) *Major incident room standard administrative procedures*, London, ACPO.

ASSOCIATION OF CHIEF POLICE OFFICERS (2006) *Manual of murder investigation*, London, ACPO.

ASSOCIATION OF CHIEF POLICE OFFICERS & CENTREX (2005) *Guidance on investigating child abuse and safeguarding children*, Bramshill, UK, Centrex NCPE.

ATTIG, T. (2001) Relearning the world: making and finding meanings. In NEIMEYER, R. (Ed.) *Meaning reconstruction and the experience of loss*. Washington, American Psychological Association.

BAJANOWSKI, T., VEGE, A., BYARD, R. W., KROUS, H. F., ARNESTAD, M., BACHS, L., BANNER, J., BLAIR, P. S., BORTHNE, A., DETTMEYER, R., FLEMING, P., GAUSTAD, P., GREGERSEN, M., GROGAARD, J., HOLTER, E., ISAKSEN, C. V., JORGENSEN, J. V., DE LANGE, C., MADEA, B., MOORE, I., MORLAND, J., OPDAL, S. H., RASTEN-ALMQVIST, P., SCHLAUD, M., SIDEBOTHAM, P., SKULLERUD, K., STOLTENBURG-DIDINGER, G., STRAY-PEDERSEN, A., SVEUM, L. & ROGNUM, T. O. (2007) Sudden infant death syndrome (SIDS) – standardised investigations and classification: recommendations. *Forensic Sci Int*, **165**, pp. 129–43.

BAJANOWSKI, T., VENNEMANN, M., BOHNERT, M., RAUCH, E., BRINKMANN, B. & MITCHELL, E. A. (2005) Unnatural causes of sudden unexpected deaths initially thought to be sudden infant death syndrome. *Int J Legal Med*, **119**, pp. 213–6.

BALL, H., HOOKER, E. & KELLY, P. (1999) Where will the baby sleep? Attitudes and practices of new and experienced parents regarding co-sleeping with their newborn infant. *American Anthropologist*, **101**, pp. 143–51.

BARNES, P. M., NORTON, C. M., DUNSTAN, F. D., KEMP, A. M., YATES, D. W. & SIBERT, J. R. (2005) Abdominal injury due to child abuse. *Lancet*, **366**, pp. 234–5.

BARROS, F. C., VICTORA, C. G., SEMER, T. C., TONIOLI FILHO, S., TOMASI, E. & WEIDERPASS, E. (1995) Use of pacifiers is associated with decreased breast-feeding duration. *Pediatrics*, **95**, pp. 497–9.

BARTICK, M. (2006) Bed sharing with unimpaired parents is not an important risk for sudden infant death syndrome: to the editor. *Pediatrics*, **117**, pp. 992–3.

BASS, M., KRAVATH, R. E. & GLASS, L. (1986) Death-scene investigation in sudden infant death. *N Engl J Med*, **315**, pp. 100–5.

BEAL, S. (1995) Sleeping position and SIDS: past, present and future. In ROGNUM, T. (Ed.) *SIDS: new trends in the nineties*. Oslo, Scandinavian University Press.

BEAL, S. M. (2000) Sudden infant death syndrome in South Australia 1968–97. Part I: changes over time. *J Paediatr Child Health*, **36**, pp. 540–7.

BEAL, S. M. & BLUNDELL, H. (1978) Sudden infant death syndrome related to position in the cot. *Med J Aust*, **2**, pp. 217–8.

BECROFT, D. M. & LOCKETT, B. K. (1997) Intra-alveolar pulmonary siderophages in sudden infant death: a marker for previous imposed suffocation. *Pathology*, **29**, pp. 60–3.

BECROFT, D. M., THOMPSON, J. M. & MITCHELL, E. A. (2001) Nasal and intrapulmonary haemorrhage in sudden infant death syndrome. *Arch Dis Child*, **85**, pp. 116–20.

BECROFT, D. M., THOMPSON, J. M. & MITCHELL, E. A. (2005) Pulmonary interstitial hemosiderin in infancy: a common consequence of normal labor. *Pediatr Dev Pathol*, **8**, pp. 448–52.

BEGLEY, S. (1997) The nursery's littlest victims. Hundreds of cases of 'crib death,' or SIDS, may in fact be infanticide. *Newsweek*, **130**, pp. 72–3.

BELSKY, J. (1993) Etiology of child maltreatment: a developmental-ecological analysis. *Psychological Bulletin*, **114**, pp. 413–34.

BENNETT, E., CUMMINGS, P., QUAN, L. & LEWIS, F. M. (1999) Evaluation of a drowning prevention campaign in King County, Washington. *Inj Prev*, **5**, pp. 109–13.

BENSLEY, L. S., SPIEKER, S. J., VAN EENWYK, J. & SCHODER, J. (1999) Self-reported abuse history and adolescent problem behaviors. II. Alcohol and drug use. *J Adolesc Health*, **24**, pp. 173–80.

BERGMAN, A. (1997) Wrong turns in sudden infant death syndrome research. *Pediatrics*, **99**, pp. 119–20.

BIRD, L. M., BILLMAN, G. F., LACRO, R. V., SPICER, R. L., JARIWALA, L. K., HOYME, H. E., ZAMORA-SALINAS, R., MORRIS, C., VISKOCHIL, D., FRIKKE, M. J. & JONES, M. C. (1996) Sudden death in Williams syndrome: report of ten cases. *J Pediatr*, **129**, pp. 926–31.

BLACKWELL, C. C. & WEIR, D. M. (1999) The role of infection in sudden infant death syndrome. *FEMS Immunol Med Microbiol*, **25**, pp. 1–6.

BLAIR, P. (2002) 'Back to Sleep' advice should be taken literally not laterally. *Italian Journal of Pediatrics*, **28**, pp. 251–3.

BLAIR, P., PLATT, M. W., SMITH, I. & FLEMING, P. (2006a) Sudden Infant Death Syndrome and the time of death: factors associated with night-time and day-time deaths. *Int J Epidemiol*, **35**, pp. 1563–9.

BLAIR, P. S. & BALL, H. L. (2004) The prevalence and characteristics associated with parent-infant bed-sharing in England. *Arch Dis Child*, **89**, pp. 1106–10.

BLAIR, P. S. & FLEMING, P. J. (2006) Dummies and SIDS: causality has not been established. *BMJ*, **332**, pp. 178.

BLAIR, P. S., FLEMING, P. J., BENSLEY, D., SMITH, I., BACON, C., TAYLOR, E., BERRY, J., GOLDING, J. & TRIPP, J. (1996) Smoking and the sudden infant death syndrome: results from 1993–5 case-control study for confidential inquiry into stillbirths and deaths in infancy. Confidential Enquiry into Stillbirths and Deaths Regional Coordinators and Researchers. *BMJ*, **313**, pp. 195–8.

BLAIR, P. S., FLEMING, P. J., SMITH, I. J., PLATT, M. W., YOUNG, J., NADIN, P., BERRY, P. J. & GOLDING, J. (1999) Babies sleeping with parents: case-control study of factors influencing the risk of the sudden infant death syndrome. CESDI SUDI research group. *BMJ*, **319**, pp. 1457–61.

BLAIR, P. S., PLATT, M. W., SMITH, I. J. & FLEMING, P. J. (2006b) Sudden infant death syndrome and sleeping position in pre-term and low birth weight infants: an opportunity for targeted intervention. *Arch Dis Child*, **91**, pp. 101–6.

BLAIR, P. S., SIDEBOTHAM, P., BERRY, P. J., EVANS, M. & FLEMING, P. J. (2006c) Major epidemiological changes in sudden infant death syndrome: a 20-year population-based study in the UK. *Lancet*, **367**, pp. 314–9.

BOHNERT, M., GROBE PERDEKAMP, M. & POLLAK, S. (2004) Three subsequent infanticides covered up as SIDS. *Int J Legal Med*, **119**, pp. 31–4.

BOLTON, D. P., TAYLOR, B. J., CAMPBELL, A. J., GALLAND, B. C. & CRESS-WELL, C. (1993) Rebreathing expired gases from bedding: a cause of cot death? *Arch Dis Child*, **69**, pp. 187–90.

BONNER, B., CROW, S. & LOGUE, M. (1999) Fatal child neglect. In DUBOWITZ, H. (Ed.) *Neglected children: research, practice and policy*. Thousand Oaks, CA, Sage.

BOURGET, D. & GAGNE, P. (2002) Maternal filicide in Quebec. *J Am Acad Psychiatry Law*, **30**, pp. 345–51.

BOURGET, D. & GAGNE, P. (2005) Paternal filicide in Quebec. *J Am Acad Psychiatry Law*, **33**, pp. 354–60.

BOUVIER-COLLE, M. H., INIZAN, J. & MICHEL, E. (1989) Postneonatal mortality, sudden infant death syndrome: factors preventing the decline of infant mortality in France from 1979 to 1985. *Paediatr Perinat Epidemiol*, **3**, pp. 256–67.

BOWDEN, K. (1950) Sudden death or alleged accidental suffocation in babies. *Med J Aust*, **1**, pp. 65–72.

BOWLBY, J. (1980) *Attachment and loss. vol 3, loss: sadness and depression*, London, Hogarth Press.

BRANDON, M. (2007) Key messages: national overviews of serious case reviews. *Preventing child death or serious injury*. East Midlands Conference Centre, Nottingham.

BREWSTER, A. L., NELSON, J. P., HYMEL, K. P., COLBY, D. R., LUCAS, D. R., MCCANNE, T. R. & MILNER, J. S. (1998) Victim, perpetrator, family, and incident characteristics of 32 infant maltreatment deaths in the United States Air Force. *Child Abuse Negl*, **22**, pp. 91–101.

BRITISH SOCIETY OF PAEDIATRIC RADIOLOGY Standard for skeletal surveys in suspected non-accidental injury (NAI) in children.

BROOKE, H., TAPPIN, D., BECKETT, C. & GIBSON, A. (2000) Dummy use on the day/night of death: case-control study of Sudden Infant Death Syndrome (SIDS) in Scotland, 1996–99. *Sixth SIDS International Conference*. Auckland, New Zealand.

BROOKMAN, F. & MAGUIRE, M. (2003) *Reducing homicide: summary of a review of the possibilities*, London, Home Office, Research, Development and Statistics Directorate.

BROTHERTON, J. M., HULL, B. P., HAYEN, A., GIDDING, H. F. & BURGESS, M. A. (2005) Probability of coincident vaccination in the 24 or 48 hours preceding sudden infant death syndrome death in Australia. *Pediatrics*, **115**, e643–6.

BRYCE, J., BOSCHI-PINTO, C., SHIBUYA, K. & BLACK, R. E. (2005) WHO estimates of the causes of death in children. *Lancet*, **365**, pp. 1147–52.

BUNTING, L. & REID, C. (2005) Reviewing child deaths – learning from the American experience. *Child Abuse Review*, **14**, pp. 82–96.

BUZZETTI, R. & D'AMICO, R. (2006) The pacifier debate. *Pediatrics*, **117**, 1850; author reply pp. 1850–3.

BYARD, R. & COHLE, S. (2004) Homicide and suicide. In BYARD, R. (Ed.) *Sudden death in infancy, childhood and adolescence*. 2nd ed. Cambridge, Cambridge University Press.

BYARD, R. W. (2004) *Sudden death in infancy, childhood, and adolescence*, Cambridge, Cambridge University Press.

BYARD, R. W. & BEAL, S. M. (1997) V-shaped pillows and unsafe infant sleeping. *J Paediatr Child Health*, **33**, pp. 171–3.

BYARD, R. W. & BEAL, S. M. (2000) Gastric aspiration and sleeping position in infancy and early childhood. *J Paediatr Child Health*, **36**, pp. 403–5.

BYARD, R. W., STEWART, W. A., TELFER, S. & BEAL, S. M. (1997) Assessment of pulmonary and intrathymic hemosiderin deposition in sudden infant death syndrome. *Pediatr Pathol Lab Med*, **17**, pp. 275–82.

CAMERON, D., BISHOP, C. & SIBERT, J. R. (1992) Farm accidents in children. *BMJ*, **305**, pp. 23–5.

CARPENTER, R. G., IRGENS, L. M., BLAIR, P. S., ENGLAND, P. D., FLEMING, P., HUBER, J., JORCH, G. & SCHREUDER, P. (2004) Sudden unexplained infant death in 20 regions in Europe: case control study. *Lancet*, **363**, pp. 185–91.

CARPENTER, R. G., WAITE, A., COOMBS, R. C., DAMAN-WILLEMS, C., MCKENZIE, A., HUBER, J. & EMERY, J. L. (2005) Repeat sudden unexpected and unexplained infant deaths: natural or unnatural? *Lancet*, **365**, pp. 29–35.

CARROLL, L. & STEADMAN, R. (1975) *Lewis Carroll's 'Through the looking glass and what Alice found there'*, London, Hart-Davis MacGibbon.

CASE, M. E., GRAHAM, M. A., HANDY, T. C., JENTZEN, J. M. & MONTELEONE, J. A. (2001) Position paper on fatal abusive head injuries in infants and young children. *Am J Forensic Med Pathol*, **22**, pp. 112–22.

CHACE, D., KALAS, T., FIERRO, M., HANNON, H., RASMUSSEN, S., WOLF, K., WILLIAMS, J. & DOTT, M. (2003) Contribution of selected metabolic diseases to early childhood deaths – Virginia, 1996–2001. *Morbidity and Mortality Weekly Report*, **52**, pp. 677–9.

CHACE, D. H., DIPERNA, J. C., MITCHELL, B. L., SGROI, B., HOFMAN, L. F. & NAYLOR, E. W. (2001) Electrospray tandem mass spectrometry for analysis of acylcarnitines in dried postmortem blood specimens collected at autopsy from infants with unexplained cause of death. *Clin Chem*, **47**, pp. 1166–82.

CHADWICK, D. L., CHIN, S., SALERNO, C., LANDSVERK, J. & KITCHEN, L. (1991) Deaths from falls in children: how far is fatal? *J Trauma*, **31**, pp. 1353–5.

CHAMP, C. S. & BYARD, R. W. (1994) Sudden death in asthma in childhood. *Forensic Sci Int*, **66**, pp. 117–27.

CHAPMAN, S., CORNWALL, J., RIGHETTI, J. & SUNG, L. (2000) Preventing dog bites in children: randomised controlled trial of an educational intervention. *BMJ*, **320**, pp. 1512–3.

CHIKRITZHS, T. & BRADY, M. (2006) Fact or fiction? A critique of the National Aboriginal and Torres Strait Islander Social Survey 2002. *Drug Alcohol Rev*, **25**, pp. 277–87.

CHILD ACCIDENT PREVENTION TRUST (2002) Burns and scalds fact sheet. London, Child Accident Prevention Trust.

CHILD ACCIDENT PREVENTION TRUST (2004) Road crashes fact sheet. London, Child Accident Prevention Trust.

CHRIST, G. H. (2000) *Healing children's grief: surviving a parent's death from cancer*, New York; Oxford, Oxford University Press.

CHRISTOFFEL, K. K. (1984) Homicide in childhood: a public health problem in need of attention. *Am J Public Health*, **74**, pp. 68–70.

CHRISTOPHERSEN, E. R., SOSLAND-EDELMAN, D. & LECLAIRE, S. (1985) Evaluation of two comprehensive infant car seat loaner programs with 1-year follow-up. *Pediatrics*, **76**, pp. 36–42.

CHURCH, N. R., ANAS, N. G., HALL, C. B. & BROOKS, J. G. (1984) Respiratory syncytial virus-related apnea in infants. Demographics and outcome. *Am J Dis Child*, **138**, pp. 247–50.

CM 5730 (2003) The Victoria Climbie inquiry. HMSO.

COMMITTEE ON FETUS AND NEWBORN (2003) Apnea, sudden infant death syndrome, and home monitoring. *Pediatrics*, **111**, pp. 914–7.

CONFIDENTIAL ENQUIRY INTO MATERNAL AND CHILD HEALTH (2004) Why mothers die 2000–2002, the sixth report of the Confidential Enquiries into Maternal Deaths in the United Kingdom. London, RCOG Press.

CONNOR, J., BROAD, J., REHM, J., VANDER HOORN, S. & JACKSON, R. (2005) The burden of death, disease, and disability due to alcohol in New Zealand. *N Z Med J*, **118**, U1412.

CORBIN, T. (2005) Investigation into sudden infant deaths and unascertained infant deaths in England and Wales, 1995–2003. *Health Stat Q*, pp. 17–23.

CORNALL, P., HOWIE, S., MUGHAL, A., SUMNER, V., DUNSTAN, F., KEMP, A. & SIBERT, J. (2005) Drowning of British children abroad. *Child Care Health Dev*, **31**, pp. 611–3.

COTE, A., RUSSO, P. & MICHAUD, J. (1999) Sudden unexpected deaths in infancy: what are the causes? *J Pediatr*, **135**, pp. 437–43.

COZZI, F., ALBANI, R. & CARDI, E. (1979) A common pathophysiology for sudden cot death and sleep apnoea. 'The vacuum-glossoptosis syndrome'. *Med Hypotheses*, **5**, pp. 329–38.

COZZI, F., MORINI, F., TOZZI, C., BONCI, E. & COZZI, D. A. (2002) Effect of pacifier use on oral breathing in healthy newborn infants. *Pediatr Pulmonol*, **33**, pp. 368–73.

CRAFT, A. W. (1983) Circumstances surrounding deaths from accidental poisoning 1974–80. *Arch Dis Child*, **58**, pp. 544–6.

CRAFT, A. W. & HALL, D. M. (2004) Munchausen syndrome by proxy and sudden infant death. *BMJ*, **328**, pp. 1309–12.

CREIGHTON, S. (1992) Child abuse trends in England and Wales 1988–1990. London, NSPCC.

CREIGHTON, S. (1995) Fatal child abuse – how preventable is it? *Child Abuse Review*, **4**, pp. 318–28.

CREIGHTON, S. (2001) Childhood deaths reported to coroners: an investigation of the contribution of abuse and neglect. *Out of sight; NSPCC report on child abuse deaths 1973–2000*. London, NSPCC.

CROSSLEY, D. & STOKES, J. A. (2001) *Beyond the rough rock: supporting a child who has been bereaved through suicide*, Gloucester, Winston's Wish.

CROWN PROSECUTION SERVICE (2004) The code For Crown Prosecutors. London, CPS.

CRUME, T. L., DIGUISEPPI, C., BYERS, T., SIROTNAK, A. P. & GARRETT, C. J. (2002) Underascertainment of child maltreatment fatalities by death certificates, 1990–1998. *Pediatrics*, **110**, e18.

CULLEN, A., KIBERD, B., MCDONNELL, M., MEHANNI, M., MATTHEWS, T. G. & O'REGAN, M. (2000) Sudden infant death syndrome – are parents getting the message? *Ir J Med Sci*, **169**, pp. 40–3.

CUSHMAN, R., DOWN, J., MACMILLAN, N. & WACLAWIK, H. (1991) Helmet promotion in the emergency room following a bicycle injury: a randomized trial. *Pediatrics*, **88**, pp. 43–7.

DALTVEIT, A. K., OYEN, N., SKJAERVEN, R. & IRGENS, L. M. (1997) The epidemic of SIDS in Norway 1967–93: changing effects of risk factors. *Arch Dis Child*, **77**, pp. 23–7.

DANCEA, A., COTE, A., ROHLICEK, C., BERNARD, C. & OLIGNY, L. L. (2002) Cardiac pathology in sudden unexpected infant death. *J Pediatr*, **141**, pp. 336–42.

DASHASH, M., PRAVICA, V., HUTCHINSON, I. V., BARSON, A. J. & DRUCKER, D. B. (2006) Association of sudden infant death syndrome with VEGF and IL-6 gene polymorphisms. *Hum Immunol*, **67**, pp. 627–33.

DATTANI, N. & COOPER, N. (2000) Trends in cot death. *Health Statistics Quarterly*. London, Office for National Statistics.

DAVIES, B. (1995) Long-term outcomes of adolescent sibling bereavement. *Journal of Adolescent Research*, **6**, pp. 83–96.

DAVIES, B. (1996) Long-term effects of sibling bereavement. Unpublished manuscript.

DAVIES, B. P. D. (1999) *Shadows in the sun: the experiences of sibling bereavement in childhood*, Philadelphia, PA, Brunner/Mazel.

DAVIES, D. P. (1985) Cot death in Hong Kong: a rare problem? *Lancet*, **2**, pp. 1346–9.

DAVIS, R. M. & PLESS, B. (2001) BMJ bans 'accidents'. *BMJ*, **322**, pp. 1320–1.

DAVISON, W. (1945) Accidental infant suffocation. *BMJ*, **25**, pp. 251–252.

DE JONGE, G. A., ENGELBERTS, A. C., KOOMEN-LIEFTING, A. J. & KOSTENSE, P. J. (1989) Cot death and prone sleeping position in The Netherlands. *BMJ*, **298**, p. 722.

DENT, A. (2002) Family support after sudden child death. *Community Practitioner*, **75**, pp. 469–73.

DENT, A. & STEWART, A. R. G. N. (2004) *Sudden death in childhood: support for the bereaved family*, Edinburgh, Butterworth-Heinemann.

DEPARTMENT OF HEALTH (1991) *Child abuse – a study of inquiry reports 1980–1989*, London, HMSO.

DEPARTMENT OF HEALTH AND SOCIAL SECURITY (1982) *Child abuse – a study of inquiry reports 1973–1981*, London, HMSO.

DIFRANZA, J. R. & LEW, R. A. (1996) Morbidity and mortality in children associated with the use of tobacco products by other people. *Pediatrics*, **97**, pp. 560–8.

DIGUISEPPI, C. & HIGGINS, J. P. (2000) Systematic review of controlled trials of interventions to promote smoke alarms. *Arch Dis Child*, **82**, pp. 341–8.

DIGUISEPPI, C., ROBERTS, I. & LI, L. (1998) Smoke alarm ownership and house fire death rates in children. *J Epidemiol Community Health*, **52**, pp. 760–1.

DIGUISEPPI, C., ROBERTS, I. & SPEIRS, N. (1999) Smoke alarm installation and function in inner London council housing. *Arch Dis Child*, **81**, pp. 400–3.

DINGWALL, R. (1986) The Jasmine Beckford affair. *The Modern Law Review*, **49**, pp. 489–507.

DIX, J. (1998) Homicide and the baby-sitter. *Am J Forensic Med Pathol*, **19**, pp. 321–3.

DOKA, K. J. (1996) *Living with grief after sudden loss: suicide, homicide, accident, heart attack, stroke*, Washington, DC, Hospice Foundation of America; [London]: Taylor & Francis [distributor].

DOKA, K. J. E. (1989) *Disenfranchised grief: recognizing hidden sorrow*, Lexington Books.

DOUGLAS, E. & FINKELHOR, D. (2007) Child maltreatment fatalities fact sheet. Durham, New Hampshire, Crimes Against Children Research Center.

DRSD (1938) The infanticide act, 1938. *The Modern Law Review*, **2**, p. 229.

DUBE, S. R., ANDA, R. F., FELITTI, V. J., CHAPMAN, D. P., WILLIAMSON, D. F. & GILES, W. H. (2001) Childhood abuse, household dysfunction, and the risk of attempted suicide throughout the life span: findings from the Adverse Childhood Experiences Study. *Jama*, **286**, pp. 3089–96.

DUHAIME, A. C., CHRISTIAN, C. W., RORKE, L. B. & ZIMMERMAN, R. A. (1998) Nonaccidental head injury in infants – the 'shaken-baby syndrome'. *N Engl J Med*, **338**, pp. 1822–9.

DURFEE, M., DURFEE, D. T. & WEST, M. P. (2002) Child fatality review: an international movement. *Child Abuse Negl*, **26**, pp. 619–36.

DYREGROV, A. & MATTHIESEN, S. B. (1987) Similarities and differences in mothers' and fathers' grief following the death of an infant. *Scand J Psychol*, **28**, pp. 1–15.

EIDELMAN, A. I. & GARTNER, L. M. (2006) Bed sharing with unimpaired parents is not an important risk for sudden infant death syndrome: to the editor. *Pediatrics*, **117**, pp. 991–2; author reply pp. 994–6.

ELLIS, P. S. (1997) The pathology of fatal child abuse. *Pathology*, **29**, pp. 113–21.

ELLISON, J. (2005) Family liaison: when once has to be enough. In MONROE, B. & KRAUS, F. (Eds.) *Brief interventions with bereaved children*. Oxford, Oxford University Press.

EWIGMAN, B., KIVLAHAN, C. & LAND, G. (1993) The Missouri child fatality study: underreporting of maltreatment fatalities among children younger than five years of age, 1983 through 1986. *Pediatrics*, **91**, pp. 330–7.

FALKOV, A. (1995) *Study of Working Together 'Part 8' reports: fatal child abuse and parental psychiatric disorders: an analysis of 100 Area Child Protection Committee case reviews conducted under the terms of Part 8 of Working Together under the Children's Act 1989*, Great Britain, Department of Health.

FAROOQI, I. S., LIP, G. Y. & BEEVERS, D. G. (1994) Bed sharing and smoking in the sudden infant death syndrome. *BMJ*, **308**, pp. 204–5.

FEDRICK, J. (1973) Sudden unexpected death in infants in the Oxford record linkage area. An analysis with respect to time and place. *Br J Prev Soc Med*, **27**, pp. 217–24.

FELDMAN, K. W., SCHALLER, R. T., FELDMAN, J. A. & MCMILLON, M. (1978) Tap water scald burns in children. *Pediatrics*, **62**, pp. 1–7.

FELDMAN, K. W. & SIMMS, R. J. (1980) Strangulation in childhood: epidemiology and clinical course. *Pediatrics*, **65**, pp. 1079–85.

FIGLEY, C. (1996) Traumatic death: treatment implications. In DOKA, K. (Ed.) *Living with grief after sudden loss*. Philadelphia, Taylor and Francis.

FILIANO, J. J. & KINNEY, H. C. (1994) A perspective on neuropathologic findings in victims of the sudden infant death syndrome: the triple-risk model. *Biol Neonate*, **65**, pp. 194–7.

FINKBEINER, A. (1996) *After the death of a child*, Baltimore, John Hopkins Press.

FLEMING, P., BLAIR, P., BACON, C. & BERRY, P. (2000) *Sudden unexpected deaths in infancy. The CESDI SUDI studies 1993–1996*, London, The Stationery Office.

FLEMING, P., BLAIR, P. & MCKENNA, J. (2006) New knowledge, new insights, and new recommendations. *Arch Dis Child*, **91**, pp. 799–801.

FLEMING, P. J. & BLAIR, P. S. (2003) Sudden unexpected deaths after discharge from the neonatal intensive care unit. *Semin Neonatol*, **8**, pp. 159–67.

FLEMING, P. J. & BLAIR, P. S. (2005) How reliable are SIDS rates? The importance of a standardised, multiprofessional approach to 'diagnosis'. *Arch Dis Child*, **90**, pp. 993–4.

FLEMING, P. J., BLAIR, P. S., BACON, C., BENSLEY, D., SMITH, I., TAYLOR, E., BERRY, J., GOLDING, J. & TRIPP, J. (1996) Environment of infants during sleep and risk of the sudden infant death syndrome: results of 1993–5 case-control study for confidential inquiry into stillbirths and deaths in infancy. Confidential Enquiry into Stillbirths and Deaths Regional Coordinators and Researchers. *BMJ*, **313**, pp. 191–5.

FLEMING, P. J., BLAIR, P. S., PLATT, M. W., TRIPP, J., SMITH, I. J. & GOLDING, J. (2001) The UK accelerated immunisation programme and sudden unexpected death in infancy: case-control study. *BMJ*, **322**, p. 822.

FLEMING, P. J., BLAIR, P. S., POLLARD, K., PLATT, M. W., LEACH, C., SMITH, I., BERRY, P. J. & GOLDING, J. (1999) Pacifier use and sudden infant death syndrome: results from the CESDI/SUDI case control study. CESDI SUDI Research Team. *Arch Dis Child*, **81**, pp. 112–6.

FLEMING, P. J., BLAIR, P. S., SIDEBOTHAM, P. D. & HAYLER, T. (2004) Investigating sudden unexpected deaths in infancy and childhood and caring for bereaved families: an integrated multiagency approach. *BMJ*, **328**, pp. 331–4.

FLEMING, P. J., BLAIR, P. S., WARDPLATT, M., TRIPP, J. & SMITH, I. J. (2003) Sudden infant death syndrome and social deprivation: assessing epidemiological factors after post-matching for deprivation. *Paediatr Perinat Epidemiol*, **17**, pp. 272–80.

FLEMING, P. J., GILBERT, R., AZAZ, Y., BERRY, P. J., RUDD, P. T., STEWART, A. & HALL, E. (1990) Interaction between bedding and sleeping position in the sudden infant death syndrome: a population based case-control study. *BMJ*, **301**, pp. 85–9.

FLEMING, P. J., MULLER, N. L., BRYAN, M. H. & BRYAN, A. C. (1979) The effects of abdominal loading on rib cage distortion in premature infants. *Pediatrics*, **64**, pp. 425–8.

FLEMING, P. J. & STEWART, A. J. (1992) What is the ideal sleeping position for infants? *Dev Med Child Neurol*, **34**, pp. 916–9.

FLICK, L., WHITE, D. K., VEMULAPALLI, C., STULAC, B. B. & KEMP, J. S. (2001) Sleep position and the use of soft bedding during bed sharing among African American infants at increased risk for sudden infant death syndrome. *J Pediatr*, **138**, pp. 338–43.

FORBES, A. & ACLAND, P. (2004) What is the significance of haemosiderin in the lungs of deceased infants? *Med Sci Law*, **44**, pp. 348–52.

FOUNDATION FOR THE STUDY OF INFANT DEATHS (2003) Police and coroners guidelines for sudden infant death. London, FSID.

FOUNDATION FOR THE STUDY OF INFANT DEATHS (2006) Babies are still dying needlessly from a range of known preventable causes [Press Release online]. FSID.

FRANCO, P., PARDOU, A., HASSID, S., LURQUIN, P., GROSWASSER, J. & KAHN, A. (1998) Auditory arousal thresholds are higher when infants sleep in the prone position. *J Pediatr*, **132**, pp. 240–3.

FRANCO, P., SCAILLET, S., WERMENBOL, V., VALENTE, F., GROSWASSER, J. & KAHN, A. (2000) The influence of a pacifier on infants' arousals from sleep. *J Pediatr*, **136**, pp. 775–9.

FREED, G. E., MENY, R., GLOMB, W. B. & HAGEMAN, J. R. (2002) Effect of home monitoring on a high-risk population. *J Perinatol*, **22**, pp. 165–7.

FROGGATT, P., LYNAS, M. A. & MACKENZIE, G. (1971) Epidemiology of sudden unexpected death in infants ('cot death') in Northern Ireland. *Br J Prev Soc Med*, **25**, pp. 119–34.

FSID (2006) Baby zone – how to keep your baby safe and healthy. London, Foundation for the Study of Infant Deaths.

GANTLEY, M., DAVIES, D. P. & MURCOTT, A. (1993) Sudden infant death syndrome: links with infant care practices. *BMJ*, **306**, pp. 16–20.

GEIB, L. T. & NUNES, M. L. (2006) The incidence of sudden death syndrome in a cohort of infants. *J Pediatr (Rio J)*, **82**, pp. 21–6.

GELLERT, G. A., MAXWELL, R. M., DURFEE, M. J. & WAGNER, G. A. (1995) Fatalities assessed by the Orange County child death review team, 1989 to 1991. *Child Abuse Negl*, **19**, pp. 875–83.

GESSNER, B. D. & PORTER, T. J. (2006) Bed sharing with unimpaired parents is not an important risk for sudden infant death syndrome. *Pediatrics*, **117**, pp. 990–1; author reply 994–6.

GILBERT-BARNESS, E. & BARNESS, L. A. (2006) Pathogenesis of cardiac conduction disorders in children genetic and histopathologic aspects. *Am J Med Genet A*, **140**, pp. 1993–2006.

GILBERT, R., RUDD, P., BERRY, P. J., FLEMING, P. J., HALL, E., WHITE, D. G., OREFFO, V. O., JAMES, P. & EVANS, J. A. (1992) Combined effect of infection and heavy wrapping on the risk of sudden unexpected infant death. *Arch Dis Child*, **67**, pp. 171–7.

GLEADHILL, D. N., ROBSON, W. J., CUDMORE, R. E. & TURNOCK, R. R. (1987) Baby walkers. Time to take a stand? *Arch Dis Child*, **62**, pp. 491–4.

GOLDEN, M. H., SAMUELS, M. P. & SOUTHALL, D. P. (2003) How to distinguish between neglect and deprivational abuse. *Arch Dis Child*, **88**, pp. 105–7.

GOLDING, J., LIMERICK, S. & MACFARLANE, A. (1985) *Sudden infant death: patterns, puzzles and problems*, Open Books.

GOLDSMITH, L. (2004) The review of infant death cases following the Court of Appeal decision in the case of R v Cannings (2004).

GOLLOB, M. H., GREEN, M. S., TANG, A. S., GOLLOB, T., KARIBE, A., ALI HASSAN, A. S., AHMAD, F., LOZADO, R., SHAH, G., FANANAPAZIR, L., BACHINSKI, L. L. & ROBERTS, R. (2001) Identification of a gene responsible for familial Wolff-Parkinson-White syndrome. *N Engl J Med*, **344**, pp. 1823–31.

GOVERNMENT OFFICE FOR THE WEST MIDLANDS (2007) Regional profile.

GRANGEOT-KEROS, L., BROYER, M., BRIAND, E., GUT, J. P., TURKOGLU, S., CHRETIEN, P., EMILIE, D., DUSSAIX, E., LAZIZI, Y. & DEHAN, M. (1996) Enterovirus in sudden unexpected deaths in infants. *Pediatr Infect Dis J*, **15**, pp. 123–8.

GRAUPMAN, P. & WINSTON, K. R. (2006) Nonaccidental head trauma as a cause of childhood death. *J Neurosurg*, **104**, pp. 245–50.

GRAY, P. (2005) Is grief counselling a waste of time? *Therapy Today*, **16**, pp. 26–8.

GREEN, M. A. (1998) A practical approach to suspicious death in infancy – a personal view. *J Clin Pathol*, **51**, pp. 561–3.

GREENE, D. (1930) Asymmetry of the head and face in infants and in children. *American Journal of Diseases in Children*, **41**, pp. 1317–26.

GRUBER, L. E., MAHONEY, M. C., LAWVERE, S., CHUNIKOVSKIY, S. P., MICHALEK, A. M., KHOTIANOV, N., ZICHITTELLA, L. J. & CARTER, C. A. (2005) Patterns of childhood mortality in a region of Belarus, 1980–2000. *Eur J Pediatr*, **164**, pp. 544–51.

GUNTHEROTH, W. & SPIERS, P. (2005) Long QT syndrome and sudden infant death syndrome. *Am J Cardiol*, **96**, p. 1034.

GUNTHEROTH, W. G., LOHMANN, R. & SPIERS, P. (1990) Risk of sudden infant death syndrome in subsequent siblings. *Journal of Pediatrics*, **116**, pp. 520–4.

GUNTHEROTH, W. G. & SPIERS, P. S. (2002) The triple risk hypotheses in sudden infant death syndrome. *Pediatrics*, **110**, e64.

GYULAY, J. E. (1975) The forgotten grievers. *Am J Nurs*, **75**, pp. 1476–9.

HAGLUND, B. & CNATTINGIUS, S. (1990) Cigarette smoking as a risk factor for sudden infant death syndrome: a population-based study. *Am J Public Health*, **80**, pp. 29–32.

HAMILTON, B. E., MININO, A. M., MARTIN, J. A., KOCHANEK, K. D., STROBINO, D. M. & GUYER, B. (2007) Annual summary of vital statistics: 2005. *Pediatrics*, **119**, pp. 345–60.

HANDLEY, M. & GREEN, R. (2004) *Safeguarding through audit: a guide to auditing case review recommendations*, Leicester, NSPCC.

HARVEY, A. S., NOLAN, T. & CARLIN, J. B. (1993) Community-based study of mortality in children with epilepsy. *Epilepsia*, **34**, pp. 597–603.

HAUCK, F. R., HERMAN, S. M., DONOVAN, M., IYASU, S., MERRICK MOORE, C., DONOGHUE, E., KIRSCHNER, R. H. & WILLINGER, M. (2003) Sleep environment and the risk of sudden infant death syndrome in an urban population: the Chicago Infant Mortality Study. *Pediatrics*, **111**, pp. 1207–14.

HEIN, H. A. & PETTIT, S. F. (2001) Back to sleep: good advice for parents but not for hospitals? *Pediatrics*, **107**, pp. 537–9.

HERMAN-GIDDENS, M. E., SMITH, J. B., MITTAL, M., CARLSON, M. & BUTTS, J. D. (2003) Newborns killed or left to die by a parent: a population-based study. *Jama*, **289**, pp. 1425–9.

HESKETH, T. & XING, Z. W. (2006) Abnormal sex ratios in human populations: causes and consequences. *Proc Natl Acad Sci USA*, **103**, pp. 13271–5.

HICKS, R. A. & GAUGHAN, D. C. (1995) Understanding fatal child abuse. *Child Abuse Negl*, **19**, pp. 855–63.

HILEY, C. (1992) Babies' sleeping position. *BMJ*, **305**, p. 115.

HINDMARCH, C. (2000) *On the death of a child*, Abingdon, Radcliffe Medical.

HM GOVERNMENT (1988) Coroners act 1988. The Stationery Office Limited.

HM GOVERNMENT (2000) Framework for the assessment of children in need and their families. London, The Stationery Office.

HM GOVERNMENT (2003) *Every child matters*. The Stationery Office.

HM GOVERNMENT (2004a) Children act 2004, London, The Stationery Office.

HM GOVERNMENT (2004b) Human tissue act 2004. The Stationery Office.

HM GOVERNMENT (2005a) Common assessment framework. In DEPARTMENT FOR EDUCATION AND SKILLS (Ed.), The Stationery Office.

HM GOVERNMENT (2005b) Statutory instrument 2005 No. 420. The coroners (amendment) rules 2005. InN OFFICE, H. (Ed.), Her Majesty's Stationery Office.

HM GOVERNMENT (2006a) Collision report form MGNCRF.

HM GOVERNMENT (2006b) Working together to safeguard children. In DEPARTMENT FOR EDUCATION AND SKILLS (Ed.) London, DfES.

HOARE, P. & BEATTIE, T. (2003) Children with attention deficit hyperactivity disorder and attendance at hospital. *Eur J Emerg Med*, **10**, pp. 98–100.

HOBBS, C. J. (1984) Skull fracture and the diagnosis of abuse. *Arch Dis Child*, **59**, pp. 246–52.

HOBBS, C. J., HANKS, H. G. I. & WYNNE, J. M. (1999) *Child abuse and neglect: a clinician's handbook*, London, Churchill Livingstone.

HOFFMAN, H.J., HUNTER, J.C., DAMUS, K., PAKTER, J., PETERSON, D.R., VAN BELLE, G. & HASSELMEYER, E. G. (1987) Diphtheria-tetanus-pertussis immunization and sudden infant death: results of the National Institute of Child Health and Human Development Cooperative Epidemiological Study of Sudden Infant Death Syndrome risk factors. *Pediatrics*, **79**, pp. 598–611.

HORNE, R.S., PARSLOW, P.M., FERENS, D., BANDOPADHAYAY, P., OSBORNE, A., WATTS, A.M., CRANAGE, S.M. & ADAMSON, T.M. (2002) Arousal responses and risk factors for sudden infant death syndrome. *Sleep Med*, **3** Suppl 2, S61–5.

HOWARD, C. R., HOWARD, F. M., LANPHEAR, B., DEBLIECK, E. A., EBERLY, S. & LAWRENCE, R. A. (1999) The effects of early pacifier use on breastfeeding duration. *Pediatrics*, **103**, E33.

HOWATSON, A. (2006) The autopsy for sudden unexpected death in infancy. *Current Diagnostic Pathology*, **12**, pp. 173–83.

HOWELLS, J. G. & COLWELL, M. (1974) *Remember Maria*, London: Butterworth.

HUBER, J. (1993) Sudden infant death syndrome: the new clothes of the emperor. *Eur J Pediatr*, **152**, pp. 93–4.

HUNT, C.E., LESKO, S.M., VEZINA, R.M., MCCOY, R., CORWIN, M.J., MANDELL, F., WILLINGER, M., HOFFMAN, H. J. & MITCHELL, A. A. (2003) Infant sleep position and associated health outcomes. *Arch Pediatr Adolesc Med*, **157**, pp. 469–74.

HUNT, L., FLEMING, P. & GOLDING, J. (1997) Does the supine sleeping position have any adverse effects on the child? I. Health in the first six months. The ALSPAC Study Team. *Pediatrics*, **100**, E11.

HUTCHISON, B. L., THOMPSON, J. M. & MITCHELL, E. A. (2003) Determinants of nonsynostotic plagiocephaly: a case-control study. *Pediatrics*, **112**, e316.

JARDINE, D. S. (1992) A mathematical model of life-threatening hyperthermia during infancy. *J Appl Physiol*, **73**, pp. 329–39.

JARVIS, S. & SIBERT, J. (1998) Action on injury. Setting the agenda for children and young people in the UK: conclusion. *Inj Prev*, **4**, S46.

JASON, J. & ANDERECK, N. D. (1983) Fatal child abuse in Georgia: the epidemiology of severe physical child abuse. *Child Abuse Negl*, **7**, pp. 1–9.

JAYAWANT, S., RAWLINSON, A., GIBBON, F., PRICE, J., SCHULTE, J., SHARPLES, P., SIBERT, J. R. & KEMP, A. M. (1998) Subdural haemorrhages in infants: population based study. *BMJ*, **317**, pp. 1558–61.

JENNY, C. & ISAAC, R. (2006) The relation between child death and child maltreatment. *Arch Dis Child*, **91**, pp. 265–9.

JHA, P., KUMAR, R., VASA, P., DHINGRA, N., THIRUCHELVAM, D. & MOINED-DIN, R. (2006) Low female-to-male sex ratio of children born in India: national survey of 1.1 million households. *Lancet*, **367**, pp. 211–8.

JONES, S. J., LYONS, R. A., JOHN, A. & PALMER, S. R. (2005) Traffic calming policy can reduce inequalities in child pedestrian injuries: database study. *Inj Prev*, **11**, pp. 152–6.

JONVILLE-BERA, A. P., AUTRET-LECA, E., BARBEILLON, F. & PARIS-LLADO, J. (2001) Sudden unexpected death in infants under 3 months of age and vaccination status – a case-control study. *Br J Clin Pharmacol*, **51**, pp. 271–6.

JORDAN, J. R., KRAUS, D. R. & WARE, E. S. (1993) Observations on loss and family development. *Fam Process*, **32**, pp. 425–40.

KAHN, A., BLUM, D., HENNART, P., SELLENS, C., SAMSON-DOLLFUS, D., TAYOT, J., GILLY, R., DUTRUGE, J., FLORES, R. & STERNBERG, B. (1984) A critical comparison of the history of sudden-death infants and infants hospitalised for near-miss for SIDS. *Eur J Pediatr*, **143**, pp. 103–7.

KAIRYS, S. W., ALEXANDER, R. C., BLOCK, R. W., EVERETT, V. D., HYMEL, K. P., JOHNSON, C. F., KANDA, M. B., MALINKOVICH, P., BELL, W. C., CORA-BRAMBLE, D., DUPLESSIS, H. M., HANDAL, G. A., HOLMBERG, R. E., LAVIN, A., TAYLOE, D. T., JR., VARRASSO, D. A. & WOOD, D. L. (1999) American Academy of Pediatrics. Committee on Child Abuse and Neglect and Committee on Community Health Services. Investigation and review of unexpected infant and child deaths. *Pediatrics*, **104**, pp. 1158–60.

KASIM, M. S., CHEAH, I. & SHAFIE, H. M. (1995) Childhood deaths from physical abuse. *Child Abuse Negl*, **19**, pp. 847–54.

KATCHER, M. L., LANDRY, G. L. & SHAPIRO, M. M. (1989) Liquid-crystal thermometer use in pediatric office counseling about tap water burn prevention. *Pediatrics*, **83**, pp. 766–71.

KEELING, J. W. & KNOWLES, S. A. (1989) Sudden death in childhood and adolescence. *J Pathol*, **159**, pp. 221–4.

KEENAN, H. T., RUNYAN, D. K., MARSHALL, S. W., NOCERA, M. A., MERTEN, D. F. & SINAL, S. H. (2003) A population-based study of inflicted traumatic brain injury in young children. *Jama*, **290**, pp. 621–6.

KELLEY, J., ALLSOPP, D. & HAWKSWORTH, D. L. (1992) Sudden infant death syndrome (SIDS) and the toxic gas hypothesis: microbiological studies of cot mattresses. *Hum Exp Toxicol*, **11**, pp. 347–55.

KELLY, S. C. (2004) Serious Case Review on Ian Huntley, North East Lincolnshire 1995–2001. North East Lincolnshire Area Child Protection Committee.

KEMP, A. & SIBERT, J. R. (1992) Drowning and near drowning in children in the United Kingdom: lessons for prevention. *BMJ*, **304**, pp. 1143–6.

KEMP, A. M. (2002) Investigating subdural haemorrhage in infants. *Arch Dis Child*, **86**, pp. 98–102.

KEMP, A. M., MOTT, A. M. & SIBERT, J. R. (1994a) Accidents and child abuse in bathtub submersions. *Arch Dis Child*, **70**, pp. 435–8.

KEMP, J. S., NELSON, V. E. & THACH, B. T. (1994b) Physical properties of bedding that may increase risk of sudden infant death syndrome in prone-sleeping infants. *Pediatr Res*, **36**, pp. 7–11.

KEMP, J. S. & THACH, B. T. (1995) Quantifying the potential of infant bedding to limit CO_2 dispersal and factors affecting rebreathing in bedding. *J Appl Physiol*, **78**, pp. 740–5.

KIECHL-KOHLENDORFER, U. (2003) [Sudden infant death – prevention programs in Austria]. *Wien Klin Wochenschr*, **115**, pp. 881–6.

KIECHL-KOHLENDORFER, U., PEGLOW, U. P., KIECHL, S., OBERAIGNER, W. & SPERL, W. (2001) Epidemiology of sudden infant death syndrome (SIDS) in the Tyrol before and after an intervention campaign. *Wien Klin Wochenschr*, **113**, pp. 27–32.

KING, W. J., LEBLANC, J. C., BARROWMAN, N. J., KLASSEN, T. P., BERNARD-BONNIN, A. C., ROBITAILLE, Y., TENENBEIN, M. & PLESS, I. B. (2005) Long term effects of a home visit to prevent childhood injury: three year follow up of a randomized trial. *Inj Prev*, **11**, pp. 106–9.

KING, W. K., KIESEL, E. L. & SIMON, H. K. (2006) Child abuse fatalities: are we missing opportunities for intervention? *Pediatr Emerg Care*, **22**, pp. 211–4.

KINNEY, H., ARMSTRONG, D., CHADWICK, A., CRANDALL, L., HILBERT, C., BELLIVEAU, R., KUPSKY, W. & KROUS, H. (2007) Sudden death in toddlers associated with developmental abnormalities of the hippocampus: a report of five cases. *Pediatr Dev Pathol*, **1**.

KLASS, D., SILVERMAN, P. R. & NICKMAN, S. L. (1996) *Continuing bonds: new understandings of grief*, London, Taylor & Francis.

KLONOFF-COHEN, H. S. & EDELSTEIN, S. L. (1995) A case-control study of routine and death scene sleep position and sudden infant death syndrome in Southern California. *Jama*, **273**, pp. 790–4.

KLONOFF-COHEN, H. S., EDELSTEIN, S. L., LEFKOWITZ, E. S., SRINIVASAN, I. P., KAEGI, D., CHANG, J. C. & WILEY, K. J. (1995) The effect of passive smoking and tobacco exposure through breast milk on sudden infant death syndrome. *Jama*, **273**, pp. 795–8.

KNEYBER, M. C., BRANDENBURG, A. H., DE GROOT, R., JOOSTEN, K. F., ROTHBARTH, P. H., OTT, A. & MOLL, H. A. (1998) Risk factors for respiratory syncytial virus associated apnoea. *Eur J Pediatr*, **157**, pp. 331–5.

KOLF, J. (1995) *Grandma's tears*, Grand Rapids, MI, Baker Books.

KOTCH, J., BROWNE, D., DUFORT, V., WINSOR, J. & CATELLIER, D. (1999) Predicting child maltreatment in the first 4 years of life from characteristics assessed in the neonatal period. *Child Abuse & Neglect*, **23**, pp. 305–319.

KOTCH, J. B., CHALMERS, D. J., FANSLOW, J. L., MARSHALL, S. & LANGLEY, J. D. (1993) Morbidity and death due to child abuse in New Zealand. *Child Abuse Negl*, **17**, pp. 233–47.

KRAUS, J. F. (1985) Effectiveness of measures to prevent unintentional deaths of infants and children from suffocation and strangulation. *Public Health Rep*, **100**, pp. 231–40.

KRAUS, J. F., GREENLAND, S. & BULTERYS, M. (1989) Risk factors for sudden infant death syndrome in the US Collaborative Perinatal Project. *Int J Epidemiol*, **18**, pp. 113–20.

KROUS, H. F. (1995) The international standardised autopsy protocol for sudden unexpected infant death. In ROGNUM, T. (Ed.) *Sudden infant death syndrome: new trends in the nineties*. Oslo, Scandinavian University Press.

KROUS, H. F., CHADWICK, A. E., CRANDALL, L. & NADEAU-MANNING, J. M. (2005) Sudden unexpected death in childhood: a report of 50 cases. *Pediatr Dev Pathol*, **8**, pp. 307–19.

KROUS, H. F., WIXOM, C., CHADWICK, A. E., HAAS, E. A., SILVA, P. D. & STANLEY, C. (2006) Pulmonary intra-alveolar siderophages in SIDS and suffocation: a San Diego SIDS/SUDC Research Project report. *Pediatr Dev Pathol*, **9**, pp. 103–14.

KRUG, E. G., MERCY, J. A., DAHLBERG, L. L. & ZWI, A. B. (2002) [World report on violence and health]. *Biomedica*, **22** Suppl 2, pp. 327–36.

KUBLER-ROSS, E. (1969) *On death and dying: what the dying have to teach doctors, nurses, clergy, and their own families*, New York, Touchstone, 1997.

KULLO, I. J., EDWARDS, W. D. & SEWARD, J. B. (1995) Right ventricular dysplasia: the Mayo Clinic experience. *Mayo Clin Proc*, **70**, pp. 541–8.

L'HOIR, M. P., ENGELBERTS, A. C., VAN WELL, G. T., DAMSTE, P. H., IDEMA, N. K., WESTERS, P., MELLENBERGH, G. J., WOLTERS, W. H. & HUBER, J. (1999) Dummy use, thumb sucking, mouth breathing and cot death. *Eur J Pediatr*, **158**, pp. 896–901.

L'HOIR, M. P., ENGELBERTS, A. C., VAN WELL, G. T., MCCLELLAND, S., WESTERS, P., DANDACHLI, T., MELLENBERGH, G. J., WOLTERS, W. H. & HUBER, J. (1998a) Risk and preventive factors for cot death in The Netherlands, a low-incidence country. *Eur J Pediatr*, **157**, pp. 681–8.

L'HOIR, M. P., ENGELBERTS, A. C., VAN WELL, G. T., WESTERS, P., MELLEN-BERGH, G. J., WOLTERS, W. H. & HUBER, J. (1998b) Case-control study of current validity of previously described risk factors for SIDS in The Netherlands. *Arch Dis Child*, **79**, pp. 386–93.

LANG, A. & GOTTLIEB, L. (1993) Parental grief reactions and marital intimacy following infant death. *Death Studies*, **17**, pp. 233–55.

LEACH, C. E., BLAIR, P. S., FLEMING, P. J., SMITH, I. J., PLATT, M. W., BERRY, P. J. & GOLDING, J. (1999) Epidemiology of SIDS and explained sudden infant deaths. CESDI SUDI Research Group. *Pediatrics*, **104**, e43.

LEACH, P. (1980) *Baby and child*, London, Michael Joseph.

LEE, A. J., MANN, N. P. & TAKRITI, R. (2000) A hospital-led promotion campaign aimed to increase bicycle helmet wearing among children aged 11–15 living in West Berkshire 1992–98. *Inj Prev*, **6**, pp. 151–3.

LEVENE, S. & BACON, C. J. (2004) Sudden unexpected death and covert homicide in infancy. *Arch Dis Child*, **89**, pp. 443–7.

LEVINE, M., FREEMAN, J. & COMPAAN, C. (1994) Maltreatment-related fatalities: issues of policy and prevention. *Law and Policy*, **16**, pp. 449–71.

LEWIS, K. W. & BOSQUE, E. M. (1995) Deficient hypoxia awakening response in infants of smoking mothers: possible relationship to sudden infant death syndrome. *J Pediatr*, **127**, pp. 691–9.

LI, D. K., PETITTI, D. B., WILLINGER, M., MCMAHON, R., ODOULI, R., VU, H. & HOFFMAN, H. J. (2003) Infant sleeping position and the risk of sudden infant death syndrome in California, 1997–2000. *Am J Epidemiol*, **157**, pp. 446–55.

LI, D. K., WILLINGER, M., PETITTI, D. B., ODOULI, R., LIU, L. & HOFFMAN, H. J. (2006) Use of a dummy (pacifier) during sleep and risk of sudden infant death syndrome (SIDS): population based case-control study. *BMJ*, **332**, pp. 18–22.

LIMERICK, S. R. (1992) Sudden infant death in historical perspective. *J Clin Pathol*, **45**, pp. 3–6.

LIMERICK, S. R. & BACON, C. J. (2004) Terminology used by pathologists in reporting on sudden infant deaths. *J Clin Pathol*, **57**, pp. 309–11.

LORD, J. (1997) America's number one killer: vehicular crashes. In DOKA, K. (Ed.) *Living with grief after sudden loss: suicide, homicide, accident, heart attack, stroke.* Washington, DC, Taylor & Francis.

LOUGHREY, C. M., PREECE, M. A. & GREEN, A. (2005) Sudden unexpected death in infancy (SUDI). *J Clin Pathol*, **58**, pp. 20–1.

LUCAS, D. R., WEZNER, K. C., MILNER, J. S., MCCANNE, T. R., HARRIS, I. N., MONROE-POSEY, C. & NELSON, J. P. (2002) Victim, perpetrator, family, and incident characteristics of infant and child homicide in the United States Air Force. *Child Abuse Negl*, **26**, pp. 167–86.

LUDINGTON-HOE, S. M., HADEED, A. J. & ANDERSON, G. C. (1991) Physiologic responses to skin-to-skin contact in hospitalized premature infants. *J Perinatol*, **11**, pp. 19–24.

LYMAN, J. M., MCGWIN, G., JR., MALONE, D. E., TAYLOR, A. J., BRISSIE, R. M., DAVIS, G. & RUE, L. W., 3RD (2003) Epidemiology of child homicide in Jefferson County, Alabama. *Child Abuse Negl*, **27**, pp. 1063–73.

LYONS, R. A., JONES, S. J., NEWCOMBE, R. G. & PALMER, S. R. (2006) The influence of local politicians on pedestrian safety. *Inj Prev*, **12**, pp. 312–5.

MACKNIN, M. L., GUSTAFSON, C., GASSMAN, J. & BARICH, D. (1987) Office education by pediatricians to increase seat belt use. *Am J Dis Child*, **141**, pp. 1305–7.

MACKWAY-JONES, K., MOLYNEUX, E., PHILLIPS, B. & WIETESKA, S. (2005) *Advanced paediatric life support: the practical approach*, Oxford, Blackwell.

MAGUIRE, S., MANN, M. K., SIBERT, J. & KEMP, A. (2005) Are there patterns of bruising in childhood which are diagnostic or suggestive of abuse? A systematic review. *Arch Dis Child*, **90**, pp. 182–6.

MAHER, J. & MACFARLANE, A. (2004) Inequalities in infant mortality: trends by social class, registration status, mother's age and birthweight, England and Wales, 1976–2000. *Health Stat Q*, pp. 14–22.

MARKESTAD, T., SKADBERG, B., HORDVIK, E., MORILD, I. & IRGENS, L. M. (1995) Sleeping position and sudden infant death syndrome (SIDS): effect of an intervention programme to avoid prone sleeping. *Acta Paediatr*, **84**, pp. 375–8.

MARKS, K. H., DEVENYI, A. G., BELLO, M. E., NARDIS, E. E., SEATON, J. F. & ULTMAN, J. S. (1985) Thermal head wrap for infants. *J Pediatr*, **107**, pp. 956–9.

MARTIN, R. J., HERRELL, N., RUBIN, D. & FANAROFF, A. (1979) Effect of supine and prone positions on arterial oxygen tension in the preterm infant. *Pediatrics*, **63**, pp. 528–31.

MATHEWS, T. J. & MACDORMAN, M. F. (2006) Infant mortality statistics from the 2003 period linked birth/infant death data set. *Natl Vital Stat Rep*, **54**, pp. 1–29.

MATTOS-GRANER, R. O., DE MORAES, A. B., RONTANI, R. M. & BIRMAN, E. G. (2001) Relation of oral yeast infection in Brazilian infants and use of a pacifier. *ASDC J Dent Child*, **68**, pp. 33–6, 10.

MC CLOWRY, S., DAVIES, E., MAY, K., KULENCAMP, E. & MARTINSON, I. (1987) The empty space phenomenon: the process of grief in the bereaved family. *Death Studies*, **11**, pp. 361–74.

MCCLURE, R. J., DAVIS, P. M., MEADOW, S. R. & SIBERT, J. R. (1996) Epidemiology of Munchausen syndrome by proxy, non-accidental poisoning, and non-accidental suffocation. *Arch Dis Child*, **75**, pp. 57–61.

MCCRACKEN, A. & SEMEL, M. (1998) *A broken heart still beats: after your child dies*, Center City, Minn., Hazelden; [Enfield: Airlift [distributor]].

MCGARVEY, C., MCDONNELL, M., CHONG, A., O'REGAN, M. & MATTHEWS, T. (2003) Factors relating to the infant's last sleep environment in sudden infant death syndrome in the Republic of Ireland. *Arch Dis Child*, **88**, pp. 1058–64.

MCGARVEY, C., MCDONNELL, M., HAMILTON, K., O'REGAN, M. & MATTHEWS, T. (2006) An 8 year study of risk factors for SIDS: bed-sharing versus non-bed-sharing. *Arch Dis Child*, **91**, pp. 318–23.

MCGLASHAN, N. D. (1989) Sudden infant deaths in Tasmania, 1980–1986: a seven year prospective study. *Soc Sci Med*, **29**, pp. 1015–26.

MCKENNA, J. (1996) Sudden Infant Death Syndrome in cross-cultural perspective. Is infant-parent co-sleeping protective? *Ann Rev of Anthropology*, **25**, pp. 201–16.

MCKENNA, J. J. (1986) An anthropological perspective on the sudden infant death syndrome (SIDS): the role of parental breathing cues and speech breathing adaptations. *Med Anthropol*, **10**, pp. 9–92.

MEADOW, R. (1998) Munchausen syndrome by proxy abuse perpetrated by men. *Arch Dis Child*, **78**, pp. 210–6.

MEADOW, R. (1999) Unnatural sudden infant death. *Arch Dis Child*, **80**, pp. 7–14.

MEADOW, R. (2002) Different interpretations of Munchausen Syndrome by Proxy. *Child Abuse Negl*, **26**, pp. 501–8.

MENDELSON, K. (2004) The Society for Pediatric Radiology – National Association of Medical Examiners: post-mortem radiography in the evaluation of unexpected death in children less than 2 years of age whose death is suspicious for fatal abuse. *Pediatr Radiol*, **34**, pp. 675–7.

MENY, R. G., CARROLL, J. L., CARBONE, M. T. & KELLY, D. H. (1994) Cardiorespiratory recordings from infants dying suddenly and unexpectedly at home. *Pediatrics*, **93**, pp. 44–9.

MESERVY, C. J., TOWBIN, R., MCLAURIN, R. L., MYERS, P. A. & BALL, W. (1987) Radiographic characteristics of skull fractures resulting from child abuse. *AJR Am J Roentgenol*, **149**, pp. 173–5.

MILLER, J. R. & PLESS, I. B. (1977) Child automobile restraints: evaluation of health education. *Pediatrics*, **59**, pp. 907–11.

MINCHOM, P. E., SIBERT, J. R., NEWCOMBE, R. G. & BOWLEY, M. A. (1984) Does health education prevent childhood accidents? *Postgrad Med J*, **60**, pp. 260–2.

MITCHELL, E., KROUS, H. F. & BYARD, R. W. (2002) Pathological findings in overlaying. *J Clin Forensic Med*, **9**, pp. 133–5.

MITCHELL, E. A., FORD, R. P., STEWART, A. W., TAYLOR, B. J., BECROFT, D. M., THOMPSON, J. M., SCRAGG, R., HASSALL, I. B., BARRY, D. M., ALLEN, E. M. ET AL. (1993a) Smoking and the sudden infant death syndrome. *Pediatrics*, **91**, pp. 893–6.

MITCHELL, E. A. & MILERAD, J. (2006) Smoking and the sudden infant death syndrome. *Rev Environ Health*, **21**, pp. 81–103.

MITCHELL, E. A., SCRAGG, L. & CLEMENTS, M. (1996) Soft cot mattresses and the sudden infant death syndrome. *N Z Med J*, **109**, pp. 206–7.

MITCHELL, E. A., SCRAGG, R., STEWART, A. W., BECROFT, D. M., TAYLOR, B. J., FORD, R. P., HASSALL, I. B., BARRY, D. M., ALLEN, E. M. & ROBERTS, A. P. (1991) Results from the first year of the New Zealand cot death study. *N Z Med J*, **104**, pp. 71–6.

MITCHELL, E. A., STEWART, A. W. & CLEMENTS, M. (1995) Immunisation and the sudden infant death syndrome. New Zealand Cot Death Study Group. *Arch Dis Child*, **73**, pp. 498–501.

MITCHELL, E. A., TAYLOR, B. J., FORD, R. P., STEWART, A. W., BECROFT, D. M., THOMPSON, J. M., SCRAGG, R., HASSALL, I. B., BARRY, D. M., ALLEN, E. M. ET AL. (1992) Four modifiable and other major risk factors for cot death: the New Zealand study. *J Paediatr Child Health*, **28** Suppl 1, S3–8.

MITCHELL, E. A., TAYLOR, B. J., FORD, R. P., STEWART, A. W., BECROFT, D. M., THOMPSON, J. M., SCRAGG, R., HASSALL, I. B., BARRY, D. M., ALLEN, E. M. ET AL. (1993b) Dummies and the sudden infant death syndrome. *Arch Dis Child*, **68**, pp. 501–4.

MONROE, B. & KRAUS, F. (2005) *Brief interventions with bereaved children*, Oxford, Oxford University Press.

MOORE, A. (2005) Changing patterns of childhood mortality in Wolverhampton. *Arch Dis Child*, **90**, pp. 687–91.

MORENTIN, B., AGUILERA, B., GARAMENDI, P. M. & SUAREZ-MIER, M. P. (2000) Sudden unexpected non-violent death between 1 and 19 years in north Spain. *Arch Dis Child*, **82**, pp. 456–61.

MORRIS, J. A. (1999) The common bacterial toxins hypothesis of sudden infant death syndrome. *FEMS Immunol Med Microbiol*, **25**, pp. 11–7.

MORRIS, J. A. (2004) Common bacterial toxins and physiological vulnerability to sudden infant death: the role of deleterious genetic mutations. *FEMS Immunol Med Microbiol*, **42**, pp. 42–7.

MORRIS, J. A., HARRISON, L. M. & PARTRIDGE, S. M. (2006) Postmortem bacteriology: a re-evaluation. *J Clin Pathol*, **59**, pp. 1–9.

MORRISON, A. & STONE, D. H. (1999) Unintentional childhood injury mortality in Europe 1984–93: a report from the EURORISC Working Group. *Inj Prev*, **5**, pp. 171–6.

MOSCOVIS, S. M., GORDON, A. E., HALL, S. T., GLEESON, M., SCOTT, R. J., ROBERTS-THOMSOM, J., WEIR, D. M., BUSUTTIL, A. & BLACKWELL, C. C. (2004) Interleukin 1-beta responses to bacterial toxins and sudden infant death syndrome. *FEMS Immunol Med Microbiol*, **42**, pp. 139–45.

MOSKO, S., MCKENNA, J., DICKEL, M. & HUNT, L. (1993) Parent-infant cosleeping: the appropriate context for the study of infant sleep and implications for sudden infant death syndrome (SIDS) research. *J Behav Med*, **16**, pp. 589–610.

MOSKOWITZ, H., LARAQUE, D., DOUCETTE, J. T. & SHELOV, E. (2005) Relationships of US youth homicide victims and their offenders, 1976–1999. *Arch Pediatr Adolesc Med*, **159**, pp. 356–61.

NADEAU, J. (2001) Family construction of meaning. In NEIMEYER, R. (Ed.) *Meaning reconstruction and the experience of loss*. Washington, American Psychological Association.

NASHEF, L., GARNER, S., SANDER, J. W., FISH, D. R. & SHORVON, S. D. (1998) Circumstances of death in sudden death in epilepsy: interviews of bereaved relatives. *J Neurol Neurosurg Psychiatry*, **64**, pp. 349–52.

NASHEF, L., HINDOCHA, N. & MAKOFF, A. (2007) Risk factors in sudden death in epilepsy (SUDEP): the quest for mechanisms. *Epilepsia*.

NATIONAL WORKING GROUP ON CHILD PROTECTION AND DISABILITY (2003) *'It doesn't happen to disabled children': child protection and disabled children*, London, NSPCC.

NEIMEYER, R. A. (2001) *Meaning reconstruction & the experience of loss*, Washington, D.C.; London, American Psychological Association.

NELSON, E. A., SERRA, A., COWAN, S. & MANGIATERRA, V. (2000) Maternity advice survey: sleeping position in Eastern Europe. MAS Study Group for WHO EURO region. *Arch Dis Child*, **83**, pp. 304–6.

NELSON, E. A., TAYLOR, B. J. & MACKAY, S. C. (1989a) Child care practices and the sudden infant death syndrome. *Aust Paediatr J*, **25**, pp. 202–4; discussion 205–6.

NELSON, E. A., TAYLOR, B. J. & WEATHERALL, I. L. (1989b) Sleeping position and infant bedding may predispose to hyperthermia and the sudden infant death syndrome. *Lancet*, **1**, pp. 199–201.

NELSON, T., TO, K. F., WONG, Y. Y., DICKINSON, J., CHOI, K. C., YU, L. M., OU, Y., CHOW, C. B., WONG, E., TANG, N., HJELM, M. & CHEN, L. (2005) Hong Kong case-control study of sudden unexpected infant death. *N Z Med J*, **118**, U1788.

NEWBERGER, E. H., REED, R. B., DANIEL, J. H., HYDE, J. N. & KOTELCHUCK, M. (1977) Pediatric social illness: toward an etiological classification. *Pediatrics*, **60**, pp. 178–85.

NEWBOULD, M. J., MALAM, J., MCILLMURRAY, J. M., MORRIS, J. A., TELFORD, D. R. & BARSON, A. J. (1989) Immunohistological localisation of staphylococcal toxic shock syndrome toxin (TSST-1) antigen in sudden infant death syndrome. *J Clin Pathol*, **42**, pp. 935–9.

NIXON, J. W., KEMP, A. M., LEVENE, S. & SIBERT, J. R. (1995) Suffocation, choking, and strangulation in childhood in England and Wales: epidemiology and prevention. *Arch Dis Child*, **72**, pp. 6–10.

O'NEILL, T. (1981) *A place called hope: caring for children in distress*, Oxford, Blackwell.

OFFICE FOR NATIONAL STATISTICS (2005a) Deaths by age, sex and underlying cause, 2004 registrations: health statistics quarterly 26. Office for National Statistics.

OFFICE FOR NATIONAL STATISTICS (2005b) Deaths: 1985–2003, deaths by sex and age group. Office for National Statistics.

OFFICE FOR NATIONAL STATISTICS (2005c) Mortality statistics: general. Office for National Statistics.

OFFICE FOR NATIONAL STATISTICS (2005d) Review of the Registrar General on deaths by cause, sex and age, in England and Wales, 2004. Office for National Statistics.

OFFICE FOR NATIONAL STATISTICS (2006a) Mortality statistics: cause 2005, London, Office for National Statistics.

OFFICE FOR NATIONAL STATISTICS (2006b) Mortality statistics: childhood, infant and perinatal. Office for National Statistics.

ONWUACHI-SAUNDERS, C., FORJUOH, S. N., WEST, P. & BROOKS, C. (1999) Child death reviews: a gold mine for injury prevention and control. *Inj Prev*, **5**, pp. 276–9.

OPESKIN, K. & BERKOVIC, S. F. (2003) Risk factors for sudden unexpected death in epilepsy: a controlled prospective study based on coroners cases. *Seizure*, **12**, pp. 456–64.

OVERPECK, M. D., BRENNER, R. A., TRUMBLE, A. C., TRIFILETTI, L. B. & BERENDES, H. W. (1998) Risk factors for infant homicide in the United States. *N Engl J Med*, **339**, pp. 1211–6.

OYEN,N.,MARKESTAD,T.,SKAERVEN,R.,IRGENS,L.M.,HELWEG-LARSEN, K., ALM, B., NORVENIUS, G. & WENNERGREN, G. (1997) Combined effects of sleeping position and prenatal risk factors in sudden infant death syndrome: the Nordic Epidemiological SIDS Study. *Pediatrics*, **100**, pp. 613–21.

OYEN, N., SKJAERVEN, R. & IRGENS, L. (1996) Population-based recurrence risk of sudden infant death syndrome compared with other fetal deaths. *American Journal of Epidemiology*, **144**, pp. 300–5.

OZANNE-SMITH,J.,DAY,L.,STATHAKIS,V.& SHERRARD,J.(2002)Controlled evaluation of a community based injury prevention program in Australia. *Inj Prev*, **8**, pp. 18–22.

PANICKAR,J. R., DODD, S. R., SMYTH, R. L. & COURIEL, J. M. (2005) Trends in deaths from respiratory illness in children in England and Wales from 1968 to 2000. *Thorax*, **60**, pp. 1035–8.

PARKES, C. (2001) A historical overview of the scientific study of bereavement. In STROEBE, M., HANSSON, R., STROEBE, W. & SCHUT, H. (Eds.) *Handbook of bereavement research*. Washington, American Psychological Association.

PARKES, C. M. (1972) *Bereavement: studies of grief in adult life*, London, Tavistock Publications.

PASTORE, G., GUALA, A. & ZAFFARONI, M. (2003) Back to sleep: risk factors for SIDS as targets for public health campaigns. *J Pediatr*, **142**, pp. 453–4.

PAULOZZI, L. & SELLS, M. (2002) Variation in homicide risk during infancy – United States, 1989–1998. *MMWR Morb Mortal Wkly Rep*, **51**, pp. 187–9.

PELAYO, R., OWENS, J., MINDELL, J. & SHELDON, S. (2006) Bed sharing with unimpaired parents is not an important risk for sudden infant death syndrome: to the editor. *Pediatrics*, **117**, pp. 993–4; author reply pp. 994–6.

PERKINS, D. F. & JONES, K. R. (2004) Risk behaviors and resiliency within physically abused adolescents. *Child Abuse Negl*, **28**, pp. 547–63.

PERY, S. R. (1998) *Expert group to investigate cot death theories: toxic gas hypothesis: final report*, Great Britain, Department of Health.

PETRIDOU, E., KOURI, N., POLYCHRONOPOULOU, A., SIAFAS, K., STOIKIDOU, M. & TRICHOPOULOS, D. (1996) Risk factors for childhood poisoning: a case-control study in Greece. *Inj Prev*, **2**, pp. 208–11.

PETROU, S., KUPEK, E., HOCKLEY, C. & GOLDACRE, M. (2006) Social class inequalities in childhood mortality and morbidity in an English population. *Paediatr Perinat Epidemiol*, **20**, pp. 14–23.

PIAGET, J. & COOK, P. (1952) *[La Naissance de l'intelligence chez l'enfant.] The origins of intelligence in children. Translated by Margaret Cook*, pp. xi. 419. International Universities Press: New York.

PICKETT, W., BRISON, R. J., BERG, R. L., ZENTNER, J., LINNEMAN, J. & MARLENGA, B. (2005) Pediatric farm injuries involving non-working children injured by a farm work hazard: five priorities for primary prevention. *Inj Prev*, **11**, pp. 6–11.

POETS, C. F. (2004) Apparent life-threatening events and sudden infant death on a monitor. *Paediatr Respir Rev*, **5** Suppl A, S383–6.

POLLANEN, M. S., SMITH, C. R., CHIASSON, D. A., CAIRNS, J. T. & YOUNG, J. (2002) Fatal child abuse-maltreatment syndrome. A retrospective study in Ontario, Canada, 1990–1995. *Forensic Sci Int*, **126**, pp. 101–4.

PONSONBY, A. L., DWYER, T. & COCHRANE, J. (2002) Population trends in sudden infant death syndrome. *Semin Perinatol*, **26**, pp. 296–305.

PONSONBY, A. L., DWYER, T. & COUPER, D. (1997) Sleeping position, infant apnea, and cyanosis: a population-based study. *Pediatrics*, **99**, E3.

PONSONBY, A. L., DWYER, T., COUPER, D. & COCHRANE, J. (1998) Association between use of a quilt and sudden infant death syndrome: case-control study. *BMJ*, **316**, pp. 195–6.

PONSONBY, A. L., DWYER, T., GIBBONS, L. E., COCHRANE, J. A., JONES, M. E. & MCCALL, M. J. (1992) Thermal environment and sudden infant death syndrome: case-control study. *BMJ*, **304**, pp. 277–82.

PONZETTI, J. & JOHNSON, M. (1991) The forgotten grievers: grandparents' reactions to the death of grandchildren. *Death Studies*, **15**, pp. 157–67.

PRIGERSON, H. (2005) Complicated grief: when the path of adjustment leads to a dead end. *Bereavement Care*, **3**, pp. 38–40.

RANDO, T. (1996) Complications in mourning traumatic death. In DOKA, K. (Ed.) *Living with grief after sudden loss*. Bristol, PA, Taylor and Francis.

RANDO, T. A. (1993) *Treatment of complicated mourning*, Champaign, IL, Research Press.

RANDO, T. A. E. (1986) *Parental loss of a child*, Champaign, IL, Research Press.

RANKIN, J., BUSH, J., BELL, R., CRESSWELL, P. & RENWICK, M. (2006) Impacts of participating in confidential enquiry panels: a qualitative study. *Bjog*, **113**, pp. 387–92.

RAPHAEL, B. (1984) *The anatomy of bereavement: a handbook for the caring professions*, London, Hutchinson.

RCPCH (2002) *Fabricated or induced illness by carers: report of the Working Party of the Royal College of Paediatrics and Child Health*, London, Royal College of Paediatrics and Child Health.

REDER, P. & DUNCAN, S. (1999) *Lost innocents: a follow-up study of fatal child abuse*, Routledge.

REDER, P., DUNCAN, S. & GRAY, M. (1993) *Beyond blame: child abuse tragedies revisited*, Routledge.

REDMOND, L. (1996) Sudden violent death. In DOKA, K. (Ed.) *Living with grief after sudden loss*. Bristol, PA, Taylor and Francis.

REEDER, C. & NICOL, C. (2004) Assessing the take up of ACPO guidelines on infant death investigations. London, Home Office.

RICHES, G. & DAWSON, P. (2000) *An intimate loneliness: supporting bereaved parents and siblings*, Buckingham; Philadelphia, PA, Open University Press.

RIGHARD, L. (1998) Sudden infant death syndrome and pacifiers: a proposed connection could be a bias. *Birth*, **25**, pp. 128–9.

RIGHARD, L. & ALADE, M. O. (1997) Breastfeeding and the use of pacifiers. *Birth*, **24**, pp. 116–20.

RIMSZA, M. E., SCHACKNER, R. A., BOWEN, K. A. & MARSHALL, W. (2002) Can child deaths be prevented? The Arizona Child Fatality Review Program experience. *Pediatrics*, **110**, e11.

RINTAHAKA, P. J. & HIRVONEN, J. (1986) The epidemiology of sudden infant death syndrome in Finland in 1969–1980. *Forensic Sci Int*, **30**, pp. 219–33.

RIVARA, F. P., THOMPSON, D. C. & THOMPSON, R. S. (1997) Epidemiology of bicycle injuries and risk factors for serious injury. *Inj Prev*, **3**, pp. 110–4.

ROBERTS, I., ASHTON, T., DUNN, R. & LEE-JOE, T. (1994) Preventing child pedestrian injury: pedestrian education or traffic calming? *Aust J Public Health*, **18**, pp. 209–12.

ROHDE, A., RAIE, D., VARCHMIN-SCHULTHEIß, K. & MARNEROS, A. (1998) Infanticide: sociobiographical background and motivational aspects. *Archives of Women's Mental Health*, **1**, pp. 125–30.

ROSE, M., MURPHY, M., MACFARLANE, J. A., SEFI, S., SHRIBMAN, S. & HALES, V. (1998) 'Back to sleep': the position in Oxfordshire and Northampton. *Paediatr Perinat Epidemiol*, **12**, pp. 217–27.

ROSE, W. & BARNES, J. (2007) Key messages: national overviews of Serious Case Reviews. *Preventing Childhood Death*. Copthorne Hotel, Newcastle.

ROSENBERG, D. A. (1987) Web of deceit: a literature review of Munchausen syndrome by proxy. *Child Abuse Negl*, **11**, pp. 547–63.

ROSENBLATT, P. C. (2000) *Parent grief: narratives of loss and relationship*, Philadelphia, PA; Hove, Brunner/Mazel.

ROYAL COLLEGE OF ANAESTHETISTS (2006) A code of practice for the diagnosis and certification of death (Draft for consultation). London, Royal College of Anaesthetists.

ROYAL COLLEGE OF PAEDIATRICS & CHILD HEALTH (2004) *Witholding or withdrawing life sustaining treatment in children*, London, RCPCH.

ROYAL COLLEGE OF PATHOLOGISTS & ROYAL COLLEGE OF PAEDIATRICS AND CHILD HEALTH (2004) *Sudden unexpected death in infancy: a multi-agency protocol for care and investigation*, London, Royal College of Pathologists, Royal College of Paediatrics and Child Health.

RUNYAN, C. W., BANGDIWALA, S. I., LINZER, M. A., SACKS, J. J. & BUTTS, J. (1992) Risk factors for fatal residential fires. *N Engl J Med*, **327**, pp. 859–63.

RUSEN, I. D., LIU, S., SAUVE, R., JOSEPH, K. S. & KRAMER, M. S. (2004) Sudden infant death syndrome in Canada: trends in rates and risk factors, 1985–1998. *Chronic Dis Can*, **25**, pp. 1–6.

SABOTTA, E. E. & DAVIS, R. L. (1992) Fatality after report to a child abuse registry in Washington State, 1973–1986. *Child Abuse Negl*, **16**, pp. 627–35.

SACKS, J. J., KRESNOW, M. & HOUSTON, B. (1996) Dog bites: how big a problem? *Inj Prev*, **2**, pp. 52–4.

SANDERS, R., COLTON, M. & ROBERTS, S. (1999) Child abuse fatalities and cases of extreme concern: lessons from reviews. *Child Abuse Negl*, **23**, pp. 257–68.

SATURNUS, K. (1985) Plotzicher Kindstod – eine Folge der Bauchlage? *Festchrift Professor Leithoff*. Heidelberg, Kriminalstatistik.

SAWCZENKO, A. & FLEMING, P. J. (1996) Thermal stress, sleeping position, and the sudden infant death syndrome. *Sleep*, **19**, S267–70.

SCHEERS, N. J., DAYTON, C. M. & KEMP, J. S. (1998) Sudden infant death with external airways covered: case-comparison study of 206 deaths in the United States. *Arch Pediatr Adolesc Med*, **152**, pp. 540–7.

SCHELLSCHEIDT, J., OTT, A. & JORCH, G. (1997) Epidemiological features of sudden infant death after a German intervention campaign in 1992. *Eur J Pediatr*, **156**, pp. 655–60.

SCHERZ, R. G. (1970) Prevention of childhood poisoning. A community project. *Pediatr Clin North Am*, **17**, pp. 713–27.

SCHLOESSER, P., PIERPONT, J. & POERTNER, J. (1992) Active surveillance of child abuse fatalities. *Child Abuse Negl*, **16**, pp. 3–10.

SCHLUCKEBIER, D. A., COOL, C. D., HENRY, T. E., MARTIN, A. & WAHE, J. W. (2002) Pulmonary siderophages and unexpected infant death. *Am J Forensic Med Pathol*, **23**, pp. 360–3.

SCHUT, H., STROEBE, M., VAN DEN BOUT, J. & TERHEGGEN, M. (2001) The efficacy of bereavement interventions. In STROEBE, M., HANSSON, R., STROEBE, W. & SCHUT, H. (Eds.) *Handbook of bereavement research*. Washington, American Psychological Association.

SCHWARTZ, F. C., FENNER, A. & WOLFSDORF, J. (1975) The influence of body position on pulmonary function in low birthweight babies. *S Afr Med J*, **49**, pp. 79–81.

SCHWARTZ, P. (2001) QT prolongation and SIDS – from theory to evidence, in sudden infant death syndrome: problems, progress, and possibilities. In BYARD, R. & KROUS, H. (Eds.) London, Arnold.

SCHWARTZ, P. J., STRAMBA-BADIALE, M., SEGANTINI, A., AUSTONI, P., BOSI, G., GIORGETTI, R., GRANCINI, F., MARNI, E. D., PERTICONE, F., ROSTI, D. & SALICE, P. (1998) Prolongation of the QT interval and the sudden infant death syndrome. *N Engl J Med*, **338**, pp. 1709–14.

SCRAGG, R. K. & MITCHELL, E. A. (1998) Side sleeping position and bed sharing in the sudden infant death syndrome. *Ann Med*, **30**, pp. 345–9.

SCRAGG, R. K., MITCHELL, E. A., STEWART, A. W., FORD, R. P., TAYLOR, B. J., HASSALL, I. B., WILLIAMS, S. M. & THOMPSON, J. M. (1996) Infant room-sharing and prone sleep position in sudden infant death syndrome. New Zealand Cot Death Study Group. *Lancet*, **347**, pp. 7–12.

SHAPIRO-MENDOZA, C. K., TOMASHEK, K. M., ANDERSON, R. N. & WINGO, J. (2006) Recent national trends in sudden, unexpected infant deaths: more evidence supporting a change in classification or reporting. *Am J Epidemiol*, **163**, pp. 762–9.

SHARPLES, P. M., STOREY, A., AYNSLEY-GREEN, A. & EYRE, J. A. (1990) Causes of fatal childhood accidents involving head injury in northern region, 1979–86. *BMJ*, **301**, 1193–7.

SHEEHAN, K. M., MCGARVEY, C., DEVANEY, D. M. & MATTHEWS, T. (2005) How reliable are SIDS rates? *Arch Dis Child*, **90**, pp. 1082–3.

SHERMAN, J. M., WINNIE, G., THOMASSEN, M. J., ABDUL-KARIM, F. W. & BOAT, T. F. (1984) Time course of hemosiderin production and clearance by human pulmonary macrophages. *Chest*, **86**, pp. 409–11.

SIBERT, J. R., CRAFT, A. W. & JACKSON, R. H. (1977) Child-resistant packaging and accidental child poisoning. *Lancet*, **2**, pp. 289–90.

SIBERT, J. R. & KEMP, A. M. (2002) Safe communities for children: only models of good practice or ways through practical difficulties in injury prevention? *Child Care Health Dev*, **28**, pp. 439–42.

SIBERT, J. R., LYONS, R. A., SMITH, B. A., CORNALL, P., SUMNER, V., CRAVEN, M. A. & KEMP, A. M. (2002) Preventing deaths by drowning in children in the United Kingdom: have we made progress in 10 years? Population based incidence study. *BMJ*, **324**, pp. 1070–1.

SIBERT, R. (1975) Stress in families of children who have ingested poisons. *Br Med J*, **3**, pp. 87–9.

SIDEBOTHAM, P. (2001) An ecological approach to child abuse: a creative use of scientific models in research and practice. *Child Abuse Review*, **10**, pp. 97–112.

SIDEBOTHAM, P., FLEMING, P. & BLAIR, P. (2005) Sudden unexpected death in infancy. In DAVID, T. (Ed.) *Recent Advances in Paediatrics 22.* London, Royal Society of Medicine.

SIDEBOTHAM, P. & HERON, J. (2006) Child maltreatment in the 'children of the nineties': a cohort study of risk factors. *Child Abuse Negl,* **30,** pp. 497–522.

SILVERMAN, P. & NICKMAN, S. (1996) Children's construction of their dead parent. In KLASS, D., SILVERMAN, P. & NICKMAN, S. (Eds.) *Continuing bonds: new understandings of grief.* Washington, DC, Taylor & Francis.

SILVERMAN, P. R. (2000) *Never too young to know: death in children's lives,* New York; Oxford, Oxford University Press.

SIMKISS, D. E., SHEPPARD, I. & PAL, B. R. (1998) Airway obstruction by a child's pacifier – could flange design be safer? *Eur J Pediatr,* **157,** pp. 252–4.

SINCLAIR, R. & BULLOCK, R. (2002) *Learning from past experience: a review of serious case reviews,* Great Britain, Department of Health.

SKADBERG, B. T., MORILD, I. & MARKESTAD, T. (1998) Abandoning prone sleeping: effect on the risk of sudden infant death syndrome. *J Pediatr,* **132,** pp. 340–3.

SMITH, D. J. (2003) The third Shipman inquiry report – chapter 4. London, The Stationary Office.

SORENSON, S. B. & PETERSON, J. G. (1994) Traumatic child death and documented maltreatment history, Los Angeles. *Am J Public Health,* **84,** pp. 623–7.

SPENCER, N. (1996) *Poverty and child health,* Abingdon, UK, Radcliffe.

SPIEGEL, C. N. & LINDAMAN, F. C. (1977) Children can't fly: a program to prevent childhood morbidity and mortality from window falls. *Am J Public Health,* **67,** pp. 1143–7.

SPOCK, B. & ROTHENBERG, M. (1985) *Baby and child care,* New York, Pocket Books.

SPOELSTRA, A. J. & SRIKASIBHANDHA, S. (1973) Dynamic pressure-volume relationship of the lung and position in healthy neonates. *Acta Paediatr Scand,* **62,** pp. 176–80.

SQUIRES, T. & BUSUTTIL, A. (1995) Child fatalities in Scottish house fires 1980–1990: a case of child neglect? *Child Abuse Negl,* **19,** pp. 865–73.

STAAB, D., WENNINGER, K., GEBERT, N., RUPPRATH, K., BISSON, S., TRETTIN, M., PAUL, K. D., KELLER, K. M. & WAHN, U. (1998) Quality of life in patients with cystic fibrosis and their parents: what is important besides disease severity? *Thorax,* **53,** pp. 727–31.

STEWART, A. (2000) When an infant grandchild dies: family matters. Wellington, New Zealand, Victoria University of Wellington.

STEWART, A. & DENT, A. (2005) Bereavement: learning from parents. In WICKHAM, S. (Ed.) *Midwifery best practice.* Edinburgh, Churchill Livingstone.

STEWART, S., FAWCETT, J. & JACOBSON, W. (1985) Interstitial haemosiderin in the lungs of sudden infant death syndrome: a histological hallmark of 'near-miss' episodes? *J Pathol,* **145,** pp. 53–8.

STROEBE, M. (1992–3) Coping with bereavement: a review of the grief work hypothesis. *Omega,* **26,** pp. 19–42.

STROEBE, M. & SCHUT, H. (1999) The dual process model of coping with bereavement: rationale and description. *Death Stud,* **23,** pp. 197–224.

STROEBE, M. & SCHUT, H. (2001) Meaning making in the dual process of coping with bereavement. In NEIMEYER, R. (Ed.) *Meaning reconstruction and the experience of loss.* Washington, American Psychological Association.

STUBBS, A. J. & ABURN, N. S. (1996) Penetrating eye injury from a rigid infant pacifier. *Aust N Z J Ophthalmol,* **24,** pp. 71–3.

STUELAND, D. T., LEE, B. C., NORDSTROM, D. L., LAYDE, P. M. & WITTMAN, L. M. (1996) A population based case-control study of agricultural injuries in children. *Inj Prev,* **2,** pp. 192–6.

SULLIVAN, P. & KNUTSON, J. (2000) Maltreatment and disabilities: a population-based epidemiological study. *Child Abuse & Neglect,* **24,** pp. 1257–73.

SVANSTROM, L. (1997) More safe communities programs in Scandinavia have been evaluated: repeating the results from Falkoping. *Inj Prev,* **3,** pp. 230–1.

SWENSEN, A., BIRNBAUM, H. G., BEN HAMADI, R., GREENBERG, P., CREMIEUX, P. Y. & SECNIK, K. (2004) Incidence and costs of accidents among attention-deficit/hyperactivity disorder patients. *J Adolesc Health,* **35,** 346 e1–9.

TAKEDA, K. (1987) A possible mechanism of sudden infant death syndrome. *Journal of Kyoto Prefecture University Medicine,* **96,** pp. 965–8.

TAPPIN, D., BROOKE, H., ECOB, R. & GIBSON, A. (2002) Used infant mattresses and sudden infant death syndrome in Scotland: case-control study. *BMJ,* **325,** p. 1007.

TAPPIN, D., ECOB, R. & BROOKE, H. (2005) Bedsharing, roomsharing, and sudden infant death syndrome in Scotland: a case-control study. *J Pediatr,* **147,** pp. 32–7.

TARLING, R. (1998) Research study 181 – coroner service survey. London, Home Office.

TESTER, D. J. & ACKERMAN, M. J. (2005) Sudden infant death syndrome: how significant are the cardiac channelopathies? *Cardiovasc Res,* **67,** pp. 388–96.

THACH, B. T. (1986) Sudden infant death syndrome: old causes rediscovered? *N Engl J Med,* **315,** pp. 126–8.

THOMPSON, R. S., RIVARA, F. P. & THOMPSON, D. C. (1989) A case-control study of the effectiveness of bicycle safety helmets. *N Engl J Med,* **320,** pp. 1361–7.

TONKIN, S. L. (1986) Epidemiology of cot deaths in Auckland. *N Z Med J,* **99,** pp. 324–6.

TOWNER, E. & DOWSWELL, T. (2002) Community-based childhood injury prevention interventions: what works? *Health Promot Int,* **17,** pp. 273–84.

TOWNER, E., DOWSWELL, T. & MACKERETH, C. (2001) *What works in preventing unintentional injuries in children and young adolescents? an updated systematic review,* Great Britain.

TROKEL, M., DISCALA, C., TERRIN, N. C. & SEGE, R. D. (2006) Patient and injury characteristics in abusive abdominal injuries. *Pediatr Emerg Care,* **22,** pp. 700–4.

TUOHY, P. G., COUNSELL, A. M. & GEDDIS, D. C. (1993) Sociodemographic factors associated with sleeping position and location. *Arch Dis Child,* **69,** pp. 664–6.

TZIOUMI, D. & OATES, R. K. (1998) Subdural hematomas in children under 2 years. Accidental or inflicted? A 10-year experience. *Child Abuse Negl,* **22,** pp. 1105–12.

UHARI, M., MANTYSAARI, K. & NIEMELA, M. (1996) A meta-analytic review of the risk factors for acute otitis media. *Clin Infect Dis,* **22,** pp. 1079–83.

UNICEF (2006) *The state of the world's children 2006,* New York, UNICEF.

VAN SCHAGEN, I. N. & BROOKHUIS, K. A. (1994) Training young cyclists to cope with dynamic traffic situations. *Accid Anal Prev,* **26,** pp. 223–30.

VEGE, A. & ROGNUM, T. O. (1997) Use of new Nordic criteria for classification of SIDS to re-evaluate diagnoses of sudden unexpected infant death in the Nordic countries. *Acta Paediatr*, **86**, pp. 391–6.

VEGE, A., ROGNUM, T. O., SCOTT, H., AASEN, A. O. & SAUGSTAD, O. D. (1995) SIDS cases have increased levels of interleukin-6 in cerebrospinal fluid. *Acta Paediatr*, **84**, pp. 193–6.

VENNEMANN, M., FISCHER, D., JORCH, G. & BAJANOWSKI, T. (2006) Prevention of sudden infant death syndrome (SIDS) due to an active health monitoring system 20 years prior to the public 'Back to Sleep' campaigns. *Arch Dis Child*, **91**, pp. 324–6.

VENNEMANN, M. M., BUTTERFASS-BAHLOUL, T., JORCH, G., BRINKMANN, B., FINDEISEN, M., SAUERLAND, C., BAJANOWSKI, T. & MITCHELL, E. A. (2007) Sudden infant death syndrome: no increased risk after immunisation. *Vaccine*, **25**, pp. 336–40.

VENNEMANN, M. M., FINDEISEN, M., BUTTERFASS-BAHLOUL, T., JORCH, G., BRINKMANN, B., KOPCKE, W., BAJANOWSKI, T. & MITCHELL, E. A. (2005) Modifiable risk factors for SIDS in Germany: results of GeSID. *Acta Paediatr*, **94**, pp. 655–60.

VICTOR, Y. H. (1975) Effect of body position on gastric emptying in the neonate. *Arch Dis Child*, **50**, pp. 500–4.

VISH, N. L., POWELL, E. C., WILTSEK, D. & SHEEHAN, K. M. (2005) Pediatric window falls: not just a problem for children in high rises. *Inj Prev*, **11**, pp. 300–3.

VOGEL, A. M., HUTCHISON, B. L. & MITCHELL, E. A. (2001) The impact of pacifier use on breastfeeding: a prospective cohort study. *J Paediatr Child Health*, **37**, pp. 58–63.

WAGNER, M., SAMSON-DOLLFUS, D. & MENARD, J. (1984) Sudden unexpected infant death in a French county. *Arch Dis Child*, **59**, pp. 1082–7.

WAILOO, M., BALL, H., FLEMING, P. & WARD PLATT, M. P. (2004) Infants bed-sharing with mothers. *Arch Dis Child*, **89**, pp. 1082–3.

WALTER, T. (1996) A new model of grief: bereavement and biography. *Mortality*, **1**, pp. 7–25.

WALTER, T. (1999) *On bereavement: the culture of grief*, Buckingham, Open University Press.

WARNOCK, D. W., DELVES, H. T., CAMPELL, C. K., CROUDACE, I. W., DAVEY, K. G., JOHNSON, E. M. & SIENIAWSKA, C. (1995) Toxic gas generation from plastic mattresses and sudden infant death syndrome. *Lancet*, **346**, pp. 1516–20.

WARREN, J. J., LEVY, S. M., KIRCHNER, H. L., NOWAK, A. J. & BERGUS, G. R. (2001) Pacifier use and the occurrence of otitis media in the first year of life. *Pediatr Dent*, **23**, pp. 103–7.

WARUIRU, C. & APPLETON, R. (2004) Febrile seizures: an update. *Arch Dis Child*, **89**, pp. 751–6.

WEBSTER, R. A., SCHNITZER, P. G., JENNY, C., EWIGMAN, B. G. & ALARIO, A. J. (2003) Child death review. The state of the nation. *Am J Prev Med*, **25**, pp. 58–64.

WEESE-MAYER, D., ACKERMAN, M., MARAZITA, M. & BERRY-KRAVIS, E. (2007) Sudden Infant Death Syndrome: Review of implicated genetic factors. *Am J Med Genet C Semin Med Genet*, **143**, pp. 771–88.

WEISS, P. P. & KERBL, R. (2001) The relatively short duration that a child retains a pacifier in the mouth during sleep: implications for sudden infant death syndrome. *Eur J Pediatr*, **160**, p. 60.

WELSH CHILD PROTECTION SYSTEMATIC REVIEW GROUP (2005) Fractures review.

WERNE, J. & GARROW, I. (1947) Sudden deaths of infants allegedly due to mechanical suffocation. *American Journal of Public Health*, **37**, p. 675.

WESTCOTT, H. & JONES, D. (1999) Annotation: the abuse of disabled children. *J Child Psychol Psychiat*, **40**, pp. 497–506.

WEST MIDLANDS PERINATAL INSTITUTE (2006) West Midlands perinatal mortality. Update 2006. Birmingham, Perinatal Institute.

WHITE, M., BECKETT, M., O'REGAN, M. & MATTHEWS, T. (1995) The effect of maternal smoking in pregnancy on autonomic function in infants. In ROGNUM, T. (Ed.) *Sudden infant death syndrome: new trends in the nineties*. Oslo, Scandinavian University Press.

WHO (1968) *The eighth revision of the international classification of diseases*, Geneva, World Health Organisation.

WIGFIELD, R. E., FLEMING, P. J., AZAZ, Y. E., HOWELL, T. E., JACOBS, D. E., NADIN, P. S., MCCABE, R. & STEWART, A. J. (1993) How much wrapping do babies need at night? *Arch Dis Child*, **69**, pp. 181–6.

WILCZYNSKI, A. (1994) The incidence of child homicide: how accurate are the official statistics? *J Clin Forensic Med*, **1**, pp. 61–6.

WILKINS, B. (1997) Head injury – abuse or accident? *Arch Dis Child*, **76**, pp. 393–6; discussion pp. 396–7.

WILLIAMS, S. M., TAYLOR, B. J. & MITCHELL, E. A. (1996) Sudden infant death syndrome: insulation from bedding and clothing and its effect modifiers. The National Cot Death Study Group. *Int J Epidemiol*, **25**, pp. 366–75.

WILLINGER, M., JAMES, L. & CATZ, C. (1991) Defining the sudden infant death syndrome (SIDS): deliberations of an expert panel convened by the National Institute of Child Health and Human Development. *Pediatric Pathology*, **11**, pp. 677–84.

WILLIS, S. (2005) Work with bereaved children. In MONROE, B. & KRAUS, F. (Eds.) *Brief interventions with bereaved children*. Oxford, Oxford University Press.

WILSON, C. A., TAYLOR, B. J., LAING, R. M., WILLIAMS, S. M. & MITCHELL, E. A. (1994) Clothing and bedding and its relevance to sudden infant death syndrome: further results from the New Zealand Cot Death Study. *J Paediatr Child Health*, **30**, pp. 506–12.

WOLKIND, S., TAYLOR, E. M., WAITE, A. J., DALTON, M. & EMERY, J. L. (1993) Recurrence of unexpected infant death. *Acta Paediatr*, **82**, pp. 873–6.

WOOLEY, P. (1945) Mechanical suffocation during infancy. *Journal of Pediatrics*, **26**, pp. 572–5.

WORDEN, J. W. (1991) *Grief counselling and grief therapy: a handbook for the mental health practitioner*, Routledge.

WORLD HEALTH ORGANISATION (1993) *The international statistical classification of diseases and related health problems – tenth revision, volumes 1, 2 and 3*, Geneva, WHO.

WORTMAN, C. & SILVER, R. (1989) The myths of coping with loss. *Journal of Consulting and Clinical Psychology*, **57**, pp. 349–57.

WORTMAN, C. & SILVER, R. (2001) The myths of coping with loss revisited. In STROEBE, M., HANSSON, R., STROEBE, W. & SCHUT, H. (Eds.) *Handbook of bereavement research.* Washington, American Psychological Association.

WREN, C., O'SULLIVAN, J. J. & WRIGHT, C. (2000) Sudden death in children and adolescents. *Heart*, **83**, pp. 410–3.

YEOH, C., NIXON, J. W., DICKSON, W., KEMP, A. & SIBERT, J. R. (1994) Patterns of scald injuries. *Arch Dis Child*, **71**, pp. 156–8.

YSTGAARD, M., HESTETUN, I., LOEB, M. & MEHLUM, L. (2004) Is there a specific relationship between childhood sexual and physical abuse and repeated suicidal behavior? *Child Abuse Negl*, **28**, pp. 863–75.

YUKAWA, N., CARTER, N., RUTTY, G. & GREEN, M. A. (1999) Intra-alveolar haemorrhage in sudden infant death syndrome: a cause for concern? *J Clin Pathol*, **52**, pp. 581–7.

ZORGANI, A., ESSERY, S. D., MADANI, O. A., BENTLEY, A. J., JAMES, V. S., MACKENZIE, D. A., KEELING, J. W., RAMBAUD, C., HILTON, J., BLACKWELL, C. C., WEIR, D. M. & BUSUTTIL, A. (1999) Detection of pyrogenic toxins of Staphylococcus aureus in sudden infant death syndrome. *FEMS Immunol Med Microbiol*, **25**, pp. 103–8.

Index